L——.ing and Development

13

Fourth edition

Rosemary Harrison is chief examiner, learning and development, the Chartered Institute of Personnel and Development (CIPD). She is a Fellow of the CIPD and of the Royal Society of Arts, member of the Society of Authors, and a leading academic and author in the learning and development field. After graduating from King's College London with an honours history degree she worked as a training officer in the National Health Service. She then joined Newcastle Polytechnic to lecture in personnel management and organisational behaviour and was for many years course leader of the Institute of Personnel Management's professional qualification programme. She was subsequently appointed Lecturer in Human Resource Management at Durham University Business School and later became director of its Human Resource Development Research Centre. She is an experienced HR consultant and speaker at conferences and universities

The CIPD would like to thank the following members of the CIPD Publishing Editorial Board for their help and advice:

Pauline Dibben, Middlesex University Business School

Edwina Hollings, Staffordshire University Business School

Caroline Hook, Huddersfield University Business School

Vincenza Priola, Wolverhampton Business School

John Sinclair, Napier University Business School

Learning and Development

Fourth edition

Rosemary Harrison

Chartered Institute of Personnel and Development

For Joseph, friend, colleague and mentor

Published by the Chartered Institute of Personnel and Development,
151 The Broadway, London SW19 1JQ

First edition published 1997
Reprinted 1998, 1999
Second edition published 2000
Reprinted 2000
Third edition published 2002
Reprinted 2002, 2003 (twice)

This edition published 2005
Reprinted 2006

Typeset by Curran Publishing Services, Norwich, Norfolk
Printed in Great Britain by Cromwell Press, Trowbridge, Wiltshire

British Library Cataloguing in Publication Data
A catalogue record of this book is available from the British Library

ISBN 1 84398 0509

The views expressed in this publication are the author's own and may not necessarily reflect those of the CIPD

The CIPD has made every effort to trace and acknowledge copyright holders. If any course has been overlooked, CIPD Enterprises Ltd would be pleased to redress this for future editions.

Chartered Institute of Personnel and Development,
151 The Broadway, London SW19 1JQ
Tel: 020 8971 9000   Fax: 020 8263 3333
Email: cipd@cipd.co.uk   Website: www.cipd.co.uk
Incorporated by Royal Charter   Registered Charity No. 1079797

Contents

Appendices

Figures

Tables

Editor's Foreword

I am very pleased to have this opportunity to introduce the latest (the fourth) edition of Rosemary Harrison's book on Learning and Development. As ever it offers a remarkable journey through this ever-expanding field, providing readers with a clear, systematic and comprehensive understanding of what has become a vast and increasingly complex area. Before writing this foreword, I looked through the contents of Rosemary's earlier editions and realised just how dramatically the learning and development agenda has changed in less than 10 years. Those readers hoping to make do with the previous edition are in for a rude shock; this book contains so much new material, it is ordered differently, and it is written in an even more engaging way than previous editions. I can see no option but to buy this edition if they want to remain ahead of the field and feel confident in their knowledge and understanding of L&D.

The book is organised into four parts. The first provides readers with an understanding of the field, introducing them to the main themes and issues, as well as providing analysis of the national frameworks and the education system. Without appreciating the mass of activity in these areas, it is impossible to see just how much has changed and its impact on employers and L&D professionals. The second part aims to help readers get to grips with practice and understand some of the theoretical and ethical considerations involved in embedding learning and development at work. This raises the key issue of how L&D may aid organisational performance. Part 3 looks in more detail at how L&D, both the specialist function and in general, can make a contribution to the business, not in terms of vague generalisations and exhortations to engage in training but from the perspective that a variety of solutions may work in the quite different circumstances faced by organisations of different sizes or in different sectors. Finally, the book turns to address how L&D can build for the future, in relation to careers, leadership and management development. Typical of Rosemary, the book ends with a series of challenges for the L&D profession and a suggestion that all professionals should understand the twin values of wisdom and humility: the wisdom to ask fundamental questions and the humility to realise some of these may never be answered. In learning and development, probably more than in any other area of HRM, the quest for lifelong learning and the ability to continue searching for ways to improve both social and human capital is critically important.

Rosemary Harrison has made a substantial contribution to the development of L&D as a field of inquiry, not just as a practical subject, and this book is one which CIPD students in particular need to read from cover to cover if they are to truly understand what the professional standards actually mean. As she is the CIPD's Chief Examiner in the field, this makes sense for all students. However, the book sets out to achieve much more than this, and it succeeds in providing a wide-ranging yet very readable account of how L&D has developed, why its practice varies between contexts and where it might be going in the future. As such it will appeal to a much wider audience, both those on formal courses and people who want to know more about L&D as a corpus of knowledge. By the end of the book, readers will be desperate for the next edition to see how she addresses the challenges posed here.

Professor Mick Marchington
Professor of Human Resource Management,
Manchester Business School,
The University of Manchester, and
Chief Moderator, Standards for the CIPD.

Preface to the Fourth Edition

The aims of the fourth edition

This fourth edition has three aims: to meet the needs of a postgraduate market; to encourage high professional standards in the L&D field; and to update readers' knowledge of that field.

The first aim means that this edition continues to provide theoretical and practical guidelines for those studying the CIPD's Learning and Development Standards (CIPD 2001a). However the book is also intended to reach a wider postgraduate market including MBA and specialist HRM and HRD students. Therefore although its content covers the 10 performance indicators in the CIPD's L&D Generalist Standard (Appendix 1) it goes beyond them to meet other needs. I write – as I have always done – as an independent author. To question, reflect and evaluate are vital tasks for anyone who seeks or holds professional status. My purpose is to promote those qualities without subordinating them to any one set of norms.

The second aim rests on an uncomfortable reality: that the L&D field can be too demanding for some. It is complex, challenging and under regular public scrutiny as awareness increases about the key role that L&D processes have in building the nation's skills base and in aiding business performance. There are always organisations whose L&D practice is exemplary. National Training Awards in 2003, for example, showed that an increasing number of businesses were by then putting their faith in training and development to see them through testing trading conditions, and the quality and value of training evident in the 1,000 entries was outstanding. In the 2004 Awards the number of finalists rose by a further 300.

Yet research indicates that despite 45 per cent of employees in the UK participating in training in 2003 compared with the international average of 27 per cent (CBI 2003), an overwhelming majority of UK employees are not sufficiently trained to do their job. Harsh criticisms are frequently levelled against trainers, and whether or not fair they gain a wide hearing. Note, for example, the publicity given to major training deficiencies in organisations as diverse as Thames Trains (in the 2004 court case over the Paddington rail crash) the Royal Mail (whose widespread delivery problems, many allegedly due to insufficient training, were exposed in a report by its official regulator early in 2004) and the BBC (accused in October 2004 of investing in a £35 million leadership training course at a prestigious management school without having established any clear links between the course and performance objectives at the BBC (Leonard 2004)). The professional response to accusations of complacency, ignorance and ineptitude in the L&D field should not be defensiveness. It should be a determination to assess the evidence, learn from it and improve.

Although I identify and analyse poor L&D practice and its contributory factors in this book I also draw attention to practice that is good and innovatory. I hope that readers will find much on both sides of the coin to encourage them in their quest for high standards in their professional practice.

The third aim of the book is to help readers to keep abreast with change. This fourth edition incorporates major developments in the field since the third edition was written, and this explains fundamental changes in its structure and content. Although each chapter contains reference sources, these are only starting points. Academic journals identify and debate new theories. Professional journals and reports evaluate current policy and practice (and with the needs of CIPD students particularly in mind I refer regularly to the CIPD's journal, *People Management*, its research projects and other publications). The Web is a crucial information source and Appendix 2 shows some of the most useful CIPD websites for those studying for CIPD professional examinations. Each chapter also identifies relevant website links relating to its subject matter.

The structure of the book

The fourth edition of this core text has four parts and incorporates 17 chapters.

Part 1 'Understanding the field' provides an introduction to L&D as an organisational process, locating it in an external context where the main challenges come from a more turbulent business environment, the emergence of a new knowledge economy, new trends in L&D practice and scope and radical changes over the past three years in national skills and life-long learning strategies. This external context has fundamental implications for the focus, management and measurement of L&D activity in organisations.

Part 2 'Getting to grips with the practice' is concerned with the need for high-quality, ethical and professional L&D practice, with learning linked to organisational as well as individual performance and practitioners who are fast-responsive to new challenges confronting them. One major thrust in Part 2 is the need, in an emerging knowledge economy, for those practitioners to promote and support not just a shift from trainers to learners but a more demanding shift from self-managed learning to learner-initiated knowledge creation in the workplace. Another is the need for attention to be paid to process. In the L&D field operational expertise alone is not enough to bring success. L&D professionals must engage stakeholders in their activity from inception to evaluation if they are to make any lasting and positive impact on the business.

Part 3 'Making a business contribution' covers the L&D agenda in different sectoral settings, major pressures in today's business environment on traditional ways of organising and managing an L&D function and some innovative responses to those pressures. It explores changing approaches to L&D strategising and planning, ways of adding value through L&D activity, and the considerations involved for L&D professionals in building and sustaining effective business partnerships both within their organisations and beyond increasingly blurred organisational boundaries.

Part 4 'Building for the future' centres on ways in which an organisation's processes for career, leadership and management development can build organisational capacity for the future. Its final chapter provides a review of key issues in the book and their implications for L&D professionals.

Learning materials

This fourth edition incorporates many learning aids, intended particularly to help those new to the field. These include:

■ An *introductory section* to each chapter explaining the chapter's purpose and the main issues with which it deals, and a *concluding section* summarising main ground covered in the chapter.

■ *'Reflection'* breaks within each chapter to encourage readers to review their understanding of material covered.

■ *Case examples* to highlight key issues covered in each chapter, many with feedback comments.

■ *Review questions* (Appendix 3) relating to the content of each chapter. They are in the style of questions set in Section B of the CIPD's Learning and Development examination but are relevant for all readers. They represent the kind of on-the-spot queries that L&D practitioners constantly have to face in real life.

■ *Further information sources* listed at the end of each chapter, wherever relevant incorporating websites as well as books and articles.

A 2005 edition of the *Learning and development revision guide* has been produced for CIPD students as a complement to the core text (Harrison 2004). In the guide I advise on the competencies and preparation needed for success in PDS exams in general and the L&D exam in particular. I explain the L&D Standard's performance indicators in detail and relate them to typical L&D exam content. Half the guide consists of past examination questions, with feedback notes incorporating examples of candidates' answers. Any tutor using the core text can also access on the CIPD's website a Tutors' Manual related to this fourth edition.

Starting out

The fourth edition focuses primarily on the strategic contribution that L&D activity could, and should, make to organisational performance. Yet to those starting out on a career in people management and development (PMD) such discussion may seem of only theoretical interest – few, after all, have any influence on strategic players in the organisation or on 'strategy' in its more obvious guises.

To think in that way is to miss a vital point – that even the newest entrants to the field should think strategically as they go about their everyday tasks and should apply that thinking to operations at their organisational level. This is why the CIPD stresses the need for PMD professionals to be 'thinking performers', reflecting on what is going on around them, looking outwards to identify and anticipate threats, challenges and opportunities, and promoting ways in which PMD processes and initiatives at their level can help to move the organisation forward.

Newly-qualified professionals with L&D responsibilities can achieve much by helping to introduce and embed initiatives to improve performance today and build organisational capacity for tomorrow. By making a mark in modest ways even the most inexperienced will gain respect. Their influence will grow as people learn to trust their knowledge and judgement. By working in business partnerships and demonstrating a real understanding of the organisation and its business environment they will build up further credibility. When the opportune moment comes they will be well equipped to become strategic players.

Rosemary Harrison
Chief examiner, Learning and Development
December 2004

Acknowledgements

All real-life material reported in the book relates only to situations current at the time. Unless otherwise indicated, comments on such material are my own and do not represent any official views within or by the organisations concerned.

I acknowledge with thanks the organisations that, through the years of this book's several editions, have allowed me to publish accounts of their business and human resource policies and practice, particularly Cummins Engine, Egg plc and Harris Associates and Hemsley Fraser. I am especially grateful to the following individuals: Dave Bevan at Harris Associates for his help with the Egg plc case in Chapter 14; Wendy Brooks, Director of Learning & Development and Consultancy and Linda Pugh, Head of Learning & Development, both at Hemsley Fraser Group Limited, for providing the first draft of the HF case in Chapter 6; Graham O'Connell, International Development & Training Consultant at CMPS Learning in Government, Sunningdale Park and Ian Healy, Trainer and Coach at University College, Northampton for their suggestions on the first draft of Chapter 9; and Helen Rainbird for advice on the first draft of the case of the local government cook-freeze centre in Chapter 5. In addition I wish to thank my editor, Ruth Lake and the anonymous reviewers of my first draft for their encouragement.

I acknowledge permission to reproduce or summarise materials as follows:

- Cambridge Strategy Publications for permission to reprint Table 9 in Chapter 13.
- CMPS for permission to reproduce the Cabinet Office Code in Appendix 5.
- CIPD, for permission to draw on material from CIPD research reports.
- Cummins Engine, for permission to publish the case in Chapter 12.
- Dr Carley Foster and Professor Lynette Harris for permission to summarise their Diversity case in Chapter 9.
- Hemsley Fraser Group Limited for permission to publish Figure 1 and their case study in Chapter 6.
- Palgrave Macmillan for permission to reproduce Table 4 in Chapter 3 and to draw substantially on the local government cook-freeze centre case in Chapter 5.
- *People Management* journal, for agreement to summarise material for many case examples in the text.

Above all, I am indebted to my husband. Trite but true to say that but for his good humoured and patient support this book certainly could not have been written.

Glossary of Terms

adding value To add value, the L&D process must achieve outcomes that significantly increase the organisation's capability to differentiate itself from other, similar organisations, and thereby enhance its progress. It must also achieve those outcomes in ways that ensure, through time, that their value will more than offset the costs that they have incurred.

assessment centre 'A systematic approach to identifying precisely what is required for success in a particular job and then labelling these requirements in terms of a short-list of tightly defined criteria' (Stevens 1985). Data collected in this way is used primarily to feed into decisions about promotion or some other form of employee redeployment.

bite-sized learning An approach to learning and training popularised by the Learning and Skills Council in its Bite Sized Learning Campaign. It refers to 'light touch' or modular work-place learning where subject matter is divided into short chunks (one or two-hour blocks are common) in order to achieve speed, reduce learning time and costs, and increase ease and motivation for learners.

Black Box Term used to describe the fact that although many studies have examined the link between HR practices and policies and shown there to be a positive relationship, few have sought to explain the nature of this connection. The Work and Employment Research Centre at the University of Bath has sought to remedy this by looking inside the black box. The resulting People and Performance model offers a way of examining and understanding how and why HR practices impact on organisational performance (Purcell et al 2003).

business partners When applied to HR practitioners, the term is a way of emphasising that in all their activities they must add value for the business, and cannot do this on their own. They must collaborate with others in the business – especially managers – in working for outcomes that will benefit that business.

career 'The total sequence of employment-related positions, roles, activities and experiences encountered by an individual' (Jackson 2000).

cognitive Concerned with the psychological processes of perception, memory, thinking and learning (Coffield et al 2004).

competencies The set of character features, knowledge and skills, attitudes, motives and traits that comprise the profile of a job-holder and enable him or her to perform effectively in his or her role.

competency framework A construct of core competencies that provides a template against which individuals and teams can be developed.

computer-based training A term that covers both e-based learning (see below) and such computerised learning tools as CD-ROMs.

cybernetics The science of control and communication in animals and machines.

decentralised Transferred from central to local control, as in 'decentralised training function'; or, in the case of educational institutions, from local authority control to self-government.

deregulated Not subject to any direct government restrictions, constraints or regulations.

develop To unfold more fully, bring out all that is contained (Onions 1973). To make or become bigger or fuller or more elaborate or systematic advancement (Pearsall and Trumble 1996).

development centre A methodology by which participants take part in a variety of job simulations, tests and exercises in front of observers who assess their performance against a number of predetermined job-related dimensions. Data thus generated is used to diagnose individual training needs, facilitate self-development or provide part of an organisational development audit (Rodger and Mabey 1987).

dialogic learning A style of learning that involves interacting with others in ways which produce a growing understanding of the culture of the organisation, and of how that organisation typically achieves its goals (Mezirow 1985).

discretionary behaviour The extent to which the individual can and does exercise control over the key parameters of his or her job, such as speed, care, innovation and style of job delivery. Recent research strongly indicates that for employees individually and collectively to engage in discretionary behaviour beneficial to the firm, they must have the needed ability, motivation and opportunity. These AMO drivers lie at the heart of the People and Performance model (Purcell et al 2003).

double-loop learning A concept to describe the style of learning that involves questioning why certain problems occur in the first place and identifying and tackling root causes instead of only surface symptoms (Argyris 1977). Contrast with single-loop learning (qv).

educate To bring up from childhood so as to form habits, manners, mental and physical aptitudes (Onions 1973). To give intellectual, moral and social instruction, especially as a formal and prolonged process (Pearsall and Trumble 1996).

e-learning Any form of electronically-based learning, whether enabled through wired or wire-free systems.

Employer Training Pilots Provide financial support to employers who give employees paid leave to study for basic skills or level 2 qualifications. They involve a small business being allocated an adviser to source on-site training that fits employers' basic skills needs.

evaluation of learning A process to identify the total value of a learning event or process, thereby putting the event or process into its organisational context and aiding future planning.

explicit knowledge Knowledge that has been articulated and codified.

external consistency Applied to L&D activity, a term that refers to the commitment, shared purpose and perceptions of stakeholders that can be achieved through actively involving them in the planning, design, delivery and evaluation of learning events and processes (Kessels 1996).

Fordism/Fordist workplace Refers to the system of mass production characteristic of private sector organisations during the 1940s–1960s. Under Fordism, mass consumption combined with mass production to produce sustained economic growth and widespread material advancement. Henry Ford's assembly-line production system drove the explosive growth of the automobile industry, still the world's largest manufacturing activity.

function The body of (for example, L&D) activity that has to be provided for an organisation, and the personnel most directly responsible for that provision.

holistic view Looking at a system, situation, organisation or collection of activities as a whole that is greater than the mere sum of its parts – taking a helicopter view.

human capital The knowledge, skills, competencies and attributes embodied in individuals that facilitate the creation of personal, social and economic well-being (OECD 2001, p18). 'Gives us an alternative view of people management where people are assets to be deployed and managing them is a value adding activity' (CIPD 2003a).

implementation The process by which strategy or plans are put into action in the workplace.

instrumental learning Learning how to do the job better once the basic standard of performance has been attained. It is helped particularly by learning on the job (Mezirow 1985).

internal consistency Applied to L&D activity, a term that refers to the outcome achieved by the effective application of a systematic approach to planning, design, delivery and evaluation tasks (Kessels 1996).

job training analysis A process of identifying the purpose of a job and its component parts, and specifying what must be learned in order for there to be effective work performance.

job training specification A key outcome of job training analysis. It describes in overall terms the job for which training is to be given, or the key problem areas in a job which training will enable learners to tackle. It then specifies the kinds and levels of knowledge, skill and, where relevant, attitudes (the 'KSA' components) needed for effective performance, together with the performance standards for the job and the criteria for measuring achievement of the standards.

Key Skills The six 'key skills' identified in the Government's educational strategy are those of communication, use of IT, use of numbers, working with others, improving own learning and performance, and problem-solving.

knowledge Knowledge can be viewed as a type of commodity – something 'out there' that can be searched out and acquired, assessed, codified and distributed across the organisation. In this sense, it is an intangible asset that can have unique competitive value for an organisation. Yet knowledge can also be viewed as a process, emerging from within the individual but intimately shaped by relations with others. In this sense knowledge is dynamic, changing as the individual's understanding and interpretation of the world around him or her changes.

knowledge economy A way of describing a world in which 'knowledge' has become the key to wealth. In this world, the application of knowledge adds more value than the traditional factors of capital, raw materials and labour, and the 'knowledge worker' has unique status.

knowledge management A term often used to describe merely the capture and storage of information, usually by electronic means, although in its broader sense it refers to 'using the ideas and experience of employees, customers and suppliers to improve the organisation's performance'. It has come into regular use for three reasons: the use of knowledge as a competitive weapon; the increasing awareness of how easy it is to lose knowledge; and new technology's facilitation of knowledge sharing (Skapinker 2002).

knowledge productivity A term coined by Professor Joseph Kessels (1996) to refer to an organisation's ability to generate, disseminate and apply knowledge to products, processes and services. Knowledge productivity should therefore enable an organisation to continuously adapt and improve and to regularly innovate.

knowledge workers Peter Drucker (1993) is thought to have been the first to use this term, to describe specialist workers such as management consultants, architects, lawyers, accountants and PR experts, whose market value lies in what they know. In its broader sense, however, the term applies to all organisational members who apply their knowledge (especially of the unique tacit kind) successfully to the improvement of operating procedures, products, services and processes and to innovate.

KSA components see job training specification.

L&D see learning and development.

learning A qualitative change in a person's way of seeing, experiencing, understanding and conceptualising something in the real world (Marton and Ramsden 1988). Also a process whereby such change occurs.

learning and development (L&D) An organisational process to aid the development of knowledge and the achievement of organisational and individual goals. It involves the collaborative stimulation and facilitation of learning and developmental processes, initiatives and relationships in ways that respect and build on human diversity in the workplace.

learning and development function The way in which the whole body of L&D activity is structured in an organisation.

learning technology A term that refers to the way in which learning media and methods are incorporated into the design and delivery of a learning event and interact with those participating in the event.

media of learning The routes, or channels, through which learning is transmitted to the learner.

methods of learning The ways in which learning is transmitted.

mission The detailed (and usually written) articulation of vision (qv), which acts as an inspiration and a guide for action. Sometimes a mission statement represents only a minority view, and mission statements also fall out of date. Many therefore now regard missions as valueless yet the process that produces them does have value, if it brings together organisational members in ways that encourage informed reflection on crucial issues and that generate innovative thinking.

monitoring of learning 'Taking the temperature' of a learning event or process from time to time, picking up any problems or emerging needs.

organisation 'Involves all the elements of organisational design; not only the formal structures of organisational charts but also the systems, processes and people dimensions that are essential to making these work' (CIPD 2003b).

organising The dynamic process needed if organisational design is to be effectively implemented and regularly renewed. The skills involved in how to organise and regularly re-organise are as important as knowing what organisational design to choose (Whittington and Mayer 2002).

organisational context The internal and external organisational circumstances that shape and help to explain the organisational situation being examined. Often, organisational context is summarised by reference to culture and structure, but they themselves emerge from the interplay of more fundamental factors. Research indicates that three of the most powerful are: top management's vision and values, line management's style and actions at all organisational levels and HR strategies and practices.

paradigm shift A permanent change in the established pattern of thinking by organisational members about their work organisation; a radical shift in the way they understand their world.

pluralist system A term that refers to the concept of an organisation as a system in which there are many and often conflicting interests, and therefore in which conflict itself is a natural occurrence. Contrast with unitary system (qv).

post-Fordism/post-Fordist workplace One where efficient operations have required the dismantling of the Fordist workplace to enable a more equal distribution of knowledge, authority and responsiblity (Zuboff 1988). See Fordism (qv).

psychological contract Concerns the social and emotional aspects of the exchange between employer and employee (Sparrow 1999, p420). It refers to that aspect of the relationship binding individual and organisation that consists of felt and perceived expectations, wants and rights. It represents a dynamic and reciprocal deal, with new expectations being added over time.

relational contract A psychological contract based on mutual commitment. See psychological contract (qv).

self-managed learning Term coined by Ian Cunningham to describe an approach he developed at the Anglian Regional Management Centre in the 1970s. SML essentially refers to the individual taking charge of their own learning, whether through independent study or in a learning group in an organisation (for example, an action learning set). In each case the individual negotiates a learning contract agreeing on learning goals and how he or she will achieve them.

self-reflective learning The kind of learning that leads individuals to redefine their current perspective in order to develop new patterns of understanding, thinking and behaving. It requires unlearning as well as new learning (Mezirow 1985). See also double-loop learning (qv).

single-loop learning A concept to describe the style of learning involved in taking a problem at its face value and therefore tackling its surface symptoms but not its root causes (Argyris 1977). Contrast with double-loop learning (qv).

skilled incompetence Term coined by Chris Argyris (1996) to describe the way in which once successful organisations rest on their laurels for too long, causing strategies and behavioural patterns to become increasingly inappropriate in the face of new challenges. The learning that once enabled them to become highly competent has become outdated and is now the biggest barrier to their survival.

social capital Networks together with shared norms, values and understandings that facilitate co-operation within or among groups (OECD 2001, p41).

strategic capability 'Strategic capability provides the vision, the rich and sustained learning and knowledge development, the integrity of purpose and the continuous direction and scope to the activities of the firm that are needed to secure long-term survival. It is based on a profound understanding of the competitive environment, of the resource-base, capacity and potential of the organisation, of the strategy process, and of the values that engender commitment from stakeholders to corporate goals' (Harrison and Miller 1999).

strategising The continuing process needed if strategy is to be effectively implemented and regularly renewed; the dynamic process by which a chosen strategy is continuously adapted and often changed to fit or exploit changes in the external and internal environment of the organisation (Whittington and Mayer 2002).

strategy A route that has been chosen for a period of time and from a range of options in order to achieve organisational and business goals.

tacit knowledge Knowledge that is embedded deep in the individual or the collective subconscious, expressing itself in habitual or intuitive ways of doing things that are exercised without conscious thought or effort (Nonaka 1991).

technology The particular way in which, in a workplace, technical systems, machinery and processes are designed to interact with human skill and knowledge in order to convert inputs into outputs.

theories Constructs that are the products of reflections on, testing of, and generalisations from, experience. Theories help to aid initial understanding, to give structure to ideas, to suggest explanations of actions and events, and to improve skill in problem-solving and practice in the 'real world'.

thinking performers Practitioners who are knowledgeable and competent in their various fields, and able to move beyond compliance to provide a critique of organisational policies and procedures and to advise on how organisations should develop in the future (CIPD 2001a).

transactional contract A psychological contract representing a mainly functional relationship between employer and organisation: specified services in return for specified compensation. See psychological contract (qv).

train To instruct and discipline in or for some particular art, profession, occupation or practice; to exercise, practise, drill (Onions 1973). To teach a specified skill especially by practice (Pearsall and Trumble 1996).

unitary system Refers to the concept of an organisation as a system in which there is one overriding goal or set of interests, and in which consensus, not conflict, is the expected norm. Contrasts with pluralist system (qv).

validation of learning An assessment of the extent to which learning objectives have been achieved.

vision The picture that people hold in their minds about what kind of organisation theirs should be. Some believe vision should be clear and shared across the organisation, in order to be an effective guide to action. Others see value in a vision that, while being compelling, also has sufficient ambiguity to cause searching questions to be asked about the organisation's direction, and to stimulate creativity in finding ways forward.

workforce development Consists of activities which increase the capacity of individuals to participate effectively in the workplace, thereby improving their productivity and employability (DfES 2003a).

Understanding the Field

Main Themes and Issues in Learning and Development

CHAPTER 1

INTRODUCTION

In *Barnaby Rudge* Charles Dickens wrote:

> **'Chroniclers are privileged to enter where they list, to come and go through keyholes, to ride upon the wind, to overcome, in their soarings up and down, all obstacles of distance, time and place.'**

Some chroniclers find it hard to decide on exactly where to list as they begin their story. 'Begin at the beginning', Alice in Wonderland would have said. But where is the beginning of learning and development?

The purpose of this four-part chapter is to present learning and development (L&D) as an organisational process, and to place it in both a historical and a current context. Because L&D is a multi-faceted field of study, the first two sections open a series of gateways into its territory. In the third section there is a discussion of current trends affecting the L&D field, and the fourth contains a story about an organisation – Procter and Gamble – that is now investing heavily in L&D, and the benefits its management hopes will flow from that.

GATEWAYS INTO LEARNING AND DEVELOPMENT TERRITORY

Figure 1 contains an advertisement picked at random from many that appeared in a single month in *People Management*.

What does the advert tell anyone new to the field of learning and development (L&D)? That it is essentially about training? Not so. The advert refers to training planning, design and delivery, but it also refers to 'learning solutions' and the professionals it seeks to attract are described not as trainers but as learning and development specialists. That it is a narrow field, dominated by a fairly small cluster of tasks? Not so. The work that its professionals are expected to do in this company is broad-based and clearly requires sophisticated behavioural as well as functional skills.

It is natural enough that high-level experience and expertise is needed to work at this level in a major global organisation. What is more significant because it applies to L&D practitioners in organisations far smaller and more localised than this one is the emphasis on how they should operate and on the results they should achieve. Processes to do with partnering and teamwork are critical to their ability to deliver added value.

The message in all of this is that L&D is a major business field. It requires passion as well as skill, the successful operation of processes as well as the design and delivery of products, and a commitment to the organisation no less than to individuals. It involves demanding and

Figure 1 *The Hemsley Fraser advertisement*
Source: Reproduced with kind permission of Hemsley Fraser Group Limited, London

interrelated areas of activity – see, for example, in Appendix 1 those identified by the CIPD as the 10 key areas in which the performance of any L&D practitioner should be measured.

In the section that follows I open four gateways into the L&D field: those of terminology, of purpose, of theories and of human resource management. The final gateway, of history, is given a subsequent section of its own.

The gateway of terminology

Terms for L&D as an organisational process
The terms that we choose to describe things matter. In the past three terms have been widely

used to describe the L&D field: 'training and development', 'employee development', and 'human resource development'.

The term *'training and development'* is still a popular one, particularly in official publications. However, training is only one way of achieving development, and to highlight it in this way is to give it a prominence that can be dangerous. It can imply that all that really counts in an organisation, or indeed in a country, is formal, planned learning activity. Some national policy implications of this view are discussed in Chapters 2 and 3.

The term *'employee development'* is now touched by political incorrectness. It smacks too much of the old 'master–servant' relationship. It is no accident that it is falling out of use at a time when many organisations are referring to their members as associates or partners rather than as employees.

The term *'human resource development'* retains its popularity amongst academics but it has never been as attractive to practitioners. They tend to dislike it because reference to people as a 'resource' is felt to be demeaning. Putting people on a par with money, materials and equipment creates the impression of 'development' as an essentially unfeeling, even manipulative activity.

What then is left? During 1999 and 2000 the CIPD was conducting a country-wide consultation process to review the professional standards it had first produced in 1996. During that process the matter of what to call the revised 'Employee Development' was endlessly debated. Many titles were rejected until only one was left: 'Learning and Development'. This term alone focused on what everyone agreed mattered most – the learning needed if organisational and individual development is to occur. It is an inclusive term too, and it came closer than any other to capturing the desired vision of shared endeavour. Like HRD, but without the pitfalls associated with that term, it conveys the scope of a process that can extend beyond those who work in the organisation to those who, although not legally its employees, make an essential contribution to its success – for example, voluntary and contracted-out workers and suppliers. Coincidentally the national occupational standards in 'Training and Development' that were being revised at the same time also emerged under the same changed title: 'Learning and Development'.

Meanings attached to 'learning'
However, using the term 'Learning and Development' is not the perfect solution. What is gained in scope is lost somewhat in generalisation. 'Learning' has so many meanings. A common view is to see it as a lifelong activity involving three processes (Onions 1973):

- *To develop*: to unfold more fully, bring out all that is contained in
- *To educate*: to bring up from childhood, so as to form habits, manners and mental and physical aptitudes
- *To train*: to instruct and discipline in or for some particular art, profession, occupation or practice; to exercise, practise, drill.

Combining these terms highlights a conditioning process and the gaining of competencies through planned instructional activity. Another kind of definition would draw more attention to learning driven by the individual's natural curiosity and by everyday experience.

So the terms that we choose to describe things do matter. They bestow identity and they influence people's perception. An organisation that uses the term 'human resource development' in preference to 'employee development', or 'training', or 'learning and development' has a reason for that choice. If in Figure 1 the advertisement had contained the word 'training' instead of 'learning and development' throughout, how differently might you have interpreted it?

The gateway of purpose

Terminology cannot take us much further. What we need now is a statement of purpose that can give real meaning to L&D as an organisational process.

L&D activity first acquired a specific organisational meaning in the USA in the 1970s. Termed 'human resource development' its purpose was regarded as primarily about short-term training, encompassing skills acquisition and behavioural change. It was defined by one of its most influential commentators (Nadler 1970) as:

> **'a series of organized activities conducted within a specified time and designed to produce behavioural change.'**

By the 1980s some commentators were moving towards a more strategic perspective. Hall (1984), another well-known American author, had this to say:

> **'Strategic human resource development is the identification of needed skills and active management of learning for the long-range future in relation to explicit corporate and business strategies.'**

By the early 1990s in the USA 'HRD' had developed into a recognisable profession, with many of its members emphasising their role as agents of organisational change. HRD was now to do less with training or with 'explicit strategies' than with a generalised task of renewal (Burack 1991):

> **'HRD people have been charged to blueprint and lead the way to organization and individual renewal.'**

However even now there was still no universally accepted definition in the USA (Nadler 1992). The situation was no clearer in the UK, where in 1998 a survey commissioned by the (then) Institute of Personnel and Development found that training and development practitioners were (Darling, Darling and Elliott 1999: xii):

> **'affected by the confusion of meanings and boundaries between such terms as human resource management, human resource development, training, learning and development.'**

In its revised professional standards, the Institute (by then chartered) laid out its statement of L&D's purpose as an organisational process. It emphasises the significance of L&D activity for the business, whether in for-profit or in not-for-profit organisations. It also recognises the need to obtain the active commitment of the learners. You cannot force people to learn, but you can encourage and help them to do so. The CIPD's definition of L&D's purpose is as follows (CIPD 2001a):

> **'The organisational process of developing people involves the integration of learning and development processes, operations and relationships. Its most powerful outcomes for the business are to do with enhanced organisational effectiveness and sustainability. For the individual they are to do with enhanced personal competence, adaptability and employability. It is therefore a critical business process, whether in for-profit or not-for-profit organisations.'**

In all its professional standards the CIPD identifies two generic roles of people and development professionals: those of thinking performer and business partner. *Thinking performers* are knowledgeable and competent in their field, able to move beyond compliance to provide a critique of organisational policies and procedures and advice on how organisations should develop in the future. A *business partner* works with others at his or her level both within and outside the organisation in order to make a strong contribution to organisational performance (for competencies associated with these roles see Harrison 2004). These roles give a strong strategic thrust to L&D activity.

My own definition of L&D's purpose is shorter than the CIPD's and has a rather different emphasis:

> **'The primary purpose of learning and development as an organisational process is to aid collective progress through the collaborative and expert stimulation and facilitation of learning and knowledge that support business goals, develop individual potential, and respect and build on diversity.'**

Implicit in this statement is a recognition of the centrality of mutuality and ethics to L&D policy and practice. In using learning to meet organisational ends we are intervening in a process that goes to the heart of human identity. We cannot expect individuals to use that process to benefit the organisation unless they believe that it will also benefit them. And we should not use it in ways that exploit human vulnerability or that cause or increase damaging divisions between people. As employees, those with L&D roles should work to add value for the business. As members of a wider professional community they must do so in ways that enact that community's ethical values.

My definition also highlights learning as the route to knowledge. It is a central theme of this book that the unique value of the learning process for any organisation is the knowledge that it can generate. Knowledge creation enables an organisation to continuously improve and from time to time radically innovate in its products, services and processes. An organisation that invests in the learning of its members without being clear what kind of value-adding return it seeks is an organisation that courts failure. As one commentator pointed out (Coulson-Thomas 2001):

> **'For many years before its break-up, Rover had championed learning at all levels in the organisation. But what was learned did little to enhance the company's competitiveness, as events subsequently proved.'**

Today there remain so many meanings attached to L&D as an organisational process that it can be arbitrary to select any one definition. Some say the confusion is caused by its inter-disciplinary nature, drawing as it does on psychology, sociology, educational theory, economics – the list goes on. For others, myself included, that is simplistic. Many factors are at work here as our final gateway, of history, will reveal.

The gateway of theories

A third gateway into L&D territory is provided by theoretical frameworks, or 'constructs' as they are often called in research studies. First, some general points:

- Theories are the products of a) reflections on experience, b) the testing of experience, and c) generalisations from experience. The experience may be taken from real life, or it may be artificially constructed before being tested in a real life situation.
- Theories can aid our understanding, give structure to our ideas, suggest explanations for actions and events that we encounter, and improve our skill in problem-solving, decision-making and practice.
- However, theories about L&D are not rules and should not be treated as such. There are no theories that explain beyond dispute how people think, learn and acquire knowledge, so there can never be black-and-white L&D prescriptions.

Theories can seem dry and academic. Stories, on the other hand, provide us with the *feel* of L&D. Without them we may study theory yet be unable to relate it to the real world. Even for the most experienced practitioner, narratives about unfamiliar situations and contexts can offer an emotional understanding of the L&D process. They also have a central role to play in developing a community's culture, bringing its members together as they reflect on their past and take pride in their unique identity.

The studies with which the following narrative is associated made a major contribution to L&D theory. As you read it, try to identify two or three concepts that seem to you to be of major importance. A commentary follows the case.

CASE EXAMPLE

The photocopier repair technicians

A group of technicians had to repair photocopier machines in customers' locations. They had been given detailed instructional manuals and training. However, it soon became clear to them that this formal knowledge was not enough. The people who had designed the machines had not understood the different social settings in which they had to be used, and so had ignored many of the everyday human errors that cause such machines to break down.

When the technicians realised this they got together to discuss the many repair problems that they were encountering. All they had to fall back on was their own experience and intuition. They had to draw on their 'tacit' knowledge – the kind of knowledge that is often buried deep in the subconscious, expressing itself in habitual ways of doing things that people often exercise without conscious thought or effort (Nonaka 1991).

The technicians shared this kind of knowledge as they exchanged stories of similar problems they had encountered in the past and of how they had dealt with them. By comparing what they knew from experience with the 'explicit' or formal knowledge contained in their training and repair manuals, they began to work out how to tackle the many repair problems they kept encountering. Uncertainty, the need to know, experimentation and discovery finally gave them an unrivalled understanding of the machines. This understanding was developed as much through their social interactions and conversations as through any technical know-how. It enabled them to combine 'tacit' and 'explicit' knowledge in ways that produced innovative ideas and led to improved work methods.

Source: ORR, J.E. (1990)

Comments

This story was one of a number that helped to give birth to three central concepts related to workplace learning and knowledge in organisations:

- learning situated in workplace communities of practice (Vygotsky 1978; Brown and Duguid 1991; Lave and Wenger 1991)
- knowledge as a process that is shaped by social interactions (Nonaka 1991; Hall 1993)
- knowledge that can be tacit or explicit (Polanyi 1966; Nonaka 1994).

Much more will be said about workplace learning later in this book. What matters here is to notice the way in which Orr's story breathes life into academic theory through the reassuringly commonplace setting in which it is located and its picture of a society in miniature, its identity developing through collective informal learning.

Stories alone are not enough, of course. The methods by which research is undertaken, the samples the researchers use, the reliance we can place on their data and its analysis – all these are critical factors in deciding which theories to use as our guides. Even the most respected constructs can prove fallible. You will find throughout this book regular statements such as 'there is evidence to suggest', 'there are statistics to indicate', 'it is logical to conclude that', or 'it may seem that'. These are all marks of uncertainty concerning the crucial question 'What is really going on here?'

Centuries ago a famous theologian wrote – naturally in a different context, but producing insights relevant to this discussion – (St Augustine):

> **'The appearance of what we do is different from the intention with which we do it, and the circumstances at the time may not be clear.'**

Many commentators have found a major disconnect between what firms claim as their human resource (HR) strategy and what happens in reality (Storey 1992; Truss and Gratton 1994; Becker and Gerhart 1996; Pettigrew et al 2002). That kind of gap can be wide and littered with intervening variables. Strategy-makers often see only what they wish to see. Those who have to put plans into action may not always be aware of, or may not wish to confess to, the many changes that those plans can go through once they reach the workplace. And those charged with strategy's implementation may be incompetent or unwilling to perform the task.

So all theories should be challenged. It is a sign of strength, not weakness, to admit that some need to be changed or abandoned in the face of new knowledge. As L&D practitioners test out theories in an increasing range of organisational situations they should become more confident in their own views. It is one of the tasks of a professional to assess where theory works, where it does not, on what evidence it is grounded and how best to apply it to the particular situation.

The HRM gateway

Our fourth gateway offers a unique perspective on L&D – that of its membership of a family of HR processes. Traditionally the term 'human resource management' has been taken to mean the practices, formal policies and overarching philosophies whereby an organisation's employees are attracted, deployed, retained, rewarded, developed and nurtured (Jackson and Schuler 1995). Figure 2 shows this family of processes and their interaction in the form of a wheel.

There are many studies in the UK and the USA going back to the 1980s whose findings support the view that L&D should be linked in appropriate ways with wider HR practices in order to make its due organisational contribution. One important CIPD-sponsored research programme currently being carried out at the University of Bath is confirming the need for this integrative approach and has produced a People and Performance framework to express it in visual form (Purcell et al 2003). You will find the framework in Chapter 5, where I explain how it relates to performance management and development in an organisation.

The Bath research findings make abundantly clear the need for people management and development professionals to work together in a shared purpose. Not all trainers accept the logic of this argument. Some seek the separation rather than the integration of 'training' and 'personnel' so that training can make a unique impact on the business. This is to fly in the face of logic. Whatever the problems in HR professionals from different fields working in partnership – and it must be admitted that there can be many – there is now a convincing weight of evidence that L&D activity has a crucial part to play in raising the skills and commitment levels needed by high-performing organisations, but that this activity needs to be supported by wider HR practices, and to link positively with organisational goals.

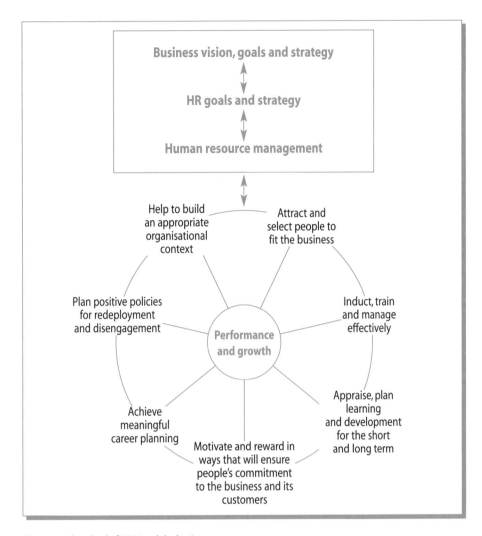

Figure 2 *The wheel of HRM and the business*

Introduction to the fifth gateway

The final L&D gateway is the biggest because it takes us into the history of L&D as a business process. Some say that history is unimportant. They claim that in a fast-changing world it can teach us little of relevance, and that its narratives are in any case biased. I disagree. No historical accounts can be completely objective, but they remain a vital key to the past. They offer us an understanding of the routes we have travelled to reach where we are today. They reveal some of the values and mindsets that have coloured past views of the world and that explain past decisions. They show the ultimate outcomes of strategies on which we have relied – often so different from those that were intended. This need to know, coupled with a willingness to take responsibility for the past and to learn from it, are vital to the healthy working of any society.

My account of L&D's history is necessarily brief. The selection and analysis of data on which it rests are coloured by the lens through which I view the L&D world. But I hope that it can still provide some useful insights.

THE GATEWAY OF HISTORY

(Note: As the term 'Learning and Development' refers to a field that is more usually known in the literature as 'Human resource development' (HRD), that term will be used throughout most of this section)

The study and practice of HRD will always be challenging because it is underpinned by so many different disciplines. Its boundaries are disputed and the needs it serves do not sit comfortably together. In organisations the demands made on it by 'the business' and by 'the individual' can never be completely reconciled. Often pressures upon it from different groups of stakeholders can cause acute conflicts of interest and a negative organisational contribution.

The foundation years

During the last century there were three distinct strands to HRD's development.

The cusp of the twentieth century: scientific management and the psychology of learning

For many this is where HRD really began. The work of American organisational psychologists from the 1950s, discussed below, was essentially the continuation of pioneering activity in industrial management and in the psychology of learning that started at the onset of the industrial age.

The American engineer F. W. Taylor (1856–1915) and his colleagues produced in those early years a body of work that has continued to influence management theory and practice down to present times. That work, expanded subsequently, came to be known as Scientific Management. Taylor believed that the chaotic conditions that he often found in industrial settings must be tackled by the application of rational, fair and systematic forms of management and organisation. He saw in scientific method a way of ensuring the orderly design and structuring of work, improved conditions for employees and greatly enhanced efficiency and productivity for the business. It could help to build mutuality of interest and effort between management and workers (Taylor 1947).

Taylor saw a need for training to be a well designed systematic process so that operators could rapidly and with minimum stress achieve competent and consistent standards of performance in their tasks. His approach here was greatly influenced by early psychological studies into animal and human behaviour that proposed stimulus–response theory as the key to learning (see Chapter 4). It was also influenced by a desire to improve the health and welfare of industrial workers.

If we place the true origins of organisational HRD in the dawn of the industrial era when management science, health and safety research and psychological theories were beginning to converge, we can more easily understand the tensions that still bedevil the L&D process. Many of them arise from trying to combine a business imperative with a genuine concern for the well-being and development of the individual, and from an excessive preoccupation with training as the key to employees' learning.

The Second World War: the growth of industrial training

For those who see the HRD process as being essentially about 'training', its historical starting-point is here. During the Second World War, training as a work-field developed a business profile in both the USA and the UK. In the UK, training officers came into being as a distinct category of staff, and the influential author G. R. Moxon (1943) linked education with training to form one of the 'six categories' of personnel management work. By 1996 the professional field in the UK had broadened to incorporate HRD at levels four and five of the new national occupational standards in training and development.

As I will explain in Chapter 4, this training strand in the history of HRD continues to be enormously influential. It has led to an over-emphasis by government and employers on learning activity that is planned, formalised and measurable, underplaying the value of more informal learning processes. The lasting popularity of the 'systematic training model' has much to do with this, and so deserves an explanation at this point.

I have already noted that the thrust to systematise training goes back to the days of Taylorism. It received a huge boost during the war years because of the need for thousands of inexperienced factory operators (many of them women entering employment for the first time) to quickly master tasks that were vital to the war effort. In the post-war reconstruction years much basic research was carried out in the UK by psychologists like Douglas Seymour (1959) and by institutions like the Department of Scientific and Industrial Research and the Industrial Training Council, all working to understand and perfect techniques by which the learning of industrial tasks in particular could best take place. In the 1960s as the UK's industrial performance began to flag, the systematic approach to training was developed into a full-blown model (Taylor 1991). It was widely publicised by the 23 Industrial Training Boards set up in 1964.

The model's purpose is to make training methodology more rigorous, consistent and scientifically based. As shown in Figure 3 it represents an orderly, sequential cycle of functional training tasks. Specific instruments used include needs assessment techniques, instructional objectives, learning strategies, training materials, guidelines for trainers, and evaluation instruments.

Work continued to be carried out on the systematic cycle of training activity, especially by Tom Boydell (1971). In the late 1990s the model underpinned the development of national occupational standards in training and development, and more recently was applied to their revision. Its weaknesses as well as its strengths are reflected there.

The major criticism of the model is that it presents training as operating in a free-standing closed system dominated by functional tasks. The underlying assumption is that these tasks should and can take place in a predetermined sequence, requiring only the application of specialist expertise to ensure their success.

Real life, of course, is not so simple. In reality training has to be carried out in contexts that can be messy, disorganised, and complicated by the interplay of powerful political forces.

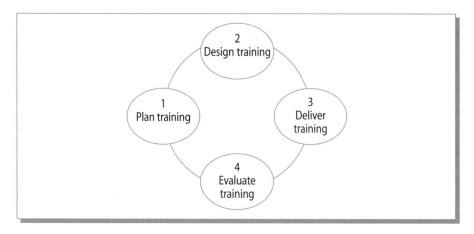

Figure 3 *The systematic training model*

No matter how perfect its design and delivery, it can still fail if it does not pay enough attention to that context. When training based on systematic principles does fail it is usually because it lacks the support of key stakeholders – especially front-line managers of learners and the learners themselves – whose buy-in is essential to its success (Kessels and Harrison 1998).

The post-war years: organisational psychology and systems theory

During the 1950s and 1960s in the USA organisational psychologists like Argyris (1957), McGregor (1960), Likert (1961) and Hertzberg (1966) were studying motivation at work. Their research drew attention to the needs of all employees for self-fulfilment, meaningful work and tasks that could engage their intelligence and develop their potential. The idea that all organisational members had a creative contribution to make and deserved the opportunity to do so no matter at what level they worked in the hierarchy became widely popularised. Coupled with a developing interest in Japanese notions of total quality management and a concern to find new ways of gaining competitive advantage, this led many organisations to innovate in their HRD practices as well as in the business more widely.

Meanwhile in the UK, researchers at the Tavistock Institute of Human Relations were exploring organisations as systems, the interaction of whose human and technical elements determined the overall capability of an organisation to adapt to its environment (Trist and Bamforth 1951). This organic view stressed the need for as much attention to be paid to human as to technical needs in organisations. It highlighted learning as the means whereby organisations continuously adapt to their environment. This added a major perspective to HRD.

Both systems thinking and organisational psychology had a powerful impact on the subsequent development of 'learning organisation' theory (Senge 1990) and indeed of HR theory more widely. They provide a link to the current preoccupation with informal workplace learning and knowledge creation as sources of unique competitive capability – a topic we will touch on again towards the end of this chapter. They also reflect much of the thinking that informs the latest HR research today concerning the links between individual and organisational performance, as will be seen in Chapter 5. As the saying goes, there is little, after all, that is new under the sun...

The push for business results

As the HRD field expanded during the second half of the twentieth century the business imperative grew steadily stronger, particularly in the USA. *Human capital theory* (Schultz 1961) was by then widely known, largely due to the writings of the economist G. Becker (1975). This theory presents people as organisational assets whose economic value derives from their skills, competence, knowledge and experience. Intangibles such as intellectual property and customer equity are all derived from human capital and are regarded as the ultimate source of competitive advantage, generating earnings that are powerful drivers of stock returns. Becker argued that investment in training and education leads to increased productivity, and thence to increased wages and business earnings. This makes HRD a value-adding process both for organisations and for individuals. Since education is a powerful means of creating a more numerate, literate and informed society, it can enable HRD to fulfil its wider social purpose.

We can see here direct links with the emphasis today on building human capital and on human capital reporting by businesses. I will return to this point later in this chapter.

The business imperative expressed itself in a strong drive for performance improvement that has continued to dominate HRD practice in the USA. In the UK, the same drive gained ground during the 1980s, notably in larger and multi-divisional organisations. A sustained period of recession had been accompanied by a collapse in manufacturing and by a rapid decline in the country's skill base as apprenticeship numbers were slashed. The outcomes of these crises highlighted the need for performance improvement and skills development. At the same time, much was being learnt about business-focused training strategies practised in successful competitor countries like Germany and Japan.

Throughout the last two decades of the twentieth century government in the UK attempted to break the old pattern of a 'stop-go' approach to vocational education and training. It encouraged organisations to invest in a more business-focused strategic approach to their training investment, particularly through the introduction of the Investors in People Standard in the early 1990s (see Chapter 2 and Appendix 4).

In the HRD profession many have been concerned at the extent to which the drive to improve short term economic performance dominates employers' HRD investment. In the USA in the early 1990s a group of HRD academics and practitioners established the Academy of Human Resource Development. It was not a physical institution but a body of people who felt that an undue preoccupation with the business drivers of HRD was undermining its potential to achieve individual and social benefits. The Academy's membership expanded over the years and it now has strong partnership ties with the more recently established University Forum for HRD in the UK. The Forum's network in this country consists of over 20 universities conducting research and providing postgraduate master's-level HRD programmes. It also incorporates EURESFORM, an international association for universities, reflective practitioners and learning-oriented organisations. Its aim is to achieve through improved research and practice a strong focus on lifelong learning that will expand the capabilities and creativity of individuals as well as of the business and the economy (www.ufhrd.com).

The importance of context

Today, although employers increasingly call for their L&D activity to be more convincingly tied to business needs, there are still many organisations where this is not happening and also where L&D professionals are failing to make a strategic contribution. Often this is because they do not relate their activity sufficiently to context. That term has two dimensions, external and internal:

The *external context* consists of the business environment of the organisation and other external factors that have a direct relevance for L&D practice within the organisation.

The *internal, organisational context*, expressed most obviously in workplace culture, is most powerfully shaped by:

- top management's vision and values, goals and leadership
- management (especially front-line management) style and actions
- HR strategies and practices.

To work effectively within context HR practitioners, including those specialising in the L&D field, must form business partnerships, working at multiple organisational levels in order to integrate their operations with business activity (Ulrich 1987; Mohrman and Lawler III 1999). The fact that much of this book is concerned with exploring L&D activity in a variety of organisational settings is an acknowledgement of the importance of context and of partnerships.

REFLECTION

This section has provided an overview of HRD's history, from its beginnings as a set of operational activities focused primarily on training to its current position as an organisational learning process with powerful but rarely realised strategic potential. If you could change one aspect of organisational context in order to improve L&D's strategic impact in your organisation, which would you choose – and why?

CURRENT TRENDS

Pressures on line managers

As far back as the early 1990s the major Cranfield European HRM survey indicated a growing awareness in organisations across Europe of the need for full integration that would create a synergy between the training and development of the individual employee, development of business strategies and plans, and development of the organisation (Larsen 1994, p121). Trends indicated an increased decentralisation of HRD to line management to achieve this.

In the UK, senior HR and training professionals in 531 organisations who responded to the CIPD's 2004 annual training and development survey (CIPD 2004a) offered a mixed message here. Although 94 per cent agreed that line managers should have a significant role to play in helping their teams to learn and develop, 60 per cent reported that HR and training departments, not line managers, were still expected to take the main responsibility for driving learning activities. While 74 per cent agreed to a somewhat vague statement about the need for a supportive culture for learning and development, only 58 per cent advocated getting managers' active commitment to L&D activities (Thomson 2004). At the same time the survey confirmed the continuance of a well documented past trend: lack of management support in evaluating training.

Restructuring of organisations now takes place on average once every three years. Pressures on line managers are therefore increasing. In June 2004, Barclays Bank announced plans to merge three internal business units into a single 'UK Banking' section. A key change would be the creation of a new type of branch manager with increased autonomy to create a branch workforce, with HR input, and according to local needs. In July 2004, the Chancellor announced a forthcoming downsizing of the Civil Service, initially by around 80,000 jobs with a further 20,000 to follow in the longer term. Once more, back office jobs were expected to feature large together with a major reliance on information technology to take up the slack. Once more, front-line managers can anticipate increased pressures and expanded responsibilities.

Research conducted at the University of Bath into the links between HR practices and organisational performance has already been mentioned in this chapter. It is throwing new light on the critical role played by front-line managers in enabling or preventing the success of L&D plans (Hutchinson and Purcell 2003). Most respondents to the CIPD's 2004 Training and Development survey made similar observations, expressing the need for:

- clear understanding by managers of their role in developing their staff
- the development of line managers with the skills and motivation to encourage and support learning
- making 'developing others' a part of line managers' annual performance objectives
- ensuring line managers are committed and rewarded for L&D activities.

Yet only 10 per cent reported that their organisations attached importance to these ways of supporting managers who held L&D responsibilities. As a further disturbing sign, two major reports have recently warned of grave deficiencies in UK firms' approach to training and developing managers, of a significant underinvestment compared with almost all European countries, and of a generally non-strategic management development process (CEML 2002; Mabey and Ramirez 2004). Chapter 16 provides further details.

Trends in the training investment

Another finding of the 2004 CIPD survey was that in 2003 a higher proportion of public sector than private sector organisations had cut their budgets, with only 13 per cent feeling any improvement in their economic circumstances despite increased public sector funding from government. In the private sector too the year had been hard. Training budgets held steadier in that sector, but there was little sign of consciously building for the future rather than simply responding to here-and-now skills needs. In most organisations L&D activity was focused only on immediate operational, technical and legislative requirements. Such findings do not suggest cultures in which learning, as distinct from short-term training, can flourish.

Human capital reporting

Human capital is officially defined as (OECD 2001, p18):

'the knowledge, skills, competencies and attributes embodied in individuals that facilitate the creation of personal, social and economic well-being.'

In the past few years there has been a resurgence of interest in the building of human capital – an interest that, in my historical outline of HRD, I noted was a dominating one in the USA in the 1970s. The US federal governments' Office of Management and Budget now insists that its agencies include human capital management in their performance plans. In 2003 the UK government launched its proposals for measuring the effects of human capital management on company performance in a consultation paper, *Accounting for People* (http://www.accountingforpeople.gov.uk). It highlights four basic areas, one of which is 'staff training and development'. From 2005 it is mandatory for all UK-based organisations to report on their management of human capital. The CIPD has worked with the Government on human capital reporting, and has now produced its own reporting framework (http://www.cipd.co.uk/changeagendas). It focuses on all the ways in which the firm adds value through its people, and recommends as one of the core components of any annual report a section on how the company develops and manages employees.

New technology can offer invaluable help here, although as Trapp (2004) points out any metrics used in HR software systems must enable comparisons to be made both inside and outside the company. The Saratoga Institute, an arm of PricewaterhouseCoopers, has developed a wide range of metrics designed to enable managers to more accurately assess the impact of changes in HR policies on their organisations.

In Chapter 13 I explore some of the issues for L&D professionals that arise from this renewed interest in developing human capital. It is enough to remark here that it holds many implications for the ways in which they set and measure outcomes for their activity.

The emergence of a new knowledge economy

One of the best documented of current trends that carry important L&D implications is the emergence of a more knowledge-based economy – that is to say, one in which the application of knowledge adds more value to the business than the application of traditional factors of capital, raw materials and labour.

By 2010 it is likely that around 30 per cent of job growth will be in specialist knowledge-based jobs, but in a knowledge economy it is not only these specialists who count. What matters most for organisations is the capability to develop and apply new knowledge to continuous improvement and radical innovation in goods, services and processes. All organisational members have a vital part to play there, so in that sense all are knowledge workers.

Organisations operating in the new knowledge economy need to make a long-term and organisation-wide investment in the kind of learning that leads to improvement and innovation. It is not enough to invest, as the majority in the UK appear to do at present, primarily in training that covers only 'key' workers. As will be seen in Chapter 2, Government policy is now actively promoting workplace learning and an expansion in workforce development.

Social capital

With the emergence of a knowledge economy it becomes vital for organisations to develop not only their human capital but also their social capital, defined officially as (OECD 2001, p41):

'networks together with shared norms, values and understandings that facilitate co-operation within or among groups. Trust may be viewed as both a source and an outcome of social capital.'

'Social capital' is about human relationships that act as the glue for society. Putnam (2000), Professor of Public Policy at Harvard University, emphasised the dangers confronting any society in which the sum of this capital shrinks: communities fragment, trust and mutual commitment are lost, commonality of purpose disappears and society itself begins to break down. Organisations failing to invest in social capital face a similar fate. Without durable social capital they cannot hope to generate the new knowledge upon which, especially in a knowledge economy, their survival depends. It is the development of social capital in an organisation that provides the conditions that nurture a willingness among individuals to connect and learn together and to apply the fruits of that learning to a shared organisational purpose (Huysman and De Wit 2002, p166).

Research in the UK indicates that most organisations today are continuing to invest only or mainly in the short-term training of human capital. The typical training and career development investment also tends to be restricted to personnel seen to be 'key' to the business, mainly managers, professionals and specialist knowledge workers. Far fewer opportunities are available for the rest (Stevens and Ashton 1999; Stevens 2000). As will be seen particularly in Chapters 5, 8, 9, 15 and 16 this raises many issues related to the management of diversity, and to the building of organisations' capacity for the future.

Focus on workplace learning

On a more hopeful note, the CIPD's 2004 Training and Development survey showed that greater attention is now being paid to workplace learning, and that on the job training and coaching/mentoring are the most popular processes here. Their main use, however, is to improve individual performance, tackle underperformance and improve productivity – again, not an indicator that value is placed on longer-term development. The survey also revealed that there is (CIPD 2004a):

- minimal evaluation of either coaching or mentoring processes against business objectives
- very little training provided for the line managers who carry the main burden of coaching roles
- uncertainty as to what activities coaching and mentoring involve.

This suggests that these processes are more the results of an act of faith than of any considered business case.

The CIPD survey also revealed a more general shift from a reliance on training to a wider variety of learning interventions in organisations. Again, though, as we shall see in Chapter 4, it is unclear whether this is due to any real change in philosophy rather than to pressures of time and money. Certainly the survey showed that time is a generally constraining factor and that the most common response is to reduce the length of training courses, provide bite-sized chunks of learning and offer employees flexible learning materials. Such measures can help employees to learn their functional tasks more rapidly and easily. However they are rarely the best ways of developing the more fundamental learning that is needed to expand people's intellectual capacity and holistic (or 'whole view') understanding of the business. Yet those qualities are essential if employees are to respond creatively to the major and unpredictable new challenges constantly being produced by the operation of today's new knowledge economy.

REFLECTION

What seem to be the most significant current trends in training and development in your own organisation? And what do you judge to be their causes and their implications for L&D practitioners and line managers?

LEARNING AND DEVELOPMENT IN CHANGING ORGANISATIONS

The Procter and Gamble story

At the start of this chapter the advertisement in Figure 1 showed what one progressive organisation – an international L&D consultancy firm – expects from its L&D professionals. To end the chapter I have chosen a different illustration in the story of Procter and Gamble. As you read through it, note the various ways in which it mirrors concepts and themes that have appeared in the chapter.

CASE EXAMPLE

Learning and Development at Procter and Gamble

Procter and Gamble (P&G) is the American personal goods giant. At the turn of the millennium it was radically restructured into a matrix organisation around global business units that drive their product groups, with HR strategy used as a key contributor to boost productivity and performance. By early 2004 the company had become revitalised, with a 30 per cent rise in productivity over four years in the UK and Ireland, consistently strong business performance even in challenging market conditions and negligible staff turnover amongst employees the company sought to retain.

HR's role in this transformation was to work in partnership with the business, fulfilling the four roles that Ulrich identified for any HR function seeking to be a true business partner: a strategic player, an administrative expert, an employee champion and a change agent. The tensions between these roles can be considerable but at P&G the historical culture of the company has worked in HR's favour. The company has always been both innovative and a high investor in training that will enable P&G to grow its own, right up to chief executive level.

Training for skill is no longer viewed as the key L&D process at P&G. The years of restructuring saw a deliberate shift from 'training' to 'learning' as part of a strategy to develop a learning culture across the company. One major vehicle has been coaching, with almost all the UK and Ireland management sector receiving training in coaching skills. The training starting at middle management level since it is there that the delivery of strategy takes place. Without front-line management's commitment, flexibility and competence, strategy cannot deliver. By early 2004 coaching had become adopted as a management technique throughout the whole organisation, from top management to shop floor level.

Learning and development has also been built into the performance management process, and the same push is evident in work done on organisational effectiveness, organisational excellence, teamworking and the structure of jobs. Determined to grow its own, the company rarely recruits from outside and its commitment to building social capital is helping it to gain and sustain leading edge.

Source: STERN, S. (2004)

CONCLUSION

Having read this chapter you should by now be able to identify the kind of contribution that the L&D process can make to a business and to individuals. You should be able to confidently tackle the review questions for this chapter (Appendix 3). The rationale of the 10 L&D performance indicators shown in Appendix 1 should also now be apparent. Finally, you should be able to form a view on which of the many definitions of L&D that you will find in your wider reading most faithfully reflects its meaning and intent in your own organisation.

To summarise the main ground covered by the chapter's four sections:

- At its start I have shown that the variety of meanings attached to the L&D process makes it difficult to settle for one in particular. However, the increasing use of that term in organisations as diverse as Hemsley Fraser and Procter and Gamble shows the value now attached to learning rather than simply to training. In such organisations L&D roles stress coaching, facilitation and the need for more active control by learners rather than by trainers over the learning process.
- The history of HRD in the USA and UK shows that many of the most important messages about the links between learning and development on the one hand, and individual and organisational performance on the other, first emerged from research carried out by social scientists many years ago. Those messages are now resurfacing in current HR research that is confirming much of their validity while taking the whole field forward in new and important directions that emphasise its critical links with the business.
- Research, however, continues to show a significant gap between strategy and its delivery across the whole HR area. To tackle this gap in their field, L&D professionals need to work with line managers to build and support learning cultures that will make L&D plans come to life in the workplace. Front-line managers in particular need help in coping with their L&D responsibilities as they come under many other pressures in organisations that are regularly restructuring in a search for competitive advantage.
- In subsequent chapters you will learn about many theories, concepts and models to aid practice in the L&D field. In this one I have included only a few, but they are important. They relate to:

L&D as part of a family of HR processes that, if they are to make a positive impact on organisational performance, need to be integrated and to support organisational goals (Figure 2).

L&D practitioners as thinking performers and business partners, two concepts emphasised by the CIPD and extensively in research as vital for all HR professionals if they are to make a strategic contribution and gain the active commitment of their clients and customers (Figure 1 and the Procter and Gamble story).

The systematic training model as a popular but limited approach to planning and organising learning events, valuable for its emphasis on the functional tasks of trainers but weak in its tendency to ignore the context within which they have to operate and the business partnerships they need to form if they are to achieve positive results (Figure 3).

The unique value of tacit knowledge acquired by individuals through ongoing experience and experimentation and often shared only in informal ways within close-knit 'communities of practice' in the workplace. If put to organisational use it can be applied in ways that result in continuous improvement and innovation in goods, processes, services and products (Orr's 1990 study of the photocopier technicians).

Communities of practice in the workplace, and their role in building social capital and organisationally valuable knowledge (again, Orr's 1990 study).

The themes covered in this chapter will all be explored in more detail in subsequent chapters.

Further information sources

MATTHEWS, J.H. AND CANDY, P.C. (1999) New dimensions in the dynamics of learning and knowledge. In D. BOUD and J. GARRICK (eds) *Understanding learning at work.* London: Routledge. 47–64.

Some relevant websites for general HR matters:

- http://www.cipd.co.uk/changeagendas [accessed 4 October 2004].
- http://www.cipd.co.uk/communities/discussions [accessed 4 October 2004].
- A lively and informative L&D virtual community: http://www.trainingzone.co.uk [accessed 16 August 2004].
- The University Forum for HRD's website: http://www.ufhrd.com [accessed 4 October 2004].

Two websites for further information on human capital reporting:

- http://www.accountingforpeople.gov.uk [accessed 3 December 2004].
- http://www.dti.gov.uk/cld/financialreview.htm [accessed 3 December 2004].

The National Framework for Workforce Development

INTRODUCTION

The Government has a wide-ranging strategy related to vocational education and the upskilling of the country's workforce. The purpose of this and the following chapter is to explain the importance of this strategy for employers, L&D professionals and individual learners. In this chapter I focus on national strategy and initiatives for workforce development, and in Chapter 3 I cover current educational reforms aimed at ensuring basic skills and lifelong learning opportunities for all.

Given their necessary scope, these two chapters are bound to be quite lengthy. I have simplified this one by focusing on government policy at the expense of opposition party policies and by omitting coverage of international comparisons, and of skills strategies in the Devolved Administrations. For those wishing to learn about those topics there is plenty of information easily accessible. Some of it is noted at the end of the chapter.

The chapter has seven 'bite-sized chunks' (an appropriate term, as you will shortly see!). In the first section I outline the state of play on national vocational education and training (NVET) when the Labour government came into power in 1997 and its policy response to that. In the second I discuss issues that underpin its Skills Strategy, and the main thrust of that strategy. The subsequent three sections explain government's plans for national workforce development, and the fourth reviews progress to date. The chapter concludes by identifying some priority tasks for L&D practitioners.

There is one further point to note: the chapter contains many abbreviations relating to government agencies and initiatives. It is a necessity that is also one of NVET policy's more irritating features.

THE NVET SYSTEM: ANOTHER OVERHAUL BEGINS

The state of play in 1997

For those interested in the key stages in the development of NVET policy in the UK, I recommend Mike Cannell's on-line paper (Cannell 2004). It is an excellent potted history. It outlines government interventions in training from the nineteenth century, considers training by employers and the recent shift in emphasis towards learning, includes a table of significant dates and gives a brief list of further reading.

As Cannell's paper explains in detail and as Figure 4 indicates in outline, NVET policy in the UK swung during post-war years from attempts to encourage employers to invest voluntarily in training that could reduce the country's severe skills gaps to a quite different regulated approach under Industrial Training Boards. It then swung back to voluntarism again with the Training and Enterprise Councils (TECs). A much clearer framework of vision, policy and aims for NVET emerged during the Thatcher and Major years, and TECs formed some fruitful partnerships with employers. However by 1997 it was clear that they would never produce their

	1958	1964	1973	1981	1983	1989–2001
Regulation		Industrial Training Act 23 Industrial Training Boards and levy-grant system (most abolished 1981)	White Paper *Training for the future* Manpower Services Commission and Training Services Agency (abolished 1990)			
Centralised funding					55 Area Manpower Boards (abolished 1989)	
Voluntarism	*Carr Report Training for skill* Industrial Training Council (abolished 1964)			White Paper *A new training initiative* Most ITBs abolished. 170 Industry Training Organisations (later reduced and incorporated into National Training Organisations, 1998)		White Paper *Employment for the 1990s* 83 Training and Enterprise Councils – legally autonomous and employer-led (abolished 2001)

Figure 4 *The changing face of the national vocational training system in the UK: 1950s to 2000*

intended outcomes. With confusion reigning across the educational system also, the scene was set for their abolition and for a further overhaul that commenced in 1999.

Lifelong learning: vision and policy

The Labour Government's NVET policy is driven by a vision of lifelong learning for all, leading to an 'interdependence of social justice and economic success' (DfES 2003a, p11). At first sight this vision seems no different from that produced by the Conservative government in 1991, which envisaged a society where (Employment Department Group 1991, p28)

> **'everyone has the opportunity and incentive to continue learning throughout life, and that the economy has the skills it needs to meet and beat the best in the world.'**

Nor is the vision unique to the UK. UNESCO adopted lifelong learning as its mission in the 1970s, and the European Community espoused it in the early 1990s. Global initiatives followed, including the World Initiative on Lifelong Learning and the European Lifelong Learning Initiative.

Labour's vision, however, rests on two specific concepts – of investing in human capital and of operating in a knowledge-based economy (DfEE 1998, p1):

> **'Investment in human capital will be the foundation of success in the knowledge-based global economy of the 21st century. That is why the government has put learning at the heart of its ambition.'**

Whereas the policy to achieve Conservative governments' lifelong learning vision rested on the achievement of seven aims, set in 1991, that were all to do with skills that would 'contribute to the economy' (EDG 1991), Labour policy focuses more powerfully on that economy and on changing it in particular ways. The policy is one of transforming the UK economy into a world leader that competes (DfES 2003a, p11):

> **'on the basis of capability for innovation, enterprise, quality and adding greater value through its products and services.'**

THE NEW SKILLS STRATEGY

The strategy in outline

In 2001 Labour announced in *Skills for Life* a strategic framework for improving employability and lifelong learning skills in England. *Skills for Life* incorporates a commitment to introduce new national standards for adult literacy, numeracy and language learning together with a national curriculum within each major strand, new entry level qualifications and national tests.

The 2003 White Paper *21st century skills: realising our potential* fleshes out the *Skills for life* framework with a detailed strategy and plan to ensure that by 2010 (DfES 2003a, p11):

'employers have the right skills to support the success of their businesses, and individuals have the skills they need to be both employable and personally fulfilled.'

Like its Conservative predecessors since the mid-1980s, the 1997 Labour Government is relying on a voluntary approach and a web of partnerships to secure employers' commitment to improving employees' skills. However the route being followed by its Skills Strategy marks a radical break with the past:

- It aims to be demand-driven rather than supply-driven.
- It is concerned not only with improving individuals' skills but with developing the contexts that shape the ways in which skills needs develop and skills once they are acquired are put to use.

I will explain the strategy in detail shortly. At this point we need to look at the skills problems that it has been designed to tackle.

The skills gap

What are the statistics?

There is a serious shortage of key skills in the UK compared with competitor countries:

- Over 20 per cent of adults in the UK have poor literacy and numeracy skills. A third of working age adults are not qualified to the level expected of a school leaver.
- Among nations of the OECD only Greece, Mexico and Turkey have lower levels of educational participation. Despite improvements made to the educational system over the past 20 or so years, by 2004 only 73 per cent of 17-year olds in England were in full-time education or training compared with over 90 per cent in France, Germany, Canada and Finland (Ryan 2004).
- Three out of four jobs in future are likely to require technical, professional or associate professional, or higher level skills compared with one out of four jobs 30 years ago.
- While the proportion of the UK workforce with level 4 skills is comparable to that in France and Germany, the big gaps are at levels 2 and 3 (DfES 2003a, p19). (A full level 2 refers to any qualification equivalent to 5 GCSEs at A*–C or a level 2 national vocational qualification. Level 3 skills are those at technician, higher craft or associate professional level. Level 4 skills are degree or equivalent and above.)
- The UK is also weak in management and leadership skills. This is often cited to explain the closure of small, young businesses, 37.5 per cent of which close within the first three years (Strategy Unit 2002).
- In a rapidly ageing society where new technology is a major force in businesses, there is an increasing need to re-skill older workers.

Why does training matter?

It matters because of the proven links between skills and productivity (SU 2002, Annex 2, point 11). Productivity refers here to adding value (Patricia Hewitt, secretary of state for trade and industry, 2004):

'Higher productivity means generating more wages and profits for each hour a person spends at work. It means developing new products, or better ways of delivering existing products, by tapping into the ingenuity of our people.'

While capital investment and Research and Development are vital keys to differences in productivity levels between firms and between countries, so too are skills and this is where training becomes important (PIU 2001):

- Research at firm and plant level shows that differences in physical and human capital can explain as much as 60 per cent of the productivity gap that exists between domestically-owned and US-owned firms in the UK and nearly all of the gap with other foreign-owned firms.
- Training is associated with greater productivity gains than wage gains, implying a significant return on investment in training for employers as well as the gains it brings to individuals in terms of their greater employability in the labour market.
- Skilled workers can increase an organisation's ability to update its work practices, products and services at a rate that rapidly changing markets demand. This benefits employers, makes the economy more flexible and productive, and enables the UK to be more competitive internationally.

Why don't employers train enough?

Employers invest too little in training that would boost skills across the economy for a mix of reasons (PIU 2001, Executive Summary point 1.3):

- For many, market failures, reduced profit levels, and the uncertain and often long-term returns on training and development investment. The small to medium sized businesses (SMEs) which account for 56 per cent of the private sector workforce and 52 per cent of the UK's total turnover are particularly vulnerable here. It is their support for NVET policies and initiatives that has always proved the most difficult to obtain.
- Fear of 'poaching'; felt especially by smaller firms that can ill afford to invest in training their workers only to see them move to other organisations.
- Employers' perception that the training government wants them to carry out does not meet their business needs.
- Employers' reliance on recruitment rather than training as the main way to get the skills they want.
- Barriers of time, money and – especially for individuals with low skills – motivation.
- Overcomplicated and constantly changing NVET institutional structures and government funding, together with lack of clear, relevant information and advice.

What makes employers train at all?

Legal compliance apart, training and development is something that most employers will do when and if it enables them to achieve their business objectives. This goes far to explain why 'managers and professionals or those with a degree [are] up to five times more likely to receive work-based training than people with no qualification and/or in an unskilled job' (Westwood 2001, p19). These are the people whom employers perceive to be the drivers of the business. The focus on a trained elite has intensified the economy's problem of lack of skills at the basic levels.

What should national Skills Strategy focus on?

The answer to this question lies in an independent report *In demand, Part I,* produced in November 2001 that fundamentally challenged and changed the government Skills Strategy. Its key arguments are (PIU 2001):

- National skills strategies in the UK were dominated throughout the last half of the twentieth century by government's, not employers', perception of what was needed. Their aim was to improve the supply of training in order to achieve a more qualified labour force. From the mid-1980s, official skills initiatives and funding have been tightly tied to national learning and development targets that involve attainment of vocational qualifications.

- This approach has consistently failed to meet employers' perceived skill needs. Too many UK firms compete on the basis of low cost/low added value. The result is 'a low skill/low wage' cycle with no incentive for employers to upskill their workforces. What is important for the economy at large is of little concern to them. What they care about is their immediate bottom line.

- For all employers the real skills problem is one of specific gaps in proficiency in the workplace, mainly at levels 2 and 3. Although the Learning and Skills Council's *National employers skills survey* in 2003 caused a major stir when it revealed that one in five posts in England remained unfilled because of skills shortages, in reality that only represents 0.6 per cent of employment. On the other hand its 2002 survey revealed that around 23 per cent of all establishments with five or more employees reported a substantial proportion of staff in one or more occupational area being less than fully proficient in their jobs (Manocha 2004).

- Employers therefore want a more demand-led NVET system that can be more responsive to their proficiency needs. But to provide one in an economy that competes primarily on a low-cost/low value-added basis will not build the skills that are needed overall by the UK economy. Too many economies across the world with cheap labour forces and high technological skills are now competing successfully on that basis. If our economy is to become a world leader – and that is government's vision – then the competitive strategy of firms needs to move much further along the high specification/high value-added route.

- Experience in the Netherlands and the USA shows that when that happens, it auto-matically drives employers to invest more heavily in vocational education and in-company training. Encouragingly, that virtuous circle has begun to develop in the UK. In 2004 the Office for National Statistics revealed in its latest figures two unexpected developments (Philpott 2004a):

  – Whereas in 1992 output per worker in the UK was almost 25 per cent below the major economy average, by 2002 the gap had shrunk to 13 per cent, reflecting a measurable improvement in UK performance rather than lower productivity in other economies.

  – Contrary to general belief, the UK is catching up with the USA and also drawing level with Germany.

  John Philpott, the CIPD's Chief Economist, reached the same conclusion in 2004 from his research as did the authors of *In demand* in 2001: that the UK's productivity levels will increase with the wider spread of high performance working, in combination with investment in new technology and people. Bringing more businesses up to that level should enable the UK to 'not only start to match the highest productivity economies but become their envy' (Philpott 2004a).

Tasks for national Skills Strategy

Following a series of green and white papers from 1998 onwards, the Government in 2003 published its skills strategy for England (DfES 2003a) to tackle the three primary tasks identified by *In demand, Part 1*:

- to ensure through lifelong learning policies that all adults have basic employability skills
- to focus on helping employers to rethink their business and organisational strategies around more ambitious high-performance/high value-added goals that, to be achieved, will require them to invest in more highly skilled workforces
- alongside that, to adopt a far more demand-led approach to NVET provision, with employers and individual learners in the driving seat.

The three skills targets

The Skills Strategy set three skills targets to be achieved by 2010. As Table 1 shows, they are less ambitious than those set by the Conservative Government in 1991, confirming just how little impact the skills strategies of the late twentieth century were able to make on the national skills gaps.

In England, to achieve these skills targets within the 2001 *Skills for Life* framework involves a range of activity across employing and voluntary organisations, the education sector and the wider community. A national *Skills Alliance* was created in 2003 to engage employers in driving the strategy forward. They have been asked to become employer champions, committed to take action to improve basic skills in their organisations. Other key partners are the Department for Education and Skills (DfES), the departments of Trade and Industry (DTI), Work and Pensions (DWP) and Customs and Excise (C&E), together with the Confederation of British Industry (CBI), Trades Union Congress (TUC), Small Business Council (SBC) and the 2001 Learning and Skills Council that I will explain in the next section (DfES 2004a).

The 2003 Skills Strategy is being pursued along two major routes, each feeding into and being supported by lifelong learning initiatives (Table 2):

- workforce development
- educational reform.

Complementary routes are being pursued by the Devolved Administrations (see endnote to this chapter).

The rest of this chapter deals with workforce development.

REFLECTION

Looking at your own organisation, or one with which you are familiar, at what levels (2, 3 or 4) do you think the most critical proficiency gaps exist and how are those proficiency gaps being tackled?

Table 1 *National adult skills targets*

National education and training targets for foundation and lifelong learning,1991 (extract)

1. By 1997 at least 80 per cent of all young people to hold by age 18 an NVQ/SVQ at level 2 or its academic equivalent.

2. All young people who can benefit should be given an entitlement to structured training, work experience or education leading to NVQ Level 3 or its academic equivalent.

3. By 2000 at least 50 per cent of that age group to be qualified to at least level 3 or equivalent.

4. By 2000 50 per cent of the employed workforce to be qualified to at least Level 3 or its academic equivalent.

National skills objectives, 2003

1. At least 28 per cent of 16 to 17 year olds to start on a Modern Apprenticeship in 2004 (tied to level 2 skills attainment).

2. By 2010, reduction by at least 40 per cent of the estimated 7 million adults who lack NVQ2 or equivalent qualifications (level 2 represents basic employability 'skills for life' to do with literacy, numeracy and ICT. It equates with five good GCSEs or the equivalent).

3. Working toward this, at least 1 million adults already in the workforce to achieve level 2 between 2003 and 2006.

Sources: *A strategy for skills*, Employment Department Group 1991; White Paper *21st century skills: realising our potential*, Department for Education and Skills 2003a.

NATIONAL WORKFORCE DEVELOPMENT

Vision and strategy for workforce development

What does workforce development mean? The official definition is (SU 2002):

> **'Workforce development consists of activities which increase the capacity of individuals to participate effectively in the workplace, thereby improving their productivity and employability.'**

Government's vision for workforce development is that (ibid.):

> **'In 2010 the UK will be a society where Government, employers and individuals actively engage in skills development to deliver sustainable economic success for all.'**

Table 2 *The NVET system: policy-making, monitoring agencies, major policy and strategy papers, implementation framework and some key initiatives*

VISION: Socio-economic – lifelong learning to boost the economy and release human potential

POLICY: A transformed economy competing on innovation, enterprise, quality and adding greater value

STRATEGY: Working in partnership in a demand-led system

National Workforce Development	Educational reform			Adult/Lifelong Learning
	Primary & Secondary	FE	HE	
Policy-making				
DfES	DfES	DfES	DfES	DfES
Also Dept. for Work & Pensions	QCA (1997)	QCA	QCA	DWP
Dept. of Trade & Industry				
Dept. for Customs and Excise				
Monitoring				
Adult Learning Inspectorate (2001)	OfSTED	OfSTED ALI	HEFC ALI Offa	Adult Basic Skills Strategy Unit (ABSSU) NIACE ALI
Health & Safety Executive				Workplace basic skills network

Table 2 *continued*

Some key reports				
Nov. 2001 *In demand:1*	Oct. 2003 QCA's *Plans to reform secondary education*	2002 *Success for all*	2000 Position Paper	2001 White Paper *Skills for life*
Nov. 2002 *In demand:2*	Jan. 2003 White Paper	2002 *Trust in FE – working in partnership*	Jan. 2003 White Paper	LSC's *Widening adult participation strategy*
2003 LSC report, *Skills in England, 2002*	Feb. 2004 Tomlinson Report, 1	July 2003 White Paper		
2003 LSC report, *The national employers' skills survey*	July 2004 5-Yr Education Plan			
July 2003 *21st century skills*				
Feb. 2004 *Skills alliance: skills strategy progress report*				
Implementation framework				
Learning and Skills Council (2001)	Local Authorities	LSC		LSCs
LSC Devel. Agency (2001)		LSCDA		ABSSU 9 regional skills coordinators
Skills for Business Network (2001)				LSCDA
Regional Devel. Agencies (1999)				Jobcentre Plus
Jobcentre Plus				ULRs
Union Learning Reps. (2000)				Ufi/learndirect
Ufi/learndirect (1999)				Connexions Service
Investors in People UK (1991)				
LSC-funded training providers				
Further education colleges				

Table 2 *continued*

Some initiatives

Employer Training Pilots	GCSEs (1985, now going out)	Foundation degrees	Foundation degrees	National Certificate in Adult Skills
IIP Standard (1990)	GNVQs (1993)	NVQs	1st degrees	NVQs
Apprenticeship (1993)	AVSEs (going out)	Learndirect	Postgraduate degrees	Adult and Community learning fund
NVQs (1986)	National Diploma			Union learning fund
learndirect 'training for the bottom line' strategy				Apprenticeships
				New Deal

Government has accepted one of the most important points made in the groundbreaking 2001 *In demand, Part 1* report (PIU 2001): that skills needs do not exist in a vacuum. They are located in a context which is shaped by an interaction between external and internal influences. As the People–Performance framework discussed in Chapter 1 identifies, it is not enough for individuals to have skills. They must also have the motivation and opportunity to use them. That requires the kind of business strategies, leadership and management, and human resource strategies and practices that will gain the commitment of employees to achieve above-average performance.

The national plan for workforce development

The White Paper *21st century skills* (DfES 2003a) sets out the priority actions government is now taking to achieve both its WfD plans and its educational reform strategies by 2010. The actions are to do with:

- raising informed demand
- improving supply
- developing the right Government framework.

In view of their unique importance to the economy, special priority is given to efforts to involve low-skilled adults and small firms, and to the public sector as employer and purchaser.

Raising employer and individual demand (SU 2002, Annex 1, pages 2 to 30)
Actions here focus on three elements:

- promoting the benefits of WfD
- providing relevant and timely information and advice
- breaking down barriers to participation faced by employers and individuals.

To ensure that in every organisation there is an 'organisational culture to innovate, change and grow' (SU 2002, Annex 1, point 18), there are actions related to:

- Improving management and leadership in organisations.
- Encouraging the development of high-performance work organisation (HPWO) to create an environment that enables more direct involvement and the resulting increased motivation of employees.
- Encouraging informal and innovative workplace learning through coaching, mentoring and e-learning.
- Promoting Human Capital Accounting in organisations, especially to highlight the value of their training investment.
- Promoting the identification and sharing of best practice by and between organisations.
- Piloting projects to test ways of breaking down barriers of time and money, with a particular concern to help SMEs, adults who lack employability skills, and those on low incomes.
- Reforming the national qualifications framework to make it more accessible to individual learners and more responsive to their varying needs.

Meeting demand with high quality provision (ibid. pages 29 to 42)
Planning here focuses on funding mechanisms and quality assurance measures that

promote flexibility and employer engagement, improve quality, reward innovation and encourage diversity in the provider market. They include:

- More purchasing power at regional, sectoral, local and individual level for consumers of training and educational programmes – especially through the Skills for Business Network (explained in the next section) and pilot initiatives to help employers and individuals meet the costs of skills development.
- More effective control over government-funded provision (see next section).
- Harnessing e-technology more effectively to learning. The DfES is responsible for implementing the delivery of an e-learning framework across the whole learning and skills sector, with a view to a powerful vision being achieved for post-16 e-learning and the confirmation of ICT as a basic skill for the economy.

Developing the right Government framework (ibid. pages 42 to 55)
Here, the aim is to provide a flexible framework to deliver the Skills Strategy – one that 'supports the development of innovative firms, multi-skilled workers, and healthy local and regional economies and labour markets'.

The government confirms that implementing its Skills Strategy will not be easy, but stresses that its action plan 'is not predominantly about new initiatives. It is about making more sense of what is already there, integrating what already exists and focusing it more effectively' (DfES 2003a, points 9 and 10). Its plan has to be delivered by 'a web of institutions' (see Table 2). They need to share a common vision of the aims of WfD policy and ensure it is realised at organisational and individual levels. The next section describes that web.

REFLECTION

How would you explain to a line manager in your organisation the distinction between workplace development and workforce development? And how far and in what ways do you think either kind of development is being pursued in your own organisation?

DELIVERING NATIONAL WORKFORCE DEVELOPMENT STRATEGY

National level: The Learning and Skills Council

(www.lsc.gov.uk)

In 1999 the *Learning to succeed* White Paper (DfEE 1999) announced the abolition of Training and Enterprise Councils in England and heralded a new – but still deregulated – system to replace them. The cornerstone of that system is a single, non-departmental public body called the National Learning and Skills Council (LSC). It has 47 local operating arms, known as Learning and Skills Councils (LSCs). Training responsibilities originally held by the TECs and funding responsibilities held by the Further Education Funding Council were brought together under the NLSC in 2001. The single biggest representation (40 per cent) on LSC boards at local as at national level is employers, joined by trade unions, government and other voluntary groups. Unions had no representation on the previous TECs, so this is a real advance for them.

LSC goals

The LSC has four goals covering WfD and lifelong learning:

- to encourage young people to stay on in learning until at least age 19, and to achieve at least a level 2 qualification
- to increase demand for learning by adults
- to maximise the contribution of education and training to economic performance
- to raise standards in teaching and training, supporting the Qualifications and Curriculum Authority (QCA, established in 1997) in its efforts to reform and harmonise educational and vocational qualifications.

To achieve these goals it is advised by two statutory committees. The independent *Adult Learning Inspectorate* (ALI) covers work-related learning and training for those over 19, to ensure coherent provision with high standards. The pre-2001 *Office for Standards in Education* (Ofsted) continues to cover 16 to 19-year-old provision in addition to its schools' inspection responsibilities. The Health and Safety Executive (HSE) has statutory responsibility for the monitoring of health and safety in the workplace and plays a particularly important role in relation to the *Apprenticeship* programme (see Chapter 3).

So the advisory and monitoring structure is complex. The Government calls this 'working in partnership'. Some wonder about that, especially when considering the many other partners with whom the LSC must work successfully if it is to achieve its goals. The following case shows the challenges it faces. The detail is not important to memorise – it is the overall picture it paints that is so striking.

CASE EXAMPLE

'Working in partnership'

The LSC's workforce development strategy, produced in 2002, fits within the national Skills Strategy framework and has three objectives:

- to stimulate demand from employers and individuals for workplace and workforce development
- to improve learning providers' responsiveness and flexibility in meeting business needs
- to build a better framework of labour market intelligence, responsive qualifications and strong links with educational providers.

Working in partnership – government departments

The LSC's emphasis on workplace as well as workforce development is a big break with the past, since until 2002 workplace development had nothing to do with skills policy or with the DfES (or, before it, with the Department for Education and Employment – DfEE). The strategy is also unique in requiring for its success the close partnership of different government departments.

For the LSC's two-pronged strategy to work, its Director of Workforce Development has to achieve close and continuous partnership between the four government departments on whose active support the whole national Skills Strategy depends – the DfES itself, the DTI, the DWP and C&E. The buy-in of the DTI is particularly important. Before November 2002 it was responsible for competitiveness, business development and support, personnel management and IR issues but had little formal interest in skills or skill formation. The latter were the responsibility of the DfES (and before it of the DfEE), which in turn could have no real involvement in, or knowledge of, how skills were used, and to what effect, within the workplace. That was the DTI's territory.

November 2002 brought a radical change, because the LSC's new WfD strategy gave an impetus for the two departments to work to a common purpose. For example: the DTIs industry forums work on a range of supply chain initiatives some of which include training. These should mesh with training activity promoted by Sector Skills Councils and with the LSCs at sectoral and local levels.

Working in partnership – funding arrangements

The LSC has responsibility to the DfES for the funding, planning, quality assurance and delivery of all post-16 education and training up to but not including higher education. Its annual budget of over £7 billion covers about 6 million learners each year in England, helping to fund vocational education and work-based learning for young people, workplace and workforce development, and adult and community learning (where it must work in partnership with local authorities).

Control over funding provision is shared between a variety of stakeholders. The LSC and its 47 arms are responsible for awarding contracts and funding to colleges and training providers that supply workbased learning programmes and projects for those in employment, while the DWP contracts its own work-based learning providers for Jobcentre Plus programmes. Both have to work closely with the DfES and the Adult Learning Inspectorate, and Ofsted is jointly responsible with the LSC for inspection of the quality and performance of FE and training provision.

Working in partnership – vision and reality

Sitting at the centre of this entire web of partnerships, the LSC has a formidable task on its hands, and while working in partnership is an essential part of Government's NVET vision, making it come to life will test the collaborative will and skills of the partners to the utmost.

Regional and sectoral levels: Regional Development Agencies and the Skills for Business network

(SSDA – http://www.ssda.org.uk)

At the next level down from national level come regional and sectoral levels. The key player in implementing both the national Skills Strategy and the LSC's WfD strategy here is the *Skills for Business* (SfB) network, launched in 2001 to deliver skills-based productivity improvements in industry and the public services.

The network comprises *Sector Skills Councils* (SSCs) and the *Sector Skills Development Agency* (SSDA). SSCs are developed at the request of employers by the SSDA (2002) which licenses and monitors their activity. It allocates funding to each licensed SSC to cover running costs, the intention being that employers will provide the rest of the money needed.

SSCs are taking over the tasks of the 72 national training organisations (NTOs) that, established in 1998 and themselves swallowing up the 170 Industry Training Organisations set up in 1981, never managed to fulfil their potential. Each SSC is intended to be the most authoritative source in the country of information and analysis about skills that its sector needs to drive up productivity and close skills gaps. The first four 'trailblazers' were created in 2001, and by mid-2004 18 SSCs were in place, with a further seven in development stage. Ultimately they should cover around 85 per cent of the country's workforce.

What are core tasks of the employer-led SSCs?

- To develop national occupational standards for their sectors and to work with various local and regional partners to shape the supply of needed training.
- To lobby government on employers' behalf in relation to current and future sector skills needs and priorities.
- To give employers real power to demand these skills from schools, colleges and universities and to get the demand-led learning agenda understood by further and higher education.
- Through Sector Skills Agreements (SSAs), to deliver tangible improvements at organisational as well as national and individual levels. Such demand-led agreements are intended to reshape public and private skills investment. By mid-2004 four SSAs were in development.

To give SSCs regional influence, 'working in partnership' is again the key. Nine regional *Sector Skills Forums* cover the country. Their business plans inform the work of Regional Skills Partnerships made up of the SfB Network, the LSC, the eight Regional Development Agencies (RDAs), Jobcentre Plus and the Small Business Service. RSPs' recommendations related to each region's skill needs are fed directly into RDAs' *Frameworks for Regional Employment and Skills Action* (FRESAs) which thus represent regional plans for collective action on skills, training, labour market services and business support. *Innovation and Growth Teams* supported by the DTI also work with SSCs to improve the overall performance of key sectors and supply chains.

So here is another complex set of partnerships that have to be made to work if national workforce development strategy is to get the support it needs at regional and sectoral levels.

Local level: the Learning and Skills Councils

(www.lsc.gov.uk)

The LSC's WFD strategy is implemented at local level by its 47 LSCs in 'Local Strategic Plans'. LSCs' vital task is to communicate local needs upwards and to deliver national priorities and policies downwards. Each has an average budget of £100 million to fund around 100,000 learners and discretion on how to allocate it locally. However the budgets are strongly tied to the government's three skills targets and therefore LSCs are under great pressure to work for the achievement of national qualifications. *The Investors in People Standard*, explained later, is key to their ability to do that while also responding to employers' specific skills and proficiency needs.

Organisational level: union learning representatives

(http://www.learning services.org.uk/national/learning)

In 1998 following the publication of *The learning age* Green Paper the Government provided a Union Learning Fund to help unions encourage and support workplace learning. In 2001 the TUC set up a network of union learning representatives (ULRs) that has become vital to the implementation of the national Skills Strategy, especially through encouraging the low skilled to engage in training. Government funding has enabled the network's rapid expansion. Under the 2002 Employment Protection Act ULRs have 'reasonable' paid time off to be specially trained for their role and to undertake their duties, namely:

- to analyse members' training needs
- to provide information and advice about learning and training
- to arrange and promote training and promote its value to individual members (this could involve brokering courses from colleges, universities or other providers with or without recourse to employers)
- to consult with employers on union members' learning and training (with any disputes likely to be settled by tribunal).

These rights are incorporated in an ACAS code of practice.

By 2003 ULRs were helping to encourage over 25,000 workers to try some form of workplace learning. The ultimate aim is to help over 250,000 workers a year with their personal training and development needs. The TUC and government hope to have 22,000 reps in place by 2010. By early 2004 there were 7,000.

ULRs are concerned with meeting individuals' needs for development, as distinct from the training they might normally receive that is closely job-related. Their concern is to engage their members actively in the learning process. However such engagement, when achieved, can then motivate employees to pursue training more in line with business needs. Certainly ULRs are now helping to take forward a wide range of activities that are also valuable to employers and the LSC, including *Employer Training Pilots, Adult Basic Skills, Sector Skills Agreements* and *Regional Skills Partnerships*. Because of their success, the LSC is looking to identify and support learning champions in non-unionised organisations especially in the SME sector.

REFLECTION

In your own organisation, who do you see to be the 'learning champions' whose main activity is to help promote individual learning – especially at basic skills level – in the workplace? And how far do you think they work effectively with management and with any L&D staff in that activity?

Before assessing the progress being made by the national Skills Strategy's sprawling partnership-based delivery framework, it is relevant to identify some of the initiatives that it offers to organisations and individuals in order to stimulate WfD.

NATIONAL WORKFORCE DEVELOPMENT: SOME INITIATIVES

As a glance at *Skills for life* (DfEE 2001) will show, the list of initiatives to promote WfD is formidable. In this section I have selected only three of those, typifying the kind that the Government is promoting in order to stimulate individual employees' demand for learning alongside employer demand: employer training pilots, bite-sized training and the Investors in People standard.

Employer training pilots

(http://www.learningservices.org.uk)

As already explained, one core task for the LSC is to open up workplace as well as workforce development, especially in the smaller organisations. One initiative here that many employers have used is *Employer Training Pilots* (ETPs).

ETPs, launched in 2002, involve a business being allocated an adviser to source on-site training that fits employers' basic skills needs. ETPs' main aim is to encourage small businesses to train low-skilled employees, thus raising the capability base of the whole organisation. They provide financial support to employers who give employees paid leave to study for basic skills (which now cover numeracy, literacy and IT skills) or level 2 qualifications. Firms with less than 50 employees pay nothing. ETPs are the Government's major initiative to offer tailored programmes for different industries and by mid-2004 twelve ETPs had enabled 10,000 participating employers, comprising a third of all employers in England, to sign up over 60,000 low-skilled employees for training to gain relevant workplace qualifications. Of those employers 93 per cent expressed satisfaction with the scheme.

Extra funding is now being given in order to extend ETPs and also – as part of workplace development strategy – to enable them to cover management training that will boost skills levels to European standards. However ETPs are tied to formal qualifications, and so do not take account of informal learning that can have a major impact on employees' performance.

Bite-size training

(http://www.learndirect.co.uk)

The National Skills Strategy emphasises the value of 'light touch' or modular workplace learning, especially in smaller firms where time is a particular constraint on training and development. The LSC introduced its national *Bite Size* campaign in 2001 and training organisations are also promoting the approach. It involves short, sharp learning hits and aims especially to provide one to three hour courses that encourage young people back into training (Roberts 2003). In the CIPD's Change Agenda paper *Focus on the learner* (Sloman 2002a) participants listed modularisation of training as a key activity and reported two days as the longest time for their training courses. A number of large organisations including the NHS, the National Grid and Royal Mail are now using the bite-sized approach.

The main advantages for employers and trainers relate to cost, speed, and speed of the transfer of learning to the job. For managers and individuals the bite-sized approach can also offer more choice and the prospect of an easier learning experience. However bite-sized learning can sometimes be facile and restricted, with insufficient opportunities for reflection and challenge in the learning situation. It is best used to train employees in straightforward techniques that they can use immediately in their work, and/or to complement, not replace, longer courses or developmental processes (Roberts 2003).

The Investors in People Standard

(http://www.iipuk.co.uk)

Established in 1990 by the Conservative government to improve the links between training and business goals, IIP did not made its intended impact under the Training and Enterprise Council system (see Figure 4 and Cannell 2004). Since then it has been extensively revamped and is a central component of national workplace development strategy as well as of upskilling (SU 2002). It is delivered through Business Link and LSCs to make it easily accessible.

Key changes in the latest version of the IIP standard unveiled in November 2004 include a simplified structure, a new focus on management and leadership at work and an indicator to encourage organisations to involve employees in decision-making. IIP UK is also working with the Department of Health to develop a new indicator on health at work. The whole Standard is now more flexible, easier to administer, focuses on outputs and has a specially tailored version for small firms (see Appendix 4 and CIPD 2003c).

By early 2002 a quarter of the UK's workforce worked in organisations that had achieved the Standard, which is probably the most successful of all the NVET initiatives in terms of attracting employers' involvement and of its business partnership process.

REFLECTION

Referring to the list of workforce and workplace development initiatives in *In demand, Part 1*, Annex 11 (PIU 2001), or on the *Skills for life* website or elsewhere as your guide:

Which initiatives does your own organisation seem to be using currently, or planning to use in the future? And what benefits do you think they have brought (or are intended to bring) for the business and for individual learners?

NATIONAL WORKFORCE DEVELOPMENT: PROGRESS

Strategy

There is no doubt that as far as national WfD strategy is concerned major changes have taken place since 1997. The most significant have been:

- Government's acceptance of the importance of the organisational context in which skills are acquired and applied. This has led it to focus its strategy on workplace development and organisational culture as well as on WfD.
- Government's concern to adopt a more demand-led approach to WfD provision.
- The ongoing delivery of the LSC's WfD strategy through a partnership process.

If the many changes first set out in the *In demand, Part 2* (SU 2002) action plan bear fruit, then their importance in helping to transform the country's economy from one of low skills and low productivity to one that can compete on innovation, enterprise, quality and adding greater value through products and services cannot be overestimated. But there are many question marks around the delivery system.

Delivery

By Government's own admission its WfD strategy stands or falls by the extent to which there is a well communicated, easily understood and effective framework of provision that is supported by:

- clear accountabilities at national, regional and local level

- excellent labour market information to enable employers, individuals and providers to make informed decisions about skills development
- sufficient funding flexibility to meet the needs of different local labour markets and to place more purchasing power for external-provided training and education directly in the hands of individuals and employers
- an improved qualifications framework.

It is still relatively early days, but the LSC's 2003 *National employers' skills survey* (LSC 2004a) showed that little progress has yet been made in closing the skills gaps that had confronted economy and employers in 1997. Of the 72,100 employers in England who were surveyed 29 per cent still blamed skills gaps on a lack of training, yet as many as one third of employers admitted to having no training budget or plan to address their skills gaps. One in five posts remain unfilled because of skills shortages.

The LSC itself and the agencies connected with it have attracted much of the blame. In the 2004 CIPD *Training and development* survey (CIPD 2004a) respondents who agreed with government's basic NVET objectives were 'far less complimentary about the official bodies it relies on for delivery' (Wolf 2004, p24). Whereas around half of the training professionals who had contacted educational institutions and *Investors in People* found those contacts productive, very few found the same in relation to the LSC. Lower contact rates noted by respondents with SSCs and other more recently established bodies are of less concern because time is needed for familiarity with them to develop. What is worrying is that LSCs are now quite widely known, that they have the most direct responsibility for delivering and funding the new Skills Strategy, yet in the CIPD survey they came very low down the scale in terms of favourable ratings from training professionals (Wolf 2004). Such findings suggest that the NVET system is not yet significantly demand-driven.

At sectoral level, the few SSCs yet fully in place have had some impressive success stories. Few of the CIPD's survey respondents knew much about them as yet, but promisingly over half agreed that skills issues should be tackled on a sectoral basis and 80 per cent thought SSCs important primarily for the action they can take on skills needs and shortages and for the funding they can provide for training projects. By contrast RDAs were not widely popular.

At organisational level ULRs' role in aiding individual learners cannot on its own have the strategic impact on employers' training investment that is needed to significantly improve skills in the economy. Nonetheless the ULR system is proving one of the most crucial spurs to individuals to take up learning opportunities in the workplace. Reps' informal links with employees matter most here. The CIPD in association with the LSC and the TUC has produced a free Guide for personnel and development practitioners and line managers who are seeking to find a positive role for ULRs within the workplace (CIPD 2004b).

Key initiatives

The CIPD's *Training and development* survey (CIPD 2004a) found that overwhelmingly its 531 respondents agreed with the four key areas which the Government has prioritised in its current skills initiatives:

- literacy and numeracy skills
- intermediate, including craft and technical, skills
- mathematics, science and technology skills
- management skills.

They confirmed that large sums of money are now coming on stream, particularly for basic skills provision in the workplace and for ETPs, and they saw real value here related to higher proficiency and improved technical skills. But at present employers and HR professionals seem to put most value on initiatives that can improve individual skills. There are few signs of any real interest in developing a high-performance work organisation with its associated high spec/high value-added business strategies. Furthermore employers are now urging Government to improve teaching in schools rather than use business to deliver basic skills training (Tyler 2004a). The Confederation of British Industry and the Engineering Employers Federation both see the growing use of the Apprenticeship scheme as an alternative way of delivering basic skills teaching as a key reason why that scheme is performing so poorly (see Chapter 3).

Findings from the CIPD's 2004 survey highlight the fact that while improved communication and high quality of providers do have an influence on take-up of initiatives, what is crucial is that employers feel the initiatives meet their immediate business needs. As a positive example here, the survey outlines work that retail store Selfridges and the trailblazer retail Sector Skills Council, Skillsmart, have done to create a new level 2 certificate in retail skills. The certificate incorporates a core unit of the retail national Occupational Standards but also in-company training (CIPD 2004a, p33). Cases like this (and the Egg case example in Chapter 14 of this book is another) send some important messages to government:

- Its WfD initiatives work best when LSCs and other providers work in partnership with employers to focus on doing what helps business goals and only as a secondary consideration on what will help to achieve national skills targets.
- Too much emphasis on 'best practice' runs the risk of neglecting the fact that what an organisation needs and responds to most are initiatives that will help it achieve its goals in unique ways.

REFLECTION

From your own desk or practical research, try to discover some more organisational stories that illustrate both the ways in which the demand-led approach to NVET delivery is working in specific cases, and the barriers that prevent it working better.

TASKS FOR HR PROFESSIONALS

Making the demand-led strategy work

The achievement of government targets related to upskilling the workforce to level 2 depends largely on activity at a very local level and involves matching local people with their particular background to local employers (Pickard 2003a). What part should HR professionals – especially those in the L&D field – play in making the demand-led strategy work to the advantage of their organisations? They should:

- Work with business partners to identify exactly where key current and anticipated proficiency gaps lie.
- Use reliable sources of information to discover what official NVET initiatives and funding may be available to help tackle those gaps.

- Use sectoral and local networks to find ways of closing those gaps and also to work on a wider front that will benefit the wider local economy.
- Use training and learning providers who can be relied on for high quality and customised service.
- Use NVET initiatives that can help to develop the workforce and the workplace in the ways that the business really needs.

In one of the most informative articles about how to use the demand-led approach at local level, Jane Pickard produced some short case studies that bring that approach to life. What general messages do you think the following case provides for L&D professionals? A commentary follows at its end.

CASE EXAMPLE

Park Royal Partnership

Park Royal Partnership is a body set up by local employers to regenerate a run-down area in West London characterised by a low-wage, low-skill cycle, poor employer engagement in training, many different training providers and 22 different funding sources for training in the area. Local employers are 'trapped in a vicious circle of lower pay, poor conditions and high staff turnover' and are in an extremely competitive market, especially the food sector (Shelley Adams, Park Royal's chief executive).

Park Royal and local colleges have formed an umbrella organisation to meet employers' HR needs and expand training places. It aims to break down barriers between training providers and employers and to get funding from the London Development Agency for a peripatetic HR consultancy. That consultancy could improve communications with employers and help them get to understand and tap into relevant funding pots.

Typical of the firms that Park Royal in 2003 was hoping to help was Hazlewood Breakwinner, employing 650 people making sandwiches for supermarkets and other outlets. The company was successful, innovative and competitive but needed to boost its workforce skills and had just invested in a training manager to this end. The workforce was composed of workers from 27 different nations and languages, principally Tamils.

The firm invested highly in training for its size, helped by the European Social Fund, and was preparing to apply for IIP status. But there was much more it would like to do but could not afford, including investing in a translator. Without that, it could not access NVQ training because, despite English language courses that it provided, such training was too difficult for most workers to tackle. With a translator, courses could be run in Tamil.

Hazlewood Breakwinner invested in training in order to retain staff, make them feel valued and give them self-respect. But for financial reasons it could only do core training that covered relatively few. It was hoping for better government funding in order to allow more people to access training and gain qualifications. Through working with the Park Royal Partnership, and given the much more demand-led strategy the government announced in July 2003, that extra funding seemed to be a real possibility.

Source: PICKARD, J. (2003a)

Comments

This case shows how important it is for HR (and especially L&D) professionals to become informed about funding streams and NVET provision locally. In the past, information and advice has in general been poorly communicated by government. Now, all L&D professionals should arm themselves with key facts accessible through, for example:

- government and agency websites such as those listed at the end of this chapter
- government policy documents – usually tediously long and dense, but their executive summaries are concise, and their annexes often provide helpful practical information
- SSCs and industry networks, helpful especially in the development of expertise and knowledge of new approaches to skill usage and work organisation
- employer networks and umbrella partnerships like Park Royal in the case study. In the CIPD's 2004 *Training and Development* survey (CIPD 2004a) employer networks gained very positive ratings, undoubtedly because they were seen to be the most relevant to organisations
- ULRs or others acting as 'learning champions' in organisations
- reliable, accessible surveys that provide information about changing trends and initiatives related to NVET and to training and development programmes in organisations
- accessible management performance assessment tools including the Investors in People (IIP) model on management and leadership, the Business Improvement Tool for Entrepreneurs and the Business Link CONNECT module on leadership.

Promoting high-performance work organisation

Like national Skills Strategy overall, the LSC's WfD strategy seeks to encourage firms to adopt the business strategies and modern work practices that will make that upskilling essential in the eyes of employers and employees. Robert Taylor, a leading researcher at the Centre for Economic Performance at the London School of Economics, explains (Manocha 2003):

> **'High skill/performance workplaces need qualified employees but also employees who are motivated and given discretion and autonomy over their jobs and their career prospects.'**

But despite the hype, what is called high-performance work organisation (HPWO) has only had a limited adoption in the UK and the scale of the LSC's task here is massive (Keep 2002). If it is to make progress it will need to develop the necessary expertise to do so, working closely with HR professionals. According again to the CIPD's 2004 *Training and development* survey, the latter are not yet taking a lead here, despite the fact that they are well qualified to promote:

- job and work design organised in such a way that workplaces provide opportunities for a skilled workforce through progression, job discretion and autonomy
- human resource strategies and practices that can help to develop employees with the skills, motivation, opportunity and discretion to achieve the high-performance working that leads to innovation.

The Government is trying to achieve a transformed economy that competes on productivity and on innovation. Unless skill levels, no matter how high, are developed in line with conditions that promote creativity and the innovation that flows from it, then that competitive capability will not be achieved. There is worrying research to show that even the companies that are pursuing a high spec/high skill/high value-added strategy in the market are not always creating those conditions (Lloyd 2003).

Promoting measures to develop the social capital that can drive such a strategy in organisations is not just a task for government. It is also a key task for the HR profession – including those who specialise in the L&D field.

To conclude, here is a case to illustrate some key points made in this section. What conclusions do you draw from it? Compare them with the comments that follow the case.

CASE EXAMPLE

Contact 24: a high-performance organisation

Contact 24 is a Bristol-based contact call centre employing 1,000 people. Changes introduced into working practices led to a 7 per cent increase in productivity in the first 10 months of 2003. Improving skills was central to this increase – the Campaign for Learning estimates that for an organisation of this size gaps in basic literacy and numeracy can cost up to £500,000 a year. However skills development was an integral part of a wider cultural change programme.

In order to develop a high-performance organisation the HR team worked with the Sector Skills Council for the IT, telecoms and contact centre industries, *E-skills UK*. On the training front they looked at every job role in a contact centre, identified the specific competencies needed for an individual to perform well, and designed a training programme around that framework.

On the wider front they tackled the whole career development system in Contact 24 and introduced a Foundation in Team Leadership programme for those interested in progressing from agent positions to team leader roles in the company. All seven who participated ultimately gained promotion, and the turnover rate at agent level reduced dramatically.

Alongside this the firm implemented a new rewards structure, moving from fixed grading to broad branding to support the new focus on training and development. Employees are now paid according to the type and level of competencies they attain. In addition new policies were introduced for benefits and incentive schemes and internal communications processes.

The next step that the HR staff want to promote is to change the qualifications available for contact centre staff – not national qualifications but industry-wide qualifications on a par with, for example, the CIPD's. That is a longer-term project that will again involve close partnership with *E-skills*, the SSC.

Source: MANOCHA, R. (2003)

Comments

Such cases point to three main conclusions:

- Attention to HR strategy and practices is essential to the development of high-performance work organisation. New business strategies and upskilling alone are not enough.
- HR professionals, including those in the L&D field, have a key role to play in working with internal and external partners in relating national Skills Strategy and initiatives to the productivity and growth needs of their organisations.
- HR professionals can and should be able to identify staff who need help and encourage them to come forward – often not an easy task – thereby bringing the problem to people's attention and acting as a resource for both individuals and managers who need support to address the issue (Hope 2004a).

CONCLUSION

Having read this chapter you should by now be able to form your own views on the vision, goals and strategy of government related to national WfD. You should also be able to confidently tackle the review questions for this chapter (Appendix 3).

To summarise the main ground covered by the chapter's seven sections, it has:

- outlined the UK's skills and productivity problem, its implications for employers and the economy, and the ways in which it is being tackled by the Labour Government's Skills Strategy
- explained and reviewed Government's strategy, plans and delivery framework for workforce development and some key WfD initiatives
- outlined a key role for HR professionals in helping to drive the demand-led approach to workforce development at local and organisational levels.

The question that remains unanswered is whether the Skills Strategy related to WfD has learned enough lessons from the past and from ongoing experience to succeed where earlier strategies have failed. At this point the jury is out. Typical concerns raised by the coverage of the chapter are these:

- Employers and L&D professionals need a flexible mix of formal and informal learning and development to achieve business goals. Government is offering a more demand-driven approach to WfD, but it is still one that is dominated by attainment of formal qualification targets to which strict funding criteria are usually tied. Because of that, the 'crop' of Government initiatives may not be enough to help meet organisations' major skills needs (Wolf 2004).
- More attention must be paid to the HR expertise and practices that firms need in order to achieve HPWO. These play a crucial part in achieving above-average organisational performance (Purcell et al 2003).
- Politicians change the course of strategies and plans. Anyone familiar with the TV series *Yes Minister* will know that official strategies get watered down or changed through time. Surveying the many redrafts of national Skills Strategy and planning documents since the watershed created by *In demand, Part 1* (2001), one of its authors has since concluded that policy proposals in their present form are unlikely to be able to deal adequately with the fundamental problems that underpin the UK skills deficit (Coffield 2002).

Yet in regard to that last point it could equally be argued that what is remarkable is not the ground that has been lost since *In demand*, but the ground retained. There is a more demand-driven system than before, there is a more promising sectoral and local infrastructure to stimulate and communicate the demand, and Government is making real attempts at joined up thinking by encouraging not only WfD but the building of new learning cultures in the workplace through promoting better leadership and management.

Further information sources

The problem with NVET as a topic of study is not lack of information, but an excess of it. Sources are best kept to those that can be consulted regularly and that provide a good balance of facts and opinions.

For more information on:

- Government approaches towards employers visit http://www.dfes.gov.uk/skillsforemployers [accessed 25 August 2004].
- Skills for Life visit http://www.dfes.gov.uk/readwriteplus/ [accessed 17 July 2004].
- National Skills Strategy visit the Department for Education and Skills' website http://www.dfes.gov.uk/skillsstrategy. It links to websites for Northern Ireland, Wales and Scotland. All government publications to which it refers can also be obtained by ordering from http://dfes@prolog.uk.com) [accessed 25 August 2004].
- International comparisons, see *In demand, Part 1* (PIU 2001, Annex 9) and Harrison and Kessels (2003a, pp61–79).

Other useful information can be found in:

- http://www.businesslink.gov.uk a central access portal introduced in April 2004 to detail all government services for employers. www.businesslink.org/ continues to act as a central access portal to advise on all small business issues and www.dti.gov.uk/manufacturing/mas is a portal for manufacturing employers.
- the CIPD's publication *People Management*, which contains updates on NVET policy and initiatives plus useful case studies illustrating take-up.
- the quality press for a range of informed views about the NVET field.

Endnote: NVET in the Devolved Administrations

Although training and skills are a devolved issue, qualifications approved in Wales, Scotland and Northern Ireland can also be offered in England (with a few exceptions). A detailed explanation of NVET policy and qualification systems in the Devolved Administrations is provided in *In demand, Part 1*, Annex 10 (PIU 2001). Updated information can be found as follows:

Wales
The National Assembly for Wales Training and Education Department is responsible for delivering all publicly funded education, training and skills activities in Wales. The Assembly Government's *Skills and employment action plan 2002* is available online at http://www.learning.wales.gov.uk (employment topic) [accessed 25 August 2004].

Northern Ireland
In Northern Ireland, the NI Department of Education, the Training and Employment Agency and the Economic Development Network are the relevant NVET bodies. The Northern Ireland

Executive's Programme for Government includes in its priorities *Investing in Education and Skills* and *Securing a Competitive Economy*. The lead on developing workforce skills is taken by the Department for Employment and Learning (http://www.delni.gov.uk) working closely with the industrial development agency for the region, Invest Northern Ireland (http://www.investni.gov.uk) [accessed 25 August 2004].

Scotland

The Scottish parliament has complete responsibility for devising and implementing education and employment strategies, and for the delivery system. Lifelong Learning and Social Inclusion are key planks of Scottish Executive policy. *'Life through learning, learning through life'*, the Executive's strategy for lifelong learning, was launched in 2003. For further information, visit http://www.scotland.gov.uk [accessed 25 August 2004].

The Education System and Lifelong Learning Opportunities

INTRODUCTION

At the start of Chapter 2 I noted that in order to achieve its vision of lifelong learning the Government's NVET policy has two broad strands, related to workforce development and educational reform. The purpose of this chapter is to explain the aims and main issues involved in its current educational reforms.

The educational system in any country influences the nature and quality of initial competence of school leavers and thence the distribution of competencies among the working population. Educational opportunities after leaving school help to further shape and expand those competencies, and employers and L&D practitioners have a leading part to play in either opening up or restricting those opportunities in the workplace.

Since the 1944 Butler Education Act no government has been able to carry through the integrated reform needed in Britain in order to approach the high quality vocational education and training systems that most European countries provide. The major changes now under way have that aim. The Government's educational reforms all fit under the umbrella of its 2003 Skills Strategy (discussed in Chapter 2) and cover the entire educational spectrum incorporating the schools, further and higher education systems.

At this point it is worth recalling the sheer scale of the issues at stake (Hackett and Woods 2004):

- Britain ranks 27th out of 30 OECD countries in terms of the proportion of 17-year-olds still at school.
- A higher percentage of 15 to 19-year-olds in Britain are not in education or work than in any other G7 country except Italy.
- Around a quarter leave school at 16, more than 5 per cent of them without any qualification and almost 60 per cent failing to secure a good GCSE pass in maths and English.
- The Confederation of British Industry reports that 42 per cent of British employers are dissatisfied with school leavers' basic numeracy and literacy.
- 55 per cent of British workers have 'low skills' compared with 30 per cent in France and 20 per cent in Germany

Given the issues, the chapter is inevitably lengthy. I have divided it into six sections. The first three cover the three main strands of UK educational policy. The fourth explores local partnership issues related to policy's implementation, looks at some work-based learning initiatives that rely on the effectiveness of those partnerships, and identifies tasks for L&D practitioners related to such initiatives. In the fifth section I discuss implications for employers of Government measures to open up lifelong learning opportunities for all. In the concluding section I assess the prospects of success for the Government's lifelong learning mission, and for the entire national skills strategy covered in this and the previous chapter.

Again, there is no scope to cover the Devolved Administrations, but information can be found on the websites shown at the end of Chapter 2.

REFORMING SCHOOLS

(www.dfes.gov.uk/14-19/documents/5YearStrategy-14-19.d.

Also http://www.literacytrust.org.uk/database.secondary/Schoolstructure)

2003/4: the state of play

The Continental model: the dual system

In most continental European countries there is a dual educational system where academic and practical learning continuously interact. Countries' vocational education systems vary widely because of the different principles that drive the role of the state, the link between education and vocational training, the responsibility of organisations to fund training, the degree to which there is a training culture, and the depth of training provision (Sparrow and Hiltrop 1994, p425). That said, the principles on which the dual system is grounded are instructive for Britain, so it is worth at this point outlining key features of the German system, regarded as the prototype.

CASE EXAMPLE

The German dual system

The German reverence for trade crafts is at the heart of its three-track high-school system, considered to be the best in the world. About one third of young people go on from gymnasium (high school) to university, the remaining two thirds to vocational and technical schools. There is a careers office in every town and city to help young people make decisions about their future education and employment.

Flexible

The education system is flexible, allowing qualified vocational and technical students to switch to the gymnasium at any point, while on the other hand some gymnasium students enrol in vocational programmes even after getting into university. It is enshrined in law that no young person should begin their working life without vocational training and this is provided through a partnership approach in which that training takes place largely on the job with less, but complementary, provision in institutions of study away from the company. In this dual system the major emphasis is on the acquisition of practical competencies, with theoretical qualifications being primarily focused on the underpinning knowledge they require. The interaction between academic and vocational pathways is co-ordinated and integrated so that both employers' and trainees' requirements and objectives are fulfilled. Training is only counted as at an end when a trainee passes final examinations and gains a vocational qualification (Sampson 1992).

Partnership-based

The dual system operates on a partnership basis. The German federal government is responsible for training regulations, the 11 Lander governments are responsible for schools, regional chambers of commerce and industry are responsible for overseeing the dual system, and employers are obliged to belong to these bodies. Vocational colleges are funded by local and regional governments. Employers collaborate with unions and the authorities to provide a high-quality, rigorously administered and controlled dual system.

Strains in the system

There is a downside, however. As the German economy continues under severe pressures, the partnership between union and employers is weakening and the dual system is proving increasingly inflexible and unaffordable not least because of failed reunification policies pursued by the two main political parties. Germany also suffers from skills shortages because 16-year-olds are increasingly opting for an academic rather than a manual education. There is a major concern to reform the education system to make it more oriented to market needs, and to spread cost and control more evenly between the state and the private sector.

Source: HARRISON, R. and KESSELS, J. (2003a, pp67–68)

The UK full-time system

In the UK, by contrast, the system is basically of the full-time kind: vocational routes begin to open up in the school system from 14 years and thereafter most vocational education takes place at a state (or independent) institution of study, with least taking place in-company. The major emphasis is on obtaining theoretical qualifications. The system broadly resembles that in the USA but is severely weakened by disparities between academic and vocational pathways, poor standards, multiplicity of providers, resource constraints and a high proportion of under-achievers.

Despite radical educational reforms introduced from the 1980s on by Conservative and Labour administrations, by 2003 the many hybrid qualifications introduced by both parties had achieved only poor take-up, lacked adequate vocational content and frequently made only low demands on students' abilities. Following a long policy development trail, in the autumn of 2003 a working group comprising representatives from education, business and other stakeholders was set up by the Government under the former chief inspector of schools, Mike Tomlinson, to review the whole 14–19 educational system. It was the first time that there had been an enquiry into the curriculum, assessment and qualifications system together.

In February 2004 the Tomlinson group presented its initial report and in October 2004, following consultation, presented the report in its final version.

The Tomlinson Report

(www.14-19reform.gov.uk)

The Tomlinson proposals addressed four problems that go to the heart of the vocational education system's continued and acute failure:

- Young people from 14 upward who become alienated from a curriculum too dominated by academic needs. Those whose skills are not academic often become uninterested in or disengaged from schooling. They perform so poorly in their GCSEs that they gain little from their education and leave school as soon as they can (Hames 2004).
- For those of 16 and over, a 'confused and devalued qualifications system in which vocational studies are regarded as inferior' (Ward 2004a) and an 'alphabet soup' of up to 5,000 vocational courses (Guardian 2004).
- A-levels that do not stretch and stimulate the brightest students enough, and do not distinguish adequately between them (Hames 2004).
- A lack of key literacy and numeracy skills in students right across the ability range.

A new diploma system

Tomlinson's proposals aimed to unify academic and vocational pathways through a new two-track, four-tier diploma system incorporating vocational and academic learning. The system would make basic skill studies compulsory, and would be tied to the levels of the national qualification framework (see Table 3).

Table 3 *The Tomlinson diploma system – a flexible ladder of progression*

What does the Tomlinson Report recommend?

A framework for a coherent set of diplomas instead of the current structure of separate subjects

What would change?

Now:	Students typically study for GCSEs (14–15), A-levels (17–18) or BTEC National or an AVCE.
In future:	Students to take courses as part of an overall award, a diploma, at one of four levels equivalent to national qualification levels.

What would a diploma's 'four-tier ladder of progression' be?

Level 1	Entry	
Level 2	Foundation	approximately equivalent to GCSE grades D–G
Level 3	Intermediate	equivalent to GCSE grades A*–C
Level 4	Advanced	equivalent to A-levels or advanced vocational courses

What would be studied in a diploma?

Core learning	To develop all students' basic employability skills, and ensure learning to know themselves, work with others and get things done. Compulsory core of new, 'functional', skills-based courses in mathematical skills, communication and ICT, plus an extended project to take the place of most current coursework, together with wider out-of-school activities, personal planning, review and guidance.

Table 3 *continued*

What would be studied in a diploma? (continued)

Main learning | To ensure progression to a higher course, into apprenticeship, or into the jobs market. Chosen by the individual from a combination of existing academic and/or vocational subjects or/and more specialised learning needed to support them so that they can lead to a particular type of work or future course.

What 'life skills' would a diploma develop?

Common skills | Teacher-assessed skills achieved in both core and main learning areas. They would be developed throughout a diploma, through independent learning, development of interpersonal skills and active citizenship, and the extended project of student's choice.

What age would students be?

Under 16 | Pupils follow the present statutory curriculum, ensuring development of basic and some common skills. They could opt for substantial elements of vocational learning, including up to two days per week placement in an SME, but cannot specialise in specific occupational areas. Some elements of learning would count towards their diploma.

From 16 | Students choose between specialised diplomas or open ones with a mix of subjects. The brightest could bypass intermediate level diploma stage. If achieving an advanced diploma at 16 they could start university then.

Main source: WARD, L. (2004b)

To facilitate the introduction of a diploma system by 2010, Tomlinson proposed that:

- GCSE and A-levels be phased out over a 10-year period, with a more differentiated grading system for A-levels in the meantime.
- Current free-standing academic and vocational qualifications be amended or redesigned as they are converted into components of the new diplomas. This would condense the 5,000 vocational courses currently on offer into 20 broad paths.

The Report emphasised the need for employers and schools to work together to achieve:

- a broadening of the curriculum to include high-quality vocational learning
- the provision of good work-related learning opportunities
- links from the education system to the rapidly expanding apprenticeship system.

Reactions to Tomlinson
On the one hand there has been widespread praise for Tomlinson's emphasis on involving employers and business and on integrating apprenticeships. All sides also appreciate the

sheer scale of the problems that the report has had to address. Crucially, employers and the CBI have given the report a cautious welcome.

On the other hand they and many others have emphasised the need for clarity about how the new qualifications will improve literacy and numeracy, and exactly how they will be implemented. They also need to be convinced that the quality of teaching needed to ensure a real improvement in literacy and numeracy standards can and will be achieved. As will be seen in the next section, that quality at present is sadly lacking.

In some quarters fundamental criticisms have been voiced, and it will be important to see whether and how these are addressed by Government when it announces its own reactions to Tomlinson early in 2005. For these critics the new diploma will not ensure parity of academic and vocational pathways but will instead fatally blur the lines between the two:

- ‘Core learning’ in the new system will cover only ‘functional’ maths, literacy and ICT, but there is as yet no clarity about what ‘functional’ means. In New Zealand three years of radical reform based on the introduction of a National Certificate of Education Achievement that is similar to the proposed Tomlinson diploma have resulted in deep divisions of opinion and some ‘functional’ qualifications of little if any value (Hackett and Woods 2004).
- Breadth of education post-16, which has already been sacrificed in the present A-level system, will be lost in the new system since maths, English, science and a foreign language can all be abandoned at age 16.
- The extended essay concept, although borrowed from the international baccalaureate, will be undermined by allowing the vague alternative of the ‘personal challenge’ instead of being – as in the IB – a stimulating, demanding exercise that tests the best pupils to the limit (Evans 2004).
- Taking 10 years to implement the new system means that there will be an over- long period of trial, error and uncertainty that may ultimately cause the system to fail.

Such criticisms reflect the view that Tomlinson’s formula is excessively complicated, and that in proposing a one-size-fits-all examination system it is attempting too much (Hames 2004). In trying to meet Government’s requirements for excellence, rigorous standards, social inclusiveness and ‘prizes for all’ Tomlinson has ended up by offering only a pale imitation of a far superior model: the international baccalaureate which represents ‘stability, rigour, breadth, coherence and philosophical vision’ (Evans 2004).

The 2004 Five-Year Education Strategy

It will be clear by this point in the chapter that reforms to vocational education can only work within the framework of an effective schools system. In July 2004 Government published its Five-Year Education Strategy for England with the aim of developing schools characterised by ‘fair admissions, full accountability and strong partnerships’ (DfES 2004b, p8). The Strategy covers the whole education system from pre-school to secondary schooling, aiming to ensure choice and quality for all without selection by ability or income.

Key measures include extending specialist status to all 3,500 secondary schools instead of the 2,000 holding it at present, encouraging all good schools to apply for foundation status, therefore gaining major control over their own destinies, and increasing City Academies in the most deprived areas to 200 by 2010. New three-year funding arrangements agreed between schools and LSCs contain measures to give schools rather than local authorities the main control over their funding. However schools' admission policies must be approved by both local authorities and local forums to ensure that there is no return to selection on ability, and that policies operate within an equal opportunity framework. Funding will receive a major boost and by 2007–8 will have risen from the £30 billion granted in 1997 when Labour came into power to over twice that sum.

CASE EXAMPLE
Building industry links with schools

In 2002 the Engineering Employers Federation headed a consortium sponsoring three schools based in Sheffield, Plymouth and Merseyside, where there were very high skills shortages. The aim was that they would gain engineering specialist schools status. To do that, they worked together to meet a list of criteria related to

- the sharing of resources and good practice with at least five other local schools
- the development of skills appropriate to industry and employers
- the building of links with local businesses through work placement for pupils and teachers.

This provides only one of many ways in which employers and schools can work together to make secondary schooling more relevant to the needs of business.

Source: TEMPLE, M. (2002)

What progress?

Since Labour came to power in 1997 its approach to educational reform has been guided by six core principles (Fullan 2001):

- ambitious standards
- devolution of responsibility to school level
- clear targets and improved data on students' achievement
- investment in teachers' professional development
- transparent accountability systems and published results
- more freedom for successful schools and targeted attention to turn failing schools around.

At the time of writing, the final shape of schools educational reform is still to be clarified by the Government. It will be in the practical detail that the devil will lie. Success will depend on:

- schools and business working in close partnership to ensure a high quality, well-balanced, demanding and involving curriculum
- industry's willingness and ability to provide effective and sufficient work placements
- very good career advice for young people
- excellent teachers and teaching resources.

History raises big question marks against all four conditions. On the last point alone, by 2001 teaching had become an 'unsustainable profession' with poor recruitment and retention rates due to 'poor pay, low status and falling morale allied to high levels of stress, bureaucracy and pupil misbehaviour' (Clare 2001). The pressures of national targets, a centrally imposed curriculum and growing levels of classroom violence and of truancy largely explained why '40 percent of trainee teachers never entered the profession and 50 percent of those who did left within five years' (ibid.).

The 2003 annual Office of Standards for Education (Ofsted) report showed that as yet measures to tackle the particularly bad educational results in deprived inner city areas had not significantly improved results across the schools system, and that in that system the historic academic–vocational divide remained as deep as ever. It will take time, of course, before the reforms that are now underway begin to make their mark, but the enormity of the task ahead should not be underestimated. One thing is certain: the quality of schools' human resource strategies will be a vital key to their progress in attracting and retaining the excellent teachers that they so badly need, especially in key science, maths and technology areas where there are acute shortages.

REFLECTION

Imagine that you have been asked by a secondary school with competent but pressured staff and only average academic results for your advice on HR strategy. What HR priorities would you urge – and why?

STRATEGY FOR FURTHER EDUCATION

(www.dfes.gov.uk/learning&skills)

2003 – the state of play

In 1993 in Britain further education (FE) colleges were removed from local authority control to become independent institutions. There are now about 400 colleges, responsible for providing more than two thirds of all vocational qualifications.

The Learning and Skills Council (LSC) is responsible for co-ordination and strategic planning mechanism relating to the FE sector. Its task is to ensure:

- a wider choice of academic and vocational learning opportunities for all
- improvement in adults' reading, writing and Information and Communications Technology skills
- responsiveness to employers' skills needs
- 50 per cent of young people participating in post-school education by 2010.

For colleges, the big issue has always been funding. They have been starved of it for years, forcing some into mergers or closures while the rest have scraped by. Yet they are still expected to meet demanding national skills targets to do with raising basic and intermediate skills levels. Greatly increased numbers of students since 2002 have put an impossible strain on resources and national targets are far from being achieved. The effects on staff recruitment and retention rates have been disastrous, with lecturers taking strike action in 2002.

By the beginning of the twenty-first century 70 per cent of companies, notably small firms, were failing to use the FE system. Causes were clear:

- The way colleges have traditionally had to deliver learning. The government funding that they receive has in the past been tied to whole, not part, qualifications, while allowances for students heavily favour full-time courses. This means that colleges have not been able to respond meaningfully to employers' and individuals' preference for bite-sized chunks and portable part-qualifications that are easier to finance.
- The fact that government has tied colleges' funding tightly to courses that lead to national vocational qualifications and skills levels related to them. Yet this does not always meet employers' and individuals' needs. A system of unitised delivery and the flexibility to provide more of what customers want would again largely resolve the problem.
- Poor quality teaching and low completion rates of students on courses, predictable results of the staffing problems endemic by now in the FE system and of colleges' lack of ability to respond adequately to learners' needs.

Between 2002 and 2004 Government took a series of measures to tackle these problems, notably through the 2002 strategy paper *Success for all* (DfES 2002a) and the 2003 Skills Strategy (DfES 2003a).

2002 – Success for all?

Success for all promised the beginning of a new era for colleges. It provided a big cash injection for all that signed up to three year plans with their local LSCs and education and training providers, agreeing to targets in four broad areas. Further funding increases will be linked to performance against those targets. Devolving to colleges more control over how they spend their funding aims to improve educational provision for learners and employers.

Colleges' four target areas relate to:

- engaging with employers and improving course choice in order to enhance skills development in the economy
- achieving excellence in teaching, training and learning
- developing and supporting the FE workforce
- developing a framework for quality and success.

Success for all also includes measures to help share good practice, with Centres of Vocational Excellence to be expanded to 400 by 2006. Other measures aim to aid professional development of staff and improve their leadership and management.

2003 – moving forward

The Skills Strategy published in 2003 (DfES 2003a) is taking forward *Success for all*. For FE and employers, the biggest changes are that whereas until 2003 the £2.5 billion being spent by the LSC on adult learning was going mainly to colleges as a 75 per cent subsidy on adult training courses that usually had to cover all elements of an NVQ to attract funding, now there is a more demand-led system that allows:

- more modular training and assessment, often taking place on employers' premises to fit in with shift patterns
- more employer input to the design of qualifications.

To reduce barriers of access its measures offer:

- free access for all adults to courses leading to NVQ level 2 or equivalent (five good GCSEs or equivalent)
- free access for those over 19 and under 30 who want to study A-level and equivalent courses (NVQ level 3), the courses chosen cover 'shortage' subjects to be determined at regional level
- permission for learners to complete NVQs in 'bite-sized chunks' through time by accumulating credits.

CASE EXAMPLE
Co-ordinating further education provision

The Association of Colleges now operates a national service, AoC Workforce Development, to co-ordinate FE provision from different colleges for employers with outlets round the country. One example is Iceland Frozen Foods. The Association has welcomed the government's decision to allow individuals to acquire NVQs through a build up of 'bite-sized chunks' of learning instead of through one-off big learning packages. It sees the next major need to be better publicity by government of learning across the board rather than just of individual programmes.

Source: PICKARD, J. (2003a)

A review of adult learning was due to be completed late in 2004. In the meantime government in its 2004 Five-Year Education Strategy (DfES 2004b) has pledged to build broader and deeper links between further and higher education and employers in the future.

What progress?

A review of funding is under way at the time of writing and it is clear that this will involve what the minister for education and skills has called 'a historic shift in expectations and practice about who pays for what' (*People Management* 2004a). Government wants employers to make a more direct contribution to building their own long-term skills supply by engaging with the educational providers and Sector Skills Councils. SSCs are crucial in helping employers to identify and articulate their skills needs to providers.

However, the optimism produced by *Success for all* and *21st century skills* is giving way to renewed concerns. LSCs have to give or withhold funding according to colleges' performance, working with them to ensure achievement of national skills targets. Given the heavy financial implications of the colleges' three-year development plans a radical switch of funds away from non-priority general adult education now seems likely in favour of free national qualification courses for all adults needing level 2 qualifications. This would reduce colleges' ability to respond to employers' and individuals' needs, since they currently offer various vocational courses that, if scrapped, would hurt industry and students (Kingston 2004). Funding is also to be substantially reduced for 225 institutions currently failing to recruit and teach the student numbers they had forecast in the three target categories (ibid.).

Since 1993 colleges have been 'riding the rollercoaster of change' (Whittaker 2003) and this introduces another critical issue: the need for effective human resource (HR) strategies and high-calibre HR managers who can successfully tackle 'huge challenges' (ibid.). Across the FE sector initiatives to improve leadership and management are being accompanied by continuing negotiations with unions to achieve much enhanced performance management through the opening up of career routes, training and development for lecturers wishing to move into management, a modernised, harmonised pay and grading scheme and an effective appraisal process. Relevant HR strategies are vital to the success of these efforts.

REFLECTION

Taking a further education college known to you or that you have read about, how far do you think its HR strategies to attract, reward and retain academic staff are successful, and what areas for improvement would you suggest in those strategies?

STRATEGY FOR HIGHER EDUCATION

(http://www.dfes.gov.uk/hegateway/hereform/index)

2003 – the state of play

In the early 1960s in the UK only 6 per cent of those under 21 had gone to university. By 2003 that figure had risen to 46 per cent, a participation rate better than that of the USA, Japan, France and Germany even though not as high as a few countries including the Netherlands, Sweden and Finland. The Government's aims for the higher education (HE) system are to:

- open up access even more, moving towards participation by 50 per cent of all 19–30 year olds and ending the social class divide between students embarking on degree courses.
- promote research, giving British universities the chance to match the best in the world in an increasingly competitive market
- promote excellence in teaching
- improve links with employers.

In 1997 the Dearing Report into higher education identified deep-rooted problems across the whole HE system (NCIHE 1997). It had been plunged into confusion after the 1988 reforms, when polytechnics lost their unique vocational status and became 'new universities' competing with the old in a challenging and expanding market place. In 2003 most of Dearing's recommendations were included in the White Paper on *The future of higher education* (DfES 2002b), and in 2004 the Higher Education Act introduced measures to assist the White Paper's implementation.

2003–4 – the big overhaul

With the Act, major changes are now being introduced relating to funding, access, research, teaching, business links and management. These include:

Funding

- By 2006, universities to have more freedom to raise their own funds, with the cap on fees removed and permission to charge and use as they see fit fees of up to £3,000 per year.

- Restoration of grants and abolition of up-front fees for all to aid the less well-off students, student loans to be repaid at more favourable rates post-qualification once graduates are in employment and salaries have reached a certain level, and funding to reward universities and colleges that attract and retain students from 'non-traditional' backgrounds.

Access

- The introduction of a new Access Regulator, the Office for Fair Access (Offa) to assess how far 'top' universities are meeting their own planned milestones for access. Universities not having a high enough proportion of students from 'disadvantaged' backgrounds can be fined and forbidden to charge top-up fees.

Research

- Providing a better infrastructure and pay scales for research staff and concentrating research funding on the best research institutions, with the main investment going to science and technology.

Teaching

- Training of all new lecturing staff, with new externally monitored teaching performance standards, rewarding the best teaching institutions and departments, and granting extra funding to 'Centres of Excellence'.
- The creation of 'teaching' universities that will not be funded for research.

Business links

- More funding for university–business knowledge networks and other measures to boost partnerships between universities, Sector Skills Councils, and RDAs – with the latter having more say in the allocation of HE funding.
- Achieving most of the targeted increase in participation rates through major funded expansion of two-year employer and work focused foundation degrees, offered through FE colleges and former polytechnics.
- The establishment of a new category of universities by private companies or public bodies engaged heavily in training, with a minimum requirement that they have 4,000 full-time students or equivalent.

Leadership and management

- Improved leadership training and development, particularly through a new Leadership Foundation, and funding for institutional-level HR plans in recognition of the importance of HR strategies in HE institutions.

What progress?

What will these sweeping changes mean in practice? It is too early to be sure, but it does seem clear already that:

- Universities will be exposed far more than in the past to market forces, although there will be more encouragement and recognition for superior performance.
- The separation of an elite research grouping of universities from the rest could create a damaging two-tier system, yet a way has to be found of keeping a small

group in the world's top cluster while at the same time making higher education affordable to non-traditional entrants. The extra resource being given to outstanding research institutions and staff should help British universities to regain that crucial international competitive edge in research.

- The expansion of foundation degrees (first introduced in 2001) within colleges and new universities sets the scene 'for a multi-tiered higher education system, from the elite and expensive to the cheap and cheerful' (Woods 2003). But these degrees should open career routes for those who currently lack the educational attainments to access them, and offer educational institutions a unique chance to engage more actively with business.
- Weaker institutions will have no option but to focus on teaching and on building links with local employers in order to survive. That raises doubts about how effective the 'business links' will actually prove to be, while the focus of research funding leaves open to question how business and management research that is vital to inform those links is to be supported.

In December 2004 the Commons science and technology committee told the science minister that the closure over the past 10 years of more than 100 university science departments represented a 'long catalogue of failures' in the way science had been directed. Government funding pressures had made it uneconomic for many universities to offer unpopular subjects, no matter how vital to the economy, or to keep open departments judged not to be doing world class research (Clare 2004). Meanwhile the University of Buckingham's vice-chancellor observed with concern that the better British universities are increasingly closing their teaching departments in order to focus on research and the rewards Government now attaches to it, worsening the plight of the lesser 'teaching' universities that, deprived of research income, facilities and resources, seemed set for further decline (Kealey 2004).

One of the most fundamental questions raised by Government's HE policy relates to its persistence in increasing participation rates for level 4 (graduate level) qualifications. Research in the dominating service sector suggests that (Mason 2002):

- The push to expand to 50 per cent participation in HE may result in an excess of young people qualified at level 4, many of whom will occupy jobs more appropriate for non-graduates with good-quality technical skills.
- Expansion of mass higher education therefore may not have the intended impact on economic performance, unless far more British employers than currently can be encouraged to adopt a high-skill, high value-added product or service strategy – the big business strategy issue discussed in Chapter 2.

EDUCATION AND EMPLOYERS: MAKING THE PARTNERSHIP WORK

Government-funded work-based programmes

Like national workforce development strategy discussed in Chapter 2, educational strategy is now moving along a more demand-led route but for this to work, local-based partnerships must take the lead. In this section I outline three of the Government's funded programmes that make particular demands on such partnerships: the University for Industry, foundation degrees, and the Apprenticeship scheme.

The University for Industry
(http://www.ufiltd.co.uk)

The University for Industry (UfI), branded *learndirect*, is central to Government's strategy to tackle acute shortage of basic skills and to achieve innovative and flexible approaches to learning. UfI is not a university in the conventional sense. It does not offer its own qualifications and it is not exclusively for industry. It operates through a network of around 1,000 'learning centres' run by a consortia of bodies – employers, unions, voluntary groups and so on – in accessible (rather than traditional educational) locations.

UfI's primary target is those who are new to learning and do not receive corporate training. It aims to cover learning at every level from elementary to postgraduate by linking businesses and individuals to information technology-based education and training underpinned by a national learning grid. The grid is intended to carry high-quality networked learning and information services to schools, libraries and museums at low cost.

The UfI's supported learning and its approach to access aim to widen lifelong learning, achieving higher social inclusion and employability. However it has been widely criticised for its poor marketing, for material that lacks depth and fails to engage learners, and for its focus on lower level skills that can devalue it in the eyes of users (Johnson 2001). Yet it offers many relevant services and products for individuals and workforces that lack basic skills, and L&D professionals need to be well informed about them in order to assess their utility for their own organisations.

Foundation degrees
(http://www.foundationdegree.org.uk/)

Foundation degrees (FDs) provide a vocationally focused higher education route for those already in employment. Positioned at level 4, their primary aim is to improve skills and knowledge at the intermediate qualifications level, including craft and technical. An FD would normally take three years of part-time study. It is a higher education qualification in its own right, but the intention is that FD graduates should also be able to proceed to a relevant honours degree in a further 12–15 months, or progress towards a professional qualification or licence to practise.

FDs must be developed by partnerships that include a degree-awarding HE institution, an employer representative (typically an L&D professional) and a delivery institution, typically an FE college. They are aimed not only at those entering vocational education after leaving school or college but also at those already in employment and at those considering a return to the labour market. What attractions do they hold?

- They promote work-based skills, key skills and generic skills like management.
- They present an opportunity for raising the organisational commitment and the motivation to learn of employees, especially those in low level work, by opening up new career routes for them.
- They involve an imaginative blend of learning methods, especially through use of e-technology combined with workplace learning and attendance at college or university, with credit given for relevant prior learning or experience.

However, there is as yet little meaningful evidence of FDs' success. Currently the picture is confused by the following issues:

■ Their funding is proving problematic. It comes through the Higher Education Funding Council for England, even though the majority of provision of FDs is actually being carried out in FE colleges, normally funded by Learning and Skills Councils. This confusion, predictably, means that LSCs are not always supportive about providing funding for FDs.

■ So far they are located in a limited and varied range of vocational areas, and take-up by employers has been poor. Most are probably uncertain about where FDs fit in the spectrum of sub-degree qualifications, adopting a 'wait and see' stance before investing in an initiative whose unique value-adding potential for a business is as yet unclear.

■ The drop-out rate amongst FD students currently is running at about one third, considerably higher than in honours degree courses.

■ The accreditation of prior learning (APL) process is fundamental to any proposal for a foundation degree, as is the need to clarify the kind of honours degrees to which FD graduates could progress, and for a clear progression map. Clarity is taking time to achieve.

The following case example outlines how FDs are being used to open up routes to being a 'semi-professional' in the NHS, the biggest spender on learning among British employers. What key points do you think it illustrates about HR professionals' role related to these degrees generally? A commentary follows the case.

CASE EXAMPLE

Foundation degrees in the National Health Service (NHS)

Foundation degrees form part of the NHS 'skills escalator' strategy for staff development (see Chapter 10). Their development for this purpose is being aided by a strategy group including representation from strategic health authorities, the LSC, the QAA (Quality Assurance Agency), the Department for Education and Skills, Foundation Degree Forward (overseeing the degrees) and the two Sector Skills Councils related to the NHS. The degrees are to be provided both for existing post-holders and for college students who wish to enter the NHS on qualifying.

Problems encountered are to do with:

■ the difficulty of finding, funding, operating and monitoring work placements for non-NHS students
■ deciding how students will be supervised and who will assess them
■ communications between NHS partners running the programmes, and between all of them and the education providers
■ the need to ensure that the degrees are driven by employers and rest on identification of a clear skills gap so that the degree doesn't just become 'another course for people to sign up to'.

The most successful courses so far are those that fill a real need, especially related to hard-to-recruit-for posts; and those that resolve the work-placement problem by drawing on existing post-holders and using their experience while offering them a degree-level route at the same time – people who are care assistants are a case in point.

Source: HISCOCK, D. (2004)

Comments

- The case illustrates the dependence of FDs on effective partnerships between many players, each with their own aims and interests to pursue.
- It shows how if HR managers and L&D professionals are to help their employers gain from investing in FDs they must work with partners to ensure 'the right fit between an individual, the right qualification at the right time and the skills needed by the organisation' (Hiscock 2004).
- They must also ensure that the organisation has the resources and the expertise needed to provide effective, well monitored and well assessed workplace experience.

Two developments that may lead to a greater take-up of FDs by employers and individuals are:

- a new (although still limited) package of financial support for part-time students from September 2004
- the withdrawal of the Higher National Diploma qualification, leaving a vacuum that FDs are ideally placed to fill.

Apprenticeship
(www.apprenticeships.org.uk)

The *Modern Apprenticeship* (MA) scheme was introduced in 1993 by the Conservative government as a publicly funded approach to rebuild youth training for skills after the abolition of Industrial Training Boards. Under the Labour Government it has been expanded to provide the major funded route for young people into vocational training and thence into skilled employment. The major revamp in May 2004 introduced a change of title to *Apprenticeships*, and coverage at three levels:

- *Apprenticeships*: equivalent to GCSE level plus Key Skills – level 2 in the national qualifications framework.
- *Advanced Apprenticeships*: equivalent to A level plus Key Skills – level 3.
- *Young Apprenticeships*: for 14–16-year-olds in a group of employment sectors, giving them up to two days a week in a workplace as part of their regular schooling.

There is also a trial extension of *Apprenticeships* for those over 25.

Apprenticeship programmes attract funding from the LSC. They involve a mix of on the job and off the job training and education, and typically take between one and four years to complete. Employers are subsidised for the costs involved in apprentices attending education courses.

All Apprenticeship frameworks contain a requirement to develop Key Skills through NVQs. Employers, through SSCs, are gaining a bigger role in design, content and entry requirements of apprenticeship programmes. Apprenticeships are being expanded into non-traditional areas and by June 2004 more than 160 frameworks were available in over 80 business sectors and 255,500 16–24 year olds had enrolled under them compared with 78,000 in 1997 when Labour came into power (Gribben 2004). About one fifth of apprentices work in large companies like Tesco, Asda or BAE Systems.

The *Apprenticeship* scheme has a complex operational framework with some worrying features. For example, the scheme costs £1 billion per year to run yet the LSC does not have any accurate list of organisations employing apprentices despite the importance of such a tool to measure the scheme's performance (Tyler 2004b). Funding and contracts with providers are the responsibility of LSCs. Training providers are paid per apprentice taken on, so the incentive to recruit is high, but they have no equivalent incentive to promote structured learning in the organisations where they place their trainees. Monitoring responsibilities are shared between providers, the ALI, the Health and Safety Executive (HSE) and the LSCs, but concerns here have been heightened by nine deaths of apprentices in the 18 months up to July 2004. All were under 23; each was with a different training provider and working in a different organisation. According to the Health and Safety Inspectorate's spokesperson in Radio 4's *File on 4* programme on 13 July 2004, all the deaths were preventable. The ALI subsequently joined the LSC and partners to establish a 'safe learner framework'.

Completion rates are another problem. In Germany two-thirds of 16-year-olds enter apprenticeships and most complete them successfully. In Denmark, around a third enter apprenticeships and around 90 per cent complete them. In England only 9 per cent of that age group enter apprenticeship and by 2004 the drop-out rate was 40 per cent (Merrick 2004). Employers too are failing to support the scheme in sufficient numbers. This is often because they do not want the complete apprenticeship package, either seeing no reason for their trainees to have to do key skills, or querying the need for all trainees to complete a full NVQ (Mackinnon 2003). Concern over the limited provision of apprenticeships by large employers in Britain is now so great that a CIPD-sponsored research project at London and Cambridge Universities has been established to investigate the issues (further information from v.gill@cipd.co.uk).

With a supposedly demand-driven national skills strategy, what the employers and the learners want should be key to provision. But there must be a balance here: if government funding is provided for an initiative, then that funding must also bring benefits for the economy and improve individuals' general employability. John Stevens (2003), then CIPD special advisor, recommended that:

- Government should provide an appropriate vocational education, then work with industry on a framework of qualifications in which young employees can be developed.
- The education system should provide the basis for key skills, leaving employers free to decide in each case whether or not to build on that to meet their particular skill needs.
- Sector skills bodies should raise awareness through international comparisons and case studies of opportunities for raising trainees' performance by extending capability.

If the Tomlinson Working Group's proposals discussed in the previous section of this chapter are accepted these features will be introduced and direct links will be created between a new 14–19 diploma system and apprenticeship. Meanwhile, Government is re-examining financial incentives for apprentices to maintain the attractiveness of the programme. It is providing help to encourage more SMEs to sign up, and introducing a portability element to allow apprentices to take partially completed programmes with them if they move employers (Gribben 2004).

REFLECTION

Taking an apprenticeship programme in your own organisation or one that you know or have read about, what measures do you see to be in place to ensure that:

- the training providers who are overseeing the programme have the necessary expertise and reliability?
- safe and high-quality workplace training is provided for the trainees?

Tasks for L&D practitioners related to funded work-based learning

LSC funding is given to many forms of work-based learning, including preparation and assessment for national vocational qualifications, and apprenticeship. The Adult Learning Inspectorate has produced highly critical reports both of those who manage, deliver and assess such learning in the workplace, and of external education and training providers.

Practitioners engaged in delivery in the workplace

In 2000 L&D practitioners involved in funded work-based learning in the workplace numbered between 95,000 and 110,000 in England. They included:

- managers, supervisors, resource and programme co-ordinators
- tutors/occupational trainers and assessors, mentors and coaches
- administrators and other support staff.

Ultimately some £7 billion per year of public funds is to be delivered into workplace training and education. In return, employers have to demonstrate that the staff they use meet the qualifications and competency requirements that are a condition of funding. To facilitate this, national occupational standards and related qualifications and units of qualifications for practitioners continue to expand.

However, reports from Training Standards Inspectors and the Adult Learning Inspectorate have identified a serious lack of competence in these practitioners and one problem, perversely, is the wide range, varying levels and skewed focus of their qualifications. Most centre on work-based assessment and verification. Other qualifications, in particular those focused on the management of training and quality and related planning activities, are much less widespread.

Practitioners engaged in workplace learning provision

By 2003 LSCs in England had issued contracts to more than 1,900 external providers, including around 400 further education colleges. In November 2003 the Adult Learning Inspectorate's (ALI) annual report concluded that despite improvement since the previous year, almost half the provision was still below standard and 40 per cent of providers had poor management and leadership, resulting in poor quality teaching and training and a high learner drop-out rate (*People Management* 2003). The number of providers has subsequently been slashed, until by mid-2004 only around 800 remained. How LSCs came to place so many contracts with below-standard providers in the first place remains an unanswered question.

The 2004 ALI annual report (ALI 2004), which covered both work-based learning and learning provided in colleges, concluded that although improvements had continued,

34 per cent of adult learning and work-based learning was still inadequate and that those in greatest need suffered most from this, including the disabled, those with low basic skills levels and those with learning disabilities. The report concluded that more training for FE teachers must be one urgent priority.

Lessons from international practice

As can be seen in Table 4, workplace learning in the UK has some distinctive features lacking in many of its competitor countries. These are explained in part by an NVET system that is still largely unregulated. It will be important to see how far government's recent attempts to make that system more demand-driven improve the weaknesses that consistently emerge in cross-national comparisons between the UK and many other countries. These are to do with (Stern and Sommerlad 1999, p79):

- the readiness or preparedness of workers for continuous training and learning in the workplace
- the organisation and management of training in the workplace including employers' attitudes.

Such comparisons identify a need for assessment of work-based learning to be in the hands of practitioners with a sound practical and a theoretical grasp of the tasks involved. They also highlight the importance of such practitioners being developed and tested, preferably by external experts, as fit to practice, with testing rigorously linked to the needs and characteristics of the workplace. This should be not only in terms of standards to be reached by the practitioners, but also of how they perform their tasks in terms of reliability, punctuality and quality.

The Government was expected to announce by the end of 2004 measures to improve the skills of external training providers and to give them stronger incentives to work with employers. All in all it is clear that L&D practitioners involved in organising and delivering internal or external LSC-funded provision have many challenging tasks to perform if essential improvements in LSC-funded work-based learning are to be achieved. These include:

- sharing responsibility with LSCs for raising work-based learning schemes' profile and demonstrating their value to businesses
- improving their own expertise and partnership skills, for example by getting centrally involved in the design of apprenticeship programmes via their SSCs
- nurturing commitment and involvement in work-based learning within their own organisations
- helping line managers and mentors to develop skills and attitudes that will improve the quality and outcomes of work-based learning in their organisations.

OPENING UP LIFELONG LEARNING OPPORTUNITIES

Barriers to access

Despite Labour's many changes to promote lifelong learning for young people and adults, by 2004 statistics still demonstrated the need for improved links between work, welfare and learning. According to the National Institute of Adult Continuing Education (NIACE, quoted in Kingston 2004):

Table 4 *A comparison of country NVET systems*

Country	VET system and funding	Training provision	Workplace learning
Netherlands	Dual. Funding shared between state and employers.	Partnership approach between the state, employers and unions. Sectoral, sub-sectoral and company networks stimulate help to deliver training.	Integral part of new ways of organising work. Managers are committed to and strongly interested in workplace learning.
Germany	Dual. Funding shared between state and employers. The university system is being reformed to make it more responsive to the market and to share funding more equally between state and private sectors.	The dual system provides the framework for training and development at company level, and training provision is overseen by regional chambers of commerce and industry.	No particular emphasis on workplace learning as a separate system. Employers have to take most of the initiative, and a focus on informal workplace learning is hampered by rigidity of the dual system.
France	Dual, but highly centralised. Funded by a training tax. Mutual funds at sectoral and multi-sectoral levels help training to meet specific industrial and cross-industrial needs.	Strong emphasis on partnership between state, employers and unions. Social partners specify training priorities and negotiate collectively for use of funds and advice from official agencies.	Strong emphasis on formal courses and vocational training. Other forms of workplace learning need more focus but this is impeded by operation of the levy system and probably also by unique organisation and management of French firms.

Table 4 *continued*

Country	VET system and funding	Training provision	Workplace learning
USA	Market-driven system with federal funding to aid special groups. Recent federal legislation has attempted to stimulate training to better meet market needs.	Partnership between state-funded Workforce Investment Boards and local governments at federal state level, and between employers and labour unions at company level.	Left to initiative of employers, but high-performance working practices and a historic culture of self-development stimulate innovation and some world-class best practice.
UK	Market-driven system with state funding to aid special groups. Recent legislation has attempted to stimulate training to better meet market needs.	New attempt at partnership between state-funded Learning and Skills Council, employers, unions, educationalists and regional development agencies. Within companies, basically determined by the employers, although unions have begun to claim a role.	Responsibility lies with employer and individuals. Emphasis has tended to focus on formal training and education and accredited competency schemes, whose quality and management national funding and standards are now trying to improve. The introduction of some high-performance working practices in organisations is leading to greater interest in work-based learning processes.

Table 4 *continued*

Country	VET system and funding	Training provision	Workplace learning
Japan	The heavily centralised state educational system sets high standards of broad-based educational attainment upon which employers can build training and development tailored to company needs and goals.	Line management, not the training function, is the major partner in employee development. Japanese companies are nested in broader economic, structural and cultural systems. They are characterised internally by integration of all business and HR strategies and their subordination to a single corporate strategic goal. The preferred strategy is to recruit well-educated workers and develop an internal labour market and career system. Japan's deep economic recession now threatens that model.	Managers are responsible for creating a learning culture and employees are expected to be active in their own development (Tjepkema, ter Horst and Mulder 2002a, p18). Strong emphasis on continued training, and strategically focused group learning and knowledge creation as integral part of everyday work. 'Nested stability and the lack of the labour mobility means that organizations are effective "social containers" for accumu lated individual and collective tacit knowledge' (Ray 2002, pp102–103).

Source: HARRISON, R. and KESSELS, J. (2003a) *Human resource development in a knowledge economy: an organisational view*. Palgrave Macmillan. 80–81. Reproduced with permission of Palgrave Macmillan.

- Fewer than a fifth of adults say they are doing some sort of organised learning, the lowest figure since before Labour took office in 1997.
- The decline in participation has been most marked among people from the skilled manual and unskilled workers and those on limited incomes, so social class still seems to operate as a divider amongst those pursuing learning.
- Only 14 per cent of 65–74 year-olds have participated in education in the past three years, compared with 19 per cent in 1996, a decline attributed by NIACE's director to a 'relentless focus of funders on achievement targets' that is narrowing the curriculum offer to adults.
- Adults without Internet access participate less than half as much as others.

While Government has the responsibility of tackling these barriers on the national scale, there is much that employers and HR professionals can do within the workplace to open up lifelong learning opportunities in ways that will benefit individuals but also bring benefits for the business. In the following section I outline some of the measures that Government is putting in place to tackle the barriers, and the rationale behind them.

Educational Maintenance Allowances

Under the Employment Rights Act, 1996, working teenagers between the ages of 16 and 17 who have not attained a certain standard of education and training have the right to paid time off in order to study for specified qualifications. Means-tested Educational Maintenance Allowances (EMAs) bring most help to students from the poorest homes, and to those on full-time courses in higher education who live at home. But for those outside those categories, or wanting to achieve a 'first' level 3, lack of adequate funding aid and incentive remains a barrier to access. Ryan (2004), drawing on the successful Australian model, urges a 'single seamless allowance' for all young people in education and training from school and college to university. This would set a reasonable minimum standard for all and could easily be combined with subsidised loans.

Within organisations, fairer recruitment and selection policies and career development planning for all employees would go a considerable way towards encouraging more participation in qualification-linked training, although many employers see no reason why they should go beyond training – whether or not qualification-linked – to fill proficiency gaps. BP has a model workforce development programme available online at http://www.dfes.gov.uk/skillsforemployers/pages/resources/index.

Skills for Life initiatives

In its *Widening adult participation strategy* (LSC 2004b), the LSC explains that since over a third of adults are still not participating in learning once they leave compulsory education, the UK clearly has a problem in getting the message across to them that lifelong learning matters. To tackle the problem Government is investing £1.6 billion from April 2003 to March 2006 in its *Skills for Life* national strategy, which works alongside the National Skills Strategy (DfES 2003a) and the LSC's strategy to improve the numbers of adults with the necessary skills and qualifications. As a priority it is targeting groups that are at most disadvantage in the labour market and in society at large. LSCs with Jobcentre Plus and the DfES's Offenders Learning and Skills Unit are charged with meeting two challenging targets:

- 750,000 adults to achieve national level 2 certificates by 2004 (470,000 had achieved them by August, 2003)
- 1.5 million to achieve the same by 2007.

The Adult Basic Skills Strategy Unit (ABSSU) within the DfES is responsible for *Skills for life* initiatives and teachers are specially trained to deliver a diverse range of learning opportunities. All basic skills classes are free to learners, including those offered online through *learndirect* and a number of organisations (BP, already mentioned, is one) are now taking positive action to improve their employees' basic skills. To provide further incentives, *Sure Start* is expanding childcare provision, and childcare allowances were introduced in the 2004 5-Year Education Act. However, there is no support as yet for other carers. Furthermore, in many organisations adults in work still find it difficult to do part-time rather than full-time courses, and also lack adequate career break opportunities.

In 2004 the *Apprenticeships* scheme was extended for a trial period to adults over 25. This too, however, has a downside, since it is unclear how the extension will be funded. Funding must also be found for the likely rolling out on a national basis from 2006 of the ETP scheme (outlined in Chapter 2). With the squeeze on LSC funds already raising concerns, it seems ever more likely that the DfES will 'raid the £2.5 billion adult FE budget' (Corney 2004).

Vocational qualification system

One of the most useful ways in which Government is now trying to encourage higher participation levels in further and higher education is in developing a flexible qualifications system that will be more attractive for individual learners and cheaper and more relevant for employers to fund, notably by:

- Dividing more vocational qualification learning programmes into units and speeding up accreditation of new qualifications.
- Moving towards the introduction of a credits framework to allow adults to gain recognition of their skills over time, enabling them to package the training programmes they want and build up a record of achievement towards qualification.
- Improving information about opportunities. The LSC, *learndirect* and the DfES are developing an integrated local and national Information and Guidance (IAG) service for adults, linking those to the wider workforce development framework.

THE FINAL VERDICT?

The vision of lifelong learning

The material covered in the previous section has highlighted the many ways in which Government is seeking to change a situation where historically the training of adults already in work has been given little meaningful attention by previous governments' skills strategies. The old priorities were the unemployed and young people, while for employers the focus tended to be on managers and professionals, leaving low-skilled adults 'in a twilight zone with no career prospects' (Pickard 2003a). Now, in national strategy at least, there is a powerful spotlight on the low-skilled and unskilled adults in work. By early 2004 the LSC-led programme of sector-based training had identified and met employer skills needs in over 30 occupational groups, helping to train some 27,000 additional adults with many progressing to level 3 qualifications and beyond.

Further steps are under way, with a review taking place through SSCs in each sector of the need for new adult learning programmes to develop generic skills for employment. At the time of writing (late 2004) a Green Paper is due to be published to pull together all the various types of support on offer to young people, to announce reforms of funding arrangements for adult learners, and to introduce measures to improve training providers' skills and give them stronger incentives to work with employers.

Will these measures prove sufficiently attractive to employers to invest meaningfully in lifelong learning opportunities for all their employees? Many doubt that they will. Lifelong learning is vital in a knowledge-based society but it needs new mindsets. It will not happen by itself. Union learning representatives are helping to achieve mutual trust related to learning in the workplace, but the biggest issue for government remains the need to fundamentally change the relationship between education and learning providers on the one hand and employers on the other. The task is formidable. It involves mediating the power relationships that exist in the firm and in the labour market. It requires employers and HR professionals becoming actively committed to substantially raising the levels of basic skills in their workforces, to reducing rigid divisions in their internal labour market, and to opening up more access to educational opportunities and career development for all their employees. Since employers have never taken the lead here, there is all the more need for the HR profession, and especially L&D practitioners within it, to take a proactive stance and work in partnerships that can produce and implement powerful, imaginative strategies and initiatives.

National Skills Strategy overall

Finally, having reviewed in this and the preceding chapter the Government's entire strategy covering workforce development and education reform, how optimistic should we be about its chances of success?

On the evidence so far, my own conclusion is guarded. The intention of strategy is clear and relevant. It makes a fundamental and positive break with the past. But the delivery is severely in doubt. It has to be achieved through an extremely complex partnership framework operating at many levels from national to local, and the strains on funding are already becoming clear. In November 2004 the King's Fund identified other kinds of problems that underlie many collaborative initiatives. Coote et al (2004) reported that the effectiveness of complex social programmes such as Local Strategic partnerships can be hampered by the competing interests of politicians, researchers and practitioners, and that there is also no reliable evaluation framework to assess the programmes' value.

These and other concerns lead many to fear that it is all a move too far. They predict that a system that relies on a voluntary approach to achieve Government's NVET vision and goals, upskill the economy and pull down intractable barriers to opportunities for adults to fully access lifelong learning opportunities will never be enough. They urge some form of regulation imposed on employers to force the pace. At present, however, Government's commitment to 'working in partnership' through a demand-driven strategy fuelled by mutual interest remains firmly in place.

CONCLUSION

Having mastered the material in this chapter, you should now understand the aims, scope and interim progress of major reforms taking place in schools and in the further and higher education sectors, and their implications for employers, L&D professionals and individuals. You should also be confident in tackling the review questions relating to this chapter, contained in Appendix 3.

In summary, the chapter's six sections have covered the following ground:

- It has explained the three core aims of the Government's educational reforms and placed them in the context of its overall 2003 National Skills Strategy to develop a demand-led and partnership-based approach to workforce development and educational provision, and to improve also the organisational and wider community contexts in which development and provision are located.
- It has outlined the key reforms in the educational system and assessed their current progress. In the schools system the most radical changes are likely to stem from the Tomlinson Report into 14–19 education and the July 2004 5-Year Education Strategy.
- In the FE and HE system the most radical changes have been introduced by *Success for all* and the National Skills Strategy, heralding in both sectors a new era of increased funding tied to improved performance and provision, enhanced links with employers and learners, and expanded student participation rates. Colleges and universities have been given more freedom to manage themselves but must discover for themselves how best to survive now that they are far more exposed to market forces. Within the university system a widening divide between research and teaching institutions offers glittering prizes for the best in each category, but an increased struggle for survival for the weakest.
- The chapter has then looked at the implications of these and other individually oriented reforms on the opening up of lifelong adult education opportunities, and their particular implications for employers and L&D professionals.
- It has raised doubts about the likely success of Government's lifelong learning mission, as about that of its national skills strategy overall, while emphasising, however, the fundamental breaks that have been made with previous governments' policies and the time it will inevitably take before real results can begin to show.

Further information sources

Alongside the various website references provided in the chapter, there are also the following:

- The Learning and Skills Council website, new in August 2004 and giving brief, clear information about government policy and initiatives related to the coverage of this chapter: http://senet.lsc.gov.uk/guide2/wideparticipationpolicy/index [accessed 25 August 2004].
- http://www.dfes.gov.uk/readwriteplus/ [accessed 25 August 2004]. Provides information on *Skills for life*, and also helpful summaries of government policy and strategies across the education and workforce development fields.
- http://www.lifelonglearning.co.uk/sitemap.htm [accessed 25 August 2004]. Useful index of site areas currently on lifelong learning, listing interesting official papers, documents and conference reports from previous years, key themes in government strategy, and links to other relevant sites.
- http://ferl.becta.org.uk for an overview of government policy and initiatives in the further education field and many useful links [accessed 27 September 2004].

For more information on basic skills policy and workplace initiatives, visit:

- http://www.dfes.gov.uk/skillsforemployers [accessed 25 August 2004].

- the Workplace basic skills network at http://www.lancs.ac.uk/wbsnet [accessed 25 August 2004].
- http://www.learningservices.org.uk/ [accessed 25 August 2004]. A TUC site where you can find out how to set up basic skills training in an organisation, and also obtain information about the Union Learning Fund.
- http://www.dfes.gov.uk/learning&skills/index.shtml [accessed 25 August 2004]. A DfES portal covering key providers such as further education and sixth form colleges, schools with sixth forms, local authority and adult education institutions and private and voluntary sector providers.

You should also regularly read:

- the CIPD's publication *People Management*, which contains updates on NVET policy and initiatives plus useful case studies illustrating take-up.
- the quality press for a range of informed views about education reform.

Getting to Grips with the Practice

Understanding Learning and the Learners

CHAPTER 4

INTRODUCTION

Part 2 of the book explores ways in which L&D practitioners can ensure high-quality and ethical learning and development practice, linked to organisational as well as individual performance and responsive to changing needs and challenges.

The focus in this chapter is on learning and the learners. Traditionally learning in organisations has been defined as 'a relatively permanent change in behaviour that occurs as a result of practice or experience' (Bass and Vaughan 1967, p8). More recently it has been given a different interpretation (Zuboff 1988, p395):

> 'The [truly successful] organization is a learning institution, and one of its principal purposes is the expansion of knowledge ... that comes to reside at the core of what it means to be productive. Learning is the heart of productive activity. To put it simply, learning is the new form of labor.'

What has happened in the past few decades to produce Zuboff's dramatically different definition? The purpose of this chapter is, essentially, to find the answer to that question.

The first two sections of the chapter cover approaches in learning theory, technological advance and environmental changes that in their interconnection are causing a shift in attention from training to learning in organisations. The last two examine the emerging age of the knowledge worker and some implications for L&D practitioners.

THE AGE OF THE TRAINER

Learning as conditioning

As we saw in Chapter 1, throughout most of the twentieth century training was the main approach to employee development in which employers invested. After the Second World War, the need to rapidly rebuild the UK's skills base increased its utility, and the advent of Industrial Training Boards in the 1960s, then of the Training Services Agency and, in the 1980s, of the Training and Enterprise Councils all further emphasised training as the dominant vehicle for employees' learning.

Throughout this era stimulus-response (SR) theory was one of a cluster of learning theories that heavily underpinned the 'trainer as driver' approach – and to a significant extent still does. It was originally developed by behavioural psychologists in the late nineteenth and early twentieth century who studied links between animal and human learning and behaviour. In the USA, F. W. Taylor and his colleagues applied its principles to industrial training programmes and it subsequently led to the development of the popular systematic training model already described in Chapter 1.

SR theory sees learning as a conditioning process that operates through an interaction in the individual of four processes:

- *Drive*: the individual must feel some fundamental need that drives them to seek new knowledge, skills or attitudes – there must be some kind of perceived learning gap to close.
- *Stimulation*: there has to be a trigger to activate and sustain that drive in a particular situation (such as a training course).
- *Response*: the aim in every planned learning situation is to ensure that the learner acquires a particular set of responses that enables him or her to perform a new task, adapt to a new situation or master new knowledge. Every learning task should be analysed and broken down into core elements of knowledge, skill and attitudes. Each element must then be further analysed to identify the set of responses that it involves. Once learnt, each set must be combined increasingly with others until all are mastered and a new pattern of behaviour has been established.
- *Reinforcement*: once correct responses are achieved in the learning situation these must be reinforced by practice, feedback and rewards whether or not material. Incorrect or unproductive responses must be put right ('unlearnt') before they become habitual, whether by the withholding of rewards or some other method.

Cybernetics has also contributed to this body of conditioning theory. Applied to training, it concerns the kind of information and feedback channels that should be used to stimulate and help people to learn. Which senses to make most use of – sight, touch, taste, sound and kinaesthetics (or the 'feel' and positioning of muscles) – all come into the equation. So does the perceptual process and the ways in which attention will shift and sharpen during a learning programme as some tasks are mastered, leaving the conscious mind freer to focus on others that are more demanding. The idea of breaking down a whole task into parts, or elements (part and whole learning) in order to design a stepped learning process is as integral to cybernetics theory as it is to SR theory.

Here is a personal case to illustrate the conditioning approach to learning.

CASE EXAMPLE

The self-instruction manual

In the 1960s I used a manual called *Principles of Management – a program for self-instruction* written by an American guru Leonard Kazmier to guide me at my own pace through essentials of management theory in preparation for the Institute of Personnel Management's business administration exam. It was designed to be completed in anything from seven to fourteen hours, and could be used as an adjunct to various management textbooks and other coursework materials.

The book divided management theory into bite-sized units, each of which commenced with a small chunk of theory, then took the reader through a series of self-test statements to ensure their understanding of it, then moved on to the next chunk. That cycle of explain, test, provide feedback and reinforcement was repeated for every element of the unit until all had been mastered and a grasp of the entire body of theory covered in the manual had been acquired.

In the final unit of the book, entitled 'Learning and employee development' (which I confess I never reached, having abandoned the manual at an earlier point where mathematics had entered too heavily into a unit on management control systems!) the author explained the conditions that, in a formal training programme, would lead to maximum progress on the part of the learners (Kazmier 1964, p225):

> These factors, called principles of learning by psychologists, include the need to maximize the individual's motivation to learn, providing feedback during learning, appropriately sequencing the materials to be learned, providing for active participation during training, and considering the individual differences among trainees.

Learning as information processing

Cognitive theories form another cluster that have had a major impact on training and learning design continuing to the present day. 'Cognitive' relates to the psychological processes of perception, memory, thinking and learning. Psychologists influenced by cybernetics theory and by cognitive psychology are interested in the brain as an information processing system that can produce high-quality knowledge.

In early cognitive theory learning was viewed as a process to do with seeking access to and mastery of a theoretically perfect body of knowledge 'out there'. It could be achieved by identifying the gaps between what could be known and what the learners actually knew, and closing them through a systematic, rational transmission process, usually in the form of training.

Technology in the age of the trainer

Training technology has changed out of all recognition since the pioneering days of the early twentieth century, but in discussing how that has happened it is important to clarify the meaning of that word 'technology'. It can be defined as:

> **'Technology – the particular way in which, in a workplace, technical systems, machinery and processes are designed to interact with human skill and knowledge in order to convert inputs into outputs.'**

From the 1960s on, computers played an increasingly important part in the technology of training. Designers were able to move from a dependence on paper-bound materials such as the Kazmier manual to the production of computerised programmes that offered the individual control over a greater variety of simulated learning situations, more rapid and involving feedback systems and an altogether more imaginative self-paced learning experience. The basic principle that drove the technology was still that of stimulus-response theory, but expressed in a more subtle and user-friendly mode.

> ## REFLECTION
>
> Reflecting on a training or educational course that you know or have read about, in which a 'conditioning' approach to learning was evident, how far did that approach seem to help or hinder the learning process and what seemed to be the reason for its use on the course?

THE AGE OF THE LEARNER

Learning as social process

In the later decades of the twentieth century the impact of much research into adult training and learning in work organisations at last began to make itself felt in industry, drawing attention to something that educationalists had always known: that to train or teach is not to achieve learning. Only the learner can learn. And learners are influenced not just by their internal cognitive processes but also by their relationships with others.

One major school of thought puts learning in the context of a world that is not a fixed external reality but a socially constructed state. To express it at its most extreme: 'There is no objective reality. Reality is socially created' (von Krogh et al 1994, p53). In this view, our learning is intimately shaped by our relations with others. Knowledge is no longer understood as a type of commodity, to be captured from the external world and transmitted by some to others in a systematic way. It is understood as at the same time the ever-changing outcome of learning and itself a stimulus to ongoing learning. Knowledge and learning are thus viewed as dynamically interacting processes.

This 'constructivist' theory (as it is called) naturally draws attention to the workplace where so many social interactions take place, and to the communities of practice that were first discussed in Chapter 1. In the workplace, learning that has value for the business can emerge from many different sources – from cross-functional groups engaged in problem solving and teamwork, from people working or discussing their work together, from online or on-the-job training, and from learning networks across related organisations such as suppliers or clients (Stewart and Tansley 2002). These and one-to-one work-based processes like mentoring, coaching, buddying and jointly negotiated performance reviews demonstrate that although the individual is the active agent in his or her learning, many of the important advances are made in a social setting (Reynolds and Sloman 2004).

Learning as experience

Social interactions are a part of our daily experience, and many psychologists have focused on that experience in its broadest sense as central to the individual's learning process. Kolb and his colleagues (1974) constructed a learning styles inventory (LSI) from their body of experiential learning theory. It is outlined in Figure 5. Honey and Mumford (1992) built on this to produce a widely popular inventory that identifies four main types of learner and of learning style – activist, reflector, analyst and pragmatist – and links them to the four stages of Kolb's learning cycle. Their inventories are used as diagnostic tools to inform the design and delivery of training responsive to a variety of individual learning styles and skills.

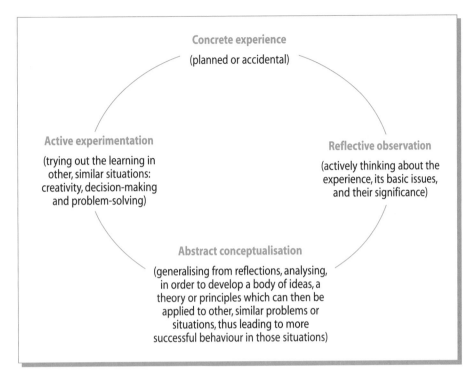

Figure 5 *The experiential cycle of learning (based on Kolb, Rubin and McIntyre 1974)*

Researchers at Newcastle University recently reported on 13 LSIs, including Honey and Mumford's (Coffield et al 2004). They found only one (by Allinson and Hayes 1996) that gave statistically meaningful and consistent results. Amongst the authors' concerns were the presentation of learning styles as relatively stable and genetically fixed, when there is much to suggest that individuals learn in quite flexible ways and may deliberately alter learning style to suit context. They advise that rather than being wedded to any one inventory it is better to encourage individuals to reflect on what they do, why they do it, how they see their learning and how they plan and monitor it.

Whatever the arguments, learning style inventories and the experiential learning theories on which some are based can provide only a partial and tentative explanation of the way in which an individual's experience interacts with their internal cognitive processes to produce learning.

The importance of unlearning

Returning to the influence of social interactions on individual learning, those interactions can of course have negative as well as positive effects. The learning that emerges from communities of practice in the workplace, for example, can bring success initially but after a time complacency can set in. That can lead to an increasing narrowness and rigidity in the ways in which organisational members see their world and make decisions about it. This fosters 'skilled incompetence' (Argyris 1996) whereby once successful organisations rest on their success for too long, causing their strategies and behavioural patterns to become ever less appropriate in the face of new challenges. When failures start to occur, defensive routines can spread across the organisation, producing a culture that avoids confrontation and resists any questioning of cherished beliefs or ways of doing things. Soon, the organisation effectively stops learning. It then locks in present methods by specifying rigid procedures that can deskill the workforce and prevent innovation (Bohn 1994, p712). Other firms then seize the competitive edge. Organisations suffering from skilled incompetence thus become dragged down by the weight of their past knowledge – a familiar example in the UK being Marks and Spencer.

After a review of relevant research Harrison and Kessels (2003a, p225) concluded:

> '**Study after study points to the impact of organisational context. Where top management's vision and values focus convincingly on knowledge productivity as an organisational capability, and where management actions, work practices and HR processes at all organisational levels support that focus and recognise the new importance of workplace learning, then a culture of learning is likely to develop and be sustained. But where context is unfavourable and/or where HR practitioners are passive, uninformed or both, culture change interventions are unlikely to take root.**'

To say, then, that learning is a social process in one sense states the obvious, but in another begs a set of complex questions. How far and in what ways can that learning be managed, directed, made productive for the organisation? What part does it play in determining an individual's performance at work? How far does it link to the performance of the organisation? There are major issues here of organisation structure, of the control employees are allowed over work-related learning and of the workplace learning culture. I will discuss them in Chapter 8.

REFLECTION

Recalling one situation you know about where skilled incompetence has developed, what seem to have been some of its most damaging effects and how they might be tackled so that new ways of thinking and doing can break through?

New technology in the age of the learner

The notion of learning as a social process that is fundamentally influenced by workplace relationships emphasises the value of learning approaches that shift control to the learner and away from the trainer. Formal training situations lack the stimulus and conviction of everyday experience. They raise transfer of learning problems that learning in its more natural setting does not meet. Instead of learning being an interactive process sparked off amongst equals by a natural desire to solve a problem or innovate, it becomes an artificial process conducted in a context where the learner is in a subordinate role, trained to learn instead of taking the initiative in the learning situation.

It is not only a greater awareness of learning theories which challenge the classical conditioning approaches that explains a growing shift of emphasis from trainer-driven to learner-driven processes in organisations. New technology has also had a major part to play. In the so-called post-Fordist workplace new information and communication technology (ICT) has brought together electronically-based hardware, human skills and knowledge in unique ways that enable individuals to rapidly and easily access information as and when they need it. ICT is still often harnessed to traditional training modes, but in an increasing number of organisations it is being used to facilitate continuous self-managed learning in the workplace.

One further influencing factor that deserves a mention here is UK government policy. From the 1960s it has had a significant part to play in promoting the application of new technology to methods of teaching and learning. The most extraordinary single achievement, initially due more to the vision of two people – the then Prime Minister Harold Wilson and Jennie Lee, the Labour politician – than to any broader policy strand, was undoubtedly the Open University. Its story provides a unique perspective on the 'age of the learner'.

CASE EXAMPLE

The Open University

The Open University (OU) was founded in the UK in the 1960s as a Labour Government initiative to open up access to degree-level education to all with the ability to benefit from it. The underpinning belief was that new communications technology could offer high-quality learning to people who normally would have no opportunity for it, especially lower income groups. Its mission was complete openness to methods.

After an initial struggle to survive in the face of considerable cynicism and of restricted financial resource, the OU became a remarkable success story. By the mid-1990s it began a comprehensive exploitation of the Internet that has gained it the position today of the world's leading e-university. Its students can access its top quality interactive materials through CD Roms and/or the web, and its net conferencing facility attracts thousands of hits daily. It continues to provide an outstanding example of a blended learning approach using media and materials that can work for students all by themselves. Every university in the land now makes some use of its materials and study methods.

The many achievements of the OU, including details of its major research projects, can be found on its historical website. Here, it is enough to note three final pieces of information that appear there: more than 40,000 employers have sponsored their staff to enrol on OU courses, the OU is the largest provider of management education in Europe, and in the UK one in five of all those studying for an MBA is doing so through the OU.

Source: *History of the Open University* (2004)

The impact of e-learning

E-learning offers a uniquely important opportunity to facilitate a self-driven learning process. By e-learning I refer to any form of electronically-based learning, whether enabled through wired or wire-free systems. At present the main gains it seems to offer are:

- to guide individuals to appropriate routes and packages that best suit their individual styles and needs
- to facilitate timing of learning

- to produce more innovative designs and delivery of learning materials
- to blend with more traditional training methods in the classroom or face to face.

But these gains come at a price. The effective harnessing of e-learning involves tailored learning events and processes that consume more time and effort, and initially often much higher costs, than do most standardised training approaches. The more choices the learner has, the more costs are likely to mount (Collis and Moonen 2001).

The Department for Education and Skills (DfES) has published a consultation document *Towards a unified e-learning strategy* with recommendations focused on the education sector but with wider relevance (DfES 2003b) The CIPD's response has implications for all L&D professionals attempting to develop a workable and productive e-learning strategy. Key points include the following (CIPD 2004c):

- E-learning is less about improving the quality of learning, more about the personalisation of learning. It enables a shift in emphasis from delivery to support in the learning process.
- Any strategy for e-learning must be driven by learning needs rather than by technology. E-learning should be delivered in support of a business need that is recognised across the organisation, with appropriate structures to support it, learners who are motivated to learn and who have good IT skills.
- The introduction of e-learning is a major change initiative and will need relevant expertise in teachers, trainers and managers involved in its implementation.
- A one-size fits all approach will not be successful, and any e-learning approach based on generic materials will likewise be limited. Research evidence suggests that the best way forward is to have a series of small-scale experiments, frequently reviewed, in a structure in which success is followed up and failure is used to aid future design.
- Research also points to the need for blended learning solutions that include varying levels of e-learning adapted to suit a variety of learning contexts. The real issue here is not how far e-learning technology is more, or less, effective than traditional approaches. It is how best to blend the two in ways that give more control to the learners over the whole learning process while ensuring that they are equipped to handle that shift and are motivated to do so.

Trainers involved in the implementation of an e-learning strategy must have the expertise to take on the facilitator role that this will involve – and they need to work with line managers and IT staff to ensure that e-learners receive support. Two examples must suffice here, but the references at the end of the chapter provide further advice.

- Online learning involves accessing much wider groups of people than is customary in traditional training situations. E-learning facilitators must therefore be competent in working cross-culturally and in building on diversity.
- Facilitators and managers must be skilled in motivating learners and have an informed knowledge of what stimulates or hinders them in an e-learning process. In the late 1990s Lloyds TSB had 450 learning centres in the UK. Researchers found some regions much better than others in achieving enthusiasm among employees for computer-based training. This was mainly because local training administrators and line managers were supportive, proactive and imaginative in their approach to learners and the learning experience (Hills and Francis 1999). It is particularly important that e-learning does not carry the image of a solitary and demotivating

experience. More sophisticated technology can avoid the problems that led in early days to such an image.

Here is an example of a learning programme that builds cleverly on learning as a social process by providing an effective blended learning experience.

CASE EXAMPLE

A blended learning programme at the House of Fraser

In May 2001 the House of Fraser launched a 12-month management training programme to help in its aim of producing more internally promoted managers. The programme combined workshops, workbooks, seminars and online learning with all types of on the job development from sitting with Nellie to assignments, coaching, job rotation, work shadowing, and mentoring.

The pilot in 2001 revealed that managers working through the modules found it helpful to get together afterwards and discuss what they had learnt. The House of Fraser's management development manager, commenting on this, stressed that online learning need not be an isolating experience. Consolidating the learning in ways that brought people together to review and expand their new knowledge was one valuable way to incorporate social interaction into the whole blended learning experience.

In terms of financial cost, £100,000 would have had to be spent on classroom workshops if the company had decided to expand its training without using computers. To that cost would have been added the costs of trainers' salaries, travel costs and so on. The organisers had to make sure that the managers on the programme were given time to do the online and offline learning that it required, but this was a cost that the company was happy to pay, given the many benefits of the blended programme.

The programme also helped to stimulate the managers to initiate further learning of their own, since after its completion, and without prompting, they began to access online learning at home on their laptops.

Source: MERRICK, N. and PICKARD, J. (2002)

To push or be pushed?

The CIPD sees e-learning as an enabler of 'a shift from top-down training interventions to learner-centred initiatives'. In so doing it makes the following distinction (CIPD 2004c):

'Learning – "a process by which a person constructs new knowledge, skills and capabilities".

Training – "an intervention by the organisation intended to advance business objectives".'

However, in laying stress on e-learning being 'delivered in support of a business need that is recognised across the organisation' the CIPD's response does not make clear quite where the claimed shift of control to learners is intended to lead – to essentially no more than the continuation of a gradual trend towards making learning a more self-managed process, or to a more radical break with the past.

The CIPD's 2004 Training and Development survey, an annual barometer of trends and views in the training field, provides clues here (CIPD 2004a). Most of the survey's 531 senior training managers (or those in equivalent positions) rated on-the-job training as the most effective way in which people learn, with coaching/mentoring coming second. Since the previous survey, e-learning had increased more than any other training or learning process apart from coaching but this increase was from a low base and most respondents also reported an increase in an already high level of formal classroom training. Furthermore while only a little less than 50 per cent of practitioners included 'training technology' as an item in their budgets, that item received by far the lowest level of investment, with only 1 per cent saying that 50 per cent or more of their budgets were allocated to it. By contrast 38 per cent spent at least half their total budgets on external training and educational events or courses.

It seems at present, then, that the 'shift to learners' is one that is relatively conservative. The trend from the 1960s in allowing learners more control over the pace, the timing, the place and the style of learning is intensifying, but the learning in question is still basically to do with learners meeting pre-defined business needs. As the CIPD paper (2004c) observes, the shift to more self-management of learning makes demands on time and work schedules and so can require a 'significant' change in workplace culture. But significant is not the same as revolutionary, and there is no evidence in the CIPD's 2004 Training and Development survey to suggest that any fundamental cultural change is as yet taking place.

The CIPD research report *How do people learn?* looks at how the dominant learning theories of the past century can be applied to new developments in learning, particularly e-learning. It raises awareness of the conditions that are essential if this shift is to become a powerful one (Reynolds et al 2002):

- Learners must have access to as many routes to learning as possible, using a blended learning approach to meet differing learning needs and overcome a dependency on a one-way information flow.
- There must be workplace cultures, leadership and management that encourage, facilitate and reward self-directed learning that has a shared organisational purpose.

While not questioning that the first of these conditions does exist now quite widely across organisations, there is little to indicate that the second is occurring in more than a few, whether in the UK or across the rest of Europe (Tjepkema 2002). One e-learning provider has concluded that what employees as well as employers really want are (Tulip 2003, p54):

'More focused packets of learning that people can do and apply in one go.... It means that individuals will have to learn to push themselves, rather than being pushed.'

The founding director of Turnkey Learning, an e-learning consultancy (Tulip 2003, p52) raises one question that goes to the heart of the matter:

> **'E-learning has overspent but under-delivered. It has its place, but are we using e-learning as a delivery mechanism, or more interactively? We haven't worked out how to engineer the learning process.'**

It is that question that raises the issues discussed in last two sections of this chapter.

REFLECTION

How far, if at all, in your own organisation, do you see evidence of a shift from 'the age of the trainer' to 'the age of the learner'? What reasons might there be for this shift, or for the lack of it?

THE AGE OF THE KNOWLEDGE WORKER

The new knowledge economy

In the age of the learner, just discussed, the focus is on the learning process. But an emerging knowledge economy is opening up further and much more radical implications for the learner.

The consequences of the 'dizzying pace' of technological change in the past few decades have included an information-rich, computation-rich, and communications-rich organisational environment (Bettis and Hitt 1995) and alongside and interacting with it, a heightened level of knowledge intensity. The CIPD notes (CIPD 2003d):

> **'Without a doubt the world of work is becoming increasingly knowledge-intensive. This brings with it a range of issues about how organisations find, keep, develop and share knowledge effectively and how this relates to their business performance.'**

In the new economy knowledge is the new key to wealth, because its application adds more value than the traditional factors of capital, raw materials and labour. Globalisation is a key factor here. In the context of this discussion it is a process directly linked with the Internet and the pricing and information revolution that the net has made possible. Through the World Wide Web buyers and sellers can come together naturally, speedily and continuously. Companies must quickly learn how to co-create value with customers who have access to information on a global scale and who can rapidly and easily compare experiences. They can experiment with and develop products, especially digital ones, and so have an unprecedented influence on value creation (Prahalad and Ramaswamy 2002).

To make progress in a knowledge economy organisations must regularly innovate as old knowledge that is vested in current products, processes and services falls quickly out of date. Organisational boundaries become blurred through the development of new cross-boundary webs of alliances, partnerships, supply chains and joint ventures that provide access to far greater resource and knowledge than any single organisation can hope to acquire (Whittington et al 2002, p483). Restructuring is no longer an infrequent activity whose outcome is a stable form of organisation design. It is a recurrent process, in which most organisations are now involved around once every three years, sometimes more often.

In like manner business strategy can no longer be cast in stone. In a knowledge economy organisations must be able to produce new strategic responses as old recipes become obsolete. 'Strategising' rather than 'producing the strategy' is the appropriate way of describing the process whereby they regularly have to find new ways of doing new things, adapt with little warning to the complex and the unfamiliar, and sometimes adopt quite new business goals (Whittington and Mayer 2002).

The twofold flexibility that organising and strategising involves rests on organisations' ability to guide and facilitate continuous individual and collective learning and knowledge creation (Sanchez 1995; Eisenhardt and Santos 2002). It explains the significance of that quote from Zuboff at the start of this chapter. He was not referring to the traditional notion of learning as conditioning or as individual behavioural change. He was referring to it as the source of knowledge that can enable organisations to continually do new things in new ways, as well as customary things better, to continuously improve and also to radically innovate in goods, processes and services. One term for such organisations is that they are knowledge-productive (Kessels 1996) and this spotlight on knowledge productivity explains why I call the final age covered in this chapter that of the knowledge worker.

E-learning in the age of the knowledge worker

In knowledge-productive organisations the role of e-learning does not end at shifting more control over learning to individuals in order to meet pre-identified business needs. It continues by helping to transform learners into their organisation's knowledge workers. In knowledge-intensive firms such as consultancies, R&D institutions and software businesses employers give unique status to their specialist knowledge workers, described by Peter Drucker in 1993 as those with high levels of education and specialist skills combined with the ability to apply these skills to identify and solve problems. But in an economy where knowledge creation is a task for all organisations, all organisational members possess uniquely valuable knowledge – especially of the tacit kind. Given the opportunity and incentive, all can become valuable knowledge workers.

To the extent that e-learning becomes an integral part of L&D activity in organisations, learning and knowledge processes will increasingly merge. It is not just a matter of the opportunities that e-learning offers for people to learn for themselves. It is that this self-directed learning is taking place in a context where more and more people are performing tasks that are facilitated by electronic means. Their ICT-dominated workplaces can provide an environment for thinking and problem-solving in which the employee's role can be transformed, so that it becomes (Schuck 1996, p199):

'not only to push buttons to control processes, but also to use the information generated by the technology to 'push the business' – to redefine process variables, to improve quality, and to reduce costs.'

In such an environment, the intelligence of employees can expand until it exceeds the intelligence of the software with which they interact. Employees can become 'smart' (Schuck 1996) – smarter, finally, than the machine that they have for so long served. They can become knowledge workers by applying knowledge that they have developed to the continuous improvement of operating procedures, products, services and processes, and to innovation.

In opening up access to the information that the learner wants, when and in the form that they want it, e-learning can offer to them a voyage of discovery that can alter the way they see and respond to the world. It can fuel the development of knowledge that can then be applied in ways that benefit the learner, the customer and the organisation. This is how learning and knowledge become fused processes. An illustration of how these processes can be stimulated by e-learning technology follows in the next case example.

CASE EXAMPLE

Knowledge working at BP

Some companies are blending informal and e-learning with structured knowledge sharing as a means of supporting communities of practice (Reynolds 2002).

One such company is BP. In his article, Reynolds describes one of BP's goals being the introduction of services that allow the individual, group or network of employees in a workplace to take charge of their own learning through 'an appropriate mix of inputs and outputs, individual and collaborative study, formal and informal processes, and a blend of face to face and virtual contact'. The idea is to provide a 'rich set of options' in terms not only of the ways in which individuals choose to learn, but also of what and why they wish to learn.

Reynolds clarifies the spectrum that can be involved here for employees, extending from fully supported learning with clear learning objectives at one extreme to a self-initiated knowledge-creating process at the other. The three applications of e-learning that he identifies as aiding this are:

- *Web-based training*: where content is delivered to the learner without significant interaction or support – a throwback, in other words, to the age of the trainer and to what is basically a stimulus-response conditioning process.
- *Supported online learning*: where the learner 'interacts intensively, supported by content as appropriate' – typifying the kind of activity involved in an age where control over the pace, place and timing of the learning process is moving significantly from trainers to learners, but where trainers still play leading albeit more design-focused, facilitative and supportive roles in the learning process.
- *Informal e-learning*: where learning occurs through self-directed communication, information retrieval and co-operation between peers during the normal course of work. It is this type of learning that has the potential to transform learners into their organisation's knowledge workers. In Reynolds' words, it marks a 'move beyond the replacement of conventional courses into richer and more fertile learning domains'.

Source: REYNOLDS, J. (2002)

Yet we must be cautious here. BP has always been in the lead for innovative L&D practice but there is a long way to go before any such similar transformation occurs in most organisations. For e-learning to turn employees from mere learners into 'smart people' (Schuck 1996, p212) there must be vision and leadership, and the context must be right.

If the workplace is of the traditional kind, where the given role of some is to think, to make decisions and to pass on instructions, and the role of others is to perform the tasks that those instructions involve, then the true potential of e-learning as a facilitator of knowledge creation cannot be realised. It is pointless for an individual to participate in a learning process through which they develop not just operational competence but 'the intellective skill required for original, independent problem-solving' (Schuck 1996, p205) if in the workplace they are allowed to use their increased operational competence but not their capability as a knowledge worker. In such a situation it is likely that their expectations will be disappointed, their motivation will decline and their commitment to high performance will disappear.

For e-learning to achieve its most powerful value-adding impact in the emerging knowledge economy, the following are essential:

- Access for all employees to learning and knowledge-creating opportunities that can enable and motivate them to move increasingly from dependency on others to dependency on themselves in the direction and operation of their learning process.
- The capital expenditure, the human expertise and the operational infrastructure to support ICT applications that can accelerate and support that shift.
- The shared vision and purpose, the leadership and management, the workplace environment and the human resource strategies that recognise and utilise employees as unique knowledge workers, committed to acting as such.

NEW TASKS FOR LEARNING AND DEVELOPMENT PROFESSIONALS

Moving from learning to knowledge productivity

By this point it should have become clear that the kind of economy in which an increasing proportion of organisations are now operating requires more than the development of human capital in order to maximise short-term performance. It requires the building of social capital as discussed in Chapter 1. But that depends on an organisational culture in which it is recognised that learning, working and knowledge creation are naturally intertwined. Key priorities for L&D professionals here are therefore to do with:

- Raising awareness across the organisation of the need for a learning culture that can lead to continuous improvement and radical innovation in goods, services and processes.
- Identifying and advising on barriers to the development of such a culture.
- Helping to develop social capital through expanding learning capacity within small groups in the workplace and through contributing to policies and practices that build commitment and trust.
- Developing the competence and motivation of leaders, managers and other employees to become actively involved in learning that leads to knowledge creation in the workplace.
- Working to ensure that training resources are focused not just on 'key' personnel but

also on all an organisation's knowledge workers, especially those at the lower skilled levels who in the past have customarily received little support from managers in their learning and development

■ Harnessing e-learning to knowledge sharing and knowledge creation.

In the rest of Part 2 I will look at how these priorities can be tackled.

REFLECTION

Reflecting on this final section of the chapter, how far do you think it is important for your organisation to invest in learning approaches that could gradually transform its employees into knowledge workers of the kind just described?

CONCLUSION

This chapter has explored the gradual shift that has been occurring in recent years from trainers to learners as prime controllers of learning in the workplace, and the further shift now in sight from learning to knowledge working as knowledge becomes the new key to competitive advantage. You will find review questions related to the chapter's content in Appendix 3.

Main themes covered in the chapter's four sections have related to:

■ An increasing awareness now in organisations of theories of learning that emphasise the role of experience and of social interactions in the learning process, and that cast doubt on the validity of the traditional trainer-dominated approach to planned learning.

■ Alongside this, a changing business environment featuring rapid technological advance, the emergence of a new and globalising knowledge economy, and a growing emphasis on organising and strategising as key processes for business organisations. It is only through these processes that an organisation can learn faster, more regularly create and apply new knowledge to continuous improvement and innovation, and quickly redeploy its internal resources in order to collaborate and compete effectively in turbulent conditions.

■ A consequent marked shift – although as yet apparently not in most organisations a radical one – to pass more control over the learning process to the individual learner, a parallel need for trainers and managers to take on facilitative and supportive learning roles, and a further shift from the learning to the knowledge process in organisations most exposed to the knowledge economy.

■ The central role played by information and communication technology in underpinning and facilitating the shift from trainers to learners, and beyond that in the transformation of learners into knowledge workers.

■ The requirement this raises for e-learning strategy to become an integral part of business strategy and to be fully supported by people management and development and ICT strategies and practices.

The chapter has ended with an introduction to the priority tasks for L&D practitioners in a new learning and knowledge age. These tasks frame the remaining chapters in Part 2.

Further information sources

HARRISON, R. and KESSELS, J. (2003a) *Human resource development in a knowledge economy: an organisational view.* Basingstoke: Palgrave Macmillan.

SLOMAN, M. (2001) *The e-learning revolution.* London: Chartered Institute of Personnel and Development.

SLOMAN, M. (2003) *Training in the age of the learner.* London: Chartered Institute of Personnel and Development.

You should also visit:

- http://www.learnonline.org.uk/ providing links to a variety of sites offering e-learning services and information [accessed 4 October 2004].
- http://www.cipd.co.uk/communities, giving CIPD members access to its online training network offering facilities for exchange of views [accessed 25 August 2004].
- http://www.trainingzone.co.uk, an online network of 45,000 members and claimed to be the UK's most popular site for training and HR professionals [accessed 4 October 2004].

Finally, the European Training and Development Federation and the European Association for Personnel Management are considering developing a project to create an Internet platform that would give their members access to good practice developed across the world. It would foster communities of practice that could lead to the creation of centres of excellence based in various countries. Their website addresses are:

- http://www.etdf-fefd.org [accessed 4 December 2004].
- http://www.eapm.org [accessed 4 December 2004].

Linking Learning and
Development to Performance

CHAPTER 5

INTRODUCTION

In Chapter 4 I explored the nature and extent of a shift in organisations from training to more individually-managed learning and knowledge processes. The purpose of this chapter is to look at ways of linking individual learning and performance to the performance of the organisation. Its primary focus is therefore L&D's role in the performance management process (PMP).

What is the aim of performance management? It is twofold: to enable, support and reward all organisational members in achieving good performance, and to retain and develop able and committed people who will help the organisation to achieve its longer-term goals.

Specifically, the PMP involves:

- setting individual targets linked to business goals, and establishing desired performance levels
- appraising and improving performance
- ensuring continuous learning and development
- giving recognition and rewards.

In responding to a CIPD survey reported in 2004, 87 per cent of HR practitioners confirmed that a formal performance management process was in place in their organisations, with 83 per cent agreeing that the focus of that process should be developmental. The survey findings strongly indicate that organisations now treat performance management as a key part of a total reward approach in which pay is only one element. That approach, furthermore, is seen as an integral part of the processes involved in running an organisation and in achieving its strategic corporate and HR management aims. In every organisation that the researchers visited, performance management was integral to the improvement of business results, and 94 per cent of respondents found it to be an essential tool in the management of organisational culture. Most telling of all, most agreed that little could be achieved unless managers were actively committed to the PMP (Armstrong and Baron 2004).

The chapter has four sections. The first explores issues of with motivation and performance at the individual level and in the second these are placed in the wider context of a new 'People–Performance framework'. The third section examines ways of achieving a developmental PMP, and tasks of L&D practitioners that this involves. The final section identifies types of learning and of helping activity that have relevance for the performance management cycle.

REFLECTION

How far does there seem to be a systematic approach to performance management in your own organisation? And who do you think is/are primarily responsible for ensuring effective performance management, whether or not that is a formalised process?

MOTIVATION AND PERFORMANCE

As we have seen in previous chapters, despite the claimed shift in attention from training to learning in organisations the main investment that employers make in their employees' development remains primarily focused on training for skills. Yet the route referred to in the CIPD's performance management survey should not be to do with increasing job or task proficiency alone. It should ensure that all organisational members have the motivation, opportunity and discretion to apply their skills effectively to a shared organisational purpose.

The AMO model

There is now much evidence that links human resource (HR) practices and organisational performance, not least the 'bundling' research of Huselid (1995) in the USA, and in the UK that of Hendry (1995), Terry and Purcell (1997), Patterson et al (1997) and Guest and King (2001). However, none has clarified what brings that link into being, or exactly how HR policies translate into performance.

That 'Black Box' is now being researched at the University of Bath. I referred to the work briefly in Chapter 1. Studies have centred so far on 12 organisations from a wide range of sectors, all known for their quality of HR management or actively seeking to improve the link between people management and performance. Findings across the 12 settings suggest that where people are performing well, that is to say beyond the minimal requirements, three conditions are necessary (CIPD 2001b):

- they have the ability to do so because they have the necessary knowledge and skills, including skills of working with others (A)
- they are motivated to do so (M)
- they are given the opportunity to use their skills both in their jobs and in contributing to their work groups and organisational success (O).

There is more to the research and I will explain that later in the chapter. In this section I want to take this AMO model and look at what goes on at its heart – human motivation.

Motivating the individual

It is not my intention to attempt a learned discussion of motivation theory. There is a mass of literature on that subject, easily accessible but impossible to summarise in the space available here. My purpose is to take one particular theory about motivation that, despite its surface simplicity, has much of relevance to offer to the AMO model.

In 1985 Charles Handy produced his concept of 'the motivation calculus' to explain the links between motivation and individual performance. He presented performance as the outcome of an ongoing interaction within the individual of felt needs, perceived and expected results and rewards, and 'e-factors':

- *Needs*. How far does the performance required or requested of the individual promise to satisfy the needs that he or she brings to work? If little satisfaction seems likely, then it is unsurprising if the individual's motivation to perform is low. But what are the individual's needs? Clues will lie in the expectations they were led to form when they were offered the job initially. What deal did they think was put on the table then – and has it subsequently been delivered?

- *Results.* How far does the individual fully understand what is wanted from him or her, and why? Has he or she had the opportunity to set work targets jointly with their manager, or have targets been unilaterally imposed? Do managers and team leaders act as good role models, give timely and accurate feedback, reinforce effective performance and deal fairly and appropriately with poor performance?
- *Rewards.* What rewards does the individual perceive to be on offer for the perform-ance required? Rewards can take many forms, financial and non-financial, and they take on different meanings in different contexts. In the particular situation, what rewards are actually available, and does the individual expect to receive them, find them worthwhile, or regard them with scepticism? What has the individual's experi-ence in the organisation thus far led him or her to expect – that promises of rewards will be honoured? Or that management cannot be trusted to deliver?
- *'E' factors.* Looking at the above, how far does the individual calculate it to be worth-while to expend effort, energy, excitement and expertise in their work? What level of those 'E' factors do they actually possess? Is their capacity correctly understood by managers, team leaders and colleagues?

This stripped-down account of the motivation calculus may give the impression that it is simplistic. It is not. In reality it has a strong underpinning base of psychological theory related to motivation – particularly expectancy theory (Vroom and Deci 1970). Yet even in outline the concept of the calculus clearly highlights the unique interplay of internal and external factors that shape and continuously change each individual's motivation in the workplace, and the powerful effects on performance of past learning (not just of skills, but learning from life experience) and of the individual's expectations.

You may find it helpful to identify the main messages that the following case suggests about the links between motivation and individual performance. Comments follow at its end.

CASE EXAMPLE

Linda, the disillusioned recruit

Pyrotem is a light engineering company employing 1,000 people and is located in an industrial conurbation in the Midlands. It is struggling to retain its leading edge, and is continuously driving down costs whilst also trying to achieve innovation and high quality in its products and excellence in its supplier and customer relationships.

Linda, who has an impressive school and university CV, was recruited immediately on her graduation two years ago to a trainee supervisory post at Pyrotem. Pyrotem's management boasts of the company's human resource practices and of its refusal to recruit any but 'the best' to work there. Starting pay, terms and conditions for supervisors and managers are above local norms. Throughout her selection process (which involved two days at an assessment centre) Linda was told that they were looking for someone with the potential to become an excellent performer and teamworker, who would be encouraged to develop by being given challenging work and a significant amount of discretion. She was delighted when she was selected.

Alas, during her induction and basic training programme Linda was given little clarification of targets and little guidance or support from managers. After six months she moved into a supervisory position where she found that her manager gave her no real discretion, expecting her to adopt his own very controlling style of management. Since Linda's preferred approach to team leadership was very different, this caused considerable tension. Try as she might to bridge the gap between them, she found it impossible both to please her boss and to achieve the best out of those working for her.

Linda soon realised that her prospects at Pyrotem were not impressive. In her part of the firm very few promotion opportunities existed. When they occurred, success seemed to depend on the subjective views of a small group of senior managers. There was no objective or meaningful performance review or staff development scheme – just a formal appraisal system to which managers gave minimal attention other than filling in annual forms in an off-hand fashion. Morale and performance levels were unsurprisingly poor. Those who got out, did so. Those who could not had little commitment to the organisation, and infected new recruits with their negative attitudes.

Linda left halfway through her second year at Pyrotem, seizing an unexpected opportunity to take a post with a well-known competitor firm with an excellent reputation as an employer. People were proud to work there. It lived up to Linda's expectations. Although management made no pretence that there would be any prospect of fast promotion the financial rewards were as good as at Pyrotem, and the work and opportunities in which she became involved offered the stimulation, development and discretionary opportunities that she had never been able to find at Pryotem.

Comments

- The case illustrates how theories of individual motivation link to the AMO model outlined at the start of this section. Linda had the skills needed to perform well in her job. She also had the initial motivation, but that declined as she realised that she had no opportunity to use her skills meaningfully, both as an individual and as a workgroup member and leader. It was this lack of opportunity and of discretion to do her job as she thought it should be done that led to Linda's loss of commitment to Pyrotem, and so to her eventual departure from the firm.
- Leadership, management and HR strategy and practices were all at fault here: what they promised at recruitment and selection stages they never delivered. The frustrated expectations that this produced in Linda and other new recruits proved damaging to their subsequent employment relationship with the firm. The deal that seemed to be on the table initially was very different from the reality that they encountered in the workplace. The outcomes were inevitable: the depreciation and often the loss of valuable human assets.

In highlighting the important effects of contextual factors – leadership, management and HR strategies and practices – on individual motivation and commitment to the organisation, and in pointing to discretion as a significant influence on an individual's performance, the case takes us beyond the AMO model to the People–Performance framework in which it is located.

LINKING PEOPLE TO ORGANISATIONAL PERFORMANCE

The Big Idea

While the AMO model explains convincingly that performance is a function of ability, motivation and opportunity that raises a further question: what sort of policies and practices are required for AMO to be turned into action? The Bath researchers have found that in the organisations they are studying the link between people policies and organisational performance is indirect but decisive (Purcell et al 2003). Key findings are that:

- Human resource policies and practices that build commitment are crucial in turning skills into action.
- High levels of commitment and of discretionary behaviour are needed to achieve above-average organisational performance. 'Discretionary behaviour' refers to the degree of choice that employees have and exercise on the ways in which they do their job and how well they do their job.

A major finding from the Bath research is the power of the 'Big Idea' as the primary source of shared organisational purpose. It refers to a clear mission, unique to each organisation and underpinned by values and a culture expressing what the organisation stands for and is trying to achieve, that draws all organisational functions and members together in a shared purpose. To have this effect, the Big Idea needs five attributes:

- *It must be embedded*: the mission must be well communicated, and the values related to it must be spread throughout the organisation, becoming deeply rooted in policies and practices. L&D practitioners have an important part to play in this process of communicating, spreading of values, and embedding of the Big Idea in training and learning activity.
- *It must be connected*: its values should link together internal and external customers, organisational culture and behaviour. By acting as this kind of glue, the Big Idea gives a collective focus to individuals' work and learning and to the application of their skills. L&D activity plays its part in this process of connecting when it demonstrates and enacts the organisation's core values, whether in formal training courses, on-the-job learning, mentoring, coaching or any other more informal learning processes.
- *It must endure*: its core values must remain clear and strong through time, helped particularly by organisational routines and practices (including training and development) that reinforce them.
- *It must be collective*: this quality can be achieved by 'the creation and continuous refinement of excellent routines so that everyone knows what to do and how to do it, time and again'. Training is one method of achieving this.
- *It must be measured and managed*: the balanced scorecard approach (to be discussed in Chapter 13) is of particular value here if used to integrate different functional areas and decisions. Selfridges expresses its Big Idea in three goals: to be the place where people want to shop, invest and work. It regularly reports on performance related to each. This scorecard approach enables an explicit link to be made between individuals' goals and those of the organisation, and can frame employees' personal development plans (Brown 2003).

CASE EXAMPLE

Tesco and the Big Idea

In April 2004 Tesco announced a record £1.6 billion pre-tax profits, an increase of almost 18 per cent in a year, with sales up by nearly 19 per cent. It did even better in the following quarter. The supermarket was way ahead of its rivals yet 15 years before no city analyst would have predicted its extraordinary and consistent rise. The 'Every little helps' campaign credited to Terry Leahy, then its marketing director and now its chief executive, is often thought to have kick-started its turnaround.

The idea was simple: take out every little thing that spoils a shopping trip for customers. Work with them continuously to make them want to come to Tesco, enjoy the shopping experience, and spend their money there. Now, £1 in every £8 spent in Britain's shops is spent at Tesco. Everything that irritates customers has been tackled: queues, problems in availability of products, unattractive premises. Customers are asked how Tesco should revamp its local stores, and a price structure referred to as 'good, better, best' plus a 'Value' line of own-brand products has broken down class barriers and helped to make Tesco popular right across the customer spectrum.

Leahy has assembled a team of bright young people around him, many of whom, like him, have only worked for the store. The whole workforce knows that complacency is the great enemy: with the cautionary tales of Marks and Spencer and Sainsbury's to remind them, employees' constant attention to customer wants and needs is held out as the best hope of ensuring that Tesco remains in the lead of a fiercely competitive race.

Source: RANKINE, K. (2004)

The Big Idea cannot operate in a vacuum. Tesco was one of the organisations studied by the Bath research team. They tracked the progress of carefully standardised HR practices at four of its stores and found marked variations in the way those practices were operated and in the employee responses and perceptions they evoked. These variations were reflected in variations in performance in each store, and some had negative, not positive, effects. The HR practices that worked best were flexible, had a robust link with the Big Idea and its values and were implemented by front-line managers who gave their teams significant opportunity for discretionary behaviour in their jobs, and supported them in using that discretion to improve store performance (Purcell et al 2003, pp28–31).

At the end of Chapter 4 I noted that employees can and will only take substantial control over their own learning and performance if managers and team leaders take a real lead in enabling this to happen. The Bath studies show how that lead can be given.

The People–Performance framework

The research carried out at Bath has produced a 'People–Performance' framework. It is shown in Figure 6.

The framework identifies 11 clusters of HR practice as having the major impact in releasing the potential of the AMO model. These clusters work through fitting with business strategy

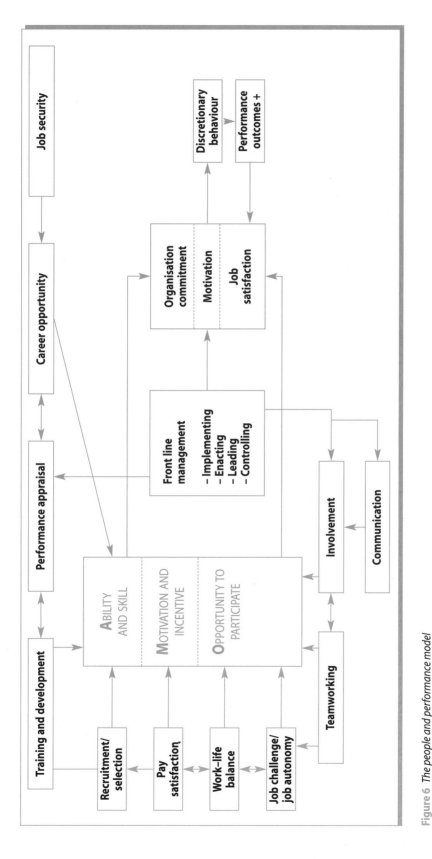

Figure 6　*The people and performance model*

Source: HUTCHINSON, S. and PURCELL, J. (2003) *Bringing Policies to Life: The vital role of front-line managers in people management.* London: Chartered Institute of Personnel Development. p2. Reproduced with kind permission of the publisher.

while being flexible enough to adapt to environmental changes, even those that put the link between people and performance under strain. They create and transmit values and culture that are unique to the organisation and bind it together.

The researchers stress that the clusters may not work as well for all organisations. HR practices need to be tailored to context. As already explained, they also found that it is not so much strategies themselves as the ways in which they are implemented in each workplace that determine how effectively the AMO model will operate.

Linking learning and development to organisational performance

So what are the L&D implications of such research? It has not yet yielded enough clear evidence of a direct link between individual learning and improvements in organisational performance (however that is defined). However, L&D activity does consistently emerge as a crucial intervening factor. In the Bath studies two HR practices were identified as being particularly powerful in influencing employee attitudes and creating positive discretionary behaviour: careers (in the sense of a 'developing future') and training. In other words, the L&D processes that help to activate the people–performance link are those that 'hold the promise of learning to do things better, or doing new things. It is the sense of progression and purpose that is important, especially in linking to organisational commitment' (Purcell et al 2003, p73).

Looking back at the case of Linda, had there been L&D activity of that kind at Pyrotem she would certainly have been motivated very differently. However if there had still been lack of good leadership and management and inadequate opportunities for discretion in the way she put learning into practice she would probably still have left the firm. L&D alone is not enough – it has to be an integral part of a cluster of appropriate HR strategies, with the leadership and management to make them come to life in the workplace.

The Bath research studies are by no means the only ones to identify the importance to organisational performance of visionary leadership, discretionary behaviour, employee commitment, and motivating and supportive front-line leadership. Particularly important earlier international research includes Ghoshal and Bartlett's (1994), Floyd and Wooldridge's (1994a) and Bartel's (2000). Similar research is also taking place at the Universities of Leicester and Birmingham. Few, however, clarify quite what the key concept of empowerment/discretion actually involves. The following case, briefly outlined here, is one that does so.

CASE EXAMPLE

Empowerment in a large supermarket chain

Research by Peccei and Rosenthal focused on a large supermarket chain where an initiative called 'Service Excellence' sought to develop employee empowerment and thereby produce better customer service values and behaviour. The HR practices used included:

- developing a more supportive management style
- redesigning jobs to allow employees greater discretion
- a training scheme to teach new service values.

A survey of 700 employees across seven of the chain's shops suggested that the initiative was successful. Those most strongly influenced by the HR practices perceived themselves to be empowered and were more likely to behave in ways that were more sensitive to customer needs. Each practice was successful in its own right, but it was the combination of the three that led to the feeling of empowerment amongst the employees. The improved relationships between customers and employees were all the more impressive for being established among service employees doing relatively routine jobs (Kessler 2001).

Source: PECCEI, R. and ROSENTHAL, P. (2001)

Building commitment

The Bath studies and many others emphasise commitment as a major variable influencing employees' performance and that of the organisation overall. Commitment can be measured by three indicators:

- the extent to which an individual identifies with, and is actively involved in, an organisation
- the extent to which employees intend to stay with the organisation
- the extent to which they would recommend it to others as a good place to work.

Findings from the 1998 *Workplace Employee Relations Survey* showed a disturbing picture here. They confirmed that workplace context has a major impact on employees' commitment to the organisation, but found that most workplaces in UK-based organisations do not pursue planned HR strategies of any kind, and that employee commitment in the UK is very low (Cully et al 1999).

The ISR 2002 worldwide survey of employees provided further data to support these findings. It revealed that levels of commitment expressed among British employees were among the very worst in the world's top 10 economies (ISR 2002). The report concluded that this is preventing the UK from competing effectively in the global marketplace. Employees surveyed identified four factors as key to commitment levels in their organisations:

- the quality of leadership
- the development opportunities provided for its employees
- the amount of empowerment (i.e. discretion) given to employees to carry out their job effectively
- supervisors' people management skills.

These findings coincide closely with those of the Bath research studies and suggest at least six major tasks for L&D practitioners in strengthening the people–performance link:

- To raise awareness through L&D activity of the negative impact of low commitment on their organisation's performance and competitive capability.
- To promote and deliver relevant leadership and management training.
- To promote the kind of learning and development that can induce or encourage better performance and can trigger positive discretionary behaviour in all employees, not just those judged to be key workers.

- As a priority, to meet the needs of front-line managers for training and development, career expectations and support from senior management. These managers have a vital role in encouraging and enabling the high levels of discretionary behaviour from their teams that will improve organisational performance (Hutchinson and Purcell 2003).
- To work with front-line managers to produce and apply well designed, consistent and appropriate L&D practices for their teams.
- To lead thinking on how to make the best of teamworking. 'Autonomous' teams –that is, those with high levels of discretion – demonstrate the highest levels of job influence and can be powerful in motivating and allowing people to act collectively. Their members work together and have responsibility for a specific product or service, they jointly decide how work is done, and they appoint their own team leaders. Yet the 1998 Workplace Employee Relations Survey showed that although in 65 per cent of workplaces most employees worked in teams, in only 3 per cent were those teams fully autonomous (Griffiths 2002).

One relevant example of an integrated HR approach to building commitment in which training and development played a major part is the UK retailer Safeway, which throughout 2003 suffered from being the subject of several bids from other supermarkets and from major uncertainties culminating in a referral to the Competition Commission. It developed an HR strategy aimed at retaining as many good people as possible and at improving morale and commitment of all employees. Management worked with the academics at the Roffey Park Institute in this task. Training and development, a leadership programme, communication, and reward and recognition formed a successful fourfold strategy to boost commitment despite the uncertainties ahead and to help all employees prepare for their future whether with the firm or outside it (Garrow 2003).

It is important to realise that raising commitment is not necessarily a complex formalised activity. In some scenarios it can be the result of a very simple L&D approach based on a sensitive understanding of what employees value most, given their work situation. The following example is a case in point.

CASE EXAMPLE
The local government cook–freeze centre

Research carried out under the Economic and Social Research Council's *Future of Work* programme to explore skills development amongst low-paid workers in the public sector involved in-depth case studies of six large public sector organisations. In a paper on the concept of 'employer demand for skill' Rainbird and colleagues (2004) discuss three small workplaces within these larger organisations, analysing the implications of different types of training interventions for performance management.

One finding was that the possession of skills demotivated workers who had no opportunity to practise them. Many of the workers studied had formal qualifications in excess of those needed for the job. Job redesign had no relevance for them, since they wanted career progression opportunities which for many did not exist. Where training was not accredited but tied tightly to a specific job, this was also demotivating because it reduced low-paid workers' employability yet further. Training was also often used to implement strategies involving new work arrangements, but this put more pressure on staff where it legitimised already unrealistic workloads. Used in this way training was not viewed as an opportunity but as an unwelcome necessity and a source of increased stress.

However in one of the three studies, the least promising at first glance, a more positive picture emerged. It centred on a small, relatively stable workforce working on a production line in the cook–freeze centre employing 14 staff, who were part of a much larger functional department of the City Council. It was the central production unit for a 'meals on wheels' service and the customer was the Social Services Department. The work was monotonous – for example, using an ice-cream scoop for an hour – and job rotation was used less as a means of making work more interesting (because there was little scope for this), more to reduce the risk of repetitive strain injury.

Despite the limited and poorly paid nature of the work, some of the staff mentioned their pride in doing a job which was socially useful and gave them a sense of responsibility and progression. The production supervisor identified a range of mechanisms for learning about the work. These included shadowing the manager, attending meetings and receiving training on new equipment from the suppliers. Part of her status derived from her recognition of the value of her own problem-solving skills and the fact that the workforce knew their own jobs extremely well. She saw an important role for herself in building their self-confidence, especially by providing reassurance in relation to off-the-job training programmes, facilitating learning opportunities for the workforce even if those opportunities did not directly relate to their jobs.

Some workers felt they had developed as a result of learning opportunities provided through the workplace or external to it, and had gained self-confidence and an enhanced potential. Some were attending such courses in their own time, and some were even paying for these themselves. Not all were relevant to their work, but they were valued for having a utility in their personal lives or for contributing to their future employability. Levels of labour turnover were extremely low and the workers had a commitment to their workplace. Its mainly female members lived locally and found the working hours and the jobs they held were good.

Lack of resources restricted the demand for skills in the organisation of production and job design, but this had not restricted staff's access to broader development opportunities. Learning was not restricted to participation in formal training events and they could point to a number of ways in which it was facilitated in the work environment, both by their supervisor and by a culture where they felt they could learn from others and ask for help if they needed it. The management style also contributed to the quality of the work environment and thence to the employees' commitment to their work.

Source: RAINBIRD, H., MUNRO, A. and HOLLY, L. (2004)

Many employees, especially those with low skills and poor educational attainment, are isolated in monotonous and unfulfilling jobs. This case example shows that the answer does not always lie in the classic government strategy of promoting basic skills accreditation. L&D interventions of a quite different kind have scope to contribute to the quality of the work environment and to job mobility within and beyond the organisation.

INTEGRATING THE MANAGEMENT AND DEVELOPMENT OF PERFORMANCE

What can L&D activity contribute?

The Bath research is based on a sample of 12 high-performing organisations already committed to excellence in HR practices. Such organisations are not the norm, and nor are high-performance workplaces that provide a natural stimulus to innovation and an investment in workplace learning (EEF and CIPD 2003). In many organisations L&D practitioners will have little say in how the performance management process is designed to operate, in what kind of 'deal', new, old or indifferent, is put on the table for new recruits, or in how the people–performance link is understood and treated. What, then, should be their starting point in contributing to the performance management process?

In real life a straightforward approach whose rationale is easy to explain and has a clear business focus is the most likely to work. Performance management is a process, certainly, and has been discussed as such up to this point. But it is also a system, the smooth functioning of whose elements depends on developmental activity as well as on a degree of management control. A developmental thrust is particularly important at those points in the performance management cycle where individuals' motivation and commitment to the organisation are most prone to dip. Figure 7 identifies induction, skills training, appraisal and continuing personal and professional development as key activities at those points.

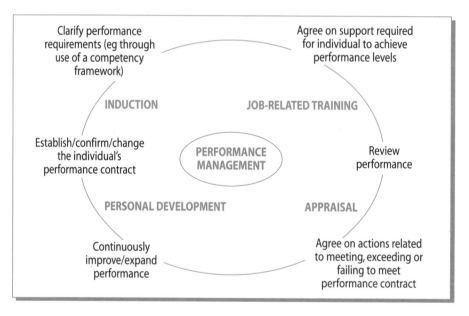

Figure 7 *The performance management process and related L&D activity*
Adapted from LOCKETT, J. (1992) *Effective performance management: a strategic guide to getting the best from people.* London: Kogan Page p38.

Induction

The purpose of induction, whether for the newcomer to the organisation or for the employee who is moving into a new job, role or organisational level, is twofold:

- to introduce newcomers to their job and to the organisational context of the workplace
- to establish a positive relationship between the new recruit and the organisation, building his or her commitment to its vision and goals – its 'Big Idea'.

Induction represents the final stage of the recruitment process and the first stage of the performance management process, so by contributing to the design and delivery of effective induction L&D practitioners are aiding both those processes (for more detailed advice see Fowler 1996).

Individuals at this stage of the performance management cycle need to understand more about their own and the organisation's values and belief systems in order to identify any tensions here and how to tackle them. They may need help in learning how to function confidently in a new context. Whatever the form and content of induction, it should lead to personal development plans that will contribute to work performance and personal growth. Mentoring is an increasingly popular process to aid induction (see below). Coaching is another, which can be carried out by a trained member of the workteam or by a high-performing member of a workgroup who has proven training skills and the disposition to foster job-related learning in others. At McDonald's, new entrants go through a three-hour induction and are then partnered with a 'buddy' who comes from a 'training squad' of specially trained employees belonging to their work team.

CASE EXAMPLE
Linking learning and performance in a small firm

In a small firm where excellent secretarial and administrative support is essential and can involve many responsibilities requiring interface with customers and clients as well as with personnel throughout the firm, resources only stretch to employing one or two people in these roles. They are recruited with a high level of existing skill and experience (since there is no time or expertise to allow much training or build up of experience in the job) and their retention and further development through time is therefore of vital importance.

The L&D activity that helps the firm to achieve those aims consists of:

- a brief but well-focused and relevant induction programme, aided by a mentor who usually comes from within the firm, but sometimes – and especially at the senior levels – may be bought in from outside.
- basic training in unique systems of the firm
- a probationary period where again a mentor helps to support, encourage and guide the new recruit in order to keep them motivated and encourage their self-development
- following confirmation in post, opportunities for continuing education and for career development that the new recruit and the firm agree to be relevant and affordable.

The firm's reward structure acts as a recognition and support system in relation to these four stages.

Skills training

Skills training is the next stage to support the performance management cycle. Sometimes the need for it may be slight and can be met within the induction period, but more usually it follows on from induction. The term is a broad one, since it can encompass the development of any special skills, attitudes or knowledge that are an essential part of the job or task the employee has to perform, and that he or she currently lacks. Common approaches include:

- mentoring to provide support and guidance
- coaching by managers or other relevant parties to develop specific skills and capability
- short training events, special assignments, projects and visits to other organisations or departments
- educational programmes to achieve an enhanced level of professional knowledge or a broadening of business or functional awareness
- flexible learning methods that blend the use of e-technology with more traditional face to face approaches.

Whatever the methods or combination of methods chosen, there must be a clear business case for the training if it is to get the full support needed from management and other key parties. The training must also be of a kind that will motivate the learner and be feasible for them to follow. Typical objectives might be to attract and retain the calibre of people needed by the organisation, to provide training that is standards-based and related to national vocational qualifications (NVQs), to establish a cost-effective way of reinforcing company culture, to build a base for flexibility of skills and for employability – and so on.

Of course throughout the employment cycle there will be many occasions when employees need to acquire new skills, and that is where the continuing development process becomes of such importance – as will be seen below.

Appraisal

Appraisal is one of the most contentious areas of the PMP but in the Bath Studies, as in many others, it has been found to have the potential to raise motivation, commitment and the extent to which employees make positive use of any discretionary power they possess. Broadening the coverage and scope for the appraisal discussion can have particularly positive outcomes (Purcell et al 2003).

Four factors consistently determine the extent to which an appraisal process realises its potential:

- *Organisational context*: for example, it is fruitless to try to introduce a developmental appraisal process into an organisation that has a rigid, divisive role structure and a controlling management style that discourage openness, the use of individual discretion and the development of potential.
- *Relationship between the parties*: this, which is itself significantly shaped by organisational context, is the single most powerful influence on the conduct and outcomes of an appraisal discussion, and constitutes one of the major areas of difficulty related to it. If the appraiser–appraisee relationship is not open and supportive it is virtually impossible for a formalised appraisal system to make it so.
- *Scope of the appraisal scheme*: where a scheme's scope is restricted to review,

planning and control of the appraisee's performance it is unlikely to have significant effect on their motivation or commitment. Where that discussion incorporates a rating of performance using structured forms, together with clear and direct links to pay and promotion, the tensions that this can introduce are also likely to produce an adverse rather than positive motivational outcome. For a scheme to be motivating for appraisees it must have objectives and a process that reflect that aim, active management commitment, the opportunity for mutual learning by themselves and their appraisers, and an emphasis on future-oriented action-planning and continuing development.

- *Methods*: some methods used within the appraisal process are more likely to produce valid information than others. An increasingly popular method, used by 14 per cent of the HR practitioners responding to the CIPD's 2004 Performance Management survey (Armstrong and Baron 2004), is 360-degree appraisal: it expands the number of sources involved in reviewing the individual's performance and if handled skilfully it can be a more effective way of helping the individual to gain a balanced perspective on their performance.

Newton and Findlay's literature review (1998) led them to conclude that the basic problem in appraisal is an assumption that an organisation is a unitary system rather than one in which there is – and it is legitimate that there should be – a multiplicity of interests and power groups. But even putting that issue aside, any appraisal discussion can produce invalid and unreliable results because it is an intensely human process. For example, as far as methods are concerned 360-degree appraisal may or may not prove useful. The value of introducing more sources of appraisal than one is that those closest to the appraisee are likely to have information that the appraiser would otherwise lack, thus contributing to a fully balanced view of the appraisee's performance. The downside is that those other informants may for whatever reasons provide biased information that distorts the picture for the appraisee.

At the end of the day while the views of peers, customers, functional bosses and other parties will all carry weight, those of the line manager are still likely to be the most powerful in determining the outcomes of appraisal. If the line manager is inept and/or ill-disposed towards the appraisee, then introducing 360-degree appraisal is unlikely to correct that fundamental bias in the appraisal discussion's outcome (see also Garrow 1997).

But not all difficulties in appraisal are intractable ones. Providing that there is the will within the organisation to develop a system that is appropriate, flexible and fair and to make it work, then a way can always be found to overcome operational problems (see Fletcher 2004).

Continuing development

The appraisal discussion should trigger a process of personal development planning, action and review that can ensure every employee's continuing personal and professional development during their time in the organisation. It is not a trouble-free process, as there may be conflicting views between appraiser and appraisee about what constitutes appropriate development. It requires a genuine collaboration between managers, any HR professionals, and individuals to produce personal development plans that are feasible, that meet the needs of individuals in ways that the organisation can, and is willing to, afford, and that will have the active support of line management and team leaders. Continuing personal development can be powerfully aided through day-to-day work activity, but that too has costs attached and must be carefully thought through.

> **REFLECTION**
>
> How far do you think appraisal in your own organisation is a motivating and develop-mental process, and what suggestions – if any are needed – might you make for its improvement as part of the organisation's performance management system?

TYPES OF LEARNING AND 'HELPING' ACTIVITY TO AID PERFORMANCE MANAGEMENT

Three types of learning

The purpose of this chapter is to look at ways of linking individual learning and performance to the performance of the organisation. There are three types of learning that can help the cycle of performance management to function smoothly: instrumental, dialogic and self-reflective (Mezirow 1985).

- *Instrumental learning*: this means learning how to perform a job or role better once the basic standard of performance has been attained. A key strategy here is learning on the job. This can be highly effective, provided that there is someone to encourage learners in the course of their daily tasks to identify problems, to formulate appropriate action and try it out, to observe the effects and learn from them.
- *Dialogic learning*: this involves interacting with others in ways that will produce a growing understanding of the culture of the organisation and of how it typically achieves its goals. Dialogic learning is particularly valuable at induction stage or when people are promoted into unfamiliar areas of the organisation. It can help individuals to quickly make sense of the organisational world they have entered and develop the confidence to operate competently in it. Mentoring is a powerful dialogic learning process.
- *Self-reflective learning*: this is the kind of learning that leads individuals to develop new patterns of understanding, thinking and behaving and thereby create new knowledge. It is needed when people have to operate in ways that are unfamiliar to them. Self-reflective learning involves unlearning and new learning and so is only possible in an environment that 'enables and empowers individuals to be responsible, productive and creative' and to see error as a positive learning vehicle (Argyris 1982). Argyris called this kind of learning 'double-loop' because whereas instrumental and dialogic learning tackle surface symptoms of a problem and only perpetuate an old loop of learning, self-reflective learning is concerned to look at root causes that explain why the problem arose in the first place. It can create a quite new learning loop. Depending on their design, educational and training programmes can generate self-reflective learning. So can work-based learning processes like quality circles, secondments, new project work, action-learning sets, mentoring and coaching, or any other approach that exposes people to new ways of thinking and new situations, encouraging them to be challenging and innovative.

Coaching and mentoring

The CIPD survey mentioned at the start of this chapter confirmed a shift from a directive to a supportive approach to the management of performance in 'best practice' organisations, with a learning-focused rather than a training-focused approach to development and frequent use of coaching, counselling and guidance. Mentoring and coaching have become 'helping' activities that are widely employed in a variety of settings. In responding to the CIPD's annual *Training and Development* survey in 2003 (CIPD 2004a) the overwhelming majority of trainers (or equivalent) believed them to be effective business tools and reported their use in their organisations. To take each in turn:

Coaching

Coaching is defined by one expert, Anthony Grant at the University of Sydney, as (http://www.psych.usyd.edu.au/coach , accessed 4 October 2004):

> **'Coaching: The research, theory and practice of the application of the behavioural science of psychology to the enhancement of life experience, work performance and personal growth of normal, non-clinical populations.'**

Coaching can take many forms, including performance coaching, life coaching, business coaching and facilitative management. Like counselling and mentoring it is about helping the individual to gain self-awareness, but it is goal focused and action is required so that the individual can move forward. The goal setting process has two components: skill development and psychological development. The outcome sought is that coachees (to use the technical if clumsy term) will achieve the goals set, and will thereafter feel able and confident to set personal goals for themselves (Passmore 2003, p31).

Many managers see coaching as 'a tool to develop skill, a simple function that can be delegated to the training department' (Johnson 2003). There is an equally mistaken view that coaching is a highly directive and supportive style only appropriate with relatively inexperienced people of moderate competence (ibid.). In business organisations coaching is commonly used to develop leadership potential, enhance individuals' influence and improve interpersonal skills. It is also widely used to promote team effectiveness and support individuals during career transitions (Lee and Pick 2004). Unlike mentoring, coaching by leaders can be available to all employees and can therefore make a direct impact on organisational climate, on motivation and performance (Goleman 1992). And unlike mentoring it is an activity through which managers can directly develop individuals and teams (see especially Burdett 1994).

CASE EXAMPLE

Coaching in local government

During 2004 a six-month coaching pilot called 'Leap' was launched to help the HR function in local government to develop its strategic skills. It was introduced by the Employers' Organisation for local government in partnership with the Institute for Employment Studies (IES), the East of England Regional Assembly (EERA) and the North West Employers' Organisation (NWEO). The programme involved 24 participants from councils in the East of England and North West regions.

Each Leap participant received eight hours of confidential one-to-one coaching with an experienced coach and attended two events, focused on developing and implementing people strategy and strategic HR delivery. A typical rationale for individuals participating in the programme was that it was flexible to both their personal needs and those of their organisations.

The scheme was so successful that a second phase was then introduced, to run from September to March 2006 with a further 50 participants.

The particular trigger to Leap was the comprehensive performance assessments by the Audit Commission, introduced in 2002 to rate councils. Leap's purpose is to quickly develop HR people who understand the theory of people management and have the confidence and support to act and be accepted as equal partners at top strategic management level.

Source: http://www.lg-employers.gov.uk/people/leap/index.html
[accessed 17 December 2004]

Mentoring

Garvey (2004, p8) defines mentoring as:

'Mentoring is a process whereby one person acts as counsellor and friend to another, usually to support them as they enter an organisation and have to familiarise themselves with its culture and processes, or as they take on new responsibilities in an unfamiliar part or level of an organisation…. The agenda is the mentee's and mentoring may have both an organisational and an individual focus.'

Mentoring is usually a face-to-face process, although it can also be delivered through a virtual medium. It is closely associated with induction, career and personal development and change. Mentors can facilitate instrumental, dialogic learning and self-reflective learning. Mentors in the work context can be 'invaluable professional allies: people with career experience and insights that they are ready to pass on' (Landale 2003). They should be both role models and guides, but they must also be able to challenge their mentees and make them think. For mentoring to succeed as a helping activity it must be founded on a close, supportive and trusting relationship. In order to avoid conflict of interests it should never be carried out by mentees' managers or by anyone else who is in authority over the mentees.

There are a variety of mentoring models, covering both individual and team mentoring. Microsoft, for example, uses the 'five Cs' model which focuses individuals on the challenges they face and achievable results, the choices open to them, the consequences of each choice, and creative solutions or conclusions. It makes use of both internal and external mentors, valuing the fresh perspectives that the latter can bring (Glover 2002a).

Standards in 'helping' activity

Alongside the good news about coaching and mentoring in the CIPD's 2004 *Training and development* survey there was some bad. As noted in Chapter 1, responses showed that despite their widespread use there was little evaluation of either process, that few managers were effectively trained in them, and that no clear business case was usually produced for their introduction. Too often they seemed to have been established as an act of faith, with no attention paid to the outcomes they were meant to achieve. The activities that each involve also appeared unclear for most respondents (CIPD 2004a). Strikingly similar findings related to coaching were reported in 2003 by change management consultancy SKAI in a survey of leaders in 300 large organisations (Lidbetter 2003).

If these 'helping' processes are to benefit the organisation as well as individuals there needs to be:

- An understanding of coaching and mentoring as processes that involve reciprocal learning, not a situation in which the coaches and mentors should be assuming a dominating or manipulative role.
- A clear business case for their introduction, with an agreed process for monitoring and evaluating operation and outcomes.
- An adequate resource base, adjustment in the workloads of the involved, and support for mentees and coachees in their continuing development.
- An up to date database of potential suitable mentors and coaches, and a skilled selection and training process against clear and relevant criteria.
- Careful piloting of initiatives, and the highlighting of their benefits across the organisation to ensure understanding of the way in which the processes operate and of their value.

Given the popularity of the two processes and the number of agencies and individuals in the open market that provide them, there is a growing concern to develop professional standards and ensure that only those adequately trained and bound by a clear code of conduct are allowed to perform coaching and mentoring roles. The industry is very fragmented and has several professional bodies and many codes of practice, but five key bodies including the CIPD and the European Mentoring and Coaching Council are now discussing accreditation and standards that could gain widespread acceptance.

E-learning can also be a helping activity, as the following highly innovative and admittedly untypical example explains.

CASE EXAMPLE

E-learning as a big tent

Allison Rosset (2002) describes the way in which e-learning can transform the process of individual performance improvement through four kinds of activity, all under the individual's control:

- *Information wraparound*: information resources can be set up in ways that resemble real world tasks, so that 'information wraparound' becomes the stuff of work, learning and knowledge all rolled into one. At the teaching resource site

> http://www.kn.pacbell.com/guide.html [accessed 4 October 2004] educators 'can find model web-based curricula by searching in ways that match how they think about things, by subject, content or grade level'.
>
> The CIPD has an interactive module on 'How People Learn' at its website http://www.cipd.co.uk/subjects/misc/_ppllrnidx.htm?IsSrchRes=1 [accessed 7 September 2004]. This enables anyone – especially training professionals – to update themselves quickly on new research into learning and knowledge creation, taking them through practical scenarios that test their understanding of how to help employees learn more or less constantly, in ways that reflect their increasingly busy and mobile patterns of work.
>
> ■ *Interaction and collaboration*: e-technology 'can engage, stir, foment, and connect people with others who share their interests and tasks' through online communities set up for that purpose.
>
> ■ *Performance support*: online guidance can 'stoke' individuals to perform 'as if they know more than they do' by providing active support through helplines and automated tools that prompt responses to typical situations.
>
> ■ *Guidance and tracking*: online technology can articulate a clear picture of what standards are expected and enable individuals to assess themselves against those standards, testing them on scenarios that reflect them and guiding indi-viduals towards critical or unmet skills and resources. Programmes can be linked to performance and career management systems.
>
> Main source: ROSSET, A. (2002)

As Sloman points out (2002b), this compelling vision of e-learning as an integral part of the performance management process is unlikely to be within the immediate reach of any but the larger organisations, generally ones with sophisticated knowledge management systems. It would also involve a major culture change for most companies and their employees. Still, it is well worth inclusion at this final point in the chapter as an example of what could one day become a realistic 'big tent' strategy to link individual learning, performance improvement and knowledge creation.

CONCLUSION

The purpose of this chapter has been to explore ways of linking individual learning and performance to the performance of the organisation. The main focus has been the perform-ance management process. You should by now understand the operation of that process, and the ways in which L&D activity can ensure that it has an appropriate developmental thrust. You can test yourself against the review questions for this chapter, in Appendix 3.

The chapter's four sections have covered the following main ground:

■ The new AMO model that explains the interaction of ability, motivation and oppor-tunity to perform well, and of the place of motivation theory in understanding that model. Handy's motivation calculus has been identified as of particular use here.

■ The placing of the AMO model within the People–Performance framework produced by Purcell and colleagues from their 'Black Box' research at Bath University. These and other studies have highlighted the crucial role of L&D activity in enhancing organisational performance when that activity is integrated with other HR practices that can raise commitment levels and stimulate the positive exercise of discretionary behaviour in the workplace.

■ A discussion of the Big Idea, described as the 'glue that binds the organisation together'. To be effective in linking people and performance the Big Idea needs the support of high quality leadership and management, and of HR strategies that can build commitment and release the potential of the AMO model. L&D practitioners have at least six awareness-raising, training and developmental tasks in contributing to those strategies.

■ The importance of a developmental performance management system. An appropriate balance between control and development can be achieved by carefully planned and expertly facilitated induction, skills training, appraisal and continuing development.

■ Types of learning – instrumental, dialogic and self-reflective – that can ease the operation of the performance management system, together with helping activity – particularly mentoring and coaching – that can underpin it. Such activity must rest on a sound business case, be well understood across the organisation and be effectively performed if it is to succeed in achieving its aims.

The most important message of this chapter has been that learning and individual performance will never make a positive contribution to performance management where organisational context is unfavourable and where levels of motivation, commitment and discretionary behaviour are low. As one chief executive commented (Bajer 2001), personnel and development professionals may work hard with their business partners to create a well-organised performance management system, manage a network of coaching and mentor relationships, generate a mass of appraisal, feedback and PDP documentation and produce accurate training plans for the coming year. The organisation may pride itself that in these ways it is being transparently people-centred. Yet all will go for nothing without the appropriate vision, leadership, management and workplace climate.

And so we have a conundrum: for a developmental PMP to work, there already has to be a developmental culture in the organisation...

Further information sources

ALRED, G., GARVEY, B. and SMITH, R. (1998) *The mentoring pocket book*. Arlesford, UK: Management Pocket Books Series.

HUTCHINSON, S. and PURCELL, J. (2003) *Bringing policies to life: the vital role of front line managers in people management*. London: Chartered Institute of Personnel and Development.

MABEY, C. and ILES, P. (eds) (1994) *Managing learning*. London: Routledge and Open University.

For fact sheets on a variety of topics covered in this chapter, go online to http://cipd.co.uk/quickfacts.

Organising Learning Events: Stages 1 to 4

INTRODUCTION

Anyone holding L&D responsibilities in an organisation should be able to organise effective learning events. I use the word 'events' throughout this and the next chapter to refer to any planned learning intervention, whether it involves training courses and educational programmes or more informal activity such as quality circles, mentoring, coaching, action learning sets, team briefing and so on. L&D professionals also need to be skilled in promoting continuous workplace learning and knowledge creation, but that is the subject of a later chapter.

The major challenge for L&D practitioners in organising learning interventions is to combine technical expertise with the business partnership skills and deep understanding of organisational context that can ensure successful delivery and impact. In this chapter I propose an 8-stage process for achieving these ends.

The first section of the chapter introduces the eight-stage process, and the subsequent four sections describe its first four stages, assessing and illustrating their implications for L&D practitioners, managers and learners. The stages cover establishing needs, agreeing purpose and objectives, identifying the learners' profile, and establishing strategy, direction and management for the event.

[Note: in this and the following chapter I am looking at how best to organise learning events that have been agreed in advance to be necessary for the organisation. Although I refer throughout to 'individuals' when discussing needs and how to meet them, many learning events of course involve teams.'Individuals' is simply a shorthand to encompass team learning also. Likewise 'training' should be taken to refer to any kind of planned learning activity.]

THE EIGHT-STAGE PROCESS FOR ORGANISING LEARNING EVENTS

The systematic training model

The traditional approach to the planning and delivery of learning events is to use the systematic training model. I have already discussed this in Chapter 1 and noted there its deficiencies, particularly its over-emphasis on a functional approach to what is to be learnt and its lack of emphasis on process. It pays scant attention to the vital need to gain support for any L&D initiative from those in the organisation – especially front-line managers – whose buy-in is essential if the learning achieved is to be transferred and put to good use in the workplace. Research has shown that even training courses that are relevant, and are expertly designed and delivered can fail in an organisation where that support is lacking (Kessels and Harrison 1998).

The eight-stage process

My own approach emphasises the value of the systematic training model's cycle of functional activity, but it places equal if not more importance on the business partnership process that L&D practitioners should operate from start to finish. The biggest challenge that they face is to achieve both internal and external consistency throughout the whole activity cycle. Those terms were coined by Kessels (ibid.) and have the following meanings:

- *Internal consistency*: refers to the outcome achieved by the effective application of a systematic approach to planning, design, delivery and evaluation tasks. The systematic training model seeks to achieve this kind of consistency.
- *External consistency*: refers to the commitment, shared purpose and perceptions of stakeholders that can be gained through actively involving them in those tasks. A business partnership approach seeks to ensure this kind of consistency.

Figure 8 shows an eight-stage process for achieving these two kinds of consistency. As with all processes, it can never in real life proceed along clear-cut sequential lines. Some stages may have to be pursued in parallel and some will have to be revisited as new contingencies arise. The successful conduct of the process draws on the L&D practitioner's technical expertise but also the skills of a thinking performer and of a business partner.

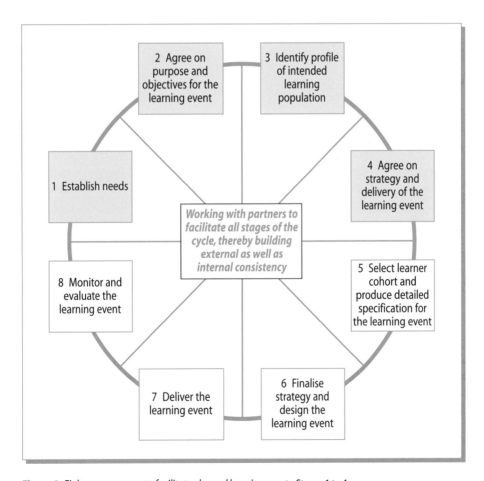

Figure 8 *Eight-stage process to facilitate planned learning events: Stages 1 to 4*

STAGE 1: ESTABLISHING NEEDS

The starting point for any decision about what kind of learning interventions to provide is to ask two questions:

- Where and why does organisational performance most need to be changed or sustained?
- For what needs are the interventions the best – that is to say, most relevant, feasible and value-adding – response?

Research of the kind discussed in Chapter 5 has repeatedly demonstrated the need to integrate L&D activity with other HR practices and align it with business strategy. In Part 3 of the book I will look at how that can be done at the strategic level. Here, my concern is with how to organise individual learning events so that they are effective for the learners and gain the support of those on whose success in the workplace they ultimately depend.

Let us assume, then, that a learning need has been agreed somewhere in the organisation and L&D staff must now arrange a learning intervention to respond to it. Their first stage must be to carry out some analysis in order to find the answer to the questions: what does successful performance look like in terms of results, and what must individuals do to achieve those results? (Brittain and Ryder 1999). In other words, they must establish the nature and cause of the learning gap.

For purposes of such analysis a job, task or role is commonly described in terms of three broad components: skills, knowledge and attitudes.

- *Skills*: skills may be, for example, manual, diagnostic, interpersonal or decision-making. They include any component of the job that involves 'doing' something.
- *Knowledge*: knowledge may be, for example, technical, procedural or concerned with company organisation. In this context, it represents the sum of what an individual knows and understands about their job.
- *Attitudes*: certain types of behaviour and the attitudes that give rise to them may be crucial to successful job performance – for example, courtesy and sensitivity in dealing with customers or clients, flexibility and co-operation when working in a close-knit team, or calmness and negotiating skill in coping with interpersonal or political tensions.

Looking at the job

I will look first at ways of clarifying the nature of the job, role or task involved and the requirements it poses if good performance is to be achieved. I do not propose to go into this 'job training analysis' process (as it is sometimes termed) in any real technical detail. There are many specialist texts that fulfil that purpose (Reid et al 2004 is particularly useful). My aim is simply to outline four of the most well-known methods and situations where each can be used to advantage:

- comprehensive analysis
- key task analysis
- problem-centred analysis
- competency-based analysis.

These four methods are not mutually exclusive and indeed it is often best to use some in combination. Thus problem-centred and key task analysis can work well together when people take up new jobs and already have most of the competence needed to perform them well, or again when new job-holders must quickly gain a firm grasp of key tasks and be able to overcome typical difficulties that they involve.

Comprehensive analysis

This approach requires a detailed examination in which every task in a job is broken down into KSA components. It must also be described by reference to its objectives, its frequency of performance, its standards of performance, and ways of measuring that performance. This kind of analysis is time-consuming and requires specialist expertise. It is therefore expensive. When should it be used? Guidelines are:

- when tasks are unfamiliar to learners, difficult, all more or less equally important, and must be learnt quickly and to standard
- when change in the job is unlikely but new recruits are fairly frequent
- when the job is closely prescribed, with little or nothing left to the initiative of the job-holders.

When the resource is available for it, comprehensive analysis is most commonly used for jobs consisting of simple, usually manual, repetitive and unchanging tasks. It leads to two typical outcomes: a job description to guide selection of learners; and a job training specification showing the skill, knowledge and (if relevant) attitudes required, the standards of performance to be reached and how performance against those standards is measured in the workplace. The specification guides training/learning design.

Key task analysis

This approach analyses only those tasks in which performance of a certain kind is critical to good performance. A brief job description needs to be produced, using the same format as in comprehensive analysis. However, the job training specification must this time be selective, covering only those tasks crucial good to job performance. Key task analysis is appropriate for any type of job where:

- a variety of tasks are involved in performing it, but not all need to be performed to the same high standard
- core tasks in a job are changing in emphasis or in content and retraining is required in those but not in others that the job involves.

Problem-centred analysis

This approach identifies any major performance problems that a particular job or role typically involves. Analysis focuses on training implications and uses a sample of job-holders to provide the necessary insights. It is an approach designed to achieve speedy resolution of problems for which training is the best solution, and to obtain the commitment of job-holders through involving them in analysis and in training design (Warr and Bird 1968). It is most appropriately used when:

- training is urgent, but analytical resources limited
- the job-holders' work is satisfactory except in one or two 'problem' areas
- it is important to gain job-holders' commitment to training.

The problem-centred approach involves recording a description of agreed problems, their typical causes and how they can best be tackled in training. Job-holders' commitment to any subsequent learning event should be a natural outcome of their involvement in the analytical process.

Competency-based analysis

The word 'competency' refers to dimensions of behaviour that are believed to lie behind competent performance (Woodruffe 1991). Like problem-centred analysis, competency analysis is both job- and person-related. It tends to be used in two main types of situation:

- when a learning intervention has to link to a competency framework (that may sometimes itself be linked to national vocational qualifications for accreditation purposes)
- when management wishes core behavioural attributes and related performance standards to be identified in order to ensure consistent and effective performance across a family of jobs or across the entire workforce.

Competency-based analysis results in the production of:

- a statement of the role or purpose of the general category of job being studied in the organisation
- a breakdown of that role into discrete areas of competence
- statements of the behavioural competencies needed to perform satisfactorily in each of those areas and criteria for measuring those competencies.

Competency frameworks are the subject of considerable debate that it is not relevant to go into here, although in a later chapter on management development (Chapter 16) there will be some discussion of its nature. While competency analysis can be useful in identifying and describing a set of desired behaviours in a range of jobs or roles, it does not of itself explain job performance adequately – as is indicated by the following comment made by a group of assessors selecting IT managers for a large financial services organisation (Brittain and Ryder 1999):

> **'She performed OK against the competencies, but she's not the one**
>
> **for the role – there's something about her that's not right for us.'**

Some might argue that all that such an observation suggests is that the firm's competency framework had been poorly designed. Others might respond that on the contrary it demonstrates the inability of any competency framework to take into account the variety of factors that explain differing performance levels in a group of job-holders who all possess the same core competencies. The fact that such arguments are common suggests that caution should be exercised in using a competency based approach in the training analysis process.

Looking at the person

In addition to establishing what is involved in successful performance in a job, the training analyst must also discover where the gaps are that currently prevent that successful performance – or that can be expected to do so in the future. For this person-centred analysis (technically termed training needs analysis – TNA) obvious data to seek will come from the performance management system, from other HR records that can throw light on reasons for good and poor job performance, from discussions with managers and team leaders of those performing the jobs in question and from job-holders themselves. But in seeking this kind of information the analyst should explain to informants exactly why it is needed and what use will be made of it, in order to obtain truthful and sufficient data from them.

In a talk at the then Institute of Personnel Management's annual Harrogate Conference in 1989 the Personnel Director at Manchester Airport made this commentary about an attempt to introduce an innovative management development programme (as it happened, one that was competency based) into the organisation (Jackson 1989):

> 'If anything we underestimated the level of inertia and opposition which faced us in this..... Throughout the process, it was noticeable that the psychological barriers were more daunting than the administrative and technical ones. Because the Company had no history of formalised and systematic Management Development, there was a degree of scepticism that the exercise would get off the ground successfully. At various stages, serious doubts were expressed as to whether we would see it through.'

They did see it through, but only after spending much time developing a good working relationship with the key parties.

In the process of obtaining information about factors that typically cause poor job performance the L&D analyst may uncover barriers to employee motivation to perform well, such as an inadequate reward system, incompetent managers or team leaders, inappropriate work schedules or workloads. Such findings highlight an organisational context that is likely to continue to produce adverse effects on job performance no matter what skills training enables the learners to acquire. Such contextual barriers will have to be tackled before the learning event goes ahead. The analyst (or the L&D professional to whom he or she reports back on findings) will therefore need the skill and credibility to put across that message to management in a way that will convince rather than make an initial situation worse.

To summarise: this first stage of the eight-stage learning design process is valuable not only because of its role in generating information to inform the design of a learning event, but also because of the way in which it tests the business case for that event. The analysis of needs may generate insights that raise doubts about the feasibility of the intended learning intervention. This is where the negotiating skills of the L&D practitioners and their ability to forge credible business partnerships become of such importance. Failure to achieve agreement on the need to tackle contextual problems will put the whole proposed intervention at risk.

STAGE 2: AGREEING PURPOSE AND OBJECTIVES

Linking purpose and learning objectives

The *purpose* of a learning event answers the question why the event is taking place, whereas its *learning objectives* define what attitudinal, behavioural or performance outcomes are to be achieved.

Any planned learning event should rest on a clear and convincing case, agreed between the L&D staff and business partners, that identifies its purpose and locates it in the context of the organisation's L&D strategy and its L&D plan (if there is one). Such a business case should record agreement between key parties on:

- The purpose and feasibility of the initiative – why it is needed, what business purpose it serves, and where it fits in the organisation's L&D strategy and plan. Where the latter do not exist in any formalised way, it should at least be clear how this event fits with other HR practices in the workplace and what support from them it will require.
- The nature of the proposed initiative and the learning strategy and outline design to deliver it.
- The outcomes set for the initiative and their value for the organisation and for the learners.
- The resource base – financial and non-financial, material and human – agreed for the initiative. It is particularly important to allow for any training that may be needed by L&D staff, managers and team leaders in order to ensure the event's successful delivery and outcomes in the workplace.
- The kind of learners who will be involved, by reference to number, types and levels of jobs and any other relevant information.
- The timescale for the initiative and how, by whom and at what points it will be monitored and evaluated.

Real life rarely conforms to the ideal. Many learning events have to be planned informally, in a rush and without much supporting documentation of the kind described here. Sometimes those who identified and analysed needs for the event are not involved in its design or delivery. Sometimes although needs have been clarified and the purpose and resourcing of the event have been agreed, little else has been settled.

Whatever the situation, those who are responsible for the design, delivery and evaluation of the event must now ensure that the kind of detail outlined above is agreed with management and any other internal or external partners. That detail must be recorded, particularly because it will be needed later to aid evaluation of the event.

To illustrate the kind of problems that can occur during this second stage, here is a case that is based on a real-life situation, with some details changed to ensure anonymity. What advice would you give to the programme's leadership after the review described in the case? Comments follow at its end.

CASE EXAMPLE

'X' University and the programme review

The business school of X University has just gone through the external teaching review process, and one of its programmes – a two-year part-time post-experience management course – had been singled out for critical comment. It has been running for many years, but in the last two had undergone a significant change of emphasis. The review panel made five main points about this programme:

1. In the past it had a sound educational purpose that was reflected appropriately in its examination-focused methods of assessment. Two years ago, however, the business school decided that, in order to reflect national trends, there must be a change in focus to the development of managerial competencies.
2. Consistent with this overall purpose, the learning objectives were made more skills-oriented. However, the main method of assessment remained the formal examination. All subjects are assessed in that way, and the format of each paper is what it has always been: a three-hour, closed-book paper, with a choice of four out of 10 or 12 questions.
3. Students who consistently do best in the programme are those who are academically the brightest, whether or not they have practical competence. The rest, however good their workplace performance and their practical assignments on the programme, tend to get poor examination results and do markedly less well on the programme overall. About a third regularly fail the programme or drop out before completion.
4. The skills-oriented objectives of the programme call for a resource level that the programme leader can rarely obtain, struggling with the large classes that she is obliged by the school's management to recruit, and with inadequate staffing. Learning resources including technical support for any form of computer-based work are patchy and unreliable.
5. Students recruited onto the programme differ widely in the relevance of their prior learning. They also enter it with widely differing levels and types of learning skills and styles and of learning expectations. By virtue of their positions at work several have no practical experience of some of the core modules that the course involves, and learning activities during class time are not varied or learner-centred enough to help them acquire such experience by proxy.

The review concluded that the examination failure rate is understandable in the circumstances but unacceptable. It noted the declining rate of recruitment coupled with increasingly poor-quality recruits. The programme staff have been advised to reconsider the overall purpose of the programme, its learning objectives and its assessment methods, and to revise its cost and activity base if they can find no other way to resolve the resource problems.

Comments

■ In this case confusion surrounding the purpose and learning objectives of the programme has started off a chain of difficulties which have finally led to highly unsatisfactory outcomes. If, two years previously, the programme leader and her colleagues had looked more critically at the educational and practical implications of running the kind of revised programme the business school wanted them to deliver – in other words, if at the start of the change process they had queried the overall purpose and objectives that the business school had set for the programme – then some at least of the problems would have been avoided. Resource issues, in particular, should have been clearly identified when making the business case for the revised programme.

- Given the disincentives that the learning process involves for many of the students it is unsurprising that little productive learning has taken place. The learning experience offered to most has been of poor quality and uninvolving.
- In this account of the case little has been said about contextual factors which, in real life, would have a direct bearing on the programme. It may prove, for example, that any restructuring of the programme or of its learning and assessment methods would require resources that the school does not have, or is not willing to allocate. So following the review what is needed is for the programme team and the school's leadership to fully assess issues and options before making any decision about the programme. Amongst the questions they need to ask themselves is one of particular importance – should the programme in fact continue? Perhaps by now it has outlived its purpose and other possibilities to support the school's goals should be explored.

Levels of objectives

The case example highlights the importance of aligning a learning initiative's purpose and its specific objectives. Except in very simple events it is helpful to formulate objectives at two levels: final and intermediate.

Final behavioural objectives

Sometimes known as 'ultimate', 'criterion', 'summative' or 'overall' objectives, these explain the kind of outcomes that the learner should have achieved once the learning event is completed.

Interim behavioural objectives

Sometimes known as 'intermediate', 'formative' or 'specific' objectives, these explain the kind of outcomes that the learner should have achieved at each key stage of the learning process.

You may have noted the use of the phrase 'behavioural objectives' in the above definitions; also the reference to 'outcomes'. The clearest guide to design can be obtained not so much by stating what the learning event aims to do in general terms but in specifying how the learner should be able to act or perform at various points. By describing the kinds of behaviour and performance to be achieved at the end of a learning event, final objectives give a clear focus to that event and link it back to its purpose. All objectives must have contextual relevance and therefore should take into careful account the specific conditions in which learners will have to perform once the learning event has concluded (Mager 1984).

REFLECTION

Consider the likely focus of a Customer Care training course for staff new to contact with the public. What kind of behavioural objectives would you suggest for such a course, and how would you justify them?

STAGE 3: IDENTIFYING THE LEARNERS' PROFILE

Information needed

If during Stage 1 analysis has not been based on the specific group of learners for whom the learning event is intended, then at this stage that kind of analysis should be undertaken. Analysis should have produced a generic profile – one that identifies the typical learning needs around which the event is to be constructed. Now, it is essential to gain more personalised information that can enable a well-tailored course design.

To establish a meaningful profile of the learners four sets of factors should be examined:

- their numbers and location
- individual performance and skill levels
- individual learning styles and learning skills
- individuals' pre-event attitudes, expectations and motivation.

Numbers and location of learners

Numbers and location of the learners affect learning strategy and methods. Small numbers should enable quite individualised learning. However, location must be considered here. A small number spread over dispersed physical locations may suggest an e-learning strategy blending with occasional workshops to bring the group together. On the other hand, it may be important to have face to face learning during all or part of the programme in order to develop a cohesive group with a strong team identity.

If the cohort is a small group from a single workplace, the best strategy may be to arrange the event around their work location, or in proximity to it. Alternatively, the purpose of the event may make it desirable to take them away from the work environment and focus their attention on wider issues. That could argue for one or more external residential events.

Performance and skill levels

What is needed here is information on variations in individual performance levels and the skills, knowledge and attitudes related to them. The following example is particularly interesting because it couples the process of job training analysis with the collection and application of precisely this kind of detailed personal information. It also takes numbers and location fully into account. It is not a method that would suit all learning situations but in the context of IT training it proved highly effective.

CASE EXAMPLE

Electronic learner profiling

The Project Manager and Technical Developer in the Learning and Development Department of Transport for London described how training needs analysis produced through using an electronic questionnaire threw up a variety of learning gaps to be filled in a programme that had to ensure the competence of 1,000 staff needing to use SAP, a new database and reporting system.

This electronic process enabled the L&D team to identify individals' exact needs and to meet them not by the customary training course but in a more flexible manner which proved timely, efficient and motivating. They used a combination of tailored workshops, email tips and one-to-one coaching.

The success of this initiative led to the introduction of a new process for all IT training. Generic IT courses had been taking people away from their workstations for up to two days and not always giving them adequate practice time. Using an expanded electronic questionnaire that checked each learner's current knowledge of a particular IT package and identified learning gaps, the L&D team was now able to group together people with similar needs and create tailored courses for them. These were designed around a single module, a combination of modules or elements of the modules – an example of bite-sized learning that reduced learning time while providing a well tailored learning strategy for groups and individuals.

In describing this initiative the authors of the article concluded that the overall dynamic and pace of delivery of the training was greatly aided by rigorous training needs analysis which ensured that participants on each course were at a similar skills level.

Source: HARLOW, T. and SMITH, A. (2003)

Learning styles and skills

Trainers often spend much time deciding how best to adapt learning design to individuals' preferred learning styles. I first looked at this topic in Chapter 4 where I noted concerns arising from recent research into the validity of learning style inventories (Coffield et al 2004). Even without using such an inventory, the type of jobs held by the proposed learners, together with their age and ability range, their length and type of experience and other such information will suggest appropriate approaches to learning.

If a learning style inventory is used to aid design, then it is important to realise that people can usually develop learning styles in more than one mode and that many may need to do so because of the nature of their present or intended future job or role. Suppose, for example, that prior to attending a 'Training the Trainers' course a group of delegates have completed the Honey and Mumford (1992) inventory and have shown a marked activist profile (and Honey and Mumford themselves have encountered this). Since trainers have to organise training for all types of learners they should be exposed to learning experiences that can develop strengths in reflector, theorist and pragmatist modes and arouse awareness of the dangers they face in relying too much on any one learning style.

Pre-event attitudes, expectations and motivation

Well over a decade ago an organisational consultant suggested that in a world of discontinuous change where we have little idea about what is coming next, we should perhaps stop looking to training needs analysis to help us to decide what training and development programmes to run. Instead we should use the process to gather tactical information about the sort of reception any learning intervention is likely to receive (Fairbairn 1991).

There is an important point here. Prior to entering a planned learning event individuals will have formed certain expectations about the quality, relevance and likely outcomes for them of that event. These expectations can come from any source – often from those who have previously attended a similar event – and they can be positive or negative. Either way they are likely to affect their performance during the event and so should be diagnosed at as early a stage as possible.

Research shows, predictably, that one factor influencing pre-event attitudes is the reputation of the L&D staff involved. Another is the extent to which, and the ways in which, training is rewarded in the organisation (Noe 1986). In their study Facteau and colleagues (1995) examined three kinds of incentive to attend training:

- intrinsic incentives (how far the learning event is expected to meet internal needs and provide learners with growth opportunities)
- extrinsic incentives (the extent to which training results in tangible external rewards such as pay, promotion)
- compliance (the extent to which learners attend a learning event because they are given no choice by the employer but to do so).

Other factors examined included managers' and colleagues' attitudes to the training, support given to it in the workplace, and its anticipated impact on career development.

The findings of Facteau's study conform with much other research (including, for example, the Black Box studies discussed in Chapter 5) in identifying the importance of managers, supervisors and team leaders in actively supporting employee development, aiding transfer of new learning to the workplace, and creating a supportive learning climate. However they also suggested that no single variable, even that of management style and actions, is enough to explain the attitudes and expectations that employees bring to a planned learning experience. It is the 'big picture' that needs particular attention from L&D staff. The scope of organisational context that influences potential learners can extend, for example, to the strategic plans for the business, layoff policies, emphasis on employee development and continual learning, creation of self-managed work teams, and organisation culture.

When seeking to understand how learners are likely to regard the learning activity in which they are going to take part, L&D staff should therefore take two major considerations into account:

- They need to be informed about organisational context. Attitudes, motivation and expectations about a learning event will be influenced by management – but the negative effects of poor management in a workplace may be balanced out by the encouragement of colleagues who have found similar learning events to be productive, or who promise their support in transferring learning to the workplace once the event is over. On the other hand even the most supportive management and work team may mean little to learners who are concerned about rumours of forthcoming downsizing or redeployment and suspicious about the part that the learning event may be playing in that organisational plan.
- As Handy's motivation calculus (Chapter 5) demonstrates, individuals' motivation, attitudes and expectations change with experience. Even the most negatively disposed learners may develop more positive attitudes and expectations once they are taking part in a stimulating event whose relevance they increasingly perceive, and where L&D staff have worked with business partners to ensure recognition for learning achieved and the opportunity to use it in the workplace.

Here is a case, again based on real life but with the identity of the organisation withheld. You may find it helpful to identify its overall message for L&D professionals related to this third stage of the eight-stage process for organising learning events. Comments follow at the end.

CASE EXAMPLE

Rewarding training or performance?

Training staff in a recently restructured company carefully planned a series of modular skills training courses related to different areas of skill, in order to promote multi-skilling in the workforce. Appropriate training of supervisors to fill new team leader roles was already taking place.

The training staff carried out a thorough analysis of the knowledge, skills and attitudes required in each module and of learning gaps that training must try to close. In the process they realised that, especially in the aftermath of restructuring, training in new skills would not work unless most employees were better motivated to undergo it. They therefore recommended to management the introduction of a financial reward system tied to successful completion of each skills module, with a final extra payment for those who went through the entire skills matrix relevant to their area of the business.

The new training matrix proved popular with employees and completion rates were excellent. However, the training subsequently proved to have far less effect on workforce flexibility than had been hoped and many of the newly acquired skills were put to little use in the workplace.

Belatedly the training staff realised that for employees the training-related reward system was motivating them to gain new skills, but not to put them into practice. A new system was devised in which successful completion of each skills module was recognised by a small financial increase, but the main rewards went to teams for subsequent effective team working in the new organisational structure.

The L&D staff also realised that although they had trained supervisors in new functional skills as team leaders, many were continuing to behave more as managers than leaders in their changed roles. Most were weak in the interpersonal skills needed to lead, inspire and support their teams, to encourage them to be more self-managing, and to work to a high standard with shared purpose. This proved a more difficult problem to resolve. Eventually it led not only to a changed type of team leadership programme but to new selection and financial reward criteria for team leader roles.

Comments

The main message in this case is that learning events may rest on an apparently secure business case and may be supported by all the parties, yet may still have a negative impact unless attention is paid at planning stage to organisational context. L&D staff should plan how best to ensure both appropriate recognition of learners' success in a learning event and the effective use of new learning in the workplace.

STAGE 4: ESTABLISHING STRATEGY, DIRECTION AND MANAGEMENT

Choosing a learning strategy

Strategy is the route to be followed in order to achieve a goal, or goals. Learning strategy therefore involves looking at alternative ways in which the goal (purpose) for a learning event can best be achieved and selecting an option that achieves best fit with the learner profile for the event, the resources available to support it and organisational context.

For example if one option is to use a work-based learning strategy then there must be the management skills, the facilitative roles and the workplace culture to support it. If another strategic option is to rely on off-the-job training, then the matter of how to ensure transfer of learning, its retention and use in the workplace must be carefully considered. Workplace cultures are slow to change, and those who have 'been away' on a course often find invisible and sometimes impenetrable barriers awaiting them on their return.

If an e-learning strategy is chosen, then as was noted in Chapter 4 a blended approach is likely to work best but again context is crucial. There must be the necessary infrastructure and skills to make e-learning feasible in the workplace, and a good partnership of L&D, management and IT staff to ensure that it is effectively introduced, embedded and monitored. Piloting is advisable to iron out any bugs and to gain understanding and active commitment from the learners, their managers and/or team leaders.

Direction and management of the learning event

Who is to lead the event, and who is to be responsible for its management? For simple events those two roles may be combined. For more complex events they may have to be shared between a number. In that scenario there must be absolute clarity about lines of accountability and responsibility, especially when in house training personnel are working in partnership with external providers.

Who and how many will be needed to carry out the work involved in design, administration, delivery and evaluation? If the learning strategy to be pursued is one of classroom-based training courses, then internal or external specialists – or a mix of both – will have to provide these, and this will need careful selection, briefing and management. If the strategy includes an educational programme using day or block release, there will have to be liaison with the educational provider.

Any requirement to assess workplace competencies for accreditation purposes will need extensive preparation and will either include training of workplace assessors or outsourcing that task. Either will be expensive in terms of finance and time. If there are to be elements of work-related learning or a strategy of continuing personal development, then again relevant experiences and how best to organise them must be agreed with the parties concerned. All options must be assessed for cost and anticipated benefits (an issue to be discussed in more detail in Chapter 11).

To conclude this chapter, the case example that follows relates to the L&D consultancy firm whose advertisement was referred to at the start of Chapter 1 – Hemsley Fraser. In engaging with clients across the world it uses a process model that ensures both internal and external consistency, involving the client throughout in the planning and design stages in order to ensure shared perceptions about learning needs and how to tackle them.

CASE EXAMPLE

Working with clients to design and deliver learning: the Hemsley Fraser process

At this international L&D consultancy firm the provision of L&D services to clients is organised around a number of interactive core processes underpinned by four principles:

- precision in identifying and responding to client needs (learner and organisational)
- ensuring that learning achieved through a project will be transferred to the workplace and contribute to business results
- the provision of a service that has built in quality and innovation
- the provision of a service underpinned by a body of professional knowledge related to workplace learning and development.

At the heart of the HF process model lies *Faculty Management*, an overarching process that builds in quality, continuous improvement and innovation throughout the relationship with the client.

Faculty Management

The title given to this process signals the professional knowledge and expertise and the educational ethos that HF consultants bring to their relationship with clients, requiring the roll-out of a learning programme to a consistent quality standard. The Head of Faculty and a team of learning consultants are selected for each such project, with selection based on:

- capacity – the scale and pace of the project
- type of client organisation – its sector, culture, geographical location and so on
- characteristics of the learners who will be involved and the nature of their work
- subject matter and nature of the delivery (e.g. a leadership programme, a modular programme, an action learning process, and so on)

The Faculty Management process frames a cycle of interactive 'plan, set up, manage and evaluate' processes to deliver the service required. Each involves the use of a set of customised HF tools.

The design process

Faculty Management is closely integrated with the HF *Design Process* which is organised around key phases, starting with capture of information that is gathered by HF sales and learning consultants, using a collaborative tool. Initial meetings with the client lead to the production of a scoping document that provides the framework for the design of the learning event, process or initiative required. Once it has been discussed and agreed with the client, detailed design and learning materials are produced.

The whole design process is structured to ensure:

- that the learning provision is backed up by quality standards and incorporates leading edge thinking

- that an 'audit trail' is produced, showing how the final design has been rooted in a shared understanding between the client and the HF learning consultants regarding organisational context, characteristics of the audience, the desired links between the learning event or programme and business goals
- a basis from which informed decisions can be made about improvements and innovations to future learning provision, and which can underpin the evaluation process.

Recruitment, selection and development of HF Learning Consultants

Key to HF's successful relationship with its clients worldwide is its ability to recruit, retain and develop high calibre L&D consultants. The firm's need is for consultants who combine a high level of specialised L&D skills with the values and behavioural competencies involved in working collaboratively with clients. In selection, the critical discriminator is values. Only those who are fully committed to HF's core values and beliefs and to working to a shared purpose with both colleagues and clients can be successfully integrated into the firm.

The selection process is documented and supported by practical tools to ensure consistency and reliability across a variety of selection scenarios. One example is a tool called 'The Design Challenges', which probes for thinking and an approach to design work that is compatible with the HF design process.

Continuing professional development for HF's staff supports its core processes. CPD strategy and practices are based on the central principle of encouraging and investing in the development of individuals who are committed both to their own CPD and to the learning of others.

With acknowledgements to Hemsley Fraser Group Limited.

The main message of this chapter has been that organising learning events requires a detailed understanding of organisational context together with the building of internal and external consistency. There must be the technical expertise to ensure a relevant, well-designed learning event and the partnership skills to secure shared perceptions as to its value and intended outcomes, and active support for it in the workplace before, during and after its delivery.

CONCLUSION

You should by now have a sound understanding of the first four stages of an eight-stage process to ensure a collaborative and expert approach to organising planned learning events and feel confident to tackle the review questions on the chapter's material, contained in Appendix 3.

The chapter has introduced the process and has covered the following main ground:

- *Stage 1: establishing needs* that the learning event must serve. Any planned learning event should tackle a learning gap agreed to be important for the business as well as for individuals. It should be integrated with overall L&D and

HR strategies whether or not these are formalised, and should be well aligned with organisational goals.

■ Establishing needs requires technical but also interpersonal and political skills. Whatever analytical methods are used, the analyst must build trust with those involved in order to obtain valid and sufficient data and build key parties' commitment to the planned learning event. Analysts must identify any problems in the workplace or wider organisational context that may put barriers in the way of the learning event's success. Failure to resolve these puts the learning event and the reputations of its providers at risk.

■ *Stage 2: establishing purpose and objectives* for learning. Any planned learning event must have an overall purpose and specific learning objectives that emerge from its business case (whether or not formally documented), placing it securely in its organisational context and providing guidelines for its design, content and evaluation.

■ *Stage 3: identifying the profile of the learners.* Those designing the event must take fully into account the learners' likely pre-event attitudes, motivation and expectation and the organisational context that has shaped them. They should also assess how far and in what ways the event could change that learner profile, and what impact the learning experience and its outcomes may have on organisational context subsequently.

■ *Stage 4: establishing learning strategy, direction and management.* All learning events should be guided by a learning strategy. They also require clearly assigned responsibility for their overall direction and day-to-day management.

Further information sources

BEE, F. and BEE, R. (2003) *Learning needs analysis and evaluation*. 2nd edn. London: Chartered Institute of Personnel and Development.

REID, M.A., BARRINGTON, H. and BROWN, M. (2004) *Human resource development*. 7th edn. London: Chartered Institute of Personnel and Development.

Organising Learning Events: Stages 5 to 8

CHAPTER 7

INTRODUCTION

In this chapter's four sections I conclude the analysis of the eight stages involved in facilitating planned learning events by looking at Stages 5 to 8 (see Figure 9). These involve the selection of learners and the design, delivery and evaluation of learning events.

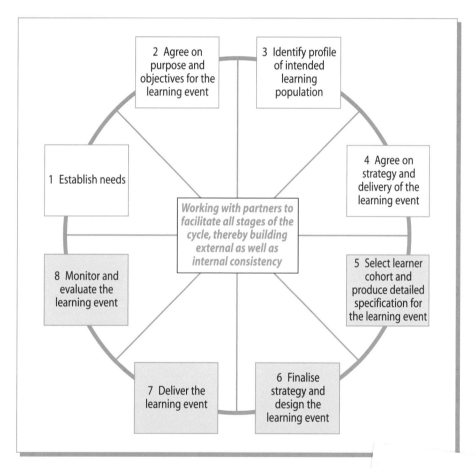

Figure 9 *Eight-stage process to facilitate planned learning events: Stages 5 to 8*

Most of the chapter is taken up with an illustrative case study, which read apply principles related to the four stages to a real-life situation and to r gained in the previous chapter. The case is in two parts, the first in r second at its end.

STAGE 5: SELECTING THE LEARNERS

The selection process

Managers are accountable for the performance and development of those reporting to them. They must, therefore, play a key part in deciding who should participate in learning events. On the other hand so should those with accountability for the provision of those events. The involvement of inappropriate participants can reduce or destroy the possibility of planned learning achieving its intended outcomes. However L&D staff sometimes have little or no say in selecting the learners, although contact with each individual before the event, as well as skilful course design and flexible delivery, can do much to remedy any problems there.

Entry to some learning events – usually educational and management development programmes – often involves some form of structured assessment. There are considerable financial, training and administrative costs associated with the use of psychometric tests, and a full development centre methodology will be particularly resource-hungry. Careful cost-benefit analysis therefore needs to be carried out to determine the most appropriate selection methods to use.

One way or another mistakes are often made in selecting participants for a training course or educational programme. The danger is probably greatest with externally provided courses, because when places are hard to fill the temptation is strong for the provider to accept people whose needs or abilities may not adequately match the course profile. Internal as well as external providers who show little concern for effective selection of learner, like those who try to 'sell' off-the-shelf products rather than produce tailored initiatives, should always be viewed with suspicion.

STAGE 6: FINALISING STRATEGY AND DESIGNING THE LEARNING EVENT

Finalising strategy

Once the participants in a learning event have been selected, it is essential to confirm or modify the learning strategy and design initially proposed. Although in most cases confir-mation will be all that is called for, from time to time the more detailed information gained when examining the needs of learners may indicate that some major change is needed. Difficult though dealing with this kind of problem can be, there will be far more likelihood of its effective resolution where L&D staff have thus far been working in close partnership with line managers and other key parties (often now including union learning representatives) than where they have neglected to do so.

Designing the event

In designing any learning event, it is essential to choose media and methods that achieve best fit:

- *Media of learning*: are the routes, or channels, through which learning is transmitted to the learner.
- *Methods of learning*: are the ways in which that learning is transmitted.

…ing technology' is a phrase commonly used to refer to the way in which learning media …ods are incorporated into the design and delivery of a learning event. I have already devoted much of Chapter 4 to a discussion of the importance of learner-centred approaches, and many texts contain specialist advice and examples. One further point is worth noting here: that often e-technology can help not only to deliver high-quality learning more cheaply and conveniently than a conventional course, but also to provide assessment of learning in a motivating way. For example, Mackinnon described how the former Polymer National Training Organisation (subsequently Cogent Sector Skills Council) delivered and assessed Level 2 vocational training knowledge through web-based technology in an approach that was both robust and popular with learners. All found that the technology was used in a way that made the questions interesting, and felt that the assessment results fairly reflected their strengths and weaknesses (Mackinnon 2004).

It is not relevant to say more here about choice of methods and media, but you may find Table 5 a useful prompt for ideas.

The following reflection point offers a way of reviewing information in Chapter 4 and applying some of its observations to a practical scenario.

REFLECTION

Imagine that you have to design a one-day workshop on time management for 20 participants. The intended outcome of the workshop is that its members should have mastered some simple techniques of time management and be able to apply them to their daily workload. Reflecting on some research findings and/or wider organisational practice, what are the main considerations that would guide your choice of media and methods?

In Chapter 4 I also discussed some limitations of classical conditioning theory. However that body of theory does have considerable value in suggesting a set of principles to aid motivation and retention of learning in a planned learning situation:

- *Clarify the purpose of learning.* There should be clarity about why the event is being offered and what needs it serves. This is important in activating individuals' drive to learn, helping them to see the event's relevance for them.
- *Ensure stimulation during learning.* The learning process should be designed to arouse and maintain the interest and energy of the learners, especially at its most difficult points. Points made in Chapter 4 about typical motivating and demotivating effects of e-learning have a particular relevance here.
- *Ensure adequate feedback and practice during learning.* Learning should be regularly checked and reinforced if learners are to gain confidence in their ability to master new skills, acquire new knowledge quickly, and competently apply it to practical situations. This is particularly important in self-directed learning. Kolb and colleagues' (1974) cycle emphasises this when it shows the stage of experimentation leading into further experience, which then generates a need for the individual to review, analyse and modify or expand their new learning. The need for reinforcement is greatest at the most difficult stages of the learning curve, and learning design should reflect that.
- *Ensure transfer and retention of learning.* The way in which learning is transferred into, as well as out of, the new learning situation has a direct impact on the ultimate

Table 5 *Designing effective learning events*

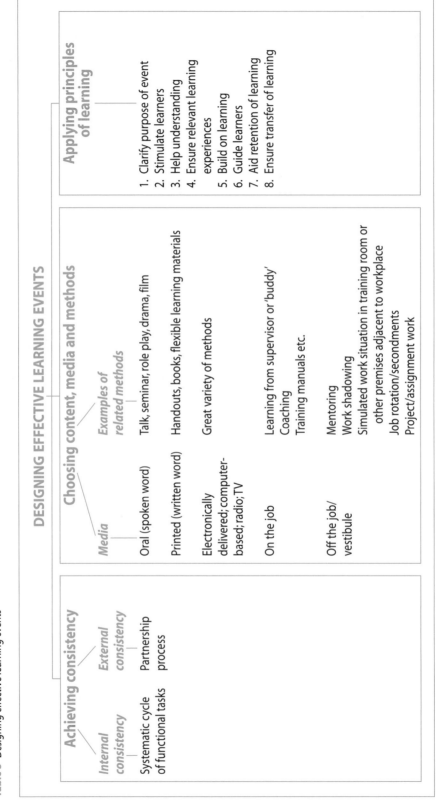

DESIGNING EFFECTIVE LEARNING EVENTS

Achieving consistency

Internal consistency	*External consistency*
Systematic cycle of functional tasks	Partnership process

Choosing content, media and methods

Media	*Examples of related methods*
Oral (spoken word)	Talk, seminar, role play, drama, film
Printed (written word)	Handouts, books, flexible learning materials
Electronically delivered; computer-based; radio; TV	Great variety of methods
On the job	Learning from supervisor or 'buddy' Coaching Training manuals etc.
Off the job/ vestibule	Mentoring Work shadowing Simulated work situation in training room or other premises adjacent to workplace Job rotation/secondments Project/assignment work

Applying principles of learning

1. Clarify purpose of event
2. Stimulate learners
3. Help understanding
4. Ensure relevant learning experiences
5. Build on learning
6. Guide learners
7. Aid retention of learning
8. Ensure transfer of learning

outcomes of the learning process. Sometimes knowledge, skills and attitudes acquired before a learner enters a new learning situation will exercise a negative influence on that situation. In the same way, learning that has been newly acquired may prove difficult to transfer to the workplace and to use effectively there. Due thought must be given at the planning stage to what learning will be most relevant, given workplace context, and to how best to ensure its effective transfer to that context (see Tennant 1999).

■ *Carry out appropriate monitoring.* Appropriateness should be determined by purpose and by availability of resources. Monitoring is not the same as evaluation (covered at a later stage). It is akin to taking a temperature – a light touch approach that enables identification of any early warning signs, and adjustments to be made in an ongoing event in order to avoid an escalation of problems. Some forms of learning generate particular monitoring problems. Mentoring, for example, is a one-to-one and highly confidential process, and in action learning sets the principle of confidentiality is also paramount. Here, ground rules have to be established in advance, with monitoring entrusted to mentors and set facilitators but exit points built into the processes at various stages for all the parties to accommodate the possibility of some relationships proving unworkable.

An integrative case study

In discussing this sixth stage of the eight-stage process it is not my purpose to provide technical advice – that can be obtained from the many texts specialising in training and learning design. It is to propose a process that can unify the performance of functional training and learning tasks with the development of partnerships that will ensure support for planned learning amongst stakeholders. When functional tasks throw up problems that go outside the L&D staff's territory into that of the wider organisation – as they will often do – a partnership process will be needed to tackle them. L&D specialists who work in silos have only themselves blame if, having devoted insufficient time up to this point to building relationships with business partners, they now find the success of their work at risk.

Instead of expanding further on this sixth stage in the text I will use a case example to illustrate some key issues. You may wish to use it to review also your understanding of the previous five stages. Comments follow at its end.

CASE EXAMPLE

A management development programme for clinical directors: Part 1

The planning and design team
During 1991 a small team at the Northern Regional Health Authority (NRHA) and Durham University Business School (DUBS) worked to plan, design and jointly manage a three-year management development initiative for clinical directors (CDs) in the region. The team initially comprised four people: a director and a programme manager from the NRHA and from DUBS. They maintained close contact throughout the three years with NHS senior management in the CDs' business units.

The programme
The programme had been designed in outline late in 1990 by an NRHA management consultant and the DUBS academic who later became one of its directors, and had been

tendered to the National Health Service's Management Executive (ME) for funding as one of nine countrywide trailblazing CD development programmes. Its purpose was to develop in senior clinicians in, or preparing to take on, CD roles the skills, motivation and disposition to perform those roles to a high standard, to the ultimate enhancement of patient care. There were to be 24 participants, split into three cohorts of eight over the 1991–94 period to enable an individualised learning system to drive the cycle of three overlapping repeat programmes. The programme design incorporated evaluation by two national bodies for the ME and the NRHA, and locally by NRHA and DUBS' staff. It concluded with a significant period of action learning – a stipulation set by the ME for all its CD programmes.

Funding was won early in 1991, tied to the above design which therefore became the programme's stable framework. Figure 10 shows the configuration of learning events in the first, prototype, programme.

Analysis of learning needs

The programme team spent much of 1991 gathering information from a wide variety of sources on learner- and job-related needs in order to produce a training specification for the programme. The CD role was a new one and was sparsely documented at any level. It was also interpreted and carried out differently across organisations. Because the programme was a trailblazer, selection of its participants was not in the team's hands but was decided by the NRHA's directorate. The 24 chosen participants proved to be very different in their professional capability, their organisational roles, their personal aptitudes and interests, and their pre-programme motivation and expectations. NRHA and DUBS staff interviewed each of them and managers of their NHS units at length, amassing a bewildering array of data that had to be related to programme design.

After considerable professional disagreement on which training analysis approach to use – the knowledge of NRHA and DUBS staff being very different, and their views on how to conduct the analytical process often in conflict – it was agreed to use a problem-centred analytical approach. Even then, however, the analytical exercise, which had to be conducted on many fronts, was immensely time-consuming and complex. Three main categories of need had to be taken into account:

- *Organisational needs* derived from the ME's concern to improve the quality of patient care through the CD programme in the North East of England. They also derived from needs expressed by the NRHA client and the participants' organisations – the NHS units who nominated them for the programme and supported their attendance. Taken together these three sets of client needs had to have a major influence on the programme's learning objectives and on its staffing and delivery. Achieving a credible and effective mix of university, business and NHS staff as tutors and mentors proved a particular challenge here.
- *Group needs* were derived from those areas of skill, knowledge and personal disposition that all programme participants – and their organisations – saw as essential in order to help them quickly master their new and demanding management tasks and, in most cases, the strategic roles at business-unit level that they would be likely to be holding by the time the programme was over.

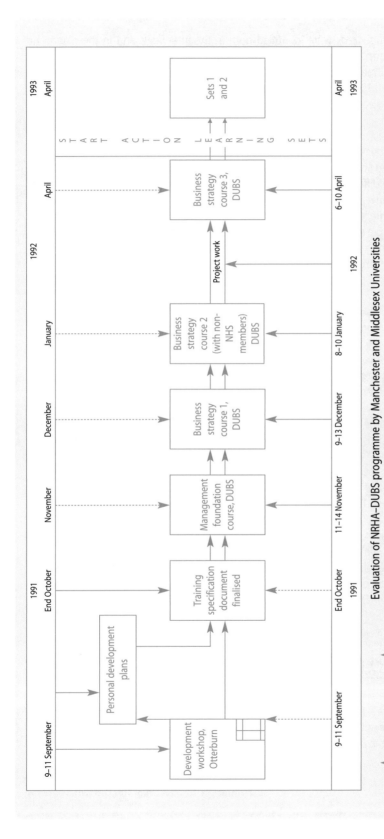

Evaluation of NRHA–DUBS programme by Manchester and Middlesex Universities

Key ◄------- = Collaborated with   ◄┃ = Controlled by

Figure 10 *NRHA–DUBS Clinical Directors' Programme: Intake 1 (1991–1993)*

■ *Individual needs* were identified both in the interviews and in the diagnostic workshop held as the first stage of the learning event (see below). They were incorporated in personal development plans (PDPs), and each CD was allocated both an NRHA and an NHS mentor for the duration of the programme. These needs were widely varied and raised many thorny issues of course design.

In mid-1991 the programme planning team was expanded to include two external management consultants recruited by DUBS to help design and deliver the programme. This introduced invaluable new expertise, but developing external consistency naturally became more difficult as team membership and organisational affiliations grew more complex. However, by making it a priority to gain a full and shared commitment to the purpose and the learning objectives of the three-year programme, the course directors achieved a stable reference point that enabled workable compromises to be reached on a number of initially divisive design issues. The core team of four was then quickly able to produce a job training specification to underpin the entire sequence of repeat programmes.

Programme design and delivery

The NRHA staff organised a three-day personal development diagnostic workshop for each of the three CD cohorts a few weeks before their formal programme began. The detailed outcomes remained confidential to the learners and their mentors, but generalised insights were passed on to DUBS staff. This led to an important final tweaking of design and content before the first cohort entered that programme.

Every programme module had its own stated purpose and three or four final objectives. Interim objectives guided each module's teaching sessions and acted as criteria for the learners to use in evaluating the modules. Their evaluations, together with the regular monitoring of each programme by DUBS and NRHA staff, were continually fed into the forward planning process, leading to more fine-tuning to adapt the programme to emergent needs. The growing cohesiveness of the core team facilitated this process.

Once its formal modules had been completed, each programme moved for its final stage into a six- to eight-month period of action-learning sets (AL, see Figure 10), each comprising four clinicians with an experienced set adviser. A substantial Action Learning component had been made a condition of ME funding for the programme. It was one about which the DUBS staff in particular had serious reservations, and in order to ensure its effectiveness they bought in two international AL experts to join the planning team, with tasks of training set facilitators and helping to design and monitor the AL component.

Their arrival was the catalyst for new tensions in the team, caused by disagreement between the core team on the one hand and the AL experts on the other about how best to integrate the formal and action-learning components of the programme. Once again, the way forward was found through agreement to subordinate divisive professional views and values to an overriding commitment to the purpose and final objectives of the programme.

Sources: HARRISON, R. and MILLER, S. (1993);
HARRISON, R., MILLER, S. and GIBSON, A. (1993)

Comments

The narrative demonstrates one important message – that flexibility and continuous learning from experience are two essential skills for any L&D professional as they struggle to reconcile the messiness of real life with the neatness of textbook theory. The eight-stage process cannot operate in an entirely sequential fashion. As with this programme, several stages may have to be conducted in parallel and some may fall out of sequence. Operating under time and other pressures, others will be subject to a variety of errors and omissions in the tasks that they involve. When an effective partnership between clients, providers and customers is forged, however, most difficulties can be resolved. I will now use the case to look briefly back at each of the five stages in the eight-stage process that have been covered so far:

Stage 1: analysing needs

Long and complex learning events like this one often involve a team of people, its members drawn from different organisations, that has to establish an effective way of operating before any real progress can be made in functional tasks. With this programme, a variety of pressures forced important agendas into the open. Once on the table, the commitment shared by all the parties to the programme's purpose and their resolve that it should be achieved enabled differences to be discussed frankly and in a way that eventually broke down barriers to progress. The partnership came at a price, but it was enduring and proved its worth thereafter.

Stage 2: agreeing purpose and objectives

In a programme like this there is always an ultimate client, often remote from the rest, who pulls the major resource strings and who determines a purpose and overall strategy for the event that must remain in place throughout. It may be corporate management in a multi-national organisation, or some public or government agency. In this case it was the ME of the NHS, but the number of other clients and the high profile of the customers (the learners) naturally complicated the setting of programme objectives and the task of programme design. Such complex learning initiatives call for a fast-responsive partnership process that can manage multiple stakeholder interests and values effectively.

Stage 3: identifying the learners' profile

The variety of the learners' pre-programme motivations, attitudes and expectations, the novelty of the CD role and the tensions and ambiguities surrounding it all complicated the task of collecting and interpreting data for a learner profile. The NRHA used a computer-based diagnostic instrument to aid the learners in a process of self-appraisal and personal development planning and this added an invaluable dimension. Today, more sophisticated e-technology can speed up the whole process but does not necessarily make such a task an easier one to handle at the human level. A mix of interpersonal, political and technical skills is required if a meaningful profile is to be assembled.

Stage 4: establishing strategy, direction and management for the learning event

When programme funding comes from an external source it always has conditions attached. In this programme the ME set a requirement for a substantial element of action learning, and stipulated that the overall strategy and structure for the programme that had been agreed when funding was granted early in 1991 must be adhered to for the duration of the programme thereafter. That strategy had deliberately been made flexible, so the crucial issue was once again one of partnership in tackling problems and challenges as they arose.

I noted in Chapters 2 and 3 the emphasis in government policy on the need for employers and educational providers to work more effectively together. This programme demonstrates that this requires much from the parties. Every significant problem, every emerging need before and during a programme for some change of focus, content or delivery, some rethinking of interim objectives or the resolution of some personal problems amongst learners – all fell to the partnership (including, once the programme was underway, the learners) to resolve. Some situations were particularly hard to resolve. All in all the core team was on a steep learning curve from start to finish of the three-year programme.

Stages 5 and 6: selecting the learners and finalising strategy

The programme provides an example of a situation where selection of the learners is not in the hands of those who are organising the learning event. Here, once programme participants had been selected at regional level, the programmes they were to join had to be closely tailored to their unique needs and characteristics while at the same time remaining well aligned with the programmes' pre-determined purpose and strategy.

STAGE 7: DELIVERING THE EVENT

All the stages until now have been a preparation for delivery, so if they have been carried out effectively then Stage 7 should not pose intractable problems. However flexibility is essential in order to cope with the unexpected. Going back to the case example, fine-tuning had to continue throughout the clinical directors' programme, since what worked well with one cohort of CDs did not always do so with the others. Furthermore as the programmes moved through the three-year period, the CD role in the NHS had become clearer in its purpose and tasks, which were not always as initially suggested, and CDs themselves were often carrying roles with a more significant strategic dimension than at first envisaged. This was reflected in the programme's later participants. It accounted for a few quite substantial changes to programme content, many of which had to be negotiated with the learners as well as within the course team.

Of course since the days of our case example training and learning delivery have acquired the potential to become transformed through e-learning. This has already been discussed in Chapter 4, but further reading in specialist texts is recommended. It is worth commenting briefly here on the importance of skills related to virtual team training and development, since these are the kinds of skills that many traditional trainers are unlikely to possess but which are crucial to success in this context. Harrison and Kessels (2003a, p197) observe that 'whenever the intention is to harness ICT to learning and knowledge processes, the key role for L&D practitioners is to act as human process mediators, who facilitate and motivate, reinforcing the groups' and the individuals' sense of identity and purpose'. Drawing on a number of international research studies they then make three specific points:

- Working with dispersed teams often requires linguistic capability and a high level of sensitivity in managing diversity. L&D practitioners must help team members to establish social contact, and to exchange information about their backgrounds, motives to participate, and perceptions on individual learning objectives and on the successful completion of the project. Not all members will find this easy, so another task is to help diverse participants in virtual teams to develop the attitudes and capabilities for engaging in virtual communities of practice.
- Collaborative ICT requires L&D practitioners to develop new conventions related to operating electronic communication modes and to promoting conceptual learning and encouraging reflection. An enthusiasm for content design is not enough.

- The L&D function should be able to supply local and global learning co-ordinators, learning facilitators and learning consultants who can connect dispersed team members and help them to align their interests and priorities.

STAGE 8: MONITORING AND EVALUATING THE EVENT

In contrast to the discussion of assessment of the L&D process and its outcomes in Chapters 4 and 5, the purpose here is to move to the micro level and look at the evaluation of specific learning events. The section does not provide a literature review or cover techniques in any detail. That kind of information will be found in specialist texts.

Four key questions

People often confuse the processes of monitoring, validation and evaluation. The purpose of monitoring is to take the temperature of a learning event from time to time, picking up any problems or emerging needs. Validation measures the achievement of learning objectives set for a learning initiative or process. Evaluation looks at the total value of that event or process, thereby placing it into its organisational context and aiding future planning. Faced with an evaluation task, there are four crucial questions to answer: why, who, when and how?

Why evaluate?

A desire to assess the value of an event can stem from many causes. Perhaps cost has to be justified, or effects on learners, or impact on job performance, or outcomes relevant to the profitability, performance, flexibility or survival of the organisation as a whole. Each aim generates a different framework for evaluation, explaining why this must be the first question to be answered.

Who should evaluate?

Depending on the answers to the first question, there will be a range of possibilities here. Trainers, line managers, the personnel function, top management, external consultants, the learners and their sponsors – all these parties will have vested interests in the evaluation process. Therefore, of course, none can be relied upon for bias-free assessments. With the CD programme there were several evaluation processes going on throughout, each for different clients and performed by different people, and each with a different purpose. This contributed to the programme's high cost – an important factor to take into account when planning an evaluation strategy.

When to evaluate?

This will depend on why the evaluation is being carried out, and on resource available for the exercise. If the purpose of evaluation is simply to validate learning outcomes at the end of the event, then assessment of learning achieved against original learning objectives, using a method agreed by the parties, will suffice. However that is rarely meaningful enough. Some measure of retention and use of learning is normally needed, and that argues for evaluation to be repeated at least once again, back in the workplace. In the CD programme it was an even longer-term evaluation that provided some of the most useful and surprising information, as the final part of the case at the end of this chapter recounts.

To evaluate in depth using sophisticated methods at several different points in time will always be costly, and rarely justified. A simple form of monitoring at intervals, together with a one or two-stage detailed evaluation is far more likely to be affordable and productive. No template can be laid down to suit all situations, however.

How to evaluate?

This is the challenging technical question. There are innumerable models of evaluation, that produced by Kirkpatrick (1960) being the most well-known. But all generic models must be tailored to fit specific needs, and even Kirkpatrick does not always suit context.

Where evaluation is being carried out to measure return on investment – always a tricky subject when applied to training and learning initiatives – Jack Phillips is an expert whose evaluation process has been used in companies worldwide (Phillips and Phillips 2001). He has produced a useful factsheet to summarise it (Phillips 2001). However it is important not to become preoccupied with technical detail at the expense of common sense: a simple, pragmatic approach designed by in-house staff can often provide all the crucial information and perspectives needed. If it has been produced in collaboration with key partners, that alone will give it the credibility that any evaluation process and methodology needs if its results are to lead to useful future action. The most sophisticated and well-known models, on the other hand, will have no value if their findings fail to gain acceptance in the organisation.

Some of the most useful work on evaluation was done many years ago by Warr and colleagues (1970) and by Hamblin (1974). Warr and his co-authors designed a CIRO framework that answers the question 'What aspects of training or learning should be evaluated?' They argued for a fourfold evaluation framework to review not only the results of a programme but also the whole training effort, beginning with training analysis. They stressed the need for evaluation to be a continuous process, planned at the outset and continuing throughout the learning cycle, not merely used as a post-training activity.

The four dimensions of their framework are:

- *context* within which the learning event has taken place
- *inputs* to the learning event
- *reactions* to the learning event
- *outcomes* of the learning event.

Context of the learning event

This involves establishing how accurately needs were initially diagnosed, why it was decided to introduce this particular event, the rationale for its purpose and objectives, what was done to prepare its path in the organisation, and especially what kind of support it was given by managers of the learners and in the learners' workplace. Recording the answers to these questions at the time they are tackled will provide the basic information against which, after the event, an evaluation can be made. That evaluation will provide a holistic view on all the ground-preparing activity that underpinned a programme, and will identify in retrospect weaknesses and strengths that may not have been apparent at the time the activity was being undertaken.

Inputs to the learning event

Here the concern is to identify what resources – human, financial and material – were needed and made available to meet training and learning requirements, and the ways in which they were used to achieve learning objectives. It involves determining how those resources were chosen and used, and how far decisions were based on sufficiently sound, accurate information. Again, records should be kept at the time to aid this evaluation. If a business case is produced at the outset of the planning process, as suggested in Stage 1 (Chapter 6), with notes kept thereafter of costs that are actually incurred and of changes in decisions made together with identification of reasons, this will be a crucial aid to evaluation. For example, in the CD programme concerns about the action learning component led to a particularly careful identification of its costs as they built up – an exercise that the team discovered is rarely carried out and that proved both revealing and disturbing when hidden costs as well as direct costs were taken into the equation.

Apart from the normal L&D staffing costs involved in any planned learning intervention, some high-cost areas of a major learning initiative or process include:

- Resources used to meet learning needs (time, money, staff and expertise, physical accommodation, materials, and the natural learning resources in the organisation).
- The cost of the chosen learning strategy and the infrastructure it requires (a factor that makes e-learning a far more expensive approach than many realise).
- The costs of lost opportunity time of learners and staff – not always essential to cost out, but in a major off-the-job event such costs can be a critical factor, especially when participants are in high-paid positions where any absence from work can create a range of problems with ripple effects spreading across the organisation.

Reactions to the learning event

This involves discovering the learners' perceptions of the event – their immediate reactions to it. Establishing what people feel, as distinct (often) from what outcomes have actually been achieved, is vital. Those views will influence others, including future potential participants, and will explain any motivational problems or successes during the event. It also involves discovering the reactions of other parties directly involved in or with the learning event, and comparing them with the reactions it was hoped the event would achieve.

In a major new programme it may be important to initially monitor reactions after every session of an event, or after every key element, or – in a modular programme – at the end of every module. What must be avoided is an indiscriminate use of 'happy sheets' that provide no value and are seen by no-one outside the course team. The identification of reactions must be tied to a significant purpose, and the information must be put to use to guide future planning. Otherwise, the exercise is pointless.

Outcomes of the learning event

This involves assessing what actually happened as a result of a learning event. Hamblin (1974) provided a detailed structure for this kind of evaluation, but he underlined the problems and practical difficulties that are involved at each of the following levels. Again, decisions need to be made well in advance of an event as to which levels matter most in the specific case.

An enquiry could cover the following four levels, but it is rare for such a comprehensive evaluation to be necessary. The broader and higher the level, the greater the range of intervening variables that could explain any changes in behaviour and performance, and the more difficult therefore to tie learning achieved to ultimate impact on the organisation:

- *The learner level*: this involves recalling the reactions of the learners and establishing whatever changes can be objectively ascertained in the their knowledge, skills and attitudes at the completion of the training. Those then need to be compared with levels that were recorded at the start of the programme (by techniques such as appraisal, tests, repertory grids, etc). What is being carried out is a validation of learning achieved against learning objectives set – it therefore presupposes that all the pre-event information it requires was in fact collected and recorded at the time. Warr and colleagues (1970) refer to measurement at this level as to do with 'immediate outcomes'.

- *The workplace level*: this involves identifying changes that take place in the learner's job behaviour back in the workplace. These can be measured by appraisal, observation, discussion with the learners' managers/peers/customers/clients, and performance records, as well as by the reactions of the learners themselves and how far these are in line with the views of others about that performance. At this level what is being identified is impact of learning on job performance. Warr and colleagues (1970) refer to measurement at this level as to do with 'intermediate outcomes'.

- *The team/department/unit level*: this involves identifying changes that take place in team working and in the learners' department or unit as a result of a learning event. What is being explored here is the wider impact of learners' changed behaviour and performance (whether favourable or unfavourable) in the workplace. Measures might cover changes in departmental output, costs, scrap rates, absenteeism, turnover, or accident frequency; improvement in productivity rates, labour costs, absenteeism and turnover rates.

- *The organisational level*: this involves identifying changes that take place in the organisation as a whole after the completion of the training programme and that appear strongly related to that programme. These could include a shift in organisational culture, more flexibility and reduced levels of conflict in relation to the introduction of change, enhanced ability to attract and retain valued workers, improved levels of employee commitment – all difficult to measure because of the number of intervening variables. Warr and colleagues refer to measurement of both departmental and organisational level impact as to do with 'ultimate' outcomes –those that cause changes in the functioning of the organisation. They can take time to emerge, and that is where longer-term evaluation becomes an important issue.

The evaluation process

It is important to distinguish between an evaluation framework (such as CIRO) with its associated techniques, and an evaluation process. The latter is the way in which the whole evaluation activity is handled. It represents the approach whereby L&D practitioners can continue to achieve external consistency.

Six factors can help to ensure an effective evaluation process:

1. *Ensure a clear purpose and objectives for the event*. Without these, meaningful evaluation will be impossible.
2. *Plan the evaluation collaboratively and well in advance* of the event, gaining agreement on measurement methods, timescale, resources and practical arrangements that will be involved. This is not only to ensure the commitment of partners to evaluation and their agreement on methods, but also because keeping the evaluative task to the fore throughout the planning and design stages will ensure that information

is gathered and collected throughout that period that will enhance the chances of effective evaluation ultimately.

3. *Identify strategic milestones* for the event, working backwards from the timing of its completion (when its final objectives should have been achieved) to its inception. This will aid both monitoring and evaluation subsequently.

4. *Identify performance standards* related to interim and final learning objectives in order to decide how the achievement of outcomes related to each milestone is to be measured. If they do not enable meaningful evaluation to be done, change them.

5. *Monitor the learning process,* using the strategic milestones already agreed. This will enable information to be shared with key parties at each stage. They can then become involved in decisions about any adjustments that may be needed to the programme or its organisational context in order that the next milestone can be met.

6. *Ensure feedback of outcomes* to the key parties in order to influence the planning of future events. The results of an evaluation process can go far beyond validation of a particular programme. Bee and Farmer (1995) described how a study that started life as a simple training evaluation task became an exercise in helping the management of change at London Underground.

Many years ago the following observation appeared in a key text on training and development (Kenny et al 1979):

> **'The majority of training ... takes place in a busy work setting and a rigorous scientific approach to evaluation ... although very desirable, is not practicable. However, if adequate resources are not made available for evaluation purposes, the effectiveness of training will remain unchecked. This is the dilemma.'**

To resolve it, the authors urged a pragmatic approach, flexible to the needs of the situation. That message remains valid today.

To complete this section and chapter, here is the final part of the case of the clinical directors' programme. Although the account focuses mainly on evaluation methods, issues of partnership remain critically important. They illustrate how essential it was long after the programme had ended to maintain the active support of all the stakeholders.

CASE EXAMPLE
The clinical directors' programme: Part 2

Because of its strategic importance nationally and regionally the programme was evaluated by two universities outside the region on behalf of the Northern Regional Health Authority (NRHA) and the Management Executive (ME). It was also monitored continuously by the programme staff at the NRHA and at DUBS. The latter used daily reaction sheets for the critical first module – the Management Foundation Course – to test perceptions of and reactions to the achievement of module objectives, and to its delivery and content. Subsequently, they distributed questionnaires only at the end of each module, testing reactions to each main component. This elicited essential information while avoiding what otherwise would have been an excess of evaluation activity.

Finally, DUBS staff organised a detailed evaluation exercise near the end of the programme in September 1993 and a longer-term evaluation in February 1995, both linked to review seminars. On each of these occasions evaluative data were obtained not only in the form of opinions from the key parties but also from specific examples provided by the clinical director (CD) participants and their managers of changes in knowledge, attitudes, behaviour and performance in their roles since attending the programme, and their perceived causes.

The information obtained demonstrated that the stakeholders had a shared perception of the purpose and objectives set for the programme, and that for the overwhelming majority both purpose and objectives were valuable and had been satisfactorily achieved. Caution must, of course, be exercised at this point. Distortions can be caused by biases of evaluators, by timing, by the design of questionnaires, and by concerns over who would see the evaluations and to what use they would put the data. That said, evidence of the programme's perceived effectiveness was wide-ranging and came from multiple sources through time.

Of particular significance was the impact of the longer-term evaluation exercise in relation to assessing the value of the action-learning (AL) component. In longer-term evaluation questionnaires, four CDs cited AL as one of the most valuable elements of the programme. The strategic role of these clinicians had steadily expanded since the conclusion of the programme. For three of them it had been fully supported by their organisational context where they received encouragement, support and, often, further training and development to fully practise that role in line with their new learning. For the fourth, the organisational context had been less favourable but by February 1995 it was at last changing in a positive way.

Of the eight other CDs who by then were also in markedly more strategic roles, but who had made no comment on AL, four rated the programme's formal modules highly, although their learning had not subsequently been supported by their organisational contexts; and one saw the programme's unique value in its 'focused, small-group, safe environment to explore and experience issues away from work'. Three had been critical of AL in their earlier evaluations. Both of the clinicians who were not by then in more strategic roles failed to mention AL in their long-term evaluations.

This information indicates the critical importance of a supportive and developmental organisational context in ensuring the long-term positive impact of an AL period. It demonstrates the unique value of obtaining evaluations at some stage after the completion of a learning event. Had the evaluation process stopped on completion of the CD programme, perceptions of the value and impact of the AL component would have been quite different, and the planners would have been reluctant to use AL again in a similar programme, given its high cost in relation to the benefits evident at that point.

Sources: HARRISON, R. (1996a); HARRISON, R. and MILLER, S. (1999)

CONCLUSION

In this chapter I have explained and discussed the final four stages of the eight-stage process for organising learning events that was introduced in Chapter 6. You should by now have a sound understanding of those stages and be able to tackle the review questions contained in Appendix 3.

The chapter's four sections have covered the following main ground:

- *Stage 5: Selecting the learners.* Selection of learners should be a process shared between the organisers of a learning event or process and the client or clients. In real life, however, the process may be taken out of the hands of the event's organisers. This will raise a particular need for them to work with business partners in identifying any difficulties generated by the selection process that are likely to rebound on the learning event, and to tailor learning design as best they can to meet and overcome those difficulties.
- *Stage 6: Finalising strategy and designing the learning event.* The need to work with business partners is particularly important when choosing a relevant and feasible learning strategy for the event, since it must be appropriately resourced and have a secure infrastructure of technical support and human resource practices. The event's design should be informed by a sound understanding of learning theory in order to stimulate the learners and ensure an effective and motivating learning process.
- *Stage 7: Delivering the event.* Flexibility should be built into the delivery process in order to respond to unexpected contingencies. A positive resolution of any problems will again rely on a partnership process, which by now should incorporate the learners.
- *Stage 8: Monitoring and evaluating the event.* Although monitoring and evaluation are shown last in the 8-stage process, both processes need to be planned during its first stage, gaining the commitment of all stakeholders and ensuring adequate record-keeping throughout. Agreement must be obtained to the purpose of both activities and on how and when to carry them out.

In this chapter and Chapter 6 I have proposed a process to aid the effective organisation of planned learning interventions. Such interventions of course form a major part of an L&D professional's work. Equally important, however, is the need to promote and facilitate continuous informal learning and knowledge creation in the workplace. That task is the subject of the next chapter.

Further information sources

BRAMLEY, P. (2003) *Evaluating training.* 2nd edn. London: Chartered Institute of Personnel and Development.

CHRISTIAN-CARTER, J. (2001) *Mastering instructional design in technology-based training.* London: Chartered Institute of Personnel and Development.

SIMMONDS, D. (2004) *Designing and delivering training.* London: Chartered Institute of Personnel and Development.

Also a highly informative site about learning processes, activities and aids: http://reviewing.co.uk/_links.htm#tools [accessed 4 October 2004].

Promoting Workplace Learning and Knowledge

INTRODUCTION

Following on from our discussion in the previous chapter, it is natural now to discuss the role of L&D professionals in promoting workplace learning and the creation of organisationally valuable knowledge.

Rylatt (2004) has proposed three 'simple questions' for any business to continually explore:

- What makes my business truly outstanding?
- What capabilities does my business generate that make it extraordinary and hard to copy?
- How can we sustain this advantage?

The answers, increasingly, lie in an organisation's know how and the people who produce it. The learning they achieve in the workplace, the knowledge that flows from that, and the extent to which that knowledge is shared across the organisation to be successfully applied to continuous improvement and radical innovation can provide the 'extraordinary capabilities' to which Rylatt refers.

However, behind these apparently straightforward statements there is uncertainty. What kind of workplace learning is envisaged here? What exactly is knowledge, and how can an organisation manage it in order to ensure that it is used to the advantage of the business?

This four-part chapter starts with a discussion of some notions of knowledge and of meanings attached to the term 'knowledge management'. The second section looks at the concept of a learning organisation and the contribution that such an organisation might make to knowledge creation, using the corporate university as a prototype. I then discuss basic building blocks for a knowledge-productive organisation. I conclude by outlining some international comparisons in the promotion of workplace learning, identifying implications for leaders, managers and L&D professionals.

NOTIONS OF KNOWLEDGE

Some definitions

Notions of knowledge are widely debated and emerge from a bewildering variety of theories. Classification systems, models and concepts are overlapping and are applied in differing ways by theorists. There are no clear-cut boundaries between the various schools of thought, nor is it invariably the case that the most meaningful theories are those produced most recently. We may have more information about 'knowledge' now, but that does not necessarily mean that we understand the subject any better than we did decades ago. Consider the following definitions:

'*Knowledge*: tacit and explicit mental models, beliefs and perspectives that influence perceptions and behaviour (after Polanyi 1966).

Knowledge: representations of facts (including generalizations) and concepts organized for future use, including problem-solving (Gregory 1998).'

Why are these definitions so different? In Chapter 4 we saw that in the traditional view of learning in organisations that was prevalent throughout most of the twentieth century, knowledge was regarded as a type of commodity – something 'out there' to be searched out and acquired, assessed, codified and distributed across the organisation, often through training. This explains Gregory's interpretation, which is lodged in a view of the world as an objective external entity, and of knowledge as a body of 'facts', truths, that explains the world.

We then saw that a relational notion of learning suggests an alternative view of knowledge: as the outcome of a distinctively social learning process, and as a process in itself. This notion of knowledge distinguishes it – as traditional notions do not – from information. Materials such as books, papers, lectures, presentations and handouts represent the knowledge of others. For the individuals who receive or access them, however, they are no more than blocks of information. Each collects, makes sense of and organises that information in a unique way, constructing individual knowledge through a learning process that is part to do with internal intellectual and emotional activity, part to do with social interactions.

Through using e-technology individuals can construct a wealth of new knowledge for themselves from an extensive bank of information. But the nature of that knowledge will still differ significantly from one person to the next. Prior knowledge, learning skills, the individual's interests and focus of attention and their ongoing relations with others – all will act as filters in their knowledge process.

Nonaka (1991) builds on Polanyi's definition to explain knowledge as a two-dimensional concept:

- *Tacit knowledge* is the knowledge that is embedded deep in the individual or collective subconscious, expressing itself in habitual or intuitive ways of doing things that are exercised without conscious thought or effort.
- *Explicit knowledge* is the knowledge that, once articulated, is written down, codified in protocols, guidelines, checklists, reports, memoranda, files, training courses or other tangible forms. At that point, it does indeed become a type of commodity, to be protected in patents and other legal formulae.

Nonaka sees tacit and explicit knowledge combining in a learning spiral to form new knowledge. This view unifies the concept of knowledge as a process (the tacit dimension) with knowledge as a commodity or resource (the explicit dimension). While not all agree with his concept it does highlight the way in which an individual's understanding of what to do and how to do it is often intuitive. An employee may be unable to express to others what explains their skilled performance, but others may still learn by observing them as they perform. The knowledge remains tacit but becomes shared across a wider community. Once tacit knowledge is made explicit it still has value for the organisation, but it also becomes vulnerable to copying and to poaching – and the individual loses exclusive ownership of it unless protecting it by patent, copyright or similar device.

This way of viewing knowledge creates a problematic scenario for management. Knowledge as process cannot be owned by the company, as tangible assets can. Individuals own it and have to want and agree to put it at the service of others. Therefore it cannot be 'managed'. It can only be encouraged, facilitated and rewarded.

REFLECTION

How far do you think that your own organisation – or the part of it with which you are most familiar – relies on tacit as well as explicit knowledge to guide its operations? And how much value do you see being placed on informal workplace learning as distinct from trained skills?

Knowledge management

What then is meant by knowledge management? Research shows a considerable range of perspectives held by different organisations here (Scarbrough et al 1999, p34). In some, especially financial institutions, knowledge is valued as intellectual capital. In some, it is exploited as intellectual property and viewed as a commodity that is essential to competitive strategy (eg pharmaceutical organisations). Some codified, explicit knowledge is of such value to an organisation that it has to be managed as a legal entity, often with property rights (for example, patents, copyright and licences). Some may be so sensitive that access to it has to be restricted. Others again may relate to particular jobs, positions, tasks or functions and so may need to be recorded in training and personnel manuals (Hall 1996). On the other hand for many organisations it is important to capture the knowledge gained from learning that has taken place in individual projects and in everyday work activity, spreading it through the organisation to promote continuous improvement and innovation.

Skapinker (2002) has avoided the difficulty of defining what knowledge matters most to an organisation by expressing knowledge management in terms of the outcome it seeks:

'Knowledge management means using the ideas and experience of employees, customers and suppliers to improve the organisation's performance.'

I have just argued that while explicit knowledge can be managed, the tacit process of knowledge creation cannot. Skapinker's type of knowledge management, however, can be achieved in large part by a workplace climate that encourages and facilitates teamwork, informal meetings and discussions, exchanges of views and observations of internal best practice (Hall 1996). When uniquely valuable tacit knowledge is shared in this way it becomes embedded in a number of people rather than a few, while still remaining tacit. Many small, flexible firms are characterised by this kind of knowledge process.

The impact of new technology

New information and communication technology (ICT) is already shifting office work increasingly away from data-processing towards various forms of knowledge management. Client-server technologies can deliver an individual's desktop and files to an employee wherever they log on to the network, while hotdesking, homeworking, remote offices and client-based desking are all the result of technologies 'that break down the physical structures and rebuild them in an online world' (Rooney 2003). New communication systems enable workers to prioritise their workflow and Instant Messaging has the potential to replace email as the most widely used method of corporate communication, giving team workers the control as to when and how to reply. Looking at such developments we can recall the discussion in Chapter 4 about a new age made possible by a more knowledge-based economy: an age when all an organisation's employees rather than just the specialists could become its knowledge workers, and increasingly need to be so.

Yet while technology may be changing the ways in which people work and redefining what work is (Rooney 2003), this is not necessarily leading organisations to become more knowledge-creative – simply to individuals becoming smarter in how they perform. Individuals' knowledge does not necessarily produce organisational knowledge.

Organisations are complex social institutions. Across them, professional and occupational networks can have a positive or negative influence on the knowledge process. Within them, formal and informal networks can operate in a similar way. In a highly segmented labour force operating in an organisation applying differentiated HR practices, work communities will be disposed to hoard rather than share knowledge. Often they will be unaware of, or uninterested in, any wider quest for knowledge than that likely to improve earnings, job-retention prospects or bargaining strengths.

Many companies are now concerned about how easy it is to lose knowledge, especially in the wake of downsizing. For them, new technology seems the obvious way to capture knowledge and spread it around the organisation, minimising the damage caused by departure of individuals. Knowledge management tools can be used in three broad areas (Merali 1999):

- To provide banks of information that enable employers to record and access explicit knowledge across the organisation
- To provide access to data across boundaries.
- To allow groups of people to interact and create new knowledge, through virtual communities where they can share expertise and tacit knowledge.

In relation to the first two points, a study by Rice and colleagues (2000) of an inter-organisational virtual engineering team indicated that sharing knowledge when using ICT requires the development of a common language, and that team members may prefer face-to-face or phone contact when seeking to resolve fundamental differences of opinion. The researchers found that ICT mainly served as an information repository. It operated as a support in exchanging ideas, opinions and preferences in the team and also facilitated developing shared cognitions. But when it came to knowledge construction there seemed to be a need for a human mediating process to facilitate, motivate and essentially reinforce group identity and purpose.

Many such studies confirm that it is the third of Merali's points that is the most problematic (Merali 1999, p62):

> **'No technology will be successfully exploited if people are not willing to use it. Collaborative tools and intranet forums are unlikely to work if the culture doesn't favour the sharing of information.... The one thing you must do before shopping for the tools is be clear about the knowledge management capabilities you will need in your organisations.'**

The following is a relevant case. You may find it helpful to identify the lessons that you learn from it. Comments follow at its end.

CASE EXAMPLE

Knowledge management at Multicorp

Multicorp is the pseudonym for a multinational food producer. In 1995 its product development department introduced the Lotus Notes groupware system, with an associated method of using it called 'the funnel'. The initiative aimed to help around 1,000 company users across the world to pool information in real time about their progress on various projects. It was hoped that it would encourage them to surface and share their tacit as well as explicit knowledge by explaining their informal work practices in writing. At a more fundamental level the aim was to aid the transformation of a functional work environment where people tended to operate mainly on an individual basis to one where employees networked in teams operating across functional boundaries.

These aims were not realised. The initiative was imposed from the top with the main emphasis on its technical features. Employees received training on those but there was no parallel move to develop a knowledge-sharing culture and so no one was prepared for the organisational implications of this major change. Three years after the introduction of the initiative the company was still organised along functional lines despite an increasing emphasis on the need for cross-functional working and collective performance. Human resource practices of reward, selection and training were still focused on individual role-specific competencies, not on the newer capabilities that were needed.

Why did knowledge-sharing fail?

Many factors came together to explain the failure of the initiative. One was that Multicorp's employees were located all over the world, yet whether or not English was their first language they all had to write out their thoughts in that language. Another was that even native English speakers sometimes found it difficult or too time-consuming to formalise in writing their ongoing work experiences and tentative thinking. When they did, much of the essence was often lost. Other barriers to knowledge-sharing included differences in national cultures, power struggles, strong departmental identities and the perceived strategic value of information. At the individual level the researchers found that employees preferred to communicate in traditional ways rather than through 'the funnel', and also that they seemed unwilling to divulge to those in other functions information about work in progress or about incomplete ideas. Most simply shared information about progress already achieved.

Source: PATRIOTTA, G. (1999) With acknowledgements to the CIPD

Comments

- The main message from this study is the confirmation that knowledge cannot be 'managed'. It can only be stimulated and its sharing facilitated.
- Sharing knowledge changes it. Attempting to write down tacit knowledge can result in the loss of the very aspects that are most likely to be the source of its uniqueness.
- One person's knowledge is no more than another's information. What matters is what kind of sense people make of that information and what they perceive its significant elements to be. Two people or 10,000 may read this chapter, but the knowledge they develop from it will be different in every case.
- Unless organisational context is changed to facilitate the introduction of a major new initiative of this kind it is most unlikely to succeed. It needs the support of organisational leadership and vision, management actions, and conducive HR strategies.

THE LEARNING ORGANISATION

What is it?

What, then, is the way forward if organisations are to become more knowledge-creative? Some would argue that it is through developing learning organisations, defined as those that facilitate the learning of all their members and that continuously transform themselves (Pedler et al 1991).

Such a statement suggests that organisations have a life of their own and are themselves capable of learning (Matthews and Candy 1999, p52). This is not the case. Only people learn, and we have just seen that spreading the learning of individuals or groups across the organisation in order to develop some kind of collective learning capability needs carefully planned processes and systems – it does not happen of its own accord. Even when new technology is drafted in to aid the process, the Multicorp case is only one of many to show that collective learning and knowledge sharing may still fail to occur. Organisations comprise many diverse and often conflicting human needs and interests. These do not conveniently converge in the common pursuit of an overriding organisational goal, or goals. To assume that they do, or will do always do so if provided with enough rational systems and procedures, is to overlook an inconvenient but stubborn reality.

In recent years there has been a reformulation of the learning organisation model (Burgoyne 1999). This new approach to the 'learning organisation' encompasses as key principles the following (Miller and Stewart 1999, p43):

- Learning and business strategy are closely linked.
- The organisation consciously learns from business opportunities and threats.
- Individuals, groups and the whole organisation are not only learning, but also continually learning how to learn.

- Information systems and technology serve to support learning rather than to control it.
- There are well-developed processes for defining, creating, capturing, sharing and acting on knowledge.
- These various systems and dimensions are balanced and managed as a whole.

Corporate universities

But how can such principles be put into practice? What would this kind of learning organisation look like? One model may be a type of corporate university. This is worth exploring here because corporate universities have moved on from being a novel fad to something approaching a significant trend, notably in large organisations that invest heavily in education and learning of their employees and that can harness sophisticated knowledge management systems to that cause.

Corporate universities began in North America. They offer a different kind of educational experience to that provided by university business schools, being tailored to the specific and immediate needs of the organisation and giving it a unique edge. However business schools increasingly welcome them and often work with them in highly effective boundary-crossing learning partnerships. Each partner is able to offer skills, experiences, perspectives and learning approaches that complement those of the other.

In corporate universities the main emphasis is on employees constantly engaging with learning and on educators designing courses that will continuously motivate them, usually and sometimes solely in a virtual environment. With knowledge in today's businesses falling rapidly out of date and needing constant renewal, employees must acquire the skill and support to learn continually rather than periodically. A corporate university that offers that facility is regarded by its investors as an ideal, and perhaps in future an essential, way of transferring knowledge fast, applying it to the business and nurturing intellectual capital. Siemens ICN established its corporate university at a time when it was undergoing a major technological transformation that required an enormous injection of learning on a continual basis in a short space of time for a widely dispersed sales force and customer base. Learning done via laptops had to be quickly applied to customer needs. With its university any employee with the knowledge needed can become an instructor who transfers his or her knowledge to other employees across the country.

The example I next describe is Unipart U, one of the best-known corporate universities. It will be helpful to identify how far it appears to meet the new criteria (above) for a learning organisation. A commentary follows at the end of the case. It is longer than usual because I relate it to each criterion in turn.

CASE EXAMPLE

Unipart University

Unipart is a UK motor components firm whose corporate slogan 'the Unipart Way' is associated with one of the best-known business success stories of the past couple of decades. It also embraces logistics, distribution and manufacturing across a variety of sectors – rail and health services included. John Neill, chief executive, has a large personal shareholding in Unipart and as a result of a buy-in in 1987 the company is owned by a partnership of employees, directors and institutional backers.

The corporate university

Unipart U, conceived by Neill, opened in 1993 as the company's in-house university and its core learning function, with Unipart's business divisions also being the University's faculties. It is a multi-million-pound complex of state-of-the-art lecture halls and computerised learning centres in the heart of the Unipart group's headquarters building at Cowley, near Oxford and serves all the company's 10,000 or so employees.

Unipart U was set up for one simple, commercial reason: the company needed to become much more competitive. Through early venture alliances with Honda and Toyota especially it realised how much it had to learn about quality and productivity. Neill decided to package the learning from those alliances to share it throughout the group. He also wanted to incorporate it in virtual lectures to suppliers to drive home the need for them to make continuous cost-down, quality-up and related improvements, and to provide them with frameworks for doing this.

In 2000 Unipart invested heavily in online training courses designed to speed up the pace of learning and to slash training costs by 20 per cent. This has been extremely successful. Employees can access training on their laptops at their workstations, or learn from home using the University for Industry's website. They can learn in bite-sized chunks rapidly, efficiently, in a location of their choice.

The university as an engine of growth

Some corporate universities are little more than e-training and e-learning centres on a grand scale. They focus mainly on specific skills training or, for those programmes that are addressed to senior executives, on specific business issues. For Neill, Unipart U is not a training centre. It is the engine to drive the company's future growth. One of its main tasks is to stimulate and support knowledge-sharing. A huge investment in information and communication technology (ICT) has enabled the company to bring structured, just-in-time learning and knowledge-building facility to the manufacturing side of the business through its 'Faculty on the Floor' initiative. This comprises computer learning and information retrieval centres often built beside assembly lines. There, employees can access sophisticated ICT systems to rapidly teach themselves about new ways to apply lean management manufacturing principles, identify opportunities for process improvements, test them out, and then record and communicate their innovations electronically to others. Unipart U's faculties are now open to outside companies, to enable them to tap into its lean manufacturing expertise.

The learning organisation

Unipart U is intended to produce strategic advantages by providing faster learning than the competition. For management, it is a way of linking continuous workplace learning to the sharing of its results across the organisation in order to improve performance and thereby support business needs. This is why Unipart calls itself a learning organisation (Miller and Stewart 1999). At Unipart strategy development hinges on 'policy deployment', and the University enables management's ideas to be quickly sent down the line with responses from employees sent back up so that their learning can inform strategy. Such responses would usually receive feedback. The major link between learning and strategy is through Neill, supported by the top management team. Miller and Stewart, however, found that although people had access to organisational knowledge at an operational level there was less evidence that they had access to strategic plans, or to the information necessary for possible future career moves.

The commercial arm

In 2000 the company established a commercial arm to develop, market and sell knowledge-based products and consultancy. It offers four 'proven frameworks for personal and organisational development' to provide a 'structured route map for clients' (Unipart U website).

In 2001 the company was named by The Vision 100 Awards (a list of the most visionary public and private sector organisations in the UK, compiled by BT and the Cranfield School of Management) as winner of the award in the category of organisational transformation – a category for organisations whose vision has produced unexpected outcomes and so allowed them to adopt radically successful ways of working (Unipart U website).

Sources: MILLER, R. and STEWART, J. (1999). Also Unipart University's website at http://www.unipart.com/learning/lea_0100.htm [accessed 8 September 2004] and the *Financial Times*' website at: http://specials.ft.com/businesseducation/march2002/FT32ELSR2ZC.html [accessed 8 September 2004].

Comments

This account, from a number of sources, does convince that Unipart meets the new LO criteria to a degree – but the misses are perhaps more significant than the hits and because of the importance of the LO concept it is worth exploring why:

Learning and business strategy are closely linked

This seems unlikely. Unipart's part-ownership by employees means that top management must be attentive to their views, but how far those views meaningfully shape policy or strategy is unclear. From Miller and Stewart's account, shop floor employees' role seems to be about implementing operational plans in the workplace and achieving continuous improvement and total quality there.

The organisation consciously learns from business opportunities and threats

This is unproven. Employees have access to superb learning and informational facilities in order to continuously improve their knowledge of business products and processes in ways that will improve their performance. They are able to rapidly transmit information about the improvements they achieve to others in order to spread best practice. But to what extent is this 'learning from business opportunities and threats'? It seems doubtful that most employees have access to the kind of information that would involve except as it relates to the immediate operational level.

Individuals, groups and the whole organisation are not only learning, but also continually learning how to learn

It is clear that every opportunity and facility is provided, and indeed considerable pressure applied, for this to happen at individual level and within local communities of practice. How far it happens across those communities, let alone at any truly collective level, is not clear. What would be the measures for any collective learning? How would it be achieved and what would be its focus? What would it look like? Individual and workgroup learning does not of itself produce organisational learning or change organisational behaviour.

Information systems and technology serve to support learning rather than to control it

In so far as a great bulk of the learning and indeed the driving rationale for the University still seems to be about training or learning for strict and immediate business needs, ICT systems and technology clearly support learning, but also significantly control it. Employees are fully enabled and encouraged to share their learning with others. But whether the ICT facility to do so is little more than a mass of online community websites organised in learning streams with random postings is unclear. It is also unclear what kind of process there may be for collecting, analysing and converting such postings into a central knowledge base.

There are well-developed processes for defining, creating, capturing, sharing and acting on knowledge

There is clear evidence of such processes but not of their precise outcomes. Miller and Stewart in their article admitted that they had not been able to research any views of shop floor workers on their one-day visit to Unipart. Information is needed to clarify: What kind of knowledge has in fact been processed in these ways? How exactly is tacit knowledge surfaced and shared? Why is the company's aim (as expressed on its website) to convert it, once captured, into explicit knowledge rather than to retain some at least in tacit form, shared across a wider virtual community?

These various systems and dimensions are balanced and managed as a whole

What is striking about the information on the Unipart U website is the extremely systematic way in which all the information processing and knowledge management tools, techniques and systems have been produced, marketed and made available to internal and external customers. The technical systems and dimensions to spread lean manufacturing management principles and ensure their expert usage have been designed with a high degree of innovation and precision. But without more knowledge of the workplace culture of the company and its HR policies and practices the answer to one major question is unclear: are the learning practices at Unipart deeply embedded and sustainable? Miller and Stewart found in 1999 that the whole initiative relied critically on one or two key and senior individuals, especially the chief executive. On the website Neill's still seems the dominating influence.

Is Unipart a learning organisation or is it also a knowledge-productive one?

In the corporate library of Unipart U a notice on the wall describes the university's concept of learning as (Miller and Stewart 1999):

> **'The exchange and development of ideas, knowledge and experience leading to improved personal and professional performance.'**

It is a curiously conservative statement. And this, in a nutshell, is precisely the concern that many have about the learning organisation concept. If even partly put into practice it can be a powerful driver of individual and of team learning and can lead to the creation of systems to aid knowledge sharing. But to share knowledge is not the same as to create it. A learning organisation is always going to be an aspiration rather than a full-blown reality – but even as an aspiration the concept falls short of providing a recipe for a truly knowledge-productive organisation.

I have mentioned that term before but it is helpful to recall its meaning here: an organisation where there is an approach to the processes of work and learning that leads to the expansion of existing knowledge and the generation of new knowledge for the organisation (Kessels 1996).

BUILDING A KNOWLEDGE-PRODUCTIVE ORGANISATION

Basic building blocks

To be a knowledge-productive organisation, a few obvious things must be done extremely well. The director of knowledge management at Thames Water described the strategy for gaining profit from its employees' knowledge as resting on four key building blocks (Lank and Windle 2003):

- *Make knowledge visible.* As part of this Thames Water has produced an internal electronic directory that helps people to find required expertise and share personal interests.
- *Increase knowledge intensity.* One key initiative was to launch cross-boundary knowledge-sharing communities early in 2002. To take two examples: one community consists of a group of professionals who share with others their knowledge on bidding, contracts and negotiations; another is of experts who share ideas on how to avoid water diversion and loss.
- *Create a knowledge infrastructure.* Each community starts with a facilitated initiation and design workshop, where members agree the scope and mission of the group, terms of membership and how they will use the electronic 'team rooms' that enable them to share information worldwide. Communities are thereafter largely self-organising and responsible for deciding how often they need to meet and what business issues to focus on. For example, a project-sifting methodology developed in the Middle East was put into immediate use in the USA.
- *Develop a knowledge culture.* Like Tesco, Thames Water explicitly encourages knowledge sharing behaviour in company value statements reinforced in core training and education programmes.

The process to build these blocks is as important as the blocks themselves. It rests on three principles:

- Have a simple communicable message of what better knowledge management can achieve for the company.
- Don't underestimate the stakeholders, both as enablers and blockers of knowledge management.
- Concentrate on the people aspects, not on IT systems.

The emphasis is therefore on an easy to explain, easy to operate and people-centred approach. Here follows an example of a knowledge-productive organisation that makes an illuminating comparison with the Unipart case. Again it is by no means a typical example. It is important to realise that there can be none such. All organisations in the new knowledge economy have to find their own unique ways of organising and strategising precisely because they are in a novel environment where learning through doing is the only reliable way to make progress.

There is no commentary on this case. It is information for you to use in order to construct your own understanding of key features of knowledge-productive organisations. However it is particularly relevant to identify the contribution of L&D activity to knowledge creation in the company, and how that activity is integrated with other HR practices. You can bring your knowledge of this case up to date by visiting Buckman Laboratories' website at http://www.knowledge-nurture.com.

CASE EXAMPLE

Learning and knowledge processes at Buckman Laboratories

The KM initiatives

Buckman Laboratories is a US-owned global chemical company. In 1989 Bob Buckman, the company's chief executive, pledged that knowledge would become the foundation of his company's competitive edge. The change strategy introduced in 1992 involved using new technology to capture and manage knowledge and innovative thinking. From the start managers realised that three factors would be critical to the knowledge management (KM) programme: advanced information technology (IT), continuous culture change, and KM-focused HRM. The technical KM initiatives were planned to emerge over time, giving flexibility to respond to new contingencies in internal and external environments.

The IT system

The KM programme is facilitated by a K'Netix network introduced in 1993. This network enables electronic sharing of knowledge between the company's 1,300 associates and from them to customers in over 90 countries. The systems connect knowledge bases worldwide to create a company knowledge base, achieved through three customer focused forums and four regional focused forums to encourage group problem-solving and sharing of new ideas and knowledge. Two technical departments are responsible for design and ongoing management of the IT network. The monitoring and processing of the knowledge generated within the forums are overseen by forum specialists and industry section leaders.

Cultural change

Traditionally Buckman was a hierarchical company where employees hoarded knowledge, with middle managers the gatekeepers. Control of scarce information was a key to power. Changing this culture was a difficult task. Bob Buckman's leadership, however, produced 'a managerial mindset that promotes internal co-operation and the efficient flow of information throughout the organisation worldwide' (Pan 1999, p82). When the KM programme was introduced, he and his top HR executives contributed regularly to forums and discussion groups, demonstrating management commitment as well as monitoring proceedings. This strong leadership created the necessary role model and provided guidelines for collecting and sharing information.

Gradually the culture began to change. Communities of practice evolved informally. Learning became a social as well as technical process, promoting the sharing of information for specific customer problems as well as gathering knowledge for widespread corporate use. Outside these communities sharing knowledge is hard to enforce, and this raises the danger that they could act as barriers to organisation-wide knowledge-sharing. However, the guidelines provided by leadership reduces that danger as does the integrated thrust of KM, cultural and human resource (HR) practices.

The role of learning and development

Until the mid-1990s training and education were delivered in traditional teacher-centred classroom fashion, but in 1996 a multi-lingual online learning centre was introduced, with content ranging from short training and reference materials to advanced academic degrees drawn from some of the best universities in the world. Primary responsibility for managing personal and career development is now with associates (the term for Buckman employees) not with specialist L&D staff, and this reinforces the associate-driven KM culture.

The reward system

At Buckman Laboratories people had to get used to a culture of knowledge sharing and of knowledge creation, as well as to a new flatter networking structure. It was therefore important to reward key behaviours as well as new competencies. New performance measurement systems were introduced, focused mainly on the outcomes of knowledge-sharing that the company and individuals found of value. Selection, rewards, recognition and compensation systems were also changed in order to gear them to the realisation that people have to be given time to adjust to KM tools, to learn how to use them and to understand the long term as well as immediate benefits they can bring. One particularly challenging task for management has been to develop a knowledge-focused reward system to replace the traditional, commission-based mechanism.

Individual monetary rewards for contribution to knowledge sharing have only been used sparingly, and as a sign of esteem by the company not as material rewards attached to specific tasks. There has also been a 'punishment' factor, especially in the early stages when top management would write to those who did not participate in the K'Netix system, asking for their reasons and suggesting that previous ways of working were now at an end and that a new way forward was necessary to the organisation's future success.

Six or seven years on, the researchers found that after a 'painful and strenuous' period of unlearning and relearning, managers at the company were continuously concentrating on facilitating knowledge creation, becoming mentors instead of barriers to the knowledge process.

Measuring results

The company has measured the results of knowledge-sharing activities against the percentage of new products sold (a key performance indicator at Buckman). On this measurement knowledge sharing by 1996 had produced a 250 per cent growth in sales in the past decade. Its global knowledge-sharing effort had helped increase the percentage of sales from products less than five years old from 14 per cent in 1987 to 34.6 per cent in 1996. The single key factor to have contributed to this success is successful cultural change that has produced a company-wide vision of knowledge sharing. Managers appreciate that once KM is embedded in the processes in which people work it can aid the knowledge process through normal corporate intranets and informal communities of practice. The incorporation of KM practices into company culture is intended to ensure that Buckman Laboratories achieves its mission to compete strategically on knowledge.

Source: PAN, S.L. (1999) With acknowledgements to CIPD

PROMOTING WORKPLACE LEARNING AND KNOWLEDGE: INTERNATIONAL COMPARISONS

Research findings

In the UK, workplace learning and innovative learning processes are receiving increasing attention in organisations that are introducing new high-performance work practices which in turn change the nature and organisation of work. The extent to which this is happening in competitor countries is generally more marked, although practices vary across organisations and across countries due to variations in national education and training policies, skill gaps, labour market trends and so on. However, research studies repeatedly show that an organisation's investment in workplace learning is most directly influenced by organisational leadership, management actions, and HR strategies and practice (Harrison and Kessels 2003a, p225).

A recent major case-based European research project has examined L&D practice in nearly 200 self-styled learning oriented organisations across Europe, including in the UK (Tjepkema et al 2002b). Where the researchers found signs of a workplace learning culture (which was quite rarely) they related its development to a number of contextual factors interacting through time (Tjepkema 2002):

- A strong push to innovation in the workplace.
- New structures that provide employees with new possibilities for linking work and learning, for example through increased contact with customers, through team working and through learning networks.
- Top management that is active in establishing and communicating new organisational vision and values.
- Clarity on L&D's new role related to learning, plus positive results of new L&D initiatives.

But the research findings showed that the combination of such a culture with the four contextual factors usually seemed accidental. Learning cultures appeared to have been introduced (like mentoring and coaching as discussed in Chapter 5) as a result of blind faith not of any reasoned business case. Also, although knowledge management, knowledge sharing and creating a favourable learning culture were all in reality big issues for the participating companies, the researchers found that (Tjepkema 2002):

- Despite considerable innovation in L&D practice, there was a generalised failure of its professionals to actively promote a learning culture in the workplace or to promote high-quality workplace learning whether in informal or formal modes.
- When they used the term 'knowledge management', L&D professionals were referring mainly to sharing knowledge more widely across the organisation. They rarely if ever used it to signify creating opportunities for knowledge-productive learning and development for all organisational members. Most L&D activity was concentrated at the individual level.

In the UK, the CIPD's 2004 *Training and Development* survey of 531 UK-based organisations yielded rather more mixed messages. It showed that organisations covered placed 'enormous importance' on creating cultures that supported learning and development and understood the critical importance of lifelong learning both for individuals and the business (CIPD 2004a, p14). Almost 60 per cent of respondents recorded that there was an appreciation in their organisations of the vital need for managers' skills and commitment if such learning was to be achieved. However, there was far less appreciation of the importance of other forms of support that could raise commitment levels, such as ensuring appropriate reward systems (10 per cent). Furthermore HR and training departments, rather than managers or individuals, were still expected to be the main drivers of learning activities (60 per cent) rather than managers or individual employees. Here too, then, the story is an ambiguous one, indicating awareness of a need for learning cultures and of how to achieve them, but too little appropriate action on the ground.

Tasks for leaders, managers and HR professionals

It is clear from research that in a new knowledge economy HR professionals should be working in partnership with management, project leaders and external partners to discover ways of effectively developing, disseminating and utilising knowledge (Scarbrough and Swan 1999; Stewart and Tansley 2002; Tjepkema et al 2002b; Harrison and Kessels 2003a). As yet, they rarely seem to be doing so. More worryingly, they are often unaware of the need to do so. Many seem unfamiliar with the KM field and have no language for entering it. General management is often hampered by a similar lack of understanding. Key features of organisational context often restrict the rapid and effective mobilisation of knowledge by all employees as and when it is most needed, and there still appears to be a preoccupation with ICT systems to process and spread information.

Companies that 'manage' knowledge most effectively – i.e. stimulate people to continuously share and apply their knowledge in ways useful to the business – are those where (Skapinker 2002, p3):

- their knowledge management programmes are an intrinsic part of their overall business strategy
- their HR and IT policies support information sharing
- they have a corporate culture that encourages people to share what they know – a difficult task when employees tend to feel insecure in the present business climate. 'Why pledge all your knowledge and expertise to a company that has no commitment to you?' (ibid., p6).

Of course HR professionals alone cannot change organisational culture or develop a knowledge-productive organisation. They must be part of a much wider partnership:

- Leadership at the top of the organisation needs to create a ' Big Idea' that motivates people through providing a clear statement purpose to engage them at an emotional level. Senior management must take the initiative and ensure that line managers carry it forward into the workplace (Purcell et al 2003).
- Leaders, managers and HR professionals at all organisational levels must work to create and sustain an environment in which the development, sharing and effective use of knowledge are signposted, facilitated and recognised as essential organisational tasks. That responsibility needs to be an explicit part of their formal roles.
- At workplace level managers and HR professionals have particularly important tasks related to encouraging and facilitating workplace learning and recognising the contribution it can make to continuous improvement and radical innovation.

Referring to research that is highlighting the need today for employees to engage in discretionary behaviour rather than simply follow instructions, John Philpott (2003a) the CIPD's Chief Economist, notes that such behaviour expands an organisation's capacity to generate knowledge and share information, add value to products and services, and satisfy consumers. This, however, requires an organisational architecture that achieves the:

> knitting (of) people management practices and employment relationships within organisational structures designed to deliver high quality products and services and respond to changing consumer demand.

This, in turn, requires the devolution of responsibility from senior management to front line management and employees. It is their role to 'make the most of these high performance architectures' (ibid.).

Tasks for L&D practitioners

Concluding their survey of research findings and of practice both good and poor in this field, Harrison and Kessels propose the following as key tasks for L&D professionals (drawing on *Human resource development in a knowledge economy: an organisational view*. Basingstoke: Palgrave Macmillan. 2003a, pp234–235):

- Working in partnerships to implement business processes and developmental activity that will equip managers and team leaders at all organisational levels to fulfil their knowledge-creating roles.
- Raising awareness across the organisation of the value of a workplace learning culture that taps into, shares and utilises explicit and tacit knowledge of organisational members, promoting continuous improvement and radical innovation in goods, services and processes.
- Producing well-contextualised processes and practical interventions that can help to transform the workplace into a learning environment conducive to knowledge creation, knowledge sharing and the development of new dynamic capabilities for the organisation.
- Working to ensure an inclusive and ethical approach to learning in the workplace. This involves building on diversity in order to access and share knowledge embedded in the grass roots of the organisational community, and contributing to a developmental performance-management process that can facilitate and value knowledge-productive learning.
- Stimulating and supporting self-managed learning at all organisational levels, utilising the support and involvement of a variety of social, occupational and professional networks to achieve this.
- Incorporating in training, learning and developmental processes opportunities for individuals to explore and invest in their personal domains of interest while also adding value through their work for the organisation.
- Providing expert learning support in becoming knowledge-productive in virtual environments, and helping dispersed team members to connect and align their interests and priorities. Whenever the intention is to harness collaborative and web-based technology to learning and knowledge processes, L&D practitioners should act as facilitative and motivating human process mediators.
- Ensuring their own continuing professional and personal development.

In this chapter the case examples have featured large organisations, some with complex, high-cost knowledge-management and learning systems. However I have already noted earlier that often it is the smaller enterprises that come closest to the ideal. Many are fast-reactive, well-informed about their external and internal environments, and foster a climate of continuous learning leading that promotes innovation. They operate like this not necessarily because there has been any conscious decision to do so, but because they have learnt intuitively that it enables them to gain a leading edge.

In their research into workplace learning practices Fuller and Unwin (2003) have produced an 'expansive learning environment' framework that is well suited to the task of raising employees' commitment to the organisation, and to stimulating knowledge creation and its application in ways that benefit the business. Key features are:

- Participation in multiple communities of practice inside and outside the workplace.
- Breadth, achieved by access to learning fostered by cross-company experiences.
- Planned time off the job including for knowledge-based courses, and for reflection.
- A vision of workplace learning as progression for a career.
- Organisational recognition of, and support for, employees as learners.
- Workforce development used as a vehicle for aligning the goals of developing the individual and organisational capability.
- Knowledge and skills of whole workforce developed and valued.
- Teamwork valued.
- Managers as facilitators of workforce and individual development.

REFLECTION

Reflecting on your own organisation, how far do you see its HR professionals (especially those with L&D responsibilities) to be working with managers and other key players to build an 'expansive learning environment'? Or what might prompt them to do so?

CONCLUSION

You should by now understand the kinds of contribution that L&D professionals should be making to promote workplace learning and the creation of organisationally valuable knowledge, and feel confident to tackle the review questions in Appendix 3 that relate to this chapter.

The subject matter contained in this chapter calls out for practical illustration. Therefore I have included a number of real-life case examples that can also act as vehicles to review and expand understanding of the learning and knowledge management field. The main issues discussed in the chapter's four sections have been:

- The notion of knowledge as comprising both tacit and explicit elements, and as an ongoing process that is shaped by individuals' learning and their workplace experience.
- The importance of this notion for organisations that seek to harness knowledge to their strategic goals and therefore need to gain the commitment of employees to put their knowledge – especially tacit – at the service of the organisation.

- The uses and shortcomings of the learning organisation concept as a way of promoting workplace learning linked to knowledge creation in an organisation, and the lessons that can be learnt here by studying both good and unsuccessful organisational practice.

- Simple, people-centred building blocks to develop genuinely knowledge-productive organisations, and the fundamental need to ensure top leadership's vision and support, line management and team leaders' active involvement, an appropriate infrastructure of HR practices and technology (not necessarily high-cost or sophisticated), and high-calibre L&D expertise.

- The importance in any organisation of linking workplace learning and knowledge creation through the application of a few straightforward people-centred principles that everyone can understand and relate to. Recent European research findings have underlined the challenges for key players in achieving the planning and culture change needed to achieve effective implementation of those principles. They require L&D professionals to apply knowledge and skills that may be new to many, but which should be part of their professional education and their continuing professional development.

Further information sources

GARVEY, B. and WILLIAMSON, B. (2002) *Beyond knowledge management: dialogue, creativity and the corporate curriculum*. Harlow: Financial Times & Prentice Hall.

HARRISON, R. and KESSELS, J. (2003a) *Human resource development in a knowledge economy: an organisational view*. Basingstoke: Palgrave Macmillan.

Achieving Ethical Practice | CHAPTER 9

INTRODUCTION

In the *Oxford English Reference Dictionary* ethics and professionalism are defined as follows (Pearsall and Trumble 1996):

> '**Ethics:** *the rules of conduct recognized as appropriate to a particular profession or area of life.*
>
> **Professionalism:** *the qualities or typical features of a profession or of professionals, esp. competence, skill, etc.'*

To be a professional therefore does not necessarily guarantee ethical practice (Dickens, with whose words this book began, would certainly agree with that, demonstrating as he did such a profound distrust of at least one group of professionals – lawyers).

It is the purpose of this chapter to explain and explore the two kind of responsibility that L&D professionals hold in relation to ethics: to ensure that they themselves are ethical as well as professional practitioners, and to work with others to build fairness and trust into the organisation's relations with its members.

Neither of these are easy tasks, and in the chapter use is made of case examples to illustrate the dilemmas that they can involve and principles to guide responses to them. There are various codes offering guidelines for HR professionals, including those established by professional bodies such as the CIPD (2000). There are also codes of practice related to UK and European legislation. However conforming to these does not guarantee ethical practice. There is always a gap that only the individual can close, using as their reference point their own reasoning, core values and beliefs. Here, though, there is a difficulty, because although a dictionary definition terms 'ethical' to mean 'morally correct; honourable' (Pearsall and Trumble 1996), that raises the question – morally correct by whose standards? Honourable in whose eyes? Whose values should prevail here? This underlines the need for clarity and ownership of an organisation's ethical values, established and enacted by its leadership and management at all levels.

In this chapter's four sections I look first at the concept of the good employer, and at the psychological contract as a way of building trust and commitment between employer and employees. I then explore the kind of L&D activity that can contribute to such a contract. The third section of the chapter identifies ways in which L&D professionals can ensure that they are ethical practitioners. The chapter ends with an examination of how to build on diversity of all kinds, including diverse values and views, in order to produce rich and inclusive learning experiences.

ETHICS, HUMAN RESOURCE PRACTICES AND THE BUSINESS

The 'good' employer

Debate about what constitutes ethical practice goes back to Aristotle and beyond. It is impossible to enter that debate here. Suffice it to outline three approaches to indicate the complexity of the arguments:

Respect for others is a duty central to morality, owed by all rational human beings to one another

This is a concept of ethics that condemns as immoral any action performed out of self-interest, and assumes morality to be a matter of the exercise of reason. It is reasonable to say that people should be treated 'with respect and as ends in their own right, not solely as means to other's ends' (Legge 1998, p23). Yet while it is difficult to argue with such a gener-alised claim, it is rarely a satisfactory guide to action. Whose 'reason' is the more valid in a contested case? That simple question has gone to the unresolved heart of the Iraq war debate, with each proposer claiming the moral superiority of their own reasoning.

Ethical behaviour is the hallmark of any civilised society

Such behaviour is characterised by the virtues of justice, charity, generosity, and its exercise brings mutual benefit to society and to all of its members. As Legge observes, this approach to ethics raises questions of how best to manage an organisation so that the rights of all its members are protected, and that all stakeholders participate in decisions relating to their welfare. This too is hardly a claim that can be contested, but it is usually too vague as a guide to action in a specific case.

Ethics is a matter of ensuring the greatest happiness or benefit of the greatest number in society

This approach defines 'ethical' by reference to the consequences of behaviour (Legge 1998), where the other two approaches view ethical behaviour as a duty or a virtue in its own right. This approach is often used as a guide to action in a business and professional context.

A number of business management authors like Barnard (1938), Simon (1945), Schendel and Hofer (1979) and Freeman and Gilbert (1988) emphasised ethics and the moral obligations of management as necessary components in the strategic planning process. However, Hosmer (1994) found that little attention had been paid subsequently in the strategic literature to this theme of integrity of common purpose among organisational stakeholders. He urged the need to return to a focus on ethics and the moral obligations of management. His context was managerial ethics as a matter not of personal virtue but of corporate strategy. In his view:

- The strategic decisions of any large-scale economic enterprise in a competitive global environment can result in both benefits and harms.
- It is the responsibility of the senior executives of the firm to distribute those benefits and allocate those harms among the stakeholders.
- Ethical principles offer the only criteria relevant for such distribution and allocation because they provide the only means of recognising and comparing the interests and rights of each of the stakeholders.
- Where this is done, this will help to develop trust in the direction of the firm.
- Stakeholders who show trust in the direction of the firm will show commitment to its future, ensuring efforts that are both co-operative and innovative and that thus lead to competitive and economic success for the firm over time.

Gratton (2003a) further argues the need for a truly democratic enterprise, involving four ethical dimensions that I will discuss further in Chapter 14:

- An adult relationship between organisation and individual.
- Individuals who can develop their natures and express their diverse qualities.
- The liberty of some individuals is not at the expense of others.
- Individuals have accountabilities and obligations both to themselves and to the organisation.

Corporate social responsibility

Cases of unethical corporate behaviour constitute just one of a number of pressures that are now forcing businesses to take seriously their social obligations. In 2003 a report produced by the Department of Trade and Industry (DTI) in association with the Corporate Social Responsibility (CSR) group and Ashridge College highlighted these obligations. Called 'Changing manager mindsets', it has led to the establishment of a CSR Academy (http://csracademy.org.uk) whose programme of activity is being developed by a government-appointed steering group. The CIPD is a member of that group.

A key conclusion of the CMM report was that CSR should be understood as a mainstream issue for all managers and that its principles should be built into the education, training and development of staff throughout all organisations. A CSR competency framework is now being developed for that purpose and HR professionals will be key to its successful implementation. The CIPD's professional standards will also be expanded to incorporate CSR standards and thinking.

CSR focuses on how companies operate: how they relate to their internal and external customers and suppliers and how they are run. However, there is at present no specific reference in the CSR framework to ethical behaviour. Instead, the emphasis is on 'responsible behaviour' and integrity, on taking a 'strategic view' and on 'harnessing diversity'.

In reality organisations treat ethics in one of two ways:

- as a tactic to ensure increased business benefits
- or as part of a genuine attempt to act as a corporate citizen with ethical responsibilities to all organisational members and to wider society.

Commitment to corporate citizenship involves ensuring an equitable distribution of benefits and of harms both within the organisation and in the wider society affected by its operations. In terms of human resource (HR) strategies, it points to not mistreating any employee, to building mutual trust and commitment to the organisation as a priority, and to gaining the support of employees to ethical standards espoused by the organisation.

That is a formidably complex task, and as Philpott (2003b) comments:

'Simply implementing lots of stakeholder initiatives in order to demonstrate corporate responsibility or reputation won't do. This is unlikely to fundamentally improve the way in which organisations

> **perform.... The tragic example of Enron, once renowned for Corporate Social Responsibility activities, yet rotten to the core, shows the limits of skin-deep ethics.'**

The task is complicated by the number and variety of stakeholder values now influencing the CSR Agenda:

- In a turbulent economic situation that has hit many institutional investors, shareholders are more anxious than ever to get quick returns on their investment in businesses. They are increasingly powerful, with commentators becoming concerned that in some companies their influence is not only leading to unprecedented changes in the boardroom but is even beginning to interfere in the legitimate role of management (Durman 2003).
- Customers are increasingly influenced by ethical and environmental considerations and expect to see these reflected in the conduct, products and services of the organisations with which they deal. Many of these stakeholders are becoming 'powerful, sophisticated and ethically-minded' (Philpott 2003b). There is now a growth of ethical investing and of investment indices such as FTSE4Good that offer an alternative to the mainstream stock market benchmarks. Pension funds are also legally obliged to make a statement of their ethical principles in their investment strategy (Cooper 2003).
- Public commentators and the media, while they may not normally be viewed as company stakeholders, nevertheless have a far-reaching influence on public opinion and their descriptions of corporate (mis)behaviour can be graphic, detailed and damning.
- Meanwhile Government as stakeholder is driving all organisations to report externally as well as internally on their investment, development and utilisation of human and social capital as major keys to their wealth, thus putting their human asset agenda on the table.

Finally the building of social capital is crucial to organisations operating in the emerging new knowledge economy – and cannot be achieved where the dominating value is the exclusively financially-driven bottom line. It depends on mutual trust and the building and sustaining of a partnership between employer and employees as key stakeholders, in order to achieve genuinely shared goals.

Therefore few organisations can now afford to risk focusing purely on values preoccupied with the short-term bottom line and/or on low-cost strategies without concern as to how these are achieved. Difficult though the task is, organisations need to find ways of engaging with all their stakeholders by building strategies that can achieve performance improvement while taking their values meaningfully into account.

The psychological contract

It is here that the concept of the psychological contract is relevant, because it is grounded in research evidence about how employees feel about their work, and the impact that specific employment practices have on their attitudes and behaviour (CIPD 2002b, p12). It therefore helps to tackle the difficulty, inherent in any discussion about ethics, of how to establish absolute values. If it is taken as the reference point, then ethics turn on the need to ensure and maintain trust and mutual respect, and how to do that can be decided on pragmatic grounds that are largely determined by contextual factors. The CIPD has found that survey evidence suggests that 90 per cent of senior HR managers see the idea of the contract as offering a useful framework for managing people, however it may be labelled (ibid.).

The term 'psychological contract' does not refer to the legal contract that binds the individual to the employer by specifying his or her duties, terms and conditions, and material rewards. It refers to the perceived expectations, wants and rights that bind him or her at a deeper psychological level. Its basic proposition is that in order to motivate and retain employees, employers have to treat them properly, and that if they do, this will raise employee satisfaction and commitment that in turn can lead to improved organisational performance (CIPD 2003e).

The psychological contract is dynamic, with new expectations being added over time as contexts and needs change. In a world where long-term job security is rare and the pace of job and organisational change can be frenetic, some refer to a 'new deal' in the employment relationship: one in which diversity management, work-life balance, flexibility and the redefinition of traditional working arrangements are all central as employers seek to attract and retain the human capital they need for their organisations. In reality, however, findings from the Economic and Social Research Council's five-year programme, completed in 2003, on the future of work in Britain do not provide any such picture (Pickard 2003b). What they do highlight is the importance of the workplace and of building commitment to the organisation there through relational rather than transactional psychological contracts (Sparrow and Cooper 2003):

- *Transactional psychological contracts* are those that represent little more than a functional relationship: the employee offers services in exchange for compensation by the employer. Such highly specific contracts typify some short-term employment relationships where work is project-driven and/or involves outsourcing arrangements. By no means all, however. Many relatively short-term relationships still want more than a purely functional bond.
- *Relational psychological contracts* are those that are based on mutual commitment. They may be less specific where they are grounded in an expectation of a relatively long-term relationship – but whatever the anticipated duration of the legal contract, the psychological one seeks a shared purpose that can be achieved through an open, trusting partnership that is there for the long haul – however 'long' is defined.

Working towards shared goals, whether in a unionised or non-unionised setting, will rarely happen naturally. Organisations are pluralist, not unitary systems. That is to say they comprise individuals and groups who have multiple goals stemming from differing values, beliefs and needs. A pluralist system is not dominated by any single logic. It is driven by a variety of non-economic as well as economic interests. But although its members are motivated by many individual interests, they will tend to respond positively to organisational strategies that can inspire co-operation by creating faith in the 'integrity of common purpose' (Barnard 1938, p259).

To summarise this section: recognising that any organisation is pluralist means recognising that all value systems of its stakeholders matter and should be reflected in the type of psychological contract established not only between employer and employees, but in a more generalised sense between the organisation and its external stakeholders. There must be a mutually acceptable 'deal' and a genuine agreement to honour it. Within the organisation, such a deal will generate the trust and commitment needed to improve organisational performance, while effective grievance and disciplinary procedures will give active expression to the aim of ensuring procedural justice and fairness (CIPD 2002b). Beyond its boundaries, blurred though they will often be, similar principles should be applied to handling customer, supplier and other stakeholder relationships.

REFLECTION

Consider organisations and movements like the following: the Body Shop, Traidcraft and the Co-Op.

What do you see to be the reasons for their ability to combine a recognised 'ethical approach' with a strong commercial thrust and a commitment to affordability and quality? And how do you think they have managed to achieve and retain customer loyalty?

L&D PRACTICE AND THE GOOD EMPLOYER

L&D and the psychological contract

The organisation's values related to CSR will inevitably frame approaches to the relationship between employer and employees at every organisational level, but within the umbrella of HR policies, a relational contract will involve paying particular attention to L&D processes and practices. They are intimately concerned with ways in which people learn together, develop their potential and build the social capital needed for knowledge creation and its application to benefit the business. The following brief case suggests the kind of contribution that the L&D process can make to relational contracts.

CASE EXAMPLE

Learning and development and relational contracts

Research recently undertaken by Roffey Park Institute into the operation of the psychological contract in a variety of organisational scenarios provides illuminating examples both of relational and transactional contracts and of the superior value of the former in building employee commitment and flexibility. The following is one of these:

The Danish company Satair Hardware, following its 2001 merger with CJ Fox, a leading supplier of hardware to aerospace equipment manufacturers in the UK, faced a severe downturn after 9/11. Redundancies became inevitable and bonuses and pay increases and other financial benefits could not be provided. The company therefore focused on non-financial rewards. Management agreed to review holiday entitlement and flexible hours and to provide increased learning and development opportunities. It regularly communicated with employees about the state of the company and involved the staff in renegotiating terms and conditions. The company weathered the storm with good levels of staff commitment throughout.

Source: GARROW, V. (2003)

As the DTI's efforts in relation to corporate responsibility described earlier illustrate, it is the values displayed by top management, and management actions and HR practices in the workplace that fundamentally shape the nature of the psychological contract between an organisation and its employees. Here, HR professionals have to be prepared to question top management's stance. As one reader of the CIPD journal *People Management* commented in a rather broader context (*People Management* 2002a):

> **'If HR professionals want to be taken seriously, we need to be able to determine for ourselves whether the organisations in which we work are actually having a benign effect on society and to take action accordingly.'**

The Institute of Business Ethics (IBE) found that in 2001 fewer organisations than before were training their staff in business ethics, fewer were reporting on ethics in annual reports, and fewer had a process for revision of their code (Glover 2002b). Employees often do not know that their organisation has an ethical code, let alone what it contains (Drummond 2004). This is bound to raise a question mark against intent. Unless ethical codes are well communicated, supported by clear guidelines for their implementation and measures to ensure their effective implementation, they mean little or nothing.

Raising ethical issues with senior management can require considerable courage. It can put the professional's career progression, even their very position, at risk, and alienate colleagues, superiors and work teams. Yet that can be the price paid for trying to maintain ethical standards. The task of HR professionals, including those operating in the L&D field, is not just to execute orders. It is also to ask questions, no matter how awkward for management or colleagues those questions may be, since it is part of their professional role to help ensure that ethical standards permeate throughout the organisation, from the board to the front line.

Assuming that there is full commitment of the board to being an ethical employer and to implementing HR strategies to support that aim (and these are big assumptions), training then has a vital contribution to make in communicating the organisation's ethical code. John Drummond (2004), chief executive of a business ethics consultancy, proposes the following type of approach:

- Since ethics is a leadership issue, the ideal starting point is education for senior management in workshops. A dilemma-based approach is most likely to be successful, since it operates on the basis of shared problem-solving between trainers and participants and can focus on real-life situations that challenge the managers to put theory into practice and that help to 'minimise the gap between rhetoric and action'.
- Providing that is successful, it can be followed by training for all other employees, co-ordinated by senor managers. They can appoint champions for each major business unit – preferably talented line managers since these are best placed to understand their front-line staff and the ethical dilemmas faced by them. Again, a dilemma-based approach is likely to work best, aided by a blend of e-learning and face to face methods.

- More specific training may be needed for those in high-risk areas such as procurement, marketing, health and safety. If training is followed by e-learning exercises to test understanding and application of learning, this will enable L&D staff and senior management to gauge the effectiveness of the training.

Such an approach can at least double employees' awareness of ethical issues (Drummond 2004). Again, though, to act on those issues is the crucial need.

Aiding legal compliance and good practice

A key task for L&D professionals, and a major way of contributing to a relational psychological contract between employer and employees, is to help achieve equality of treatment and opportunity for all employees in the workplace. The aim should be for legal compliance as no more than a base reference point from which to build and maintain good practice. There are three main tasks here: to raise awareness and improve practice, to ensure equality of access to training and development opportunities, and to contribute to affirmative action.

Raising awareness

In the UK, it is unlawful to treat any person less favourably than other people for a reason related to their race, ethnic origin, gender or disability. Currently there is a radical overhaul taking place of equality legislation, and by 2006 under various European Directives it will also have become unlawful to discriminate against any person on grounds of their religion or belief, age or sexual orientation. This wholesale reform will lead to what has been described as a 'seismic change in the management of equality in the workplace' (Javaid 2002). For L&D professionals it underlines the urgency of the need to ensure that training and guidance is given to everyone who makes policies and procedures, and administers or is in any way actively involved in the management and development of people across the organisation.

Such training and guidance should aim to achieve, through a collaborative process:

- A sound and practical understanding by all organisational members of what inequality, direct and indirect discrimination mean.
- A similar understanding of the organisation's equal opportunity policy, and the competence and commitment of those charged with its implementation to carry out the responsibilities and tasks that it involves.
- The development of a culture that supports the identification and notification to relevant personnel of any discriminatory attitudes that may affect decision-making and action at various organisational levels.
- Management's understanding of the need to keep records of how recruitment, selection, promotion and reward processes are handled, and of their outcomes. Claims of unlawful treatment can be won on a failure by the employer to provide records demonstrating that all reasonable practical steps have been taken to avoid discrimination occurring. This particularly applies in the case of claims of sex discrimination, because under the Sex Discrimination Regulations 2001 the burden of proof shifted from the complainant to the respondent, who must show that no discrimination has occurred.
- Regular monitoring of the outcomes achieved by training and the taking of necessary action when these do not achieve intended objectives.

The final point is of crucial importance but often overlooked. The consequences can be that the persistence of a culture in which discrimination is deeply embedded fails to be identified until it is too late, and incalculable damage has been incurred in financial, reputational and human terms.

CASE EXAMPLE

Race awareness training at the Metropolitan Police Force

In 2000, a 'damning report' was published by Her Majesty's Inspectorate of Constabulary on the Metropolitan Police's efforts to erase racism (Cooper 2000a). The race awareness training introduced since the Macpherson report on the Stephen Lawrence murder investigation was found to be particularly inadequate. The report also criticised the Met's previous record of training, on the grounds that 'from 1989 to 1998 it wasted £780,000 on training community race relations trainers whom it then failed to use' (ibid.) to give them the influence they needed. The reasons eventually found for failure of training on such a scale had striking similarity to those operating in the Paddington case: senior personnel chiefs did not exercise enough influence in the decision and delegation process, and they lacked the necessary power and organisational credibility; serious deficiencies in training expertise at strategic and operational levels led to a lack of:

- clarity on overall training strategy and how it fitted with wider HR functions
- clarity about where responsibility lay for training at a senior level
- understanding as to who would be trained to what standard, and when
- rigorous training needs analysis
- an effective and long-term evaluation process.

Despite significant effort and expense put into police diversity training since the Lawrence Inquiry, a Commission for Racial Equality investigation revealed in 2004 that more than 90 per cent of police race-equality schemes in England and Wales had failed to meet the minimum legal requirements of the Race Relations Act. Out of a sample of 15 police force schemes and five police authority schemes assessed, only one police force was found to be complying with the law. The bodies could now face enforcement action by the CRE, with a penalty of fine or ultimately jail for failing to do so. The bigger issue, however, is how to tackle problems that have remained so stubbornly resistant to all the methods used.

Source: COOPER, C. (2000a); *People Management* (2004b)

Ensuring equal access

Official surveys and other research regularly reveal that in the UK there are still great inequalities in access to training and workforce development. It is easy to state that everyone in an organisation should have equal access to training and development related to their and the organisation's needs. It is far more difficult to achieve that aim. In the face of such a deep training divide, it is a particular responsibility of L&D professionals to ensure that:

- L&D specialist staff, managers, and all others with L&D responsibilities, fully understand the law relating to ensuring access to opportunities for training, promotion and other forms of development.
- All employees know how to access information about training, educational and other developmental opportunities, and how to apply for them. Such opportunities must

not be communicated to employees in ways that could exclude or disproportion-ately reduce the numbers of applicants from a particular minority or racial group or gender.

■ There is no direct or indirect discrimination in selecting people for training and development. There should be regular monitoring to see whether, through time, people from a particular group or gender are failing to apply for certain kinds of training or assessment for promotion; are not trained, assessed or promoted at all; or are trained, assessed or promoted, but in significantly lower proportions than their rate of application or their representation in the workforce suggest should be the case. If such checks show that problems are occurring, causes must be established and remedial action taken.

Contributing to affirmative action

It is unlawful to discriminate against some groups in order to improve the position of others previously disadvantaged. However, it is lawful to take affirmative action to help those in the latter category and training and educational activity have a central part to play in such action. Where in a previous 12-month period there have been no or proportionately few employees of a particular sex or racial group in certain jobs, areas, or level of work, then it is lawful for:

■ The employer to provide access to training facilities that will help to fit those ethnic group members for such work or responsibilities.
■ The employer to encourage them to apply for training or education, whether it is provided internally or externally.
■ The training manager to design training schemes for school-leavers designed to reach members of such ethnic groups; and to arrange training for promotion or skills training for those who lack particular expertise but show potential (supervisory training may include language training).

REFLECTION

A workforce includes employees whose English is limited. Such employees are disad-vantaged because of this, particularly in relation to attempting to undertake educational qualification courses that would help their chances of promotion. What kind of affirmative action do you think would be most appropriate in this case, and why?

ETHICAL ISSUES IN L&D PRACTICE

Tackling bad practice

The L&D profession needs to have an informed understanding about its primary ethical as well as professional responsibilities – to individual learners, to client organisations, and to all who are ultimately affected by their activity and who put their trust in its benefi-cial outcomes. Twenty years ago, in 1985, a damning report on training in the UK was published. I mentioned this report – 'Challenge to complacency' (Coopers and Lybrand) – at the start of my first book on training and development, to draw attention to the dangers inherent in 'a combination of complacent, ill-informed and sceptical attitudes to training at all organizational levels, including that of personnel practitioners themselves' (Harrison 1988, p2).

Grave failures in developmental provision across public and private sectors continue to haunt L&D practitioners. In 1999/2000 alone there were damaging reports on training in the prison service, the Metropolitan Police, the care sector, and in hotel, catering, rail and agriculture workforces. The Health and Safety Commission's report on the 1997 Southall train crash in which seven died was highly critical of training procedures in rail companies across the country. The criticism related to failure to focus on key areas of skill and knowledge needed by drivers, to lack of consistency of practice between drivers, to absence of any centralised core training programme, and to lack of a unified training record system (Cooper 2000b). What kind of failures are we looking at here? Of professionalism? Of ethics?

In most cases of bad practice in the L&D field the failures of L&D practitioners are due in part to others, usually those who plan and provide the practitioners' education and training, and those who manage and are ultimately accountable for their performance. But the individual cannot entirely pass the ethical buck. No professional, HR or otherwise, should venture into areas of work where they are uncertain of their own competence, if in so doing they are likely to jeopardise the duty of care they have for others. Nor should they stand silently by in situations where that duty of care is jeopardised by the incompetence of others. These are ethical issues.

Ethical codes and standards

Identifying what is an ethical issue and how to tackle it can be difficult. For example, how should the trainer act in the following case? Comments follow at its end.

CASE EXAMPLE
Problems out of hours

Working in a residential training centre and regularly working in hotels, there are odd occasions when it is hard to know where the bounds of responsibility end for some trainers. One senior L&D professional found that the main challenges came when, relaxing in the evenings with course delegates, scenarios like the following unfolded:

- inappropriate humour
- over-exuberance and boisterousness, to the extent of embarrassing others
- unwanted sexual attention
- excess alcohol and late nights leading to tiredness and ineffectiveness during the day.

She found herself having to resolve the following questions:

- Should I or should I not intervene? If I do intervene, when and how should I do so?
- I am off duty. Is it my professional obligation to intervene, or do I have an ethical obligation as a 'responsible person'?
- Should I feel responsible anyway? After all, the students are adults. If I feel uncomfortable, why shouldn't I just leave and go off to bed?

Comments

This trainer recounting this case said that in such a situation she tended to let things run a little but ultimately did intervene, not as a trainer but as a fellow adult. This usually produced a positive outcome. For her, it was a matter of reflecting on her own ethical boundaries and on whether there were organisational or professional boundaries, conventions or rules that might apply in the situation.

This suggests a simple framework, based on that suggested for mentors facing ethical dilemmas in their relationships with mentees (Alred et al 1998):

- *Explore* (identifying all the critical aspects of a situation that point to its having an ethical dimension).
- *Reflect* (consider options in order to decide what course of action would bring the greatest benefit and the least adverse outcomes to those involved in the situation and to the organisation of which the trainer is a business partner).
- *Act* (taking that action, and monitoring its outcome).

What would be of most help to L&D practitioners is a generalised framework for professional and ethical practice, together with appropriate diagnostic tools and aids to problem-solving and access to wise advice (for example, from a mentor) when confronting ethical dilemmas. Some urge a need for detailed standards for the L&D profession, but the danger there is of imposing on practitioners a particular set of ethical values, spelt out in definitions of what is and is not right. By their very comprehensiveness detailed standards tend to exclude from consideration any situation falling outside their boundaries and any values but the ones they espouse. They can also overload the individual with information and advice. This is the main problem with the UK's weighty new code of practice on avoiding race discrimination. It aims to build on the old code by providing greater accessibility, an accurate explanation of current legislation and more real life case studies, while also giving detailed guidance on a variety of topics. But the code's all-embracing nature may render it virtually unusable (Spencer 2004).

The CMPS, part of the Cabinet Office in England, has produced a Code of Ethical Practice for L&D practitioners that strikes a healthy balance between a generalised framework and guidelines to aid problem-solving in the specific instance. It is reproduced in Appendix 4 and is also available online at the website shown there.

To summarise: codes, professional standards and qualifications clarify and support ethical practice but they can never guarantee it. The final choice is with the individual, who must develop his or her own well-grounded understanding of what is ethical in the particular situation, and of what actions to take.

WORKPLACE LEARNING AND THE MANAGEMENT OF DIVERSITY

New pressures in workplace learning

The knowledge economy, with the need it creates for collaborative and inclusive modes of learning, poses challenges for L&D specialists. As work becomes the new classroom, organisations must develop a more organic and dynamic model of learning as a social process. But L&D professionals need to understand that this learning process is difficult to disentangle from its context, since it is embedded in institutional cultures and structures and tied to social relationships (Rana 2002).

The operation of a knowledge economy threatens to intensify old labour market divisions in those countries where most new jobs are in the low-skill, low-paid sector and knowledge workers form at present only a small minority of the labour force. This is the situation in the UK, where the fastest-growing occupational groups include hairdressers, shelf-fillers, drivers and care assistants. There, data from the ESRC's *Future of Work Programme* suggest that knowledge workers will form the top half of an hourglass economy that will see a proportional growth in low-paid, low-skilled work (http://www.leeds.ac.uk/asrcfutureofwork). In the UK's flexible labour market there are major income disparities between the better trained and educated and the less well trained. As the skilled continue to get the good jobs, the unskilled either fall out of work or adapt by taking on the low-paid work that, increasingly, is all that is left for them. It is a real possibility that in the new knowledge economy for all the rhetoric of the learning organisation and the breakdown of hierarchy, in reality most employees will face an experience of continued subordination (Field 2000, p84).

Of course every workplace is characterised by differences between those who work there. The obvious differences are those identified in equal opportunities legislation, but those created by differing work contracts can be just as powerful. In a workforce where people have to work side by side yet are contracted to different employers, the differences will be multiple – in pay, in terms and conditions, and in commitment levels and ethical values. Other kinds of difference will also have an immediate impact on any L&D process – for example:

- differences in individuals' learning style, skills and preferences
- differences in their attitudes to change
- differences in their ability or disposition to fit into the culture of the workplace.

These last three types of differences are subtle, but they can result in some individuals feeling (or in fact being) isolated from the majority, being under pressure to conform to values they do not share, or experiencing stress and confusion in situations where they cannot play to their strengths. Although in the so-called post-Fordist workplace the emphasis is on collaboration, trust, self-managing teams, abolition of hierarchy, self-development and visions of the 'learning organisation', many argue that new forms of control have simply replaced the old and that new inequalities have emerged (Butler 1999, pp144–145).

Here I will look at four features that characterise many lean, high-performing organisations (Terry and Purcell 1997). The benefits that such a cluster of HR practices can bring to a business has been repeatedly identified in research. Yet the ability of the majority of employees to adjust relatively easily to such practices can lead those who feel disadvantaged in such a workplace to be sidelined, or dismissed as 'difficult':

- competency frameworks to identify and foster behaviour needed
- team structures
- group-based reward systems
- appraisal systems to monitor and measure performance.

Competency frameworks
There is now a widespread use across Europe of national vocational training systems that use competency-based training frameworks. Solomon (1999) observes that such systems seem at first sight to liberate learners in the workplace, since competency-focused training is intended to give learners a sense of control over their learning. It involves learner-centred approaches that emphasise group-based learning, collaboration, participation

and negotiation in the learning process. It also aids equality of treatment through its consistent approach to standards.

Yet by its very preoccupation with a particular set of learning processes and a particular approach to workplace learning, competency-based training can introduce new divisions in that workplace, socialising people to become certain kinds of learners, just as new high-performance work practices are socialising them to be certain kinds of workers (Solomon 1999, p123). Even systems offering accreditation of prior learning often focus on particular kinds of knowledge and experience, thus excluding others. The shift at national levels towards centralised vocational curricula is yet another reinforcer of sameness.

Teamwork and group-based reward systems

Effective, high-performing teams bring obvious benefits for the business, and can offer individual members social support, clarity of role and a buffer from the wider organisation. Yet not everyone can work well in a team, particularly one that is self-managing and internally controlled, or whose leadership is divisive. The 2004 NHS staff survey of 200,000 NHS employees showed that 89 per cent worked in a team but that only 41 per cent of such teams met criteria involved in being well-structured and effective (Griffiths 2004a). Where teams fail to function effectively, some individuals can find themselves in a stressful and isolated position, singled out as being unacceptably different from other team members. The stress on those who fail to fully conform to group norms is likely to be reinforced by group-based reward systems.

Appraisal

The appraisal process too can be divisive if it aims to achieve strict conformity of all employees to centralised norms relating to performance and learning, or if it is administered with a discriminatory bias. I have already noted in Chapter 5 that for cultural reasons a 360-degree feedback appraisal process can be offensive to some ethnic minorities. Other weaknesses have been revealed by a report in local government warning that the sector stood in danger of breaking race equality laws (Rana 2003). It showed that bosses' performance ratings of ethnic minority senior and middle managers were lower than ratings given by peers and direct reports. In contrast the ratings for white managers from the three groups – senior bosses, peers and juniors – tended to concur. The researchers found that bosses were being discriminatory and failing to give ethnic minority managers feedback on performance – sometimes perhaps because of a fear that negative feedback would be seen as racist. Ethnic minority managers rated themselves higher than their colleagues did, because they were not getting feedback on their strengths and weaknesses (ibid.).

While it is important not to underplay the many benefits offered by modern industrial society, L&D practitioners need to identify factors in today's workplace and in L&D processes that can intensify old patterns of difference between people and create new. These factors, if ignored, can foster in many individuals and groups attitudes that lead to alienation from workplace learning. A dispiriting downward spiral can then occur, as Figure 11 shows.

Self-managed learning

One valuable way of achieving new learning goals without magnifying differences between individuals or groups is through self-managed learning. New technology, as we have seen in previous chapters, is of exceptional value here. Self-managed learning builds on, and draws benefits from, diversity by allowing participants to design their own learning agenda and curriculum to suit their specific needs, as the following case shows.

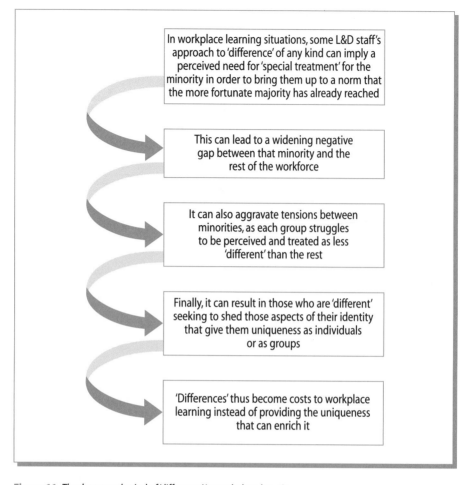

In workplace learning situations, some L&D staff's approach to 'difference' of any kind can imply a perceived need for 'special treatment' for the minority in order to bring them up to a norm that the more fortunate majority has already reached

This can lead to a widening negative gap between that minority and the rest of the workforce

It can also aggravate tensions between minorities, as each group struggles to be perceived and treated as less 'different' than the rest

Finally, it can result in those who are 'different' seeking to shed those aspects of their identity that give them uniqueness as individuals or as groups

'Differences' thus become costs to workplace learning instead of providing the uniqueness that can enrich it

Figure 11 *The downward spiral of 'difference' in workplace learning*

CASE EXAMPLE

Birmingham City Council and race relations training

Birmingham City Council in the UK places a strong emphasis on race awareness. In the past the council ran a number of conventional training programmes, but its workforce still failed to reflect local demographics.

A consultancy firm was then appointed to tackle the problem. It introduced a self-managed learning programme at the council to support managers outside the male/white stereotype. Under the scheme, managers were offered the chance to design their own learning programmes to meet their specific needs. The programme resulted in a big positive shift in attitudes, and staff started volunteering to take part in the initiative.

Source: *People Management* (2002b)

At BT and BP there is an emphasis on individual autonomy. Self-managed career development policies and flexible working policies signal to their employees a belief that they are mature enough to make their own decisions about how they develop, how they organise their work, and how they express their diverse qualities. Organisational leadership creates a sense of purpose and of a just and fair organisation, while HR professionals have key roles in building an understanding of individuals based on an acknowledgement of the variety of individual potential and motivation. They also trial policies that may involve some risk for the company but could also bring value-adding returns in many ways (Gratton 2003a).

Building on diversity

Such examples show that, despite the concerns of many commentators, workplace learning can be a liberating process. What is essential is that those who organise and deliver such learning have valid insights into the preferences of learners, and that they pursue learning approaches that harness diversity in imaginative ways to the pursuit of learning goals. L&D practitioners must also work with other HR colleagues and with line managers to ensure that across the organisation there is an active commitment to, and understanding of, good diversity practices, and that front-line managers especially are given support to achieve this.

Organisational variety is an important building block of a knowledge-productive and high performing organisation. When organisational members are able to exercise a significant degree of choice and degree of freedom in their work and in their learning, the enabling of each individual to express themselves uniquely in this way can be a stimulus to excitement and commitment to the organisation. 'We grow through engaging with the world in many different ways…We may do this by shaping our careers, crafting our development and having a voice in the rewards we receive' (Gratton 2003a).

Yet the task of managing diversity is a demanding one, whether that diversity springs from differences in learning styles and skills, from personality differences, from differences in employment contracts, ethical values, or any of the other numerous possible causes. It requires a deep understanding of the pressures under which employees, especially front-line managers, work if L&D activity is to build on diversity rather than risk adding to divisions among employees. The following case is an illustration.

CASE EXAMPLE
Managing diversity and equal opportunities in a retail store

Diversity has been defined as an approach to fair treatment that involves harnessing and valuing a wide range of visible and invisible differences in employees (Kersten 2000). The business case advocates employing a diverse work force to maximise the available labour market talent, create business opportunities by drawing on wider perspectives, and thriving in different cultures. Being known as an inclusive place to work can lead to becoming an employer of choice, thus bringing reputational benefits also, as B&Q has shown.

However in the UK anti-discrimination legislation aims to reduce inequalities in the attraction, selection, retention, training and development of employees, 'freeing individuals from stereotypical group characteristics' in order that people can work and make progress on the basis of individual merit (Foster and Harris 2004) Trying to conform to both sets of requirements – diversity and equality – creates confusion for many managers.

Training has an essential task here in ensuring that they are well informed about individual legal rights at work and are also able to accommodate individual differences in their decision-making. Yet the researchers quote survey evidence (Kandola and Fullerton 1998) to indicate that only 7.5 per cent of employers provide diversity training to staff and fewer than 10 per cent conduct it specifically for managers. In the retail organisation studied by Foster and Harris, fear of legal consequences prompted managers to opt for a compliance approach to equality issues, at the expense of effective management of diversity. Organisational context was what tended to influence their behaviour most, and this often led to expediency, favouring a policy of 'sameness' rather than effective diversity management. This could undermine progressive HR policies related to diversity management.

Where training did take place it often increased instead of reduced the problems because of a tendency to focus heavily on legal compliance and 'what not to do', intensifying the pressure to opt for equality of treatment and thereby avoid the danger of litigation. Case studies worked poorly as a training method unless based on actual dilemmas that had already taken place and on managers' decisions in those situations, both because artificial cases had little meaning for participants, and because there could be a real gap between the reactions they would propose and those that, in real life, they were likely to display.

The best solution to this dilemma, even though an imperfect one, was achieved by operational management and HR professionals working together to fully discuss all the issues and agree on a pragmatic way forward that best suited the particular organisation, its employers and its external context.

Source: FOSTER, C. and HARRIS, L. (2004)

An agenda for L&D professionals

The 2003 CIPD *Training and development* survey (CIPD 2003f) found a gulf between the rhetoric and reality of managing diversity in many organisations. Three of its findings are of special concern here:

- Diversity training had significantly increased in quantitative terms, but was more to do with legal content than with changing skills, attitudes and emotions related to diversity.
- It had little concern to look at diversity in the outside world, and especially at relations with customers.
- It was not extensively evaluated, so its impact and value was hard to determine.

This suggests an important agenda for L&D professionals. As Thacker (2002) remarks, 'diversity is about the development of individuals. It is about capitalising on individual approaches to life and styles of work'. The kind of diversity training that the CIPD survey suggests is currently being undertaken in many organisations is unlikely to achieve those aims, since it is not founded on any attempt to uncover and deal with deep-rooted differences in values, cultures and emotions, nor are its outcomes clear.

One of the problems about the push for 'sameness' no matter how it manifests itself is that intangible sources of human difference which are so important to each individual's identity can come under a sometimes relentless pressure to conform to some group or organisational norm. In a pluralist system all viewpoints should be accorded equal value and respect, and for professionals engaged in aiding one of the most sensitive of all human processes – learning – that value and respect must be accorded and used to enrich the learning experience.

A 'Valuing Differences' model such as Barbara Walker's (1994) can greatly aid the process of learning from diversity and using that learning to produce positive learning experiences. Its use by Digital Equipment Corporation proved a powerful adjunct to the company's Affirmative Action and Equal Employment Opportunity work. Its five steps are to do with:

- stripping away stereotypes
- learning to listen and probe for the differences in people's assumptions
- building strong relationships with people one regards as 'different'
- empowering oneself in order to become more open to learning from 'differences'
- exploring and identifying group differences.

In their research, Ely and Thomas (2001), looking at race and culture in professional service organisations, produced one finding that could have a generalised applicability: that linking diversity with the way employees work can make it a learning and integration resource. In the work situation this 'learning and integration' strategy can encourage better relations between work groups, make employees feel more valued and produce more efficient functioning, especially through bringing many different perspectives to bear on problem-solving. In a learning programme – for example, one where representatives from suppliers, customers and outsource partners are all learning alongside the organisation's core employees – that same approach could yield rich learning and development opportunities.

REFLECTION

Consider a learning event or educational programme with which you are familiar (whether directly or indirectly). How far do you think that it built positively on diversity amongst its participants, providing a rich learning experience for all – or failed to do so, losing the potential for a rich learning experience?

CONCLUSION

You should now have a sound understanding of the two kinds of responsibility that L&D professionals hold in relation to ethics: to ensure that they themselves are ethical as well as professional practitioners, and to work with others to build fairness and trust into the organisation's relations with its members. You should also feel confident to tackle the review questions related to this chapter that are shown in Appendix 3.

The main themes covered by this chapter's four sections have been the following:

- There are two ways in which ethics can be treated by an organisation: as a tactic to ensure increased business benefits, or as part of a genuine attempt to be a good employer and a good citizen. Corporate citizenship involves meeting social responsibilities both within the organisation and in the wider community, and human resource strategies – especially those in the L&D field – have a major part to play in building relationships of trust and mutual commitment between employers and their employees.

- L&D activity should ensure that all organisational members are aware and know how to achieve compliance with the law on equality and non-discrimination, but should go further and promote good practice. Ensuring equal access to training and development opportunities and working to achieve an equitable spread of such opportunities across the workforce is part of this task, as is contributing to affirmative action where this is clearly needed.

- A central issue for L&D professionals is how to identify and tackle ethical dilemmas in their own field, including practice that has damaging outcomes whether within or beyond the organisation. Codes of practice and standards are helpful here, but in the end it is the judgement of the individual that must be the deciding factor. That judgement must be informed by personal values, by strategic thinking, and by an understanding of how to achieve the greatest good and least harm in the particular context, both for individuals and for the organisation. Unless L&D professionals develop their own understanding of business ethics and apply their insights to their professional activity, they will find it difficult to respond appropriately and convincingly to ethical dilemmas (Harrison and Kessels 2003a, p221).

- This in turn points to the need, evident especially in the cases of bad practice included in this chapter, for an organisation's core ethical values to be clearly identified, communicated and enacted by its leadership and management at all levels in order to demonstrate their importance in guiding everyday activity and behaviour of all organisational members. L&D practitioners have a unique contribution to make to the development, communication and embedding of these values. Where values are espoused but not practised by those who should be role models, the whole organisation can become contaminated – as cases like Enron and Shell have shown in striking form. L&D professionals cannot take on the burden of acting as the conscience of their organisation, but they do have a significant part to play in shaping ethical values and culture within their own sphere of operations.

- In the new knowledge economy there is some evidence that old labour market divisions are being perpetuated and new barriers being created between the privileged knowledge workers and the non-knowledge workers in the workplace. Other pressures for 'sameness' can include clusters of HR practice that often characterise high-performing organisations. L&D professionals need to understand the ways such pressures arise, and how to minimise their negative impact on the learning process through skilfully building on diversity.

Further information sources

http://www.cipd.co.uk CIPD Homepage, links to CIPD Code of Conduct and to useful sources of legal information [accessed 26 August 2004].

http://www.eoc.org.uk/ The Equal Opportunities Commission website, whose links page connects to specialist equal opportunities sites [accessed 18 September 2004].

http://globalsullivanprinciples.org/principles.htm. An organisation that supports economic, social and political justice by companies and provides detailed principles for companies to follow to that end [accessed 18 September 2004].

http://www.abi.org.uk ABI disclosure guidelines for investors wishing to assess company management of social, environmental and ethical risks [accessed 18 September 2004].

Making a Business Contribution

The L&D Agenda in Different Sectoral Settings

INTRODUCTION

In Part 2 of the book I explored the basics of good practice in L&D activity. In Part 3 the concern is with ways in which L&D activity can be organised, managed and focused to make a value-adding contribution to the business, and with the business partnerships on which those processes depend for success.

The purpose of this chapter is to look at the impact of different organisational settings on the L&D agenda. I have already discussed, especially in Chapter 5, three primary influences on internal organisational context:

- top management's vision, values and leadership
- management style and actions at different organisational levels
- human resource strategies and practices.

Later in Part 3 I will take that discussion further. However the location of the organisation in a wider world also has significant influence on its L&D agenda, and this provides the rationale for this chapter. Having focused mainly on private sector organisations of the larger kind up to this point, in this chapter I look at other types and sectors.

In the first of the chapter's three sections I review the L&D agenda in small to medium-size enterprises. The focus of the second section is the public sector, which is the UK's major employer (and which, of course, also incorporates many SMEs). The final section deals with the voluntary and community sector upon whose workforce many organisations increasingly rely.

ORGANISATIONAL SETTINGS: SMALL AND MEDIUM-SIZED ENTERPRISES

Understanding external context

Using European Union definitions the SME sector comprises:

- Micro firms (up to nine staff).
- Small enterprise (from 10 to 49 staff).
- Medium enterprise (between 50 and 249 staff).

According to Department of Trade and Industry statistics SMEs (i.e. those with fewer than 250 employees) account for just over 99 per cent of UK firms and employ 12.6 million people, or over half the private sector workforce (Hall 2004). About one third of these work in companies with fewer than 10 employees.

Although the literature concerning people management and development draws mainly on studies in larger organisations, there is no evidence that the conclusions reached in that context apply to managing people in smaller organisations. Life in SMEs can be very different. They can be harsh and demanding places to work, poorly organised and managed and with a high rate of failure in business start-ups. On the other hand as I have noted in earlier chapters, some are close to being natural 'learning organisations', being fast-reactive, well-informed about their external and internal environments, and fostering a climate of continuous learning, improvement and innovation.

Learning and development in SMEs

SMEs generate 52 per cent of the UK's total turnover and maximising productivity is crucial to their survival. A skilled and continuously developing workforce is therefore essential to their success, yet although training is the most common form of planned L&D activity in the smaller organisation it is not necessarily a priority for investment. Many factors come together to explain this, but the stage that a firm has reached in its life-cycle is particularly important (Hendry et al 1991):

In start-up ventures there is a need for labour flexibility and loosely defined tasks. Recruitment takes place in that context, and training will tend to be informal and on-the-job, restricted to teaching or showing people how to reach required performance levels.

During the period of initial growth, other pressures make it inevitable that any except the most obviously necessary training will tend to receive little attention. In the early stages of the SME's life-cycle the factors most likely to influence people management policies are the values and style of the entrepreneur and an interacting range of product market structure and industry structure factors. In so far as human resource (HR) processes are recognised as being important, most attention will usually be paid to recruitment, pay and termination.

As the firm becomes more mature, it often undergoes change of ownership, organisational structure and managerial style. At this point, the need to develop people for the future is likely to become more apparent. However, this will not always be the case, especially because at the time no one may be aware of what stage of development a firm is entering or leaving – such stages are easier to identify once they have taken place. Also progress through stages of the life-cycle is not a neat linear process. A deliberate choice may be taken not to 'go for growth'. An owner-manager may decide to close the firm down prematurely, or for no apparent reason let it be acquired at some stage.

In assessing the form that planned learning takes in smaller organisations, some commentators tend to regard 'high' (planned, strategic) training as superior to 'low' (informal, fragmented) training. This is misleading because these two forms of training are different and the critical issue is whether the training undertaken – no matter whether high or low – will aid the performance of the firm. There is a good deal of informal training in SMEs, and it can be highly effective and efficient (Jones and Goss 1991, p25). For example, in a sector such as the free house, restaurant and wine bar informal training is widely prevalent for obvious reasons to do with the nature of the job, the small workforces and the wide geographical distribution of the sites.

Informal training and learning can also be the best option for developing and sharing the tacit skills that are particularly important to smaller businesses (Manwaring and Wood 1985, pp172–173). Their uniqueness and value give competitive advantage. Research has shown a high proportion of genuinely unique jobs in many smaller firms, with a 'desire of SMEs to hang onto and keep hidden specific skills and competences developed within the firm' (Hendry et al 1991, p84). Once a skill becomes explicit, and systematically based training can be provided to develop it, the skill can be poached or copied by other organisations. Loss of valuable tacit skills represents a loss of strategic assets that SMEs can ill afford.

External L&D provision for the smaller organisation

We have seen in Chapters 2 and 3 the effort now being devoted by Government to the training and development needs of SMEs. The Investors in People (IIP) standard is one of the most successful examples of a national initiative that has been tailored to their context. In 2004 Government published an action plan for small businesses, with seven strategic themes related to making the UK a model enterprise culture (DTI 2004). It is working with partners including Ufl Learndirect, the Sector Skills Development Agency and the Learning and Skills Council to provide access to relevant training, management and leadership development.

However as noted in Chapter 2, all Government initiatives are threatened by delivery problems, not least that of sustaining required or promised funding levels. In November 2004 the Chancellor was found to be clawing back funding promised to small businesses by tweaking the tax status of its support service, Business Link. By depriving it of the ability to continue to recover VAT on items that it bought, millions of pounds that would otherwise have been available to help small firms with tax and employment advice were now to go back to the Chancellor instead. Business Link was already criticised by many organisations for providing a patchy service. Now, its struggles to improve met with yet another barrier to its credibility (Judge 2004).

One way in which some small firms are combining economies of scale with increased training is through joining 'training clusters', working together in business parks or retail malls. Larger firms also often open up their training facilities to smaller firms in the supply chain or in their area. Business consultants with a good record of working with SMEs can also help smaller organisations to resolve any confusion they experience about the cost and value of such external provision, and can advise on L&D activity to best suit their needs.

As a small firm expands, it becomes more likely that it will appoint a part-time or full-time HR professional. However, during 2003–4 many with fewer than 50 employees received professional HR support through the DTI's nine 'Shared HR' pilot schemes, developed in collaboration with the CIPD and incorporating a High Performance Workplace Model for small businesses (Emmot and Harris 2004, and also http://www.ecdti.co.uk/CGIBIN/PERLCON.PL, accessed 8 November 2004). The pilots showed 'real change and improvement' in working practices, legal compliance, productivity, recruitment and manager confidence and as a result the Government is considering a model to roll out across the UK (Sutcliffe 2004).

In the SME sector there are varied and stimulating L&D challenges to confront, but any interventions must produce customised solutions. SMEs will tend to judge the success of an L&D investment by the extent to which it (Pettigrew et al 1990, p25):

- *Enhances organisational performance*, as indicated by a range of measures. This will be the vital consideration for firms at the early stage of their life-cycle.
- *Enhances employees' ability to cope effectively with* planned internal changes and to respond rapidly and effectively to changes in the external environment.

- *Contributes to the firm's overall ability to achieve longer-term goals.* The impact of L&D interventions here will be to do with helping the firm to cope better with crises and/or make the big strategic leap forward at the opportune time.

Delivering the L&D agenda in SMEs

There can be all kinds of triggers to a more formalised and strategic approach to training in the smaller enterprise but their interactions are unique to the particular firm. However research in the SME sector has shown that in planning employment practices, including those related to L&D, four factors need to be carefully analysed (Hendry et al 1991):

- the history of the firm, that has shaped its employment practices to date
- its survival and growth strategies, that will significantly determine the kind of employees it needs
- its strategies to obtain skills, and the external factors and internal organisational context that influence those strategies
- its approach to training and development, that will tend to focus either on 'topping up' imported skills or on building an internal labour market.

Constrained resources can prevent the development of a more systematic, formalised approach to L&D in the smaller firm. Money is an obvious issue here, but so too is time and the difficulty of releasing people for off-the-job training. The cost of any L&D provision in an SME always has to be balanced carefully against the extent to which it can give fast payback. For the smaller organisation the longer-term benefits may be clear and agreed, but there must be enough immediate benefit also (Cambridge University Small Business Research Centre 1992, p54).

REFLECTION

The owner-manager of a small firm feels that the time is coming when he will need to take a more systematic, planned approach to training. What do you think are the factors that he should look at in order to be sure about this?

ORGANISATIONAL SETTINGS: THE PUBLIC SECTOR

The modernisation programme

In Chapter 3 I explained the wide-ranging reforms taking place across the education system in order to make it more demand-led, offering high quality provision and universal access to educational opportunities, and achieving increased participation rates. The same thrust of reform is driving across the rest of the public sector, and in this section I discuss three key areas, each with a major L&D agenda: the National Health Service, central government and local government. A fourth, which there is no space to cover here, is also significant: the Armed Forces. Traditionally it has provided some excellent models for training and development, although it has recently suffered from localised adverse publicity. It too is a committed part of the Government's modernisation programme.

First, though, an overview. In the 1980s and 1990s the public services were cash starved and poorly managed. The Labour Government is now injecting a massive amount of public funding to enhance service delivery through much improved quality of services, management and working practices. Caulkin (2003) concluded from his research review that there is a need in the public sector for a fundamental shift from traditional command and control styles of management to a high-performance model based on autonomy and trust. He argues for public sector reform based on producing customer-facing, high-performance, people-centred organisations.

Customer-facing organisations

This requires a reduction in the number of centralised targets, regulators and auditing regimes that have resulted in 'Tayloristic, mass production systems in which employees face the wrong way, focusing on what their managers want (the targets) rather than what the customer or citizen wants' (Caulkin 2003, p5). There is a particular need for more consultation on targets that are set, more accountability at local levels, and more discretion for individuals and teams over their work and how they do it in order to develop services around local people.

High-performance organisations

High-trust, high-discretion, high-ambition and flexible organisations are essential for 'a complex, shifting environment where all organisations are joined up to many others' (ibid.). This will require a substantial reduction in centralised targets and wholesale reform to work practices, incentives and rewards, leadership and management, job design, and training and development programmes. CIPD research has found that the psychological contract is more variable in the public than private sector, with levels of satisfaction, trust and commitment all lower in the former, most especially in central government. The need for a relational type of contract (as discussed in Chapter 9) is paramount (CIPD 2002c).

People-centred organisations

These are the organisations that put effective people management at the heart of the reform process. Large UK organisations in both public and private sectors experience many problems in aligning their leadership development with their new performance goals and requirements (ibid.) and in ensuring that large-scale organisational change is underpinned by appropriate HR practices and developmental initiatives (CIPD 2003g). In the public sector, these problems are complicated by high stress levels, long working hours and large amounts of change across the whole sector. Work is being constantly monitored and measured and workloads are often excessive. Difficulties in attracting, retaining and motivating staff to work in such settings once again underline the need for the development of HR practices that can build and implement a relational psychological contract. What are needed are reforms that are (Caulkin 2003, p26):

> 'the result of implementing initiatives to improve service to customers on the ground, at the point of delivery, not of abstract restructuring imposed from above. In the same way, the cultural changes needed to sustain improvement grow out of a myriad of small-scale initiatives and experiments – they are a consequence, not a cause, and come from within, not from outside.'

Workforce development

Public sector employees are a priority group in the 2001 Labour *Skills for life* strategy discussed in Chapters 2 and 3 (DfEE 2001). In all areas there are action plans to improve the literacy and numeracy skills of staff, and public sector organisations are also being encouraged to extend basic skills training opportunities to contracted-in staff.

One of the most significant changes in the management of the public sector has been the replacement of a requirement for competitive tendering by one to seek 'Best Value' in the letting of public sector contracts. This requires a search for high service quality, but it also emphasises cost and the monitoring of services against performance targets. This creates tension in deciding where to place the focus of L&D activity. Where detailed contract specification is used to standardise the quality of services, research indicates that this reduces worker discretion and limits training to that needed for narrowly defined job roles (Grugulis et al 2003; Rainbird et al 2003). We have already seen in Chapter 5 that in such a context a drive to enhance skill levels is often not only irrelevant but can actually make things worse by reducing staff motivation and increasing stress levels. The longer such employees stay in such positions the less employable they become – a situation which the possession of qualifications does nothing to alter and which can further reduce motivation and commitment (Rainbird et al 2004).

REFLECTION

Given all the challenges facing people management and development in the public sector, what do you think are to be the main barriers in achieving a powerful and positive link between people and organisational performance?

The National Health Service

The NHS workforce currently numbers 1.3 million. The Department of Health's (DoH) Lifelong Learning Framework for the NHS *Working together, learning together* (DoH 2001) aims to ensure that staff are equipped with the skills and knowledge to work flexibly in support of patients and to continuously develop their own potential. Within this overarching framework the *HR in the National Health Service plan* is a 10-year reform programme with two key objectives: a major expansion in staff numbers and a major redesign of jobs (DoH 2003). *New ways of working*, a self-managed team within the NHS Modernisation Agency, is supporting the delivery of major targets in the NHS Plan to improve access to, and the quality of, patient services through the many initiatives that the HR Plan involves.

The HR Plan comprises a detailed HR strategy to:

- Enable the NHS to become a model employer – better, fairer and more flexible.
- Achieve model career planning through lifelong learning and regular role renewal for employees.
- Build a new knowledge and skills framework linked to annual development reviews and personal development plans, to support personal development and career progression.
- Produce flexible learning programmes to support new ways of patient-centred working.
- Modernise pay, professional regulation and performance management systems across the NHS.
- Improve employee morale and produce a highly skilled HR for the NHS.

In England the framework for lifelong learning is designed to replace outdated demarcations, so that staff can progress by taking on new responsibilities and jobs can be designed around patient and staff needs. It operates through a workforce *Skills Escalator* strategy that links competency assessment to a national knowledge and skills framework, setting benchmarks for the profession. Personal development plans are being produced for every employee. The aim is to achieve continuous development of professional staff, to enable those without professional qualifications to access an NHS Learning Account or NVQ training, and to identify and address adult literacy, numeracy and language gaps. There is also a major programme of reform across pre-registration and post-registration/undergraduate health professional programmes.

Another initiative in implementing lifelong learning was the 2003 launch of the NHS corporate university (NHSU), intended to become a full degree-awarding university open to those outside the NHS as well as to its employees, and planning to offer staff access to foundation degree pathways within five years of their employment. However in December 2004 the university disappeared, merged with the NHS Modernisation Agency and NHS Leadership Centre and incorporating the new Innovation Board to create the NHS Institute for Learning, Skills and Innovation. Even for a Government educational initiative this one had an unprecedentedly short life.

Government is making a particularly substantial investment in management development that will improve the workplace within which skills are acquired and applied. There are about 130,000 employees in a management role in the NHS, but few have management training. The Leadership Centre, part of the Modernisation Agency, will be providing leadership skills to frontline teams and developing leaders at all NHS levels (Higginbottom and Pickard 2003, p46). There is also to be greater support for team working through harmonised, out-of-hours and overtime arrangements.

The desired approach to HR in the NHS is one of partnership, working alongside employees and line managers. However the barriers are considerable, with a tension in the NHS as across the whole of the public sector between the political pressure to improve quality of service and the drive to achieve centralised standards and reduce costs, especially staffing costs (Rainbird et al 2004). One Trust director listed the main barriers to effective implementation of reform as (Watson 2004):

- the huge scale and scope of change
- excessive lists of nationally derived and driven targets
- lack of local autonomy for trusts
- inadequate levels of funding and support for implementation.

But progress is being made in a number of NHS organisations. Two brief examples suggest types of possibilities here.

CASE EXAMPLES

Modernising the NHS: tasks for HR professionals

Leeds Teaching Hospitals Trust, the biggest in the NHS, is successfully pioneering many of the Department of Health initiatives to support modernisation, working with internal and external HR professionals and incorporating ideas of its own managers.

> The Royal West Sussex Hospital, working in partnership with the University of Portsmouth, has introduced a highly successful programme to enable radiographer assistants to do some of the work of radiographers in order to reduce skills gaps caused by shortage of radiologists and radiographers and enable radiographers to concentrate on more complex procedures. The programme is also enhancing the career structure of radiographers and giving financial recognition for their new skills.
>
> Awards to hospitals such as these help to spread good practice and inspire L&D strategies.
>
> Source: HIGGINBOTTOM, K. and PICKARD, J. (2003)

One senior NHS management consultant accepts the potential of the NHS' modernisation programme to significantly change the psychological contract between the service and its staff, but doubts the capability of HR staff to deliver the plan (Birchenhough 2004). Be that as it may, there is no doubting the importance of the HR agenda, which was dramatically emphasised in 2001 with the publication of research that suggested strong associations between HR practices and patient mortality (West and Johnson 2002). While the findings have been questioned by some doctors, they still carry a strong credibility. They have also given a powerful edge to the L&D agenda in the NHS since the research identified as particularly critical factors the extent and sophistication of appraisal systems, the quality and sophistication of training, and the number of staff trained to work in teams.

Can the NHS deliver its L&D agenda?

The NHS reforms aim to achieve a totally modernised service through reforming pay, development and job evaluation and establishing a learning-based system so that people grow in the job and are rewarded for doing so (Higginbottom and Pickard 2003, p46). However cracks are already appearing in plans to implement the L&D agenda. A recent study carried out by the NHSU showed that despite the NHS spending more than £3 billion annually on training, 40 per cent of support staff have received no training or development since joining. One factor contributing to the problem is a segmented professional workforce in which professionals are allied to separate professional bodies. Taking the lead in building a learning culture across the service is one of the major tasks for L&D practitioners working in the embattled NHS sector (Hope 2004b).

Central Government

The publication of the White Paper *Modernising Government* (Cabinet Office 1999) announced a long-term programme of renewal and reform with a focus on public service users rather than providers. It set the scene for thoroughgoing modernisation of the Civil Service (Griffiths 2004b).

Central Government is committed to taking action to tackle basic skills needs where they occur, especially through a continuing commitment to IIP (SU 2002). Almost all central Government employees work for departments and agencies with IIP status. It will benchmark performance against other employers, to ensure that best practice is reflected in training and development. However the modernisation programme goes much further than this. Plans for change announced in 2004 include the movement of 20,000 civil servants out of London and the South East in the short term and a further 60,000 in the medium term. This and Sir Peter Gershon's review of government efficiency have emphasised the need for civil servants to be more professional, be given better developmental opportunities and be subject to more rigorous performance management than in the past. Recruitment and career routes are to be opened up to candidates from a wider variety of backgrounds.

Such strategies set a demanding agenda for HR specialists, and the modernisation of their own profession is one major thrust of the reforms. A 'Modernising People Management' unit at the Cabinet Office is concentrating on that task, using e-HR as a central tool. The Department of Environment, Food and Rural Affairs (Defra) is a much publicised example of the rapid transformation of an HR function from a model comprising devolved personnel to a modern, shared service approach. An HR capability framework has also been designed to develop experts with a deep knowledge of the business who will apply their HR skills to solve its real problems and be able to work effectively in public and in private sectors (Griffiths 2004b). Typical of many innovations is that in the Office for Government Commerce the HR function now has workforce development managers to anticipate future business changes and the implications for the workforce. Team coaching and strategic secondment programmes are also helping HR staff, many of them new recruits to the Service, to quickly acquire new capabilities (Griffiths 2004b).

Keys to delivering the Central Government's L&D agenda

The government's modernisation programme for the Civil Service has set a demanding agenda for the L&D field, both in terms of culture change issues and service delivery. In previous initiatives there was a push towards departments being broken into smaller and autonomous agencies with responsibility for their own functions, including HR. That has changed. In line with the wider public sector reform process, the emphasis now is on working in partnership, with services shared between departments to increase efficiency (Griffiths 2004b). Business partnership and a customer-facing service are two essentials for L&D professionals working in the central government area.

Local government

Two million people work for the 467 local councils throughout the UK, and every council has dozens of different departments. Local authorities are increasingly promoting themselves as progressive employers, offering flexitime, part-time work, job sharing, career breaks, training and career development. However there are the same acute pressures operating here as elsewhere in the public sector, and this means that employees have to be both creative and flexible, aided by an ethos of public service that is not normally found in the private sector.

The objective of the modernisation programme is described on the local government website (see end of chapter) as:

> **'To support and strengthen local government capacity to fulfil its responsibilities with good democratic decision making, human resource, and financial planning and management systems; a modern electoral and statutory framework and a strengthened focus on community development and social inclusion.'**

The recently published city/county strategies for economic, social and cultural development provide the platform from which to move forward in tackling the two big challenges facing local government and its partners:

- to work together in a more integrated way towards strategic goals
- to develop more open decision-making processes.

The radical changes in local government's functioning and power base in relation to the education system have been discussed in Chapter 3. Here, there is space only for a brief commentary on HR and L&D issues involved in the local government modernisation programme overall.

A total of 13 key performance indicators is being applied to the monitoring of local authorities by the Local Government Modernisation Agency. One of these is progress in implementing initiatives and effective support for best practice in HRM in local authorities. There is a long road to travel here. In its performance assessment (CPA) carried out during 2002 the Audit Commission identified an 'alarming patchiness' in the development and implementation of HR strategies, with 20 per cent of councils having either no strategy or only fragmented systems. Only 10 per cent won praise. Even where councils have had an HR strategy it seems to have been owned by the HR team but not by the organisation. HR staff appear to have formed very few business partnerships, most of them having had little involvement in their authority's CPA work (Mahoney 2003).

In the substantial improvement plans produced subsequently by most local authorities over-haul of the whole HR function looms large (ibid.). As in other areas of the public sector, before HR can make its needed contribution to the business it needs to dramatically improve its own skills base – and that includes its L&D capability.

As an illustration of what a business-focused and capable HR team can achieve, there is the example of one of the councils that has until recently been 'derided' for its abysmal perform-ance – the London Borough of Camden. However, the council achieved an 'excellent' ranking in the 2002 CPA league tables. Its HR staff had long been working to improve performance there, and the building of a clear performance management framework and the gaining of Investors in People status has given staff the clarity they wanted, leading to a steady rise in staff satisfaction and performance. The council is convinced that the ranking achieved by Camden in 2002 was linked directly to its greatly improved performance management process (Mahoney 2003).

Another and closely related key area for improvement in councils generally is senior management's competence, the quality and style of managerial leadership and training for councillors in strategic awareness and skills. Time and again performance indicators and CPA results have shown that where these are lacking, the whole modernisation programme is particularly vulnerable.

Priorities for L&D professionals in local government

The L&D agenda in local government must prioritise the introduction and embedding of cultural and structural change, a major drive in leadership and management development, and support for a modernised performance management system especially through the appraisal and continuing development processes. The Society of Personnel Officers in Local Government is working with Sector Skills Councils to tackle that agenda. Another element of it, of course, is to rapidly upgrade the functional skills and business capability of those charged with its delivery.

Can the public sector L&D agenda be delivered?

The public sector modernisation programme is intended to provide all parts of the sector with a clear signal regarding how it should develop, allowing institutions and public author-ities to develop initiatives of their own that accord with the government's aims. The programme's overarching purpose is to provide the foundation for the public sector of the future and for a welfare society that offers:

- freedom of choice
- a sector that is open, simple and responsive
- value for money.

Reforms on a scale unprecedented in recent history are now underway and the L&D agenda is one of exceptional challenge. It is complicated by a fundamental tension – that operates across all other areas of HRM and management in the sector – between the push to achieve demand-ing centralised targets and drive down costs and the pull to build high-skill, high-performing organisations working in partnership with clients and customers to meet local needs.

One disturbing L&D trend has emerged. Despite heavy government investment in the public sector overall in 2003, the CIPD's 2004 *Training and Development* survey showed that training departments experienced more budget cuts than the private sector in 2003 and expected more to come (CIPD 2004a). The public sector seems to be diverting money from training into pay awards to improve recruitment and retention of staff. This short-term approach will work directly against the longer-term aims of the modernisation programme. It will harm recruitment and retention over the long-term since training and development opportunities are not only essential to enable and motivate employees to achieve high performance but 'the offer of training is itself a useful recruitment and retention tool' (Philpott 2004b, p8).

If the public sector reform programme is to succeed, investment in skills is vital and the preservation of value-adding training budgets must be a priority. It remains to be seen whether that will be sufficiently well understood at top decision-making levels or whether –as in so much of the private sector – short-termism will prevail with the L&D process used primarily to meet immediate proficiency gaps, and its budget regularly raided to shore up other HR areas.

REFLECTION

What example can you identify in any area of the public sector with which you are familiar that shows good L&D practice in supporting the modernisation agenda, and what general lessons do you think should be learnt from it?

THE VOLUNTARY AND COMMUNITY SECTOR

Little is said in research or textbooks about L&D in the voluntary and community sector (VCS), yet the charity area alone is now of major importance to the economy, accounting for an estimated 2 per cent to 9 per cent of GDP. Although the two areas of the sector overlap,

I will comment on each separately in this short section before producing some integrated conclusions.

The vision for active communities

A Home Office Active Community Unit (ACU) has been established to realise the government's vision for 'strong, active, empowered and inclusive' communities (ACU website). The sector's ability to help drive improvements in public services was boosted with the publication in 2004 of *ChangeUp*, a framework produced by the Home Office in collaboration with the sector, for capacity building and infrastructure development (ACU 2004).

Investors in People (IIP) is again being used by Government to aid flexible demand-led provision of training and development. An 'Investors in Communities' (IiC) scheme aims to improve the economic, social and environmental quality of life of neighbourhoods. Based on IIP principles, it is funded by the training Office of the Deputy Prime Minister, the Housing Corporation, and the Countryside Agency and is being piloted by 12 housing organisations across the UK.

A crucial key to progress in such community-based projects is to create and sustain a socially inclusive environment that facilitates learning and knowledge creation. L&D activity here should prioritise (Bromiley et al 1999):

- Initiatives that emerge from a collaboration with community stakeholders that ensures the emergence and development of ideas from the grass roots and equal consideration for all values.
- Ensuring a sound resource base that enables the project to develop organically through time, wherever possible through a community-led organisation rather than being driven by any statutory bodies.
- The measuring of added value achieved by projects by reference to their qualitative outcomes as well as quantitative outputs. We saw in Chapters 2 and 3 how too many government-funded L&D initiatives have achieved poor take-up because of being tied tightly to centralised targets that are inappropriate to meet local organisational needs. The same is true here. Targets set by funders are often inappropriate to community-based and charitable initiatives in that they specify quantifiable outputs such as number of jobs created, of NVQs achieved, of clients receiving advice. Valuable qualitative outcomes of community projects are to do with confidence-building, community cohesion, pride, and the psychological benefits of participation, and these are more likely to be identified by social auditing than by traditional evaluation methods.

Improving performance in the voluntary area

Employee costs can total up to 70 per cent of a voluntary organisation's budget, yet people management in the sector has a poor record, with attention traditionally preoccupied with fundraising and service delivery. However with the advent of care in the community in 1993 many new jobs began to be created in the sector, the majority as a result of transferring social care activities from the public sector. So the push to modernise and upskill the HR profession is now as great here as it is in any area in that sector. In organisations like the crime reduction charity Nacro and the Leonard Cheshire Foundation, once tiny HR sections are now significant departments in what have become big businesses with large turnovers (Zacharias 2003).

In the charity area four areas of priority for L&D are charity performance, management, governance and staff development. One of the major priorities is leadership training at board level, because of the importance of boards in ensuring (Bruce 2004):

- effective strategic planning and marketing
- skills development plans incorporating a wide range of learning approaches including coaching, mentoring and peer group learning
- the promotion of a learning culture
- ensuring that operational managers are skilled in their people management and development roles and committed to performing them well.

Modernisation of the charity sector is a long-term issue. According to one expert the Voluntary and Community Organisation (VCO) workforce is undertrained and too transient, spending too little time on L&D activity when compared with public and private sector organisations. The ACU has commissioned a performance improvement strategy, but money – including modernised pay systems that incorporate pay for board members – has to follow if anything meaningful is to be achieved on the ground (Bruce 2004).

The Charity Commission has a wide span of control and one essential is to reduce the burden of regulation of standards, relying instead on fewer inspections shared between interested parties. Another is the need for VCOs to have easy access to appropriate information, especially about knowledge and resources for performance improvement. VCOs at local level also need more support.

Since 1997 the Government's focus on wider service delivery in its voluntary sector agenda has led to not-for-profit organisations now providing most social housing and 40 per cent of social care. In November 2004 the Association of Chief Executives of Voluntary Organisations (Acevo) criticised the present system as inefficient and bureaucratic, causing chronic financial insecurity for charities that deliver services contracted out to them by councils and health authorities. Most charities (92 per cent) were found to be on contracts of a year or less, with many facing draconian short-term deals. The Aveco Chief Executive called for (Bubb 2004):

> **'A funding revolution that recognised the voluntary sector, not at patronage level, but as a delivery partner.'**

Conclusion: implementing the L&D agenda in the VCS

Across the VCS there is a highly variegated agenda for L&D, offering much to stimulate L&D professionals but much also to challenge their skills and creativity. At present, however, there are the usual worrying signs related to funding and therefore to L&D provision. Access to L&D opportunities is also problematic. Larger charities tend to have more in-house programmes, yet a survey carried out for the Charities HR Network showed that they were spending on average only £172 per year per staff member on external training. Respondents also reported staff retention rates half those in public and private sectors (Bruce 2004).

Despite these discouraging statistics, there are always some benchmarks of innovative practice, as the two following examples show.

CASE EXAMPLES

The PILCOM Programme

The PILCOM Programme, sponsored by Jaguar Cars and supported by the Department of Trade and Industry with Community Action Network as a key community partner offers one to one support for senior managers who are community leaders from leaders in the business sector. The programme is a way of VCOs at senior level building new skills and networks. It also raises the business sector's awareness of key social issues, and engages VCOs in reflecting on and tackling them through a mentoring process.

A foundation degree for VCO

A partnership between four colleges of further/adult education – Bournville, Sandwell, Fircroft and Newnham – has produced a part-time work-based foundation degree in VCO Development for people involved as staff or volunteers in the not-for-profit sector. Its content is designed to develop the required skills as an existing or aspiring manager in the voluntary sector. The foundation degree is organised flexibly, using blended learning and a mix of classroom and independent learning modes. Accreditation is achieved through coursework and practical projects.

Sources:
BUSINESS IN THE COMMUNITY website at http://www.bitc.org.uk/programmes/ programme_directory/cares/london_cares/support.html [accessed 16 September 2004]

NEWNHAM COLLEGE website at http://www.newman.ac.uk/Courses/Foundation/FD_ VCOD.asp – 28k [accessed 16 September 2004]

CONCLUSION

In this chapter the purpose has been to explore the L&D agenda in a range of organisational settings. By now you should have a broad-based understanding of the pressures, challenges and expectations that are shaping that agenda in smaller businesses, in the public sector, and in the voluntary and community sector. You should also be confident in tackling the review questions for this chapter, contained in Appendix 3.

The main ground covered by the chapter's three sections has been:

- The variegated L&D agenda across the small and medium-sized enterprise sector, where the crucial skill required of L&D practitioners is that of promoting highly tailored strategies and initiatives that can enhance performance at different stages of an SME's growth cycle.
- The wide-ranging and demanding L&D agenda across the whole of the public sector, created by the government's modernisation programme. In every area of that sector the same drive is aiming to transform outmoded, hierarchical and bureaucratic structures into customer-facing partnerships characterised by high quality, flexibility and adaptability to change. The challenges here are immense. Wherever they work in the sector, HR professionals are having to rapidly learn new skills and values in order to implement innovative HR strategies to tackle human tensions between the push to achieve centralised targets and the pull to respond to local needs.

■ The unique L&D agenda in the voluntary and community sector where, despite increased public funding, the main need is still for enough resource to produce tailored, partnership-based L&D initiatives to meet needs at the local level while also responding to targets set by government and other sponsors.

Further information sources

Helpful websites for smaller organisations include:

■ the Department of Trade and Industry's website for SMEs with links to similar websites for the Devolved Administrations:
http://www.businesslink.gov.uk/bdotg/action/home [accessed 15 September 2004].

■ the government's Small Business Service website at http://www.sbs.gov.uk/ [accessed 15 September 2004].

For the public sector, various websites give detailed updates on the modernisation programme, including:

■ A website with links to all public sector modernisation issues:
http://www.info4local.gov.uk/relatedlinks.asp?fromPage=subjects&subj=17 [accessed 15 September 2004].

■ NHS New Ways of Working website at:
http://www.dh.gov.uk/PolicyAndGuidance/HumanResourcesAndTraining/fs/en [accessed 15 September 2004].

■ The NHS Learning and Personal Development Division website which gives examples of the skills escalator in practice (including career pathways) at:
http://www.doh.gov.uk/hrinthenhs/learning/ [accessed 16 September 2004].

■ The Prime Minister's Office of Public Services reform website at:
http://www.pm.gov.uk/output/Page249.asp [accessed 16 September 2004].

■ The Local Government modernisation programme website at:
http://www.environ.ie/DOEI/DOEIPol.nsf/wvNavView/wwdLocalGov?Open Document&Lang=en [accessed 16 September 2004].

For the voluntary sector the following are useful websites:

■ The Home Office Active Community website at:
http://www.homeoffice.gov.uk/ comrace/active/index.asp [accessed 15 September 2004].

■ The Charity Commission's website at:
http://www.charity-commission.gov.uk/ [accessed 16 September 2004].

Shaping and Managing the L&D Function

CHAPTER 11

INTRODUCTION

The purpose of this chapter is to explore ways in which an L&D function can be organised, the changing roles of L&D practitioners, and principles related to the effective management of the L&D function. By 'function' I do not imply a specialist unit. I simply mean the body of L&D activity that has to be provided for an organisation, and the personnel most directly responsible for that provision.

The chapter is not intended as a technical guide, and much of the detail concerning the routine management of resources (including staff) that has appeared in previous editions does not appear here. Such detail is readily accessible in short texts and through specialist websites and online training communities. Some information sources are noted at the end of the chapter.

The chapter has five sections. The first looks at some general issues related to organising principles in turbulent times. The second then explores ways of organising the L&D function. The third examines tensions facing the function as it struggles between a push to fragmentation and a pull towards centralisation, leading into the fourth section where I review changing and proposed new roles for L&D practitioners. The final section discusses key issues to do with the management of the function.

STRUCTURE AS AN ORGANISING PROCESS

What is the 'organising process'?

In Chapter 4 I discussed a shift in today's organisations to a more or less continuous organising process. In this section I want to explore exactly what that means and its implications for the L&D function.

Harrison and Kessels (2003a, p42) have defined structure as:

> **'Structure: an organising process, both proactive and reactive, whose aim is to achieve a continuous alignment of people, other resources, tasks and routines with strategic requirements in order to maximise current performance and generate options whereby to best position the organisation for the future.'**

The primary resources for structure as a process are (Pennings 2001, p241):

- hard-to-copy technologies
- organisational routines (such as budgeting, research and development arrangements, templates for organising work and control and planning routines)

- culture and socialisation processes
- relational competencies that allow the organisation to combine its unique resources with those of other firms, particularly those belonging to its value chain.

Today's business environment is so fast-moving that organisations have to be highly flexible to respond effectively to its pressures and opportunities. Structures can no longer be regarded as products cast in stone at a particular point in time. In his research into ICI during its period of successful turnaround in the 1980s Pettigrew (1985, 1987) found that periodical but radical eras of transformation featuring an interplay of substantial cultural, structural and business strategy were underpinned by a continuing organising process. Many studies have subsequently supported those findings (Brickley and Van Drunen 1990; Whittington 2002, p121). They indicate that the norm, regardless of size or type of organisation, tends to be an incremental organising and re-organising process rather than sudden and irregular leaps from one design of structure to another.

Network and partnership forms

In search of fluid and flexible organisational forms, Miles and Snow (1995) identified a spherical or network approach that they rightly forecast would soon become common. Firms with a spherical structure 'rotate competent, self-managing teams and other resources around a common knowledge base', use strategic alliances and outsourcing to enhance core competences, and often link together in a multifirm network (Miles and Snow 1995, pp5–6). Outsourcing is now an extensively used strategy, although not always a successful one. At Abbey National in the UK it has become almost outmoded as the company invests in the newer forms of partnership to which Miles and Snow referred, including franchises and joint ventures (Pickard 2001).

Organising through co-operative alliances, networks, cellular structures and other such flexible arrangements is now common in public and private sectors and can effectively create clusters of separate small businesses that are held together by a strong company brand. Keywords are partnership, trust and mutual dependency. Such alliances enable partners to access new knowledge that each on their own could not produce, to rapidly share it, and to apply it through their core competencies to innovation in goods, processes, products and services. These more flexible ways of organising, however, need great skill in order to ensure enough, but not excessive, formal controls to monitor exchanges of competence or capital assets (Koenig and Van Wijk 2001, p126). Without that, participating organisations' core competencies and unique knowledge can be poached and competitors can gain a unique means of assessing a partner's strengths and weaknesses (Hamel 1991). The skill, however, must go beyond that and extend to binding together people who, in the increasing number of multi-employer situations, work side by side in a single workplace yet are contracted and paid by different employers (Rubery et al 2002).

Reviewing research and practice across Europe Whittington and Mayer (2002) explored various frameworks for organisations working in conditions of rapid change and identified a need for a mix of stable and fluid features, of which five are crucial:

- clear formal structures and reporting relationships
- clear, standardised performance metrics across the organisation
- consistent, standardised compensation policies across the organisation
- propensity to organise in small, performance-oriented units
- culture of change within the organisation.

They explain that in these five key dimensions organisations need to be hard to be flexible. Too soft just adds to the confusion of change. What matters most is that managers concentrate on ways of organising people, rather than of controlling systems, in order to achieve desired performance. Yet as the whole of this section has indicated, where organisational boundaries are increasingly blurred and the notion of the single employer is no longer always an accurate reflection of employment contracts and work relationships, that task is extremely complex. Ultimately, each organisation must find its own best way of organising activity and of managing its employment system through flexible HR strategies and psychological contracts that may have to be hybrid. The historical path that the organisation has travelled will be one factor to guide but often to constrain its path. Others will include its customary routines, its sense of identity, its knowledge base and learning processes, the challenges it faces and its long-term goals.

As a follow-up to Whittington's research, the CIPD published in 2004 findings from a survey it had carried out across private and public sectors, incorporating views from 594 senior executives and HR professionals who had been heavily involved in reorganisations. The report confirmed that major restructuring was occurring every three years or so but also found that a large proportion was unsuccessful. Six key factors appeared crucial to success (CIPD 2004d, pp3–4):

- *A holistic approach*: reorganisation should not be carried out piecemeal. Its wider implications should be comprehensively considered in advance. Reorganisations can be wide-ranging, involving culture and leadership styles, but critical elements of the HR process such as reward and career management are often neglected. They need to be effectively championed by HR professionals. Even where heavy redundancies are involved, HR professionals should anticipate the need for hiring and training.
- *Effective project management*: project management skills to carry out the changes needed were found lacking in almost half of the reported reorganisations.
- *Meaningful employee involvement*: HR professionals must ensure that employee communications and involvement are real and substantial, not a token gesture by management. There should be clear milestones and effective project management.
- *Effective leadership*: the reorganisation team must set clear objectives and possess the skills needed to achieve them. Key skills are to do with managing culture, project management, organisational design and political astuteness.
- *Regular communication with external stakeholders*: it is essential to keep stakeholders (for example key customers and shareholders) fully informed of reorganisation and its progress.
- *Learning from internal and external experience*: internal learning through researching and benchmarking previous experience in other parts of an organisation was found to lead to the most significant improvements in performance, including stronger financial performance, better cost positions and enhanced capabilities for future change. Looking outside of the organisation's sector can significantly improve the organisation's ability to conduct future reorganisations.

Issues for L&D professionals

In the CIPD's 2004 survey above, HR was identified as playing a key role in 62 per cent of reorganisations. There are crucial tasks here for L&D practitioners. They are now working in a context where organising and re-organising is going on more or less all the time, and so must be fast-adaptive. They must be able to operate outside the protective walls of a specialist function as they help to produce initiatives that, while focused adequately on corporate goals, can also meet local needs. They must be skilled in 'relationship management' (Miles and Snow 1995, p11) and be able to contribute to the building and sustaining of the relational psychological contract between organisation and employees that is essential to trust, mutual commitment and a shared purpose. Finally, they must become credible, expert business partners or they have no hope of influencing the leaders, managers and HR colleagues whose strategies and actions have such a major impact on internal organisational context.

ORGANISING THE L&D FUNCTION

What decides the shape?

Imagine that you have been asked to review an organisation's current L&D function in order to decide whether its shape needs to change – or, if there is no formal pattern to L&D activity overall at present, how it should best be organised. What are the most obvious kinds of analysis that you would carry out initially? It should not take much thought to suggest the following:

- Analyse the external environment and identify any big issues that have implications for L&D in the business.
- Analyse internal organisational context and major organisational issues, and identify where the L&D process could add most value. Key here will be vision, values and business goals of top management related to the L&D investment; the L&D roles and responsibilities of management (especially line management) and their general competence, commitment and discretion related to these; and HR strategies and practices that have a bearing on L&D activity.
- Identify the key players in the organisation whose support is needed if L&D initiatives are to succeed, and their attitudes towards the function.
- Identify external and internal people with whom the L&D function should form partnerships and those (for example union learning representatives) who could be 'learning champions' in the workplace.
- Assess resources available, financial and non-financial, material and human, for L&D activity.
- Assess the way in which L&D activity is currently organised in the business and the reasons for its present structural arrangements.
- Identify any weaknesses in the current relationship between corporate structure and the organisation of the L&D function – for example, if managers carry significant L&D responsibilities, is that role included in their business targets, job descriptions and appraisals? It should be.

Such analysis is now being applied to many L&D functions that hitherto have been organised along traditional departmentalised lines. This is often leading to a radical rethink in order to create more flexible forms that can give better value. What options are there? In the following section I outline some customary forms before exploring more innovative approaches.

What shape should it be?

The cost or profit centre

Traditionally in textbooks much discussion has revolved around whether to organise the L&D function as a cost centre or a profit centre:

- *A cost centre* has its costs paid by the organisation. Its key task is to provide cost-efficient as well as cost-effective L&D activity for the organisation. A cost centre approach has been typical in hierarchically-designed organisations and others where the range of L&D operations is relatively stable through time.

- *A profit centre* has to generate and sustain its own financial base, although there is often some form of financial support from the organisation, usually during the centre's start-up stage. Profit centres require a strong profile for the centre and a strong client base, preferably drawn from outside as well as from within the organisation. In delayered organisations it is common to organise L&D operations using the profit centre approach, often with a small central function holding a corporate budget to cover organisation-wide and emergency training and learning activity, and line managers holding their own L&D budgets to purchase services from the centre and externally.

The consultancy function

The principle here is one of organising L&D activity as an internal consultancy, and the practice can take a more, or less, decentralised form. In some organisations there is a central team of professionals whose members move out at various points in time to work with internal customers on a variety of L&D projects. In others there is a small strategic and co-ordinating core at the centre, with the rest of the L&D staff permanently outposted across the organisation working within its strategic business units.

An outposting system often involves tension. Basically the issue is one of 'fit': how best to strike a balance between central and localised needs – the same kind of tension, in fact, that we have already seen in relation to government skills strategy (Chapters 2 and 3). If L&D strategy in an organisation has to stretch too far in attempting to meet local needs, the result can be that every SBU pursues its own L&D practices regardless of corporate L&D strategy – it pays lip service to the latter but in reality finds ways around it.

The line-managed function

With this model, line managers are handed the main responsibility for their L&D activity, leaving only a small core of it to be handled on a corporate basis at centre, whether by L&D specialists or in some other way (by the HR function, by external strategic advisers, by a senior line executive, and so on). This 'devolved' model requires particularly careful consideration if it is to work. There are five 'must-haves' as a starting point:

- *Vision and strategy*: have a clear L&D corporate vision and strategy that is in line with overall HR and business goals and strategy, and corporate leadership's active and regularly communicated commitment to a high quality line-managed L&D function.
- *Objectives*: have strategic L&D objectives that can be carried through by divisional and unit managers into straightforward, practical plans for implementation of the policies that serve those objectives.
- *Structure and systems*: have an organisational structure and company-wide systems and procedures to ensure that all who carry L&D roles and responsibilities have a clear understanding of their tasks and the competence, commitment and discretionary power to carry them out effectively and fairly.
- *Performance management*: have a performance management process that ensures effective training, appraisal, recognition and continuing development of those carrying L&D responsibilities.
- *Learning culture in the workplace*: so that vision, values and management actions

all give active support to the learning and development of employees as the organisation's human and social capital.

How well does devolution work in reality? In too many cases, not well at all. The following case illustrates some of the difficulties that it can involve for a human resource (HR) function more widely.

CASE EXAMPLE
Devolving HR to the line

In a study involving three large retail chains, Lynch found that store managers responsible for people management tended to neglect 'softer' policies in order to meet hard budgetary and performance targets.

Centre set budgets and targets and evaluated their results in numerical terms, while corporate strategy focused on cost-cutting and improving customer service. Given the tensions involved in that focus, and given that budgets and targets were the real bottom line for stores managers, they became principally concerned with efficiency and with what was measurable.

Outside budgetary targets their HR responsibilities were subject to few tangible measurements and were less closely monitored at the centre. This invariably led to a focus on hard HRM techniques. Even where soft high-commitment policies were in place at corporate level they were not always implemented at local level, on the rationale that the needs of the business must take precedence over the needs of employees. Often, in fact, this was an excuse to indulge in tactics that enabled managers to meet measurable targets at the expense of the non-measurable or far less tightly measured targets. Thus there were unauthorised recruitment freezes, use of overtime, the increased use of non-standard labour and scheduling practices – all contrary to company policy but not subjected to rigorous monitoring and therefore likely to be overlooked.

As Lynch (2003) concluded:

> If HR becomes the main discretionary area for all line managers, will soft HRM practices be forfeited in the drive to fulfil tangible targets set by central management?

Source: LYNCH, S. (2003)

I will return to the issue of building learning cultures in Chapter 14. As noted earlier in the book, research so far indicates a distinct lack of leadership and action here by L&D professionals. This confirms that handing over L&D to the line is a risky business. It requires active and continued support and facilitation by top management, any L&D professionals and line managers if it is to work.

The outsourcing function

The trend at present seems to be a partial reshaping of the L&D function to incorporate use of service centres, competence centres and various external partners. The key issues in outsourcing are about cost efficiency, added value, control and partnership. Handled well, outsourcing can result in a small, expert core L&D team remaining in the organisation, with its staff working as internal consultants, buying in what services it seems advantageous to the organisation to import, and providing strategic advice to business leaders. The team may also be operating a commercial consultancy service that reaches outside the organisation and brings in valued revenue as well as developing the L&D team's professional and business skills. Handled badly, outsourcing can become the catalyst for a slide to either a completely fragmented L&D function or to the disappearance of any specialist L&D function in the organisation.

The shared services model

Shared services is an innovative model with real significance for the future. When successful it can achieve economies of scale by the bundling together into a multi-disciplinary service centre of many HR services including those to do with L&D. It represents a form of recentralising L&D services that is likely to exclude many if not all of an organisation's previous L&D staff, but when successful it can provide an efficient, coherent, strategic thrust for the whole L&D brand.

CASE EXAMPLE

Shared services at PricewaterhouseCoopers, UK

PwC has not only passed all HR standardised transactional shared services to a centre but has also outsourced 'professional shared services' (PSS) – a more unusual move. PSS offers advice in areas including learning and education, delivering those services at an agreed price and quality across the firm's five UK businesses.

What was the rationale? Certainly much of it was to stop duplication of effort and to downsize the overstaffed HR function. But it was also to bring more consistency to the whole HR process and ensure flexible, high-quality services with a clear brand. The few personnel and development professionals who remained at PwC after the cull were identified as the 'human capital consultants' who were to make a new professional team. Their job is to make PwC 'a great place to work' through their strategic input across the range of people management disciplines that include development, recruitment, reward and relations (Arkin 2001).

In another sign of the changing shape of HR functions in many organisations, more than half the 107 people working at the PwC employee service centre in Birmingham when it opened were hired externally. They came from jobs as diverse as a former customer services manager at McAlpine Homes and a mortgage adviser for NatWest. The commonality was the service ethic they all shared and the skills and expertise associated with it.

It was foreseen that once the services centre got underway, administrative HR work in a conventional HR centralised function would no longer be a route into HR professional areas, including L&D, at PwC. Instead, junior staff would be able to gain experience through implementing advice given by the human capital consultants. In due course they could be trained into more senior roles.

Source: ARKIN, A. (2001)

WHICH WAY FOR THE L&D FUNCTION?

Fragmentation or integration?

Findings from a CIPD HR survey reported in 2003 covering over 1,000 organisations of all types and sectors in England and Northern Ireland showed senior HR and development professionals to be significantly upbeat about their functions. Most felt that a corner had at last been turned. They saw the shape and content of HR to be expanding, with outsourcing and internal shared service centres playing a positive part in a move that was making HR business partners significant strategic players (CIPD 2003h).

However, total reliance can never be placed on self-reports. More impartial observers tend to be more critical. At London Business School Gratton (2003b) sees HR roles and responsibilities to have become fragmented, in large part because of the 'bloated, introverted state that many functions had reached' – no exaggeration, if we recall for example the 2002 findings of the Audit Commission concerning the state of HR in local government, reported in Chapter 10. Here is another case that shows the difference that can exist between the rhetoric and the reality, this time the reality of the relationship between training and the wider personnel function.

CASE EXAMPLE

The training function in a public sector organisation

Two researchers were recently asked to review the effectiveness of a training function in a large public sector organisation. They used a comprehensive blended methodology to ensure that reliable information was obtained from those managing the personnel and training functions and from their organisational customers.

HR was structured in a traditional way, with training part of a personnel function that was headed by a generalist. Training activity and those responsible for it held a significantly lower status than elsewhere in the personnel function. Training itself was characterised by a traditional approach dominated by courses held and managed at centre.

Some responsibility for personnel and training had been devolved, and the staff who worked in line departments were independent of the centre, often combining their HR role with other resource management duties. At centre, little attention seemed to be paid to training issues. The impression was of training operating independently of personnel matters, mainly because of a disinterest by personnel generalists in getting involved. Some of them were more concerned with the efficient use of the organisation's training centre than with establishing the most effective approach for a given need. Overall there were few signs of a professional partnership or of shared professional values between the personnel and training staff.

In this organisation training was the Cinderella of the HR function. The researchers commented that this is not an uncommon scenario and that the relationship between personnel and training seems likely to continue for some time to be 'fractured rather than integrated'.

Source: STEWART, J. and HARRIS, L. (2003)

Gratton concludes from her own reflections on the state of many HR functions today that (2003b):

> **'Senior managers look at all the fragments and are not clear how the function as a whole adds value.'**

She then asks:

- Why not outsource the lower value end to low cost providers?
- And the top value end to strategic consulting firms?
- And the employee-facing part to line managers?

And there's the rub: if such steps can be taken, why keep any specialist HR function in the organisation?

The answer seems cruelly simple: why indeed! That answer has already led to the downsizing and sometimes the disappearance of once-powerful, stable HR functions. They have been found wanting in a business environment where many companies, after decades of cost-cutting and human asset stripping to improve short-term performance, seem at last to be starting to understand the need to build their human and social capital. Looking to their HR functions for the expertise to help here, too many look in vain. Companies now spend an estimated 36 per cent of revenues on human capital pay, benefits, training and other expenses related to their workforces. Asked in one survey where the spend was going to, only 16 per cent of financial directors seemed to have any real idea (Rogers 2004).

Such a survey carried out on an L&D function is likely produce similar findings, given the oft-asserted difficulty of measuring any but its short-term quantifiable training outcomes. We already know from the 2004 CIPD's *Training and Development* survey that despite an extraordinary recent increase in mentoring and coaching processes (both carrying heavy intangible costs) very few organisations are even attempting to measure outcomes, let alone provide a business case for the investment (CIPD 2004a).

Hardly surprising, then, to find an increasing number of cases where organisations are radically changing their way of providing L&D services. One such is the following.

CASE EXAMPLE
The first national Rail Academy

In 2003 the Strategic Rail Authority announced the establishment by York College and the National Railway Museum, in partnership with City of York Council and rail companies across the industry, of the Yorkshire Rail Academy. It will be a centre of excellence for all aspects of rail education, training and research. Funding comes from the Yorkshire Regional Development Agency and the Learning and Skills Council.

An SRA report in 2002 had admitted that experience and skills had often been lost as a result of downsizing, that it needed to better use the skills it had, that there was a significant skills gap, and that recruitment and training had been poorly organised.

Sources: MANOCHA, R. (2002) Also http://www.nrm.org.uk/html/ newsarch_pb/academy.asp [accessed 19 September 2004]

I will be discussing ways of setting and measuring the L&D investment in Chapter 13. It is enough to say here that if an L&D function cannot and does not communicate clearly to the business what added value it provides, then it can only expect to be dismantled. Echoing Rogers' (2004) advice to HR professionals more widely, its professionals must move the function into a position of power and avoid it (and them) becoming obsolete. Drawing on her ideas I see three steps to be essential starting points in any attempt to transform any hitherto ineffective L&D function:

- *Build a vision* for what the function should be: one that helps the board with strategies to improve the performance and capability of all organisational members and build human and social capital for the long-term.
- *Strip out non-core activities* and focus on what is really important – strategic people development and knowledge-productive learning in the workplace.
- *Develop new ways* to assess and develop the skills, talent and learning capability in the organisation in line with its long-term goals.

That is only the start. A core function, no matter how small or wherever it is located, must ensure that a strong purpose – a Big Idea – (Purcell et al 2003) embedded in an organisation-wide learning culture pulls together the clusters of localised L&D activity into a coherent whole. Putting Lynda Gratton's ideas into an L&D context, what is needed is (Gratton 2003b):

- *'Operational integration'* around a common employee brand, utilising new technology. An obvious example is Unipart University, described in Chapter 8, but any force that can be used to integrate L&D operations around a strong brand will be relevant. Portals can aid this common front. With skill, so can a shared professional services centre on the lines of that at PcW.
- *'Performance integration'*, through a clear sense in the L&D function of what it wants to achieve, of the streams of projects and processes that it needs to pursue in order to meet its goals, and of its current progress in each together with measures to establish outcomes. Essentially performance integration as described here is about effective, co-ordinated project management and interlocking activities all focused on a common goal or small cluster of goals for the L&D function across the business.
- *'Professional integration'*, described by Gratton as 'the capacity of the whole team to move into collective action through shared bonds of friendship and reciprocity'. This is to do with binding L&D specialists together as a professional group. When they are working on a variety of projects for or across an organisation, there is a danger that they will become professionally isolated. They may then lose their identity, threatening the corporate L&D brand. Someone needs to take on the role of professional leader, ensuring regular opportunities to meet whether virtually or face to face in

order to refresh their knowledge of the function's progress in supporting the aims of the business and of the different initiatives that they are all engaged in to that end, to review their own professional development, and for purposes of social interaction. Again, new technology can be a major aid to this process. Interestingly in the PcW case, at the time of its publication in 2001 the members of the new professional shared services team were not yet sure where they would be based or whether they would form a physical rather than a virtual team (Arkin 2001).

■ *'Intellectual integration'*, through a shared knowledge base. This kind of integration is about accessing, sharing and building on best practice in L&D whether within or outside the organisation in order to increase the power of its impact and, again, to reinforce its organisational identity. The NHS's IDeA Learning Pool is one example of this kind of integrative device.

CASE EXAMPLE

Knowledge sharing in local government

The Improvement and Development Agency (IDeA) is a not-for-profit organisation that acts as local government's in-house HR consultancy. Its staff have carried out peer reviews with many local authorities to support modernisation and good practice. The Agency has a knowledge and learning function that supports IDeA's consultancy arm with knowledge and e-learning databases and runs 'what used to be called training but is now referred to as learning, or, more grandly, "capacity building"' for change and modernisation (Pickard 2002, p34).

IDeA Knowledge is a website that contains good ideas from local authorities that are intended to share information about good practice and improved performance across local government. In 2002 IDeA launched the *Learning Pool* to enable local authorities and their employees to create, pool and exchange e-learning materials, enabling the creation of a virtual private network.

In another initiative, an IDeA consultant has been working with Ipswich Council in a pioneering organisation development and learning programme involving councillors and officers. During the programme maintenance engineers who are experts at project management were brought in to teach the rest of the council, typifying an approach to learning that sees it as a matter of exchanging knowledge in ways that actively involve all participants in the teaching and learning process.

The major drive behind all such IDeA initiatives is to transform a system from one primarily focused on controlling training budgets to one making an active contribution to how people learn and grow and to shifting the control over that process from trainers to learners.

Source: PICKARD, J. (2002)

Challenging traditional concepts of how to organise the L&D function fits with the discussion at the start of this chapter about the growing irrelevance of a concept of structure as a fixed state or infrequently redesigned product. Rigid structures cannot deliver the kind of demanding L&D agenda now common across all employment sectors. Continuous organising, fluid relationships, fuzzy organisational boundaries are the way forward. Judging by the results of research covered in this chapter alone, they require very different kinds of skills to those that currently typify L&D practitioners. Time is running out now. Unless L&D professionals equip themselves with those skills many could face redundancy.

DETERMINING L&D ROLES

Issues of power and politics

The same forces that influence the organisation of the L&D function also shape L&D roles. In both cases radical changes are now taking place. First, though, what do we mean by 'role'? One dictionary definition is (Allen 1990):

> **'*Role*: an actor's part ... a person's or thing's characteristic or expected function.'**

This is a useful way of thinking about 'role' because of the emphasis on playing a part, on interacting in a particular way with others, as well as on functions to be performed. It also highlights the concept of dynamism. Every actor differs in his or her interpretation of a given part and makes of it something unique, as well as fulfilling its formal requirements. These related ideas of a given and a developed element are emphasised in much of the published research about training roles.

Morgan (1997, pp169) illuminates the ways in which roles can be affected by role-holders' attempts to maintain or increase their own status, self-respect and political influence at the expense of those of others. He describes how people can identify with and protect the responsibilities and objectives associated with their specific role, work group, department, or project team, to the point where they 'value achievement of these responsibilities and objectives over and above the achievement of wider organizational goals'.

Fascinating though it would be to extend this discussion by moving into sociological theory in more depth, there is no space here to do so. Suffice to agree with Morgan that 'the potential complexity of organizational politics is mind-boggling, even before we take account of the personalities and personality clashes that usually bring roles and their conflict to life'.

Changing typologies

Turning now to the formal roles that L&D practitioners occupy: for a surprisingly long time the typology (that is to say, classification framework) produced by Pettigrew and colleagues in 1982 remained a meaningful reflection of the range of activity in which trainers have been involved across different organisational settings. Even today, many trainers can identify with its descriptors. Of the five roles – change agent, provider, training manager, role in transition and 'passive provider' – the last often strikes a particular chord. This is the practitioner who performs a purely reactive role, operating at a low level of activity and influence. He or she provides services and systems when asked but never proposes challenging ways of improving organisational performance (Pettigrew et al 1982, p8).

However, such a typology can no longer adequately reflect a shifting reality and a world that goes beyond the bounds of 'training' into the broader territory of learning and knowledge productivity. New roles have been identified over the past two decades, often using such terms as 'strategic facilitators' and 'internal consultants'. Now, even these descriptions may be falling out of date. As Alex Wilson, group HR director at BT (Morton and Wilson 2003) points out, in many organisations managers are being trained to take on specialist development roles themselves, so that they can act as 'people development consultants' who work with their teams to make sure that people 'make the best of themselves'. Line experts or external agencies can also take over roles of administrative expert and even strategic partner.

In a summary that applies as much to the L&D function as to any other field of HR activity Lynda Gratton observes (2003b):

> **'We have outsourced the lower-value operational work, and we are beginning to develop the staff profiling work that will enable us to act as 'employee champions'. We are also putting the 'change agent' roles back into the streams of business to work closely with their line managers' partners. Meanwhile the 'business partners' are either going into the business or clustering around 'best practice' centres, which may be located in different places...'**

A new typology

Drawing on Morton and Wilson's (2003) suggestions, but also reflecting on material covered in the previous section, I have produced a future-oriented typology of L&D roles, shown in Table 6.

To say something about each of the professional roles shown in Table 6:

Professional adviser
This is the term used by PricewaterhouseCoopers to describe their senior, most highly qual-ified L&D staff who are now working in the HR shared professional services centre, but used here it could operate at any organisational level. An alternative term would be 'consultant' but that is now in such common use that it is losing meaning. Advisers should be able to operate alone or in teams, self-managing or leading others. They must be deeply informed not only about the L&D field but also about all areas of the business. They must also ensure that the projects for which they are responsible are delivered on time and to specification, making appropriate use of service-level agreements (identifying how the relationship will work through responsibilities, timescales and measurement criteria based on the specific services to be provided).

Knowledge architect
This could be part of the professional adviser role or a distinctive role in itself. The term is borrowed from Lank (2002) to describe those senior strategic people who are able to provide advice, skills and solutions related to 'knowledge management'. They would be deeply informed in how people use and share knowledge and information, and in the creation and enhancement of collective and individual learning processes supported and stimulated by e-based technology.

Table 6 *A new typology of L&D roles*

Role	National Occupational Standards level at which it is commonly practised	Major focus of role
Professional adviser	3, 4, 5	Business partner, working in or for the organisation to achieve tailored, value-adding solutions to meet the client's needs. Adviser who helps to prepare the organisation for change and supports increased strategic alliance activity.
Knowledge architect	4, 5	Senior strategic adviser on training and learning processes and solutions to aid knowledge creation, sharing, transfer and application to add value.
Brand manager	4, 5	Shapes and maintains a clear and consistent brand image for all L&D activity and ensures L&D staff are engaging with and motivating those who use their services. Manages L&D resources and any L&D professional staff.
Commercial lead	4, 5	Creates revenue streams from the organisation's L&D processes and products selling them to internal and external customers.
Learning specialist	3, 4, 5	Expert specialist in design, delivery and evaluation of learning events and processes.
Administrator	3	Supports L&D activity at all levels.

Brand manager

If L&D activity, however fragmented it may be in an organisation, is to survive as a meaningful collective programme for an organisation, then it must have a clear brand, with which an L&D mission, set of values and code of behaviour is consistently associated. The brand manager would be the prime mover here, responsible for managing and marketing the L&D function within and beyond the organisation. A related task would be to ensure that those belonging to the L&D professional team, however far flung they may be, share a collective identity, holding and putting into practice a set of values that represent the way that the function should behave towards clients and customers in and outside the organisation.

Commercial lead

This role would require entrepreneurial flair, product development and marketing skills, and financial expertise, although not necessarily specialist L&D qualifications. In many organisations now, helped especially by web-based technology, there is a trend to convert the fruits of L&D activity and experience within the organisation into knowledge-based commodities with commercial appeal.

Learning specialist

This role would involve specialist training, learning and development functional tasks but acquires a new dimension with the rapid growth of innovative e-learning and e-training technology. Learning specialists must be able to work closely with all other types of L&D role-holders as their work supports and informs elements of each.

This typology is only tentative, intended as a starting point for debate. L&D professionals need to take the lead in proposing new shapes for their function and new roles for themselves. In a tough, demanding world, standing still is not an option if they want to avoid the fate that, according to Gratton (2003a), has already overtaken some HR functions:

> '.... a Humpty Dumpty, fallen from the wall and shattered into fragments on the hard pavement below.'

REFLECTION

Build a vision, strip out non-core activities, develop new ways to assess and develop skills and learning capability in the organisation.

Reflecting on these three requirements for a lean, focused, value-adding L&D function, how far do you think they have been met in your organisation, and what kind of roles would you recommend in the future for its L&D professionals?

MANAGING THE L&D FUNCTION

The managerial role

The accountability for employee training and learning belongs squarely with line management, but they should be able to call on the support of L&D professionals in carrying out whatever L&D tasks may have been devolved to them. The development of L&D strategy and plans across the business may or may not involve an L&D manager. However the accountability for the running of a specialist L&D function no matter what its type or size lies with the L&D manager or equivalent role. Like any other manager, he or she must have a mastery of skills to do with planning, direction, communication and control, since the key tasks that the role involves are about:

- Clarifying the function's mission and plans.
- Determining how its plans are to be implemented and ensuring a sufficient, but no more than sufficient, resource base in order to implement them.
- Providing training for those who will be responsible for carrying out the plans.
- Working to ensure that line managers' basic L&D responsibilities are taken seriously and are competently performed in the organisation.
- Taking a proactive stance in the development of a learning culture in the organisation.
- Ensuring that the L&D function is a centre of excellence and a benchmark for L&D products, processes and services.

In this final section of the chapter the aim is to look at the management of the L&D function not in any technical way, but to identify critical tasks and some strategic implications.

Leading and managing the people

Leadership and teamwork

As we have seen earlier, innovative structural forms offer a way of combining a strategic core and a strong L&D brand with flexibility, adaptability and knowledge productivity for the L&D function. For this to work, however, there must be high quality leadership and management to ensure the recruitment, building and sustaining of effective L&D teams. Increasingly these are likely to contain a shifting population drawn from across the organisation and outside it.

Good leadership and teamwork requires (drawing broadly on Gratton 2003c):

- *A holistic approach*, based on the building of an accurate overall picture of L&D activity in the organisation. This means creating and maintaining a database that captures the organisation's skills base, what is happening to L&D plans on the ground, what value is being achieved, and what links are being made with other HR policies and practices. A variety of L&D initiatives may be being pursued across an organisation, but all will need some overall co-ordination. Fragmentation must not mean disintegration.
- *Translation of policies into practice through realistic plans*. Project teams, service level agreements, business partnerships all have a part to play here. But although the L&D manager holds ultimate accountability for plans, skilled delegation is crucial. Recalling the principles embedded in the People Performance framework discussed in Chapter 5, the emphasis should be on giving maximum discretion to competent and committed L&D staff to exercise their skills as they judge best.
- *Keeping the best and scrapping the rest*. L&D strategies, processes and initiatives need to be regularly monitored so that they can be changed, even abandoned, if business partners agree that they are no longer fulfilling a useful purpose.

Continuing professional development and career planning

Pressures of time and financial resource mean that self-development is the most reliable way for core L&D staff to remain expert. In the shift from training to learning in organisations it is also a process that they should encourage and support in others. They should be the role models.

In career planning, it is important to pay attention to the needs of all L&D staff, not just those likely to be moving up or moving on. Offering some form of career development to all will make an important statement about the many ways in which they can develop within as well as beyond the boundaries and levels of their present positions. It will give impetus to building a learning culture and relational psychological contracts within the L&D function. Achieving and updating qualifications is crucial for professionals, but the L&D manager should also promote continuous learning opportunities in and outside the organisation that will support and stimulate continuing professional development.

The principles that apply to the management of specialist L&D staff apply equally to the support of others, especially line managers, who carry responsibility for L&D in or for the organisation. The L&D manager therefore needs to work with senior management on the tasks already outlined in the section on 'the line managed function' to ensure that a devolved L&D process is fully effective.

Using national and professional standards

We have seen in earlier chapters the major emphasis in today's organisations on targets of performance, measurement of outcomes and professional expertise in the HR area. It is therefore inevitable for national, professional and other awarding bodies to be constantly expanding and updating standards of competency that specify clear performance outcomes expected at different levels, and qualification and assessment structures related to those standards. In the UK the national L&D occupational standards and the CIPD's L&D professional standards are key in the L&D field.

National occupational standards

The national professional qualification structure for those involved in L&D activity is shown in Table 7. There are in addition nine certificate or 'entry level' level units covering formal workplace training and learning activities. Although roles are not explicitly identified in the structure, I have suggested in the table the kind indicated by the standards (not shown here) underpinning the framework.

CIPD professional standards

The CIPD identifies two generic roles for all those with personnel and development responsibilities: those of business partner and of thinking performer. It offers a set of practitioner-level standards across four fields. Each Standard contains performance indicators to guide educational design and competent professional performance at a basic practitioner level in the workplace (CIPD 2001a). Its various L&D-related standards focus on the kinds of contribution that anyone operating in the L&D field must be able to make at that level.

It can be argued that to emphasise generic standards is to become a slave to compliance and to stifle innovation and challenges to 'the norm'. However, in a field like L&D where poor practice is widespread their provision is essential to aid improved performance. Other benefits that can be achieved through the use of national and professional standards in an L&D function include:

■ clarification of what is involved in the exercise of L&D roles at different levels
■ the provision of job descriptions for L&D staff to guide their recruitment and selection
■ improved individual development, career-planning and progression
■ benchmarks for good practice
■ effective evaluation of L&D performance as a basis for appraisal
■ the measurement of skills gaps in the function and subsequent identification of suitable vocational courses to tackle these.

Table 7 *The national vocational qualification structure in Learning and Development*

Level		Title	Role indicated
5	Higher level qualification	Learning and Development	L&D director or equivalent role. Holds senior executive responsibility for L&D or is a consultant at corporate strategic level.
4	Advanced level qualifications	Learning and Development Management of L&D provision Co-ordination of L&D provision.	Roles to do with the management and improvement of a range of programmes and delivery or facilitation of a broader range of learning opportunities than those at Level 3. They incorporate various forms of workplace learning.
3	Advanced level qualifications	Direct training and support Learning and Development	Roles to do with identifying learning needs, agreeing programmes with learners, and monitoring, supporting, facilitating or delivering those and other work-based learning activity.

REFLECTION

Imagine that you have been asked to make some well-justified recommendations to enhance the leadership and management of the L&D function's staff in an organisation known to you. What would they be?

Managing the budget

I will be discussing the measurement and assessment of the added value that an effective L&D function can produce in Chapter 13. As explained at the start of this chapter it is not my purpose to go into the practical detail of how to cost training and learning activity. What is relevant at this point is a brief discussion of the L&D budget, since it is central to the effective financial management of the function, and is a crucial aid to planning and prioritising its activity.

Financial management is a big issue now for L&D managers and project leaders, especially with such a wide variety of funding sources now available, ranging from Learning and Skills Councils to the European Social Fund. However all funding whether from internal or external sources is increasingly tightly tied to targets, with funders and sponsors having high expectations of accountability and unique accounting procedures. In whatever context, the L&D

budget is a crucial tool and its central purpose is always the same: to identify what is being spent, under what headings, why, and with what intended and actual outcomes.

A budget's format and coverage should make it possible to quickly identify changing trends in L&D activity from one financial period to the next, and to highlight areas of activity that, cost-wise, are problematic. Where priority needs cannot be met within planned budgetary limits, a business case must be put forward for obtaining more money or for meeting needs through a changed pattern of activity. A good L&D budget will identify the annual running costs of the L&D function (personnel, overheads and administrative) together with L&D activity areas, the significant costs associated with them and their projected returns. Returns can flow from L&D commercial enterprise, from line managers with devolved budgets who decide to purchase the function's services, from external funders, and from reduction in quantifiable costs that can be confidently traced to the success of L&D initiatives (reduced turnover rates, improved production rates, increased sales and so on).

There is no one best way to produce an L&D budget whether for a company, an L&D function or a single L&D project. It is a practical document and has to be adapted to context. It must clarify in a format and language that suits its envisaged audience what are the costs of the L&D investment, how far they vary from costs in the previous budget period, how they are going to be recouped, and what if any gaps there are between finance available and needed. Those gaps will then become the subject for discussion. In sum: the budget is core to financial accounting but it also informs options for action and aids decisions about the L&D function's operation and the organisation's L&D investment.

Budgeting is therefore a crucial responsibility of any L&D manager. Yet during 2001 when the CIPD sent a questionnaire to 7,000 training managers concerning their management of budgets only 129 replied and their responses revealed that few had anything like a complete picture of their training costs (Cannell 2002). Presumably they had even less idea of costs associated with their less quantifiable L&D activity. How then could they hope to prove the worth of their functions or the added value of the L&D investment?

Managing the marketing and data base

In the CIPD's L&D Standard the need for competent marketing of L&D activity is stressed, but equal emphasis is placed on the need for collaborative working with stakeholders. Marketing in this sense is not to do with glossy brochures or expensive public relations efforts. It is to do with developing the right kind of products and services for clients and customers, and involving them throughout in that process.

Any L&D marketing plan therefore needs to clarify:

- How the L&D function fits into the organisation's value chain, and serves the organisation's vision and goals.
- How L&D specialists will work with internal customers in order to identify their L&D needs, relate them to overall business needs, and agree on how best to respond to them.
- How the L&D function will offer the most appropriate and cost-effective L&D products, services and processes for the organisation.
- How L&D plans will be collaboratively implemented, monitored and evaluated across the organisation.

The success of marketing depends to a large extent on having an accurate, up-to-date and appropriate information system, but that is essential for far more than marketing purposes alone. A good database will aid the identification of training and learning needs, supply evidence of L&D activity, provide details of when, where, why, for whom and for what purposes that activity has been undertaken, and act as a centralised source of up-to-date knowledge, experience, practices and ideas.

In a multi-site organisation, training records will probably be kept at each site but there must also be a centralised database, and with progress in information and communication technology the potential tensions between two systems should be much reduced. Failure to adequately reconcile the local with the central in the interests of a unified system can give rise to any or all of the following problems:

- L&D activity across the organisation will not be adequately identified and monitored, leading to the possibility of irrelevant, costly, or needlessly duplicated initiatives.
- The organisation will lack adequate evidence to show that all its L&D activity is legally compliant and ethical.
- There will be no central store of knowledge to show outcomes of L&D activity initiatives across the organisation, and this will impair the quality of the L&D planning process.
- There will be no integration of L&D and personnel records held in different parts of the organisation, thus hampering achievement of consistency of overall human resource policy-making.
- There will be insufficient attention to core organisation-wide L&D needs.
- Individuals' records of training (and associated data on any problems in their performance during or after training) may get lost when they move from one part of the organisation to another, or from one organisational level to another.
- There will be a lack of coherent organisational policies on qualification structures, career and succession planning.

The importance of an L&D database that is fit for purpose and that meshes well with wider HR information systems cannot be overemphasised, as the following case illustrates.

CASE EXAMPLE
The Southall train crash

In its report into the 1997 rail crash in Southall in which seven people lost their lives, the Health and Safety Commission extensively criticised the training function. One of the most disturbing deficiencies that the report highlighted was a failure to maintain and pass on drivers' records, so that key performance errors which training should have remedied were not always identified. Another was a 'surprising absence' of any unified record system. One of the recommendations was that Railtrack and the Association of Train Operating Companies set up a national qualification and accreditation system for drivers. This would enable centrally held records to be made available to the current employer.

Source: COOPER, C. (2000b)

What is particularly worrying in this case is that clearly the 'surprising absence' continued, since in subsequent major train crashes in England (notably Paddington) similar training records failures were identified.

An L&D resource management cycle

To conclude this entire section on managing an L&D function, in Figure 12 I have adapted the learning cycle first produced by Kolb et al (1974) to produce a resource management process for the L&D function.

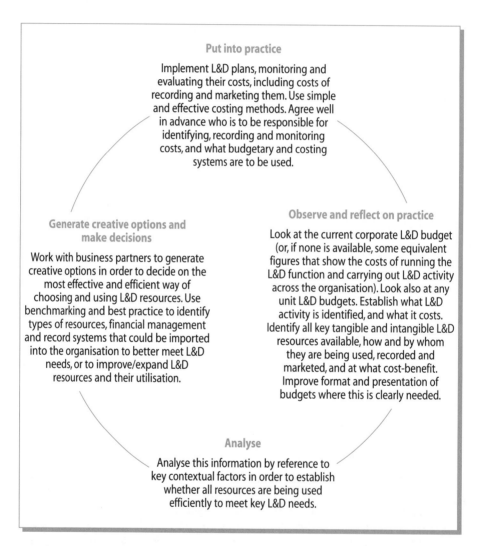

Put into practice

Implement L&D plans, monitoring and evaluating their costs, including costs of recording and marketing them. Use simple and effective costing methods. Agree well in advance who is to be responsible for identifying, recording and monitoring costs, and what budgetary and costing systems are to be used.

Observe and reflect on practice

Look at the current corporate L&D budget (or, if none is available, some equivalent figures that show the costs of running the L&D function and carrying out L&D activity across the organisation). Look also at any unit L&D budgets. Establish what L&D activity is identified, and what it costs. Identify all key tangible and intangible L&D resources available, how and by whom they are being used, recorded and marketed, and at what cost-benefit. Improve format and presentation of budgets where this is clearly needed.

Generate creative options and make decisions

Work with business partners to generate creative options in order to decide on the most effective and efficient way of choosing and using L&D resources. Use benchmarking and best practice to identify types of resources, financial management and record systems that could be imported into the organisation to better meet L&D needs, or to improve/expand L&D resources and their utilisation.

Analyse

Analyse this information by reference to key contextual factors in order to establish whether all resources are being used efficiently to meet key L&D needs.

Figure 12 *The cycle of L&D resource management*

CONCLUSION

You should by now have a broad-based understanding of key issues effecting the organisation and management of the L&D function, and feel confident in tackling the review questions on this chapter that are provided in Appendix 3.

The chapter's five sections have covered the following main ground:

- The nature of the changing structural arrangements evident in many organisations today, and some implications for L&D practitioners working in a context where organising and re-organising is going on regularly.
- Key influences on the ways in which L&D functions are organised in different settings, and various options for its shape. Any move into shared services will be of particular significance for a function, since it could mean either its complete down-sizing, or a brighter future with new developmental and business opportunities for competent L&D staff.
- Two opposite directions in which L&D functions are moving in today's fast-changing and turbulent business environment: some towards further fragmentation and serving little purpose in their organisations, others towards a new kind of integration with real strategic and commercial thrust.
- The pressures and opportunities that newer organisational forms for the function are placing on L&D roles. L&D professionals need to take the lead in proposing relevant and innovative roles for themselves if they are to move forward instead of face possible redundancy. A new typology has been proposed in the chapter as a starting point for debate.
- The need for L&D managers to lead as well as manage their core staff and bind together all who operate under an organisation's L&D brand. This involves a high level of managerial expertise, both in the leadership and management of people and in the management of non-personnel resources. A model of the resource management cycle has been proposed in the chapter for an L&D function.

Further information sources

KARTEN, N. (2001). *How to establish service level agreements*. Randolph, MA: Karten Associates. Order from slaO@nkarten.com, or see excerpts on:
htttp://www.ServiceLevel Agreements.com [accessed 19 September 2004].

The ENTO website for the national Learning and Development vocational qualification structure: http://www.ento.co.uk/standards/landd_qs.php?catalogue=landd [accessed 19 September 2004].

The CIPD's website for its professional standards:
http://www.cipd.co.uk/mandq/standards/prac/sgpd/ [accessed 19 September 2004].

The CIPD website's link for ways of calculating the cost of developing and delivering a training programme:
http://www.cipd.co.uk/subjects/training/general/cstngtrain.htm?IsSrchRes=1 [accessed 24 September 2004].

Producing and Implementing L&D Strategy

INTRODUCTION

The purpose of this chapter is to explore ways of ensuring that L&D activity in an organisation is underpinned by a sound planning process, and incorporates powerful value-adding activity with strategic thrust. The gap between strategy and its implementation on the ground is a significant one for HR professionals. Looking at the frequent criticisms of L&D practice in organisations it seems clear that the strategy and planning processes are often poorly understood and that plans in consequence add little if no value.

The chapter has six sections. The first explores concepts relating to the strategic integration of L&D activity. The second looks at ways of producing L&D strategy for an organisation and the barriers and aids to the process. Three approaches to planning an organisation's L&D activity are then identified and illustrated, together with their different implications for L&D professionals. The chapter ends with a reflection on problems of implementation and some practical issues for L&D professionals.

ISSUES OF INTEGRATION

Achieving 'fit'

It is a classic principle in the human resource (HR) literature that any HR strategy should achieve horizontal and vertical integration. Applied to an L&D strategy this means:

- *Horizontal integration*: integrating L&D activity with other HR practices so that there is consistency across the whole HR area (as shown in Figure 2 in Chapter 1), with all its activity supporting organisational goals.
- *Vertical integration*: integrating L&D strategy with overarching HR strategy and with business strategy at corporate and business unit levels.

The integrating principles are clear but the practice is difficult. Sometimes the task may prove impossible. There has been much discussion about the problems of alignment, or fit, in the HR literature, notably by Karen Legge (1995). It is irrelevant to reproduce it here, but a few points indicate the challenges involved for an L&D function.

Horizontal integration

- If other HR practices and processes in the organisation are of poor quality and inappropriate focus, then to align L&D practices and processes with them will compound activity that can harm the business.
- When adjustments or radical changes are needed to any aspect of L&D practices, consequent adjustments need to be made to other HR practices. Likewise L&D activity must give continuing support to HR practices. Such co-ordination is rare. We saw in the previous chapter the gloomy observations of Stewart and Harris (2003) in their review of an HR function in local government in the UK. There are many other

such cases to indicate lack of joined-up thinking in the HR area and of L&D's frequent status as poor relation in the HR family.

■ If there is no attempt to integrate, then one HR process (L&D) will be operating independently of – and perhaps in opposition to – other HR processes. The dangers here are obvious: silo mentalities and lost opportunities for adding major value through a coherent thrust.

■ Where L&D is a stand-alone function in the business the L&D professional must convince the organisation's management of the need for first priority to be given to establishing a framework of HR policy and action, must if required advise on what that framework might be, and must then ensure that it is implemented. Barratt the builders was just such a case in the North East of England in the 1980s (Harrison 1996b, pp1–53).

Vertical integration

The command to 'align L&D strategy with business strategy' (let alone with HR strategy) begs some awkward questions about the type of strategy in mind: corporate or divisional? Short or long-term? Of high quality, or merely any strategy – good or bad – that is formally in place at the time? And who produces it?

A number of major reports (WF 2003, Holbeche 2003, EEF and CIPD 2003, Purcell et al 2003) all agree that there is 'a worrying gap between effective management and what is actually happening in UK organisations' (Philpott 2003c). Few firms adopt a joined-up approach to managing across five performance categories: customers and market, shareholders, stakeholders, employees, and creativity and innovation. Few invest in state of the art people management practices. Few understand that in order to achieve high organisational performance there must be 'a workforce that sees the big picture and is enabled and motivated to act, with middle managers able to translate strategy into workforce goals' (WF 2003). The CIPD's survey 'Voices from the boardroom' painted a particularly discouraging picture, with very few board-level members having any awareness of the links that can be made between HR strategy and organisational performance (Guest et al 2001). Strategy expert Gordon Hewitt (2003) confirms the poor quality of many business strategies and therefore questions the wisdom of any tight vertical integration of HR strategy. Such integration can put HR into a purely reactive role, delivering value through carrying out the requirements of business strategy but not co-creating that strategy and therefore unable to influence it at the developmental stage.

Yet there is evidence on the other side of the coin too. The ESRC's *Future of Work* programme (see end of chapter) offers in its scale and credibility some of the most reliable information available on the state of the UK's labour market. Reviewing one of its surveys carried out towards the end of 2002, Emmott (2004) found that HR practices, especially those related to reward and to career development, were showing a significant trend by many employers to develop 'intelligent flexibility' through more versatile and interchangeable employees. In their organisations there was increased job quality and higher levels of discretionary power by employees over their work. Although the Workplace Employment Relations Survey (Wood and de Menezes 1998) found that very few employers had adopted so-called high-commitment practices wholeheartedly, by late 2002 a subsequent survey indicated that nearly three in ten workplaces had by then put such a strategy in place. These organisations had a clear HR agenda at strategic level, demonstrating serious efforts to link HR and business strategies (White et al 2004).

Overall, then, it does seem to be the case that HR is a truly strategic partner only in a small minority of organisations. The size of that minority is steadily increasing and where that is happening HR strategy appears to be making a valuable contribution to organisational performance. However, the bulk of evidence suggests that the gap between the ideal and the reality remains wide.

Achieving strategic thrust

Given the difficulties involved in achieving 'fit', what is the way forward for strategies in the HR area? Research findings suggest that there are two different approaches in use: tight coupling and loose coupling.

The tight-coupled approach

Tight-coupled models involved a close interconnection between different types of business strategy and organisational structure on the one hand, and of HR activity on the other. The type and content of selection, appraisal, reward and developmental policies should, in this view, follow the specific type of business strategy and organisational structure.

So-called 'hard' tight-coupled models come predominantly from the Michigan School of business management theory in the USA. The approach advocated by HR writers such as Galbraith and Nathanson (1978) and Fombrun, Tichy and Devanna (1984) appeals through its surface rationality and its operational detail. However it depends for its success on a relevant, clear and detailed business strategy that is agreed by all the parties, that remains fairly stable through time, and that consistently guides action throughout the organisation. In today's fast-moving and complex business world such conditions are increasingly unlikely to be present. Even where strategy is appropriate and has the commitment of most of the parties for much of the time, many contingencies can throw it out of line – together with any HR strategies that are tied to its coat tails.

The loose-coupled approach

Chris Hendry (1995) urged HR professionals to develop a deep knowledge of the business, its attributes and its environment, and to work with management on flexible HR strategies that best fit current needs and can be quickly adapted to meet new contingencies. His 'loose coupling' approach relies on HR practitioners, working in business partnerships, to operate pragmatically. They must produce HR plans for business units that respond to their needs while being in line with the overall goals and drivers of the business rather than lining up with every element of business strategy.

A loose-coupled approach thus focuses on expanding an organisation's capacity through practices that fit its context. Organisational capacity is produced by organisational structure and culture, routines and procedures, budgetary controls and corrective actions, business processes and organisational networks. Research has shown that it can be enhanced by many HR practices, especially in the L&D field (Huselid 1995; Patterson et al 1997; Terry and Purcell 1997; Guest and King 2001; Purcell et al 2003). However it needs considerable skill. I have already described in Chapter 5 the different ways in which Tesco's corporate HR policy and strategy was recently implemented in four of its stores, in some cases producing effective loose coupling, in other cases not. The HR practices that worked best were flexible, had a robust link with the 'Big Idea' and its values, and were implemented by front-line managers who gave their teams significant opportunity for discretionary behaviour in their jobs, and supported them in using that discretion to improve store performance (Purcell et al 2003, pp28–31).

Table 8 shows the way a loose-coupled approach to L&D strategy and implementation could work. Later in the chapter you will find a case example that illustrates a continuous strategising and planning process that achieves this kind of integration.

Table 8 *Building L&D into the business*

Strategic level	L&D's strategic focus is on	L&D must	Crucial processes for L&D	L&D specialist/manager needs to
1 Corporate	■ formulating L&D mission, goals and strategy to achieve corporate goals ■ influencing and developing strategic thinking and planning	■ 'fit' with wider HR strategy ■ be aligned with corporate strategy ■ help to secure appropriate balance between corporate goals for survival and for advancement ■ produce L&D strategy that is capable of implementation at Level 2	■ collaboratively developing mission and goals for L&D ■ strategic planning and thinking ■ influencing key stakeholders ■ adding value through L&D activity	■ have board-level position/access and skills ■ be pro-active as well as reactive ■ have deep knowledge of competitive environment ■ fully understand the value chain and strategic assets of the business ■ speak the language and logic of the business ■ work in business partnerships
2 Business unit/ managerial	■ developing L&D policies and systems in line with strategic needs of the business unit ■ ensuring achievement of business targets ■ influencing and developing strategic thinking, organisational capacity and human capability	■ 'fit' with wider HR policies and systems ■ be aligned with business unit policy ■ have a clear plan within the overall business plan, with agreed evaluation measures ■ ensure feedback on policies to Level 1	■ working with HR and business unit managers to produce policies and plans for acquisition, retention, growth/ redeployment of workforce ■ developing key performance indicators ■ strategic thinking and business planning ■ adding value through L&D activity	■ work in business partnership with managers and others ■ have collaborative relationships with other HR specialists ■ have deep knowledge of competitive environment of company and of business units ■ fully understand how strategic assets can be developed ■ speak the language and logic of the business units
3 Operational	■ ensuring individual and team performance targets are met ■ improving acquisition, quality and motivation of people for the business.	■ adapt to needs of the business and needs and aspirations of people ■ ensure L&D activity is expertly carried out and appropriately evaluated ■ ensure feedback of outcomes to Level 2.	■ working with teams and individuals to implement business plans for L&D ■ appraisal, personal development planning to achieve targets and improve core competencies and capabilities.	■ work in partnership with internal and external stakeholders ■ have effective and efficient systems and procedures ■ have deep knowledge of culture of the workforce ■ be expert and continuously self-developing.

PRODUCING L&D STRATEGY

A five-step process

The textbook approach to developing an L&D strategy involves five steps:

1. *Agree on the strategy-making team*: this should involve a broad-based group incorporating not only the key functional players but also a range of mindsets to challenge accepted thinking and generate fresh thinking about L&D strategy.
2. *Clarify organisational mission*: identify the espoused purpose of the organisation and its long-term goals.
3. *Explore core values*: carry out internal and external stakeholder analysis to clarify:
   - the organisation's identity in the eyes of its employees and of the outside world
   - its vision and values, and whether or not they are shared across the organisation. Values espoused at the top but not reflected in actions and behaviours in the organisation (whether at the top itself or elsewhere) will hinder the implementation of any strategy that is underpinned by those values
   - the basic needs it exists to meet, and its ultimate clients. If organisations in the National Health Service, for example, could truly achieve their mission, what would the world then look like for their patients and the communities that they serve?
   - what currently stands in the way of the organisation meeting those needs?
   - what makes the L&D function distinctive in this organisation, either in positive or negative ways?
4. *Carry out SWOT or PESTLE analysis to identify the strategic issues facing the organisation*: draw on professional and business knowledge to analyse the data, relating to the then information generated about the organisation's espoused and enacted mission and values to diagnose the strategic issues faced by the organisation. Then prioritise these, for example in terms of:
   - issues to keep an eye on for the future – they do not need immediate action but they may throw up problems or opportunities at some later point in time
   - issues that the organisation can handle within its ongoing plans and activity and so need no new strategies to tackle them
   - issues that are relevant to the HR area – these will provide the frame for the next and final step.
5. *Agree an L&D strategy and strategic plan*: agree on L&D goals and strategy to tackle long and short-term issues that have L&D implications. Long-term goals for the function should be set, and then a strategy for the shorter term to guide progress towards them. 'Long-term' and 'shorter-term' are subjective terms. For a small firm 'long term' may only be a couple of years, for a large organisation considerably longer.

This stage involves generating options, with careful analysis of what each would involve, its feasibility and the added value it would bring before agreeing on a strategy and then on a corporate L&D plan to carry it out. Scenario planning is often used at this stage. Its purpose is to confront uncertainty by thinking of different possible future scenarios, in this case both for the organisation and for the L&D function. A team that includes lateral thinkers from a wide variety of backgrounds is chosen, ideally from outside as well as from within the organisation, so that contrasting mindsets and bodies of knowledge are brought to bear on the planning process. The process aims to produce a clearer understanding of the forces that drive change in the organisation and in the L&D function by generating a variety of strongly contrasting possible future paths for both. Through a thorough exploration of these multiple perspectives, a strategy and plan for L&D can ultimately be agreed that has a built-in adaptability and sufficient loose-coupling from current business strategy.

Reason has its limits

The logic of the textbook approach to L&D planning that I have just described is clear. It can work, but it needs L&D strategy to be given full support by top management, robust business partnerships between the key players, challenging, innovative thinking and a high-quality, proactive L&D service. In many organisations that scenario does not exist, and here we have to return to the problems associated with the strategic management of the business. The classical view of the strategy process rests on two assumptions:

- That decision-makers share a common purpose and are driven by a shared economic logic when making strategic decisions: all seek to maximise economic rewards and minimise costs for the business.
- That decision-makers systematically 'collect and sort information about alternative potential solutions, compare each solution against predetermined criteria to asses degree of fit, arrange solutions in order of preference and make an optimizing choice which they then equally systematically draw up plans to implement' (Miller et al 1999, p44).

In reality, as Simon famously identified (1945), all decision-making is severely limited by the bounded economic rationality of the players involved. In organisational life as more widely decisions are not 'arrived at by a step by step process which is both logical and linear' (Miller et al 1999, p44). An organisation is not a unitary system, with the players coming together naturally in pursuit of a common goal. It is a pluralist system, where 'rationality' often breaks down in the confusion caused by conflicting interests and by diverse perceptions as to 'what matters here' and how to tackle it.

The concept of bounded rationality does not refer to people behaving irrationally in the broad sense of that word. Quite the reverse: for most of the time, most people are, by their own lights, very reasoned in their behaviour. What it means is that the reasoning underpinning their behaviour is influenced by many non-economic arguments and by 'human frailties and demands from both within and outside the organization' (Miller et al 1999, p45). Some of the factors that pull players away from a purely rational approach include confused, excessive, incomplete or unreliable data, incompetent processing or communicating of information, pressures of time, human emotions, and differences in individuals' cognitive processes, mental maps and reasoning capacity (Simon 1955; Cyert and March 1963). Decision-making is further limited by the power play that becomes intense the more the issues under discussion are controversial and important for the organisation and for various powerful groups and individuals involved.

The strategy process is further complicated by the fact that in any organisation some members have the automatic right to sit at the strategy table, others are excluded from it and many have little or no access to or influence over those who make the big strategic decisions that relate to their field – a fate that often typifies L&D professionals' position, even when there is an HR director at board level.

Planning the delivery

The strategic management process therefore is an uncertain one and is highly politicised. However, once a strategic framework however imperfect has been agreed – or imposed –

for L&D activity, planning has to take place to determine how best to implement strategic intent.

There is no one best way to carry out L&D planning and in consequence no handy generic template. Each L&D practitioner has to find his or her own approach, depending on their organisational context and level, the role, status and structuring of L&D in the business, and other such variables. In this section I outline three types of approach that can be found in organisations today. They range from the highly systematic centralised 'plan as product' approach to a more or less continuous planning process. The latter reflects that wider movement in organisations, noted in Chapter 4 and again in Chapter 11, away from a preoccupation with strategy and structure as fixed and relatively stable commodities to fluid strategising and organising processes.

THE CENTRALISED PLANNING APPROACH

Linking to business strategy

This represents the traditional approach to training and development (T&D) planning. It typifies an era of relatively stable, quite powerful centralised training functions (the use of the term T&D is deliberate, because training was the main focus of learning and development activity in this era). The approach is still used, especially in the public sector, as can be seen on the *Employers' Organisation for local government* website in its 60-page workforce development planning guide (EOLG 2003).

The aim of this approach is to provide a database on a large and diverse workforce and use it to produce an agreed and detailed T&D plan covering the entire workforce, with sub-plans catering for specific needs related to different occupational groups, business units and individuals' personal development plans. The local government workforce planning guidelines, for example, stress the need to identify action to enhance basic skills of the workforce in line with government skills strategy and to improve specific areas of skill in line with the public sector reform agenda.

The corporate T&D plan brings together in a practical document T&D needs derived from the business and staffing plans, the performance appraisal process and any other relevant sources. It prioritises needs, shows standards or targets to meet related to them, how those will be achieved, and estimated timescales. It specifies those carrying accountability for T&D in the organisation, and shows budget allocations per division and for the main areas of T&D activity that the plan encompasses. The aim is to apply a management by objectives approach at all levels, with clearly defined objectives and SMART methods of measuring T&D's outcomes (see Appendix 6). The plan and its sub-plans operate on a rolling basis, and are updated annually or at other agreed intervals. Monitoring aims to capture any needs for adjustment or new activity in the face of new contingencies. Often it incorporates the use of milestones, as in the following example.

CASE EXAMPLE

HRM strategic milestones in a British investment bank

During 1990–91 County NatWest, an investment bank, asked all its business units, including its personnel department, to establish strategic milestones for a five-year period. Their performance was to be measured against those milestones at specified target dates.

The requirement to produce strategic milestones as an input to the bank's five-year business plan 'marked an important watershed in defining the contribution of personnel to the business at a strategic level. It forced the department to reflect on the nature of that contribution.' (Riley and Sloman 1991).

Senior management of the bank duly authorised 18 separate strategic milestones. The milestones were consistent one with the other, and overall addressed issues that consultation within business units and across the three personnel teams had shown to be critical to business success. Each milestone was assigned to a designated individual and was incorporated into his or her own targets of performance. Quarterly reviews on progress, involving the whole department, were subsequently held to ensure that the milestones were on target.

Source: RILEY, K. and SLOMAN, M. (1991)

The operational tasks that a centralised T&D planning process involves seek to ensure that:

- T&D considerations are taken fully into account when business strategy is formulated.
- They form part of a human resource plan within the wider business plan.
- At business unit/divisional level there are policies to ensure people are trained and developed in line with the needs of the business.
- At the individual level T&D is an integrated part of daily routine and procedures, helping people to achieve performance standards and behavioural objectives and building up the kind of workforce needed in terms of productivity, quality and flexibility.
- T&D staff operate a collaborative approach to planning at every stage in order to ensure a high level of buy-in from line management and other stakeholders.

Here is a case study to illustrate this approach. It relates to a real organisation. Only the name of the Trust has been changed to ensure anonymity.

CASE EXAMPLE

Wesdale Acute Hospitals NHS Trust during the 1990s

Wesdale Acute Hospitals NHS Trust was a major provider of health care, catering for the needs of around 300,000 people in its area. It had many stakeholders – patients, staff, the local Health Commission, Community Health Council, Community Healthcare and general practitioners. The Trust's philosophy was 'Partners in Quality – working together to deliver a sensitive, caring health service, changing to meet your individual needs – today and in the future'. Its priorities during the 1990s were the building of a new District General Hospital (DGH) over five years through a controversial private finance initiative, and implementing an interim rationalisation plan related to that radical organisational change.

The Trust had four strategic goals, of which one was explicitly related to its people: 'valuing all those who work with and for us, and developing their capability and commitment through a wide range of individual and corporate training and development opportunities and programmes'. Triggered by the business goals and strategy put in place in the early 1990s, the Trust established a strategic approach to training and development at three levels: corporate, business unit and operational.

At corporate level, the HR director to whom the training manager reported had a seat on the board and was responsible for HR policy. This, and a major HR agenda leading up to the opening of the new DGH, ensured that training goals and strategy were continually related to the goals of the Trust. As part of the Trust's Annual Plan, a training plan identified a range of activities to be undertaken within the framework of overall corporate strategy and ensured evaluation of past activities as well as assessment of future investment needed.

At unit level, clinical directorates' business plans had to include the training needed to support changes and developments in services. A multidisciplinary Training and Development Group was established to oversee the implementation of a corporate approach to the delivery of all initiatives. The Group identified training responses to organisational requirements identified in the Annual Plan.

At operational level, the Trust was recognised early on as an 'Investor in People' and was successfully re-accredited. It ran its own national vocational qualification (NVQ) programmes. There was a business-led framework for the training and development process that, in the devolved management structure, was the primary responsibility of line management. That process involved identification of training needs through annual appraisal, personal development plans for all staff, encouragement to achieve NVQs, monitoring of staff performance and development, and evaluation of training events. Together, these activities enabled a 'bottom-up' as well as 'top-down' approach to be taken to developing training strategy in the Trust.

The Trust's T&D process was strategically driven and its outcomes informed the planning process. Key principles were:

- All T&D activities are goal-driven – they arise out of and feed back into T&D goals that in turn support the wider goals of the business.
- T&D has real strategic status – it is formally supported by corporate, unit level and operational management, and there is a real belief at those levels that it is supporting and also helping to drive business strategy.
- There is a clear T&D strategy – and all T&D activities, including appraisal, training, continuous development, programmes to achieve multiskilling, total quality and culture change, are being brought increasingly into line with that strategy.
- There is increasing consistency with other HR policies – whether related to recruitment and selection, recognition and rewards, or redundancy and redeployment, all support and are supported by T&D policies.

The T&D function was fully integrated within the wider HR function, with collaborative relationships between all staff and a high level of expertise both in the leadership of HR at the Trust and in the leadership and management of the T&D function. HR at the Trust was a highly successful business partner, despite great tensions involved in operating the Trust's private finance initiative and the major reorganisation programme it involved.

Issues for T&D professionals

The centralised planning approach is essentially one of tight-coupling L&D strategy to business strategy. It is a rational process that attempts to take every relevant consideration fully into account (the EOLG guide, for example, specifically refers to scenario planning as a useful tool in order to generate a variety of future-oriented visions of the kind of workforce outcomes that different kind of HR strategies might produce). As the Wesdale Trust case shows (see Figure 13) it relies on:

- T&D strategy being closely linked to corporate strategy yet capable of adaptation to local needs.
- A clear, relevant and well communicated T&D vision, mission, policy and strategy that supports and is supported by other HR strategies and practices.
- Agreement of stakeholders on specific, measurable and well-costed T&D implementation plans.
- All down the line, managerial expertise and commitment and a high level of T&D professional capability to deliver the plans.
- Agreed mechanisms for monitoring, feedback and further relevant action on T&D activity.

However, the centralised planning approach suffers from the inherent risks involved in any tight-coupling of HR activity to central business strategy. As discussed earlier, if an organisation's business strategy itself is inappropriate, incomplete or in some other way deficient, then taking this approach to L&D planning risks reinforcing some fatal flaws or getting caught up in their negative outcomes. At Wesdale Trust fundamental problems subsequently unrolled for the Trust and their seeds were sown during the 1990s. They were rooted in the strategic and especially the financial management of the Trust, the impact of the private finance initiative on beds and services, and external community, political and regional planning issues. HR strategy in such scenarios typically becomes increasingly difficult to hold in place. Ultimately Wesdale Trust was forced to merge with another, further complicating its problems and with consequent radical staffing and policy changes across the whole business.

REFLECTION

How far does the planning process for L&D activity in your organisation resemble or differ from the centralised approach discussed in this section? And to what extent do you think that process – whatever its kind – is effective in meeting key business needs?

SUPPORTING BUSINESS DRIVERS

Linking to business drivers

This approach focuses not on linking to business strategy as a commodity that is produced or updated each year but on loose-coupling with business drivers.

At Cummins Engine UK the HR function has always been at the leading edge with its HR practices. Here is a case that illustrates a point in time – the mid-1980s – when radical changes were taking place in Cummins worldwide, and when at Darlington its HR department was producing new strategies and plans to help drive the plant forward. In this case, the spotlight is on what was termed in the account written at the time 'Human Resource Development (HRD)'.

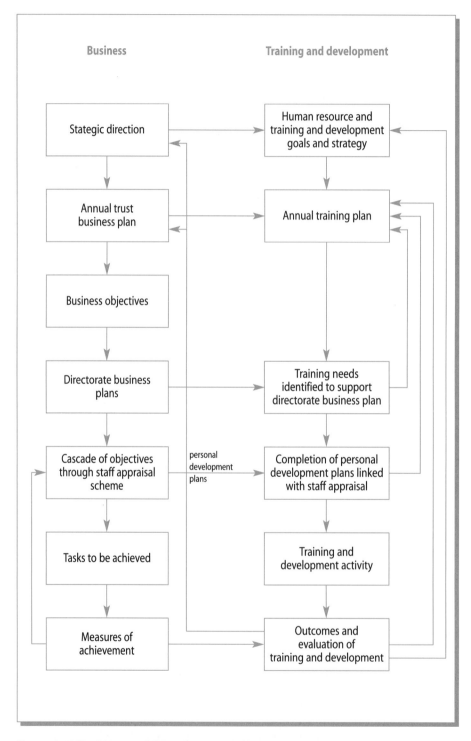

Figure 13 *Linking T&D to Wesdale Trust's strategic and business planning cycle*

CASE EXAMPLE

Human resource development (HRD) planning and delivery at Cummins Engine, Darlington, 1984

Business strategy

Cummins Engine Company Inc. is the world's largest independent manufacturer of diesel engines. Cummins Engine Co. Ltd is the UK subsidiary of the company, and has three manufacturing locations, one of which is at Darlington, in the northeast of England.

In 1979 the workforce at Darlington numbered around 3,000. By l984 the company worldwide was suffering from overcapacity and new competition in a stagnant market. In the previous year the chairman had announced a new strategy, driven by restructuring, high investment in new technology, research and engineering, immediate price-cutting and a compensatory 30 per cent cost-reduction target. The strategy was to be achieved by mid-1986, with the long-term aim of growth in the 1990s and beyond. The company's top management stressed from the beginning that 'we are in it for the long haul'.

HR strategy at Darlington, 1984

In 1984 Darlington's HR strategy had to be closely aligned with the new UK-wide HR strategy, and this raised three priorities with big HRD implications:

- *To achieve a lean, high-quality and efficient workforce.* Reducing materials costs would make the most impact on the Cummins worldwide target of 30 per cent reduction in costs, since those costs accounted for 80 per cent of turnover, whereas labour costs accounted for only 20 per cent. The aim was to achieve a more efficient rather than a smaller labour force (although some downsizing was necessary). All unit labour costs had to be reduced, especially those related to production time, turnover and absenteeism, time-keeping, working methods and procedures, accidents, materials wastage, quality, and inefficiencies due to demarcation.
- *To ensure that the workforce had the skills needed to operate the new technology.* A new product, the 'B' series engine, was to be introduced at the Darlington site. Its smooth and fast installation was essential in order to achieve full operational efficiency quickly.
- *To develop a workforce with high added value.* With a target of growth in the 1990s, an immediate start had to be made on improving the company's skills base and employees' ability to learn fast and be flexible. The aim was both to reduce labour costs and to expand employees' capability, thus adding to their own value while adding value to the business.

HRD goals

Three HRD goals were therefore established:

- To help people acquire and apply the new competencies needed to operate more efficiently, and to adapt to the new culture aimed at meeting the challenges of change.

- To encourage and enable people to work effectively in teams.
- To develop managers, especially supervisors, who could lead as well as manage teams effectively.

HRD strategy and its implementation

Flowing from these three HRD goals, a path had to be agreed in order to reach them. The new HRD strategy had three key features, linked to the drivers of the business:

- *To build an enhanced quality of basic skills*, by providing training for those with the capacity and desire to acquire the skills needed to operate the new technology. For the others, there were favourable opportunities for early retirement. It was an essential part of building commitment during a difficult period that those who left should feel they had been treated generously and fairly, and that those who remained, retained their faith in the company as a good employer in bad times as well as good.
- *To provide training for all, geared to business needs*, by giving all employees the opportunity to learn one new skill every year over the following few years, with a commensurate pay progression.
- *To achieve effective teamworking*, by developing a new breed of supervisors who would operate quite differently from the way they had before, and who, given initial training, would adapt quickly and become leaders rather than merely managers. This proved to be one of the most challenging areas of HRD strategy to implement.

HRD activity thereafter had four defining characteristics:

- *It derived from the clear definition and measurement of 'productivity'* in different sectors of the workforce, and from agreement between stakeholders on where the introduction of HRD initiatives would produce the most added value for the organisation.
- *It was consistent* with the business drivers and with HR policy and practices – most crucially, those related to achieving integrated pay systems and harmonisation of the entire workforce (Pottinger 1989).
- *It sought to build commitment* while not minimising the need for an often painful long haul approach.
- *It was in the hands of expert professionals.* Generalist and specialist HR staff worked as full business partners with managers and unions. They based their value-adding initiatives on data that were as sound and comprehensive as possible, and regularly monitored and adapted those initiatives.

Source: HARRISON R. (1996b)

Issues for L&D professionals

The 'business driver' process is significantly more loose-coupled than the centralised approach examined in the previous section. It is far more appropriate for both multi-divisional and international organisations like Cummins, where HR is largely devolved to the line, and where the term 'adapting to local needs' assumes a special meaning – local to the country, to the region of the country, and to business units. It calls for flexible, politically skilled and expert L&D professionals who know the business inside out and can manage the business partnerships and the co-ordinating processes that are involved.

In his text on creating an L&D strategy Andrew Mayo (2004) produces practical guidelines to link L&D strategy to business drivers, trying to capture all key influences on them in order to make the links secure. On the evidence of his guide's popularity alone, it seems clear that a significant number of L&D functions are convinced of the value of the business driver approach.

THE CUSTOMER-FACING APPROACH

Aiding sustainable growth

This approach typifies another kind of loose coupling. The focus is on continuously achieving an excellent service to all HR's different customers whether within or outside the organisation. This model is unlikely to typify many L&D functions as yet, but it does point the way ahead.

A later stage in Cummins history – the late 1990s – provides one way in which the approach can be carried out.

CASE EXAMPLE

HR seeking excellence at Cummins Engine in the late 1990s

The Cummins story now moves forward to 1997. By then, 'customer-led quality' was the vision that drove Cummins' new production system, providing the focus for goals, standards, performance and recognition. At the Darlington plant in 1997 human resource management and development (HRMD) was identified as one of seven 'functional excellence' functions. HRMD was regarded as a core function in the business because management believed that it was only through its HR policies that it could achieve the human capability needed to maintain its world-class competitive edge.

In 1997, the HRMD function at Darlington operated in relation to 11 policy areas where standards of performance were set:

- leadership
- environment
- health, safety and security
- administration
- staffing
- performance management
- training and development
- organisational design
- compensation and benefits
- employee relations
- community.

Measuring through standards

Standards to be achieved in each of these policy areas were expressed in terms of performance indicators with points allocated to each. Every year the HRMD function was rated by its internal and external customers against those indicators. A score was achieved in this way for the department's performance in each of the 11 policy areas. To take an example: 'Performance management' had seven performance indicators, which together carried a total possible score of 10.

Measuring L&D outcomes

The plant had five business goals to do with customer-led quality, and HRMD staff had to make a contribution each year to those goals. They also had to take lead responsibility for the goal related to 'Developing outstanding people'. They contributed to goals through projects that they managed, and that also formed the basis for their appraisal as individuals. In one year, for example, the training and development manager had a number of projects, each with its targets, timescale and methods of measurement. Taken together, these constituted her individual responsibility for contributing to the business goal of 'Developing outstanding people'.

At Cummins in the late 1990s the presumption in the company was that if HRMD outcomes were agreed by business partners to be materialising, and if the function and its staff continued to have the confidence and support of management and workforce, then that was enough – the HRMD investment was clearly being justified. Only if planned outcomes failed to materialise, or poor ratings were received on the annual customer survey of the HRMD function, would there be a special exercise to measure the value of that investment.

(With acknowledgements to the company)

A similar approach to HR activity is evident at BAE systems, where 11 key strategic goals were launched as part of the company's 2003 business plan. Work on each is owned by the relevant board member but championed by another. The HR director owns the 'people capability' strategy, aimed at optimising resource management and reward, and champions 'material flow' which is about the better management of customer requirements throughout the supply chain. Success is measured throughout the company on a balanced scorecard system.

Issues for L&D professionals

At BAE as at Cummins Engine the customer-facing process aims to make the corporate strategy team more cohesive, with no one function dominating the rest, given that the company's mandate is to deliver sustainable growth. Previously HR at BAE tended to be developing things that 'look good from an HR perspective' (quoting its director) but did not necessarily drive the business forward. Now, HR at BAE is about 'helping business to maximise performance through people'. The new strategic management and planning process is thus aiding full integration of all HR activity with the business (Pickard 2003c).

One further example of this process approach is important to include. It shows how the proactive customer service approach can operate in a very different kind of setting to any yet described: a company formed from a merger, with a consequent need to completely rethink goals, strategy and operation of its L&D activity.

CASE EXAMPLE

HRD at Westpac Bank, New Zealand

Today Westpac is New Zealand's largest bank with almost 1.3 million customers and around 30,000 New Zealand shareholders. In 2004 it was awarded by NBR the title Bank of the Year for the second year in succession (the awards were created in 2003). Its CEO is the first female to lead a bank in New Zealand's history. The bank is leading the field too in actively embracing Corporate Social Responsibility as a way of doing business that it believes all banks must now follow.

The new development centre

The brand was launched in 1996 from a merger of Westpac and Trust banks to form WestpacTrust, later changed to Westpac.

As a result of a radical review of the HRD function, the two banks' high-cost, fragmented and heavily staffed training units were combined and restructured to create a so-called 'Development Centre' to be run as a business adding strategic value to the bank. The new philosophy related to HRD required a major shift in attitudes throughout the company from learning as something gained by going on a course, to learning as an integral part of work, with the crucial questions for all employees to be: 'How and where do we learn, and how does this support my business objectives?'

By 2000 the Development Centre was operating as a specialist function within HR. Most of its products and services were promoted through or used by HR portfolio managers and their teams of HR consultants. They worked with line managers to whom many day to day HR tasks had been devolved. The centre held strategic accountability for learning and training, with agreed criteria against which to measure itself including spend per employee, cost per training day and goals for training delivery through formal and informal learning. Benchmarking was used to establish these goals and to guide the creation of an infrastructure for training administration.

In the early days of the new company the centre played a vital role in aiding the change process and creating a sense of direction for the workplace. A range of planning and monitoring tools helped people to understand how their roles had changed, what skills they had and what they needed, and to track their L&D progress. Through time new L&D standards were produced to reinforce the Development Centre brand and ensure competent staff and L&D activity that provided excellence, innovation and a coherent approach in its service to its customers.

L&D strategising

The centre was linked to the business at strategic level so that the bank could develop the corporate and individual capabilities required to achieve the WestpacTrust vision of 'a great New Zealand company'. The vehicle for this was a 'virtual' strategic learning advisory team (SLAT) that was formed as a decision-making and policy body. Its brief was to look at issues in the context of the wider organisation and to give key stakeholders, mostly executives and senior managers, the opportunity and vehicle to contribute to the strategic direction of learning and training. It formed, disbanded and reformed through time to deal with specific strategic issues that emerged and that required a corporate perspective and response. SLAT helped the centre to develop strategic partnerships with other key business functions including strategic planning and finance so that the centre could play its part in the bank's decision-making processes as well as creating performance support tools for staff. This approach means better forecasting of corporate capability requirements, smoother implementation of changes in products or procedures, and better integration of training into mainstream business decisions, projects and processes.

L&D planning

Planning and monitoring was informed by a computer system feeding into the HR information system, downloading into a central bank system where financial information could be added, enabling the centre to contribute to balanced scorecard measurement and reporting. An insourcing policy was formed with key suppliers that in effect enlisted them as part of the bank's development team, enabling better management of staff costs, access to a unique range of skills, and access also to new knowledge from around the world that led innovative learning processes and products.

The centre was soon negotiating and monitoring all supplier agreements and working with business unit heads to identify how to share training staff, resources and information to reduce duplication and costs. A universal 'training estimator tool' was produced to enable a broad-brush preview of training requirements that could be updated every six months. This linked to the bank's performance management framework, and also linked skills requirements to development solutions.

Sources: SIMMONS, C. and VALENTINE, E. (2000) and the company's website at: http://westpac.co.nz [accessed 25 September 2004]

The customer-facing planning approach comes closest to the kind that Gordon Hewitt (2003) would recommend for HR in any organisation (see earlier comments). It relies on HR professionals working in a close-knit, proactive collaboration, with each fully versed in all the core fields of HR and with a deep understanding of their organisation, the big strategic issues it faces, and opportunities to give it leading edge. The approach is essentially one that combines strategising and planning as a continuous creative activity.

While both the 'business drivers' and the customer-facing approaches to planning and delivering L&D strategy and activity can be highly effective depending on context, each involves its own risks and challenges. The customer-facing process may seem to offer the best key to the future for the L&D function in an increasing number of organisations, but it also makes the highest demands on L&D professionals.

THE IMPLEMENTATION PROBLEM

HR professionals: strategic players?

In conclusion, it is salutary to return to the issue of implementation. If that does not work, then strategy and plans are worthless whatever their qualities.

Many implementation problems should be picked up when business strategies are being developed, especially if scenario planning is used. If such problems are intelligently debated at that stage there is a far better chance that feasible HR strategies will be produced, including a strategy to cover the L&D field. While there is a long way to go before a significant proportion of L&D professionals have seats at the boardroom table, elsewhere in the HR area the picture seems more promising. In 2003 the CIPD carried out a survey of senior HR practitioners across various types and sectors of organisations (CIPD 2003h). The survey showed that 75 per cent of respondents were functional heads or board members. It revealed 'a confident profession that knows where it wants to get to and is making rapid progress' (Brown and Emmott 2003). The signs were of a 'more high-powered function displaying specialist expertise and with a clear business strategy mission' (ibid.), with HR professionals wanting to add value by developing tailored solutions to business issues. Most believed their influence to have increased, with a growth in total numbers working in the function and a greater emphasis in HR activities that have a strategic business input. The CIPD's survey showed that HR professionals had a much increased confidence in the importance of their activity to the business.

If this picture is a realistic one, surely it means that there will be a better quality of HR strategies produced, and fewer implementation problems? Unfortunately as I have already noted earlier in the chapter and before that in Chapter 11, this does not seem to reflect what is happening in the real world and the way the HR profession sees itself is not necessarily reflected in the views of other players.

What is really going on here? As we have seen earlier in the chapter, there are some signal successes in the HR strategy field, but as yet they are in the minority. The biggest failure – for whatever reason – is a continuing 'real gap' between strategic intent and delivery (Brown and Emmott 2003). One HR commentator, reviewing research findings, wrote (Baron 2000, p31):

> **'It seems that few now doubt that people management can make a difference. They merely question how the difference can be achieved. It appears that we do not yet know enough about translating strategic intentions into implementation and action, or why a particular course of action might prove successful in one situation but not in another.'**

In April 2004 Tesco announced record sales and profits that put it even further ahead as Britain's favourite retail store. Terry Leahy, its chief executive, commenting on reasons for its astonishing success, said (Rankine 2004):

> **'We don't stand out by our strategy. It's the execution that has been better.'**

Respondents to the CIPD's 2003 survey acknowledged that implementation was a problem. They cited daily workloads, legislative and administrative pressures as major barriers to carrying out HR strategies effectively in the workplace. They also cast doubt on the extent to which line managers to whom HR roles are increasingly being devolved have the necessary commitment and skills to carry out their HR roles competently. They admitted their own weaknesses too: most felt that strategic thinking was a challenge that they needed to tackle, together with improving their business knowledge, negotiating skills and innovative capability.

Issues for L&D professionals

It should by now be clear that many of the problems related to L&D strategy and its implementation are probably built into the strategic management process itself. Many, however, could be avoided by a better relationship between HR practitioners and front-line managers whose actions have such a direct effect on the skills, motivation and discretionary behaviour of employees. What, then, should L&D professionals do in order to ensure as best they can that there is a sound, feasible L&D strategy to guide L&D activity in their organisations?

- It *is* important to analyse, to diagnose, to produce goals and plans that fit context, and to work with business partners in setting a clear path for L&D as a key business process. But a pragmatic approach to implementation is essential. Given the many differing interests of the parties, there will always be constraints on collaboration. L&D professionals should identify at the start the likely aids and barriers and should develop the functional expertise, the business knowledge, the creativity and political skill to promote and achieve value-adding results for the business.
- By adopting a proactive approach and achieving excellence in services, products and processes that their activity provides, L&D professionals can build a springboard for their increasing credibility and political power in the business at all organisational levels. Their way forward is to have a proven record of achievement that is rooted in a real knowledge of the business, the big issues that confront it, and strong partnerships with those who manage it.
- Throughout the organisation people's perceptions, actions and influence related to L&D strategy will be different and will affect its implementation profoundly in each workplace. L&D professionals need to be in constant touch with strategy on the ground, communicating the purpose and monitoring the progress of L&D plans and helping to train front-line managers in their devolved HR roles.
- Much of strategy emerges in an ongoing manner from individual and collective learning. As time goes on, new threats and opportunities develop. These will call for adjustments, sometimes radical, to be made to the strategic route originally agreed. As we saw in Chapter 11, in today's business environment a continuous strategising process makes more sense than reliance on strategy and plans as products that are fixed at one point in time and resistant to change thereafter.

REFLECTION

An organisation's L&D manager complains that although she produces drafts for an L&D strategy that fully supports business goals and strategy, and provides logical arguments to underpin her proposals, she still doesn't seem to be a strategic player in the organisation. She often finds herself having to try to implement an L&D strategy that she finds unsatisfactory. 'Where am I failing and what should I do?' she asks you. What do you think would be an effective response to her concerns?

CONCLUSION

By now you should have a sound general understanding of different ways in which an L&D strategy and strategic plan can be produced and implemented, together with barriers and aids to the strategy and planning processes. You should also feel confident in tackling the review questions contained in Appendix 3.

The main themes in this six-section chapter have related to:

- Issues of integration: the problems that complicate the task of integrating L&D strategy and plans with wider HR strategy and practices and with business strategy; the meaning and value of a loose-coupled rather than tight-coupled approach and the need for all HR professionals to be proactive rather than reactive, promoting strategies to enhance organisational performance.
- A five-step process to produce an L&D strategy that is relevant to the business and has the support of key stakeholders; the effects of bounded rationality on the strategy process, and the problems encountered by HR professionals in achieving strategies that are valued in the business and feasible on the ground.
- Three different approaches to L&D planning: by linking plans to business strategy; by linking them to business drivers; and by a loose-coupled customer-facing process whose aim is to continuously deliver excellence and contribute to the organisation's sustained growth.
- The gap between strategy and its implementation, and problems of the HR profession in tackling this; some implications for L&D professionals.

Further information sources

MAYO A. (2004) *Creating a learning and development strategy: the HR partner's guide to developing people*. 2nd edn. London: Chartered Institute of Personnel and Development.

Also:

- Details of the ESRC's Future of Work programme and of the 2004 WERS survey due for initial publication in February 2005 can be found on http://www.dti.gov.uk/er/emar/wers5.htm [accessed 28 September 2004].
- The Work Foundation's website: http://www.theworkfoundation.com/ [accessed 28 September 2004].
- The Employers' Organisation website for details of its workforce planning guide: http://www.lg-employers.gov.uk/recruit/working_planning/ [accessed 28 September 2004].
- An interesting Canadian website giving advice on HR strategic planning for small organisations in the voluntary sector. The advice has a wider applicability: http://www.hrvs-rhsbc.ca/hr_practices/pg005_e.cfm [accessed 28 September 2004].

Adding Value

CHAPTER 13

INTRODUCTION

The purpose of this chapter is to explain the concept of 'adding value' and to relate it to the provision of L&D activity in an organisation. The task of adding value is central to any L&D practitioner's role because to add value is to increase the organisation's capability to achieve its goals. It is to make a difference where it matters most. It involves producing outcomes that enable the organisation to deal better than it could before with challenges and threats, and generating returns over and above the cost of the L&D investment.

From 2005 there is a legal requirement for employers to report on human capital management in their operating and financial reviews. The DTI Human Capital accounting framework highlights four basic areas on which directors must report their HR activity. The framework is disappointing in that its requirement is fairly non-specific. This is likely to mean that in many reports the link between people and performance will be left vaguely defined, and that in some only minimal information will be provided. However the CIPD has also produced a human capital reporting framework, to be discussed in this chapter, and it is more rigorous. Since human capital reporting is rarely done at present it will pose many challenges for HR professionals (Higginbottom 2003). L&D practitioners therefore need to start thinking now in practical ways about how their operations add value to the business.

The managing director of a strategic HR consultancy has offered the following advice to ensure 'added value' and I use it as the framework for this chapter (Green 1999):

- *align*: point people in the right direction
- *engage*: develop their belief and commitment to the organisation's purpose and direction
- *measure*: provide the data that demonstrate the improved results you achieve.

The chapter has four sections. The first clarifies what is involved in adding value, both in general terms and for an L&D function. The following three then relate the 'align, engage, measure' framework to L&D activity.

REFLECTION

Before starting this chapter, and perhaps knowing little at this point about what a value-adding L&D function might look like, try to identify how far it would resemble, or be very different from, the function in your own organisation and where you think the biggest gaps lie.

CLARIFYING 'ADDED VALUE'

Is best value the same as added value?

The simple answer to this question is no. To explain why, it is helpful to look first at the Best Value framework that the Audit Commission applied to the assessment of local authority services during 2002. It used four criteria (Gorman 2000):

- *Challenge* – Why is the service carried out at all?
- *Consult* – What do customers think about our service and the level of performance?
- *Compare* – How does our performance compare against the best of the public and private sector?
- *Compete* – Can the service be delivered more effectively by alternative providers?

Benchmarking and best practice processes are widely used to help establish what is 'best value'. Benchmarking involves finding a particular standard, whether internal or external, and using that as a continuous marker for a strategy, process or initiative. It is not merely a technique for copying. It is about planning comparisons in order to decide how to enhance performance. Organisations agree to be benchmarked because they acquire insight and information from the process too, and because it gives them a higher profile in the competitive environment.

There are three main types of benchmarking:

- *Internal benchmarking* looks at and compares similar processes within an organisation to achieve internal best practice. For L&D, examples might be the induction, appraisal or management development processes. The exercise of ascertaining how a process is carried out in different parts of the organisation offers two benefits: the highlighting of inconsistencies and the identification of internal best practice that can then be used as a marker across the organisation.
- *Competitive benchmarking* is where organisations in the same sector – for example, a hospital trust and a community healthcare trust – agree to work together to compare best practice in key areas, for example the matter of privacy and dignity or the complaints process.
- *Functional benchmarking* involves identifying a particular process and then comparing it to best practice outside the organisation. An organisation that wishes to improve its measurements of customer satisfaction may take two or three external organisations of different types as comparators, and finally select one to use for benchmarking.

Best practice involves gathering information across the academic and practitioner fields in order to produce general principles to guide the implementation of a process or initiative. It is illustrated in the following example.

CASE EXAMPLE
English Nature's use of best practice

English Nature, the Government's adviser on nature and conservation, aspires to be a learning organisation, and so decided to benchmark approaches to training with a wide range of companies in order to achieve that transformation. The account produced by S. Dolan, its training manager, illustrates the many ways in which examining practice in other organisations can help an L&D department to set standards, decide creative approaches and monitor progress.

A total of 12 companies across all sectors were visited because they had adopted innovative approaches to learning and business development. Their beliefs, strategies and a range of key features were analysed and compared with those noted in the 'learning organisation' literature that had already been studied at English Nature. Common traits soon became evident, and it emerged that in a number of respects English Nature already had the elements needed. The company introduced many initiatives to develop the rest, at the heart of which was a range of programmes to strengthen the links between learning and action across the organisation. Company personnel also continued to develop external learning networks with other organisations in conservation and business.

Source: DOLAN, S. (1995)

Going back to the Audit Commission's Best Value framework, as I explained in Chapter 10 the HR function emerged badly from the Commission's 2002 assessment of its activity across the local government sector. The verdict was that most HR functions offered poor value for money. But it was not informative about value-adding outcomes of HR activity because that would have meant posing – and answering – a different question: What critical difference has the service made to the organisation's capability to differentiate itself from other, similar organisations, thereby giving it a leading edge?

Thus while giving value for money is of course important, it is not the same as adding value. Green (1999) urges HR professionals to move away from their 'obsession with best practice' and concentrate on adding value instead. Failure to do so results in an inadequate focus on the key drivers of organisational performance, and in a tendency to measure HR inputs rather than organisational outputs.

Adding value through L&D activity

For an L&D function to provide added value for its organisation it needs to meet three conditions:

- It must focus its operations on areas that will make a critical difference to the organisation's ability to achieve its goals. No L&D function can meet all L&D needs in an organisation. It must prioritise to achieve added value.
- It must be organised in such a way that it can make that critical difference. Chapter 11 has already made clear what is involved here.-
- Those carrying L&D roles in the organisation must be expert and ethical business partners, and must know the business inside out.

The following examples show how the rationale for adding value works in HR and L&D terms.

CASE EXAMPLES

Adding value through L&D initiatives

Company A is delayering and downsizing in order to become leaner and move faster in a tough competitive market. It needs a highly adaptive, flexible workforce. The HR function can produce added value by producing and implementing policies related to harmonising pay and conditions, and to disengagement and redeployment of people. Recruitment and promotion policies will also have to change, as will the company's performance management process and its reward policies.

For the L&D function, this creates a need for various supporting and awareness raising initiatives. The company's new scenario makes clear the critical importance of effective team leadership and teamwork. Multiskilling is essential so that employees can operate the new type of matrix structure where what matters is collaborative horizontal relationships and self-managing cross-functional teams instead of the traditional managerial structure and emphasis on vertical relationships. Finally managers themselves will need appraisal, training and development to acquire the task and behavioural competencies involved in managing in a changed work system.

Company B is breaking into new markets in a turbulent environment where progress depends on rapidly responding to new and unfamiliar challenges. It has to be able to repeatedly group and regroup its human, financial and physical resources, and produce new organisational capabilities that can respond innovatively to changing customer demands and can stimulate new customer wants.

Again, there will be implications for HR policies to do with recruitment, promotion, rewards and performance management. In addition, HR and L&D staff need to work together to add value by helping to change and embed new organisational structure and culture, and to stimulate knowledge creation. L&D professionals must work with managers and team leaders to build a learning culture in the organisation, form learning networks both within the organisation and across its boundaries, and stimulate knowledge-productive communities of practice in the workplace.

Source: HARRISON, R. and KESSELS, J. (2003a, p25)

In the following three sections I use Green's 'align, engage and measure' framework to discuss specific ways in which the L&D function can become value adding.

ALIGNING THE PEOPLE

L&D: pointing people in the right direction

By 'right direction' is meant pointing people in the direction of the organisation's purpose and overarching goals. L&D practitioners can help to achieve this by ensuring that their activity is both business-led and proactive:

■ *Business-led L&D* is development aimed at aligning people with business targets – their own, their unit's, and ultimately the organisation's. Business-led L&D must be a dynamic process, continuously interacting with the cycle of business change in order to provide services and initiatives that are relevant to the business.

■ *Proactive L&D* is development that incorporates unique, innovative ways of directing people along a shared path towards the organisation's longer-term goals. By promoting and helping to deliver powerful L&D solutions that help the organisation respond to the big challenges that confront it, the L&D process can also make possible a widening choice of business strategies and ultimately of business goals as employees at various organisational levels begin to achieve their full potential.

Throughout the book I have stressed the critical role played by HR strategies in engaging employees fully with the organisation's vision and goals. The L&D function too needs its vision and goals, but these must not exist in some separate dimension. Here is an example of what not to do.

CASE EXAMPLE
My worst mistake

John Garnett, director of the Industrial Society from 1962 to 1986, admitted that his worst mistake was trying to sell ideas in relation to his own objectives rather than the objectives of the people to whom he was selling. He described how his passionate vision about the value of developing people's abilities and potential blinded him during his time as personnel manager of the plastics division of ICI to the equally important need to relate what he did to the objectives of the business. It led to the loss of his job because, he explained:

> My work, in the view of the board, was irrelevant and, more seriously, distracting. They were in the business of making profits in plastics, while I seemed to be in the business of developing people, which took their eyes off the main purpose.

Source: GARNETT, J. (1992)

If an L&D function in an organisation reflects Garnett's mistake, then it will be unable to engage people in ways that sufficiently help the business. It will point them in irrelevant directions and impede the building of commitment to tackling the organisation's most critical learning and performance needs. Table 9 spells out the differences between an L&D function that is directing people down the right path, and one that is not.

Using the balanced scorecard

I have referred in the Introduction to this chapter to the pressure now on all HR professionals to be able to show that they are helping to build human capital. Historically organisations have made little progress or effort in really gauging the value of their employees. They have concentrated their efforts on recruiting and deploying hands rather than brains, as Scarbrough explains (2003, p32):

'When firms compete simply through their processes, the skills of their employees are merely inputs to the process; beyond the

training needed to conform to the job description, there is little interest in the depth or range of their competencies.'

Contrast this with the following approach.

CASE EXAMPLE
Pointing people in the right direction

Marks and Spencer, whatever its problems as a business, continues to focus its developmental activity on the whole of its workforce because of the importance of high quality of customer service. In seeking to develop the talent and capability that are key to its future growth, it is interested in mapping the skills and attitudes of employees at all levels. It surveys employees on the progress they make in different types of skills, whether portable (those needed by every employee, such as planning, influencing and communicating) or technical (such as product knowledge, visual presentation and dealing with stock). These skills are then related to 20 job families that represent activity areas necessary to achieve business strategy. Information on skills and capabilities is linked to changing business needs through addressing skills gaps, highlighting strengths, and ensuring that appropriate attitudes and commitment are being applied to the exercise of skills.

Source: SCARBROUGH, H. (2003)

That is one way of aligning people with business goals. It could be incorporated within another, widely used method – the balanced scorecard approach. Kaplan and Norton's is the best known. In explaining it they make the point that what is important to achieve is clarity about the organisation's goals and the will to work towards them (2001, p52):

'Employees may feel well compensated and well treated, but that does not imply that they understand the organisation's goals and are committed to helping it to achieve them.'

They point to the need to actively engage employees in the strategic process, looking to front-line staff for new ideas and information about market opportunities, competitive threats and technological possibilities. Their balanced scorecard approach highlights an integrated set of measurements that link customers, internal processes, employees and systems to long-term financial success. It shows how these measures relate to each other and the firm's strategic objectives. The 'learning and growth' perspective is one of four around which the scorecard's measures are grouped. The others are financial, internal business process and customer.

Because the use of the scorecard focuses attention on the firm's overall business strategy and objectives it has a direct impact on the performance management process, which of course must itself be linked very clearly to business objectives if the whole approach is to work as

Table 9 *Matrix to identify training and development role and contribution to the business*

T&D activity	Alignment with business goals	T&D seen financially by management as	T&D formal responsibility of	Ownership of T&D felt mainly by	Focus and purpose of T&D mainly	Main mode of delivery
Peripheral to the business	Negligible	A cost to the business, one of the first that can be cut back in contingency	Specialist T&D/ personnel staff or some individual on full/part-time basis	Specialist staff of whoever holds formal T&D responsiblity	No systematic focus, and *ad hoc* purposes	Formal and knowledge-based courses and/or picking up skills on the job from more experienced individuals
Business-led	Linked to current business goals and targets	An essential 'bottom-line' business cost	Specialist staff/ managers	Top and line managers, specialist staff, and to some extent workforce generally	Job-related, for individuals and teams, to improve current performance and prepare for specific changes in jobs, systems and workplace practices	Systematically designed internal learning events, and job-related external courses, skill and knowledge-based
Strategically focused	Linked to strategic goals at corporate and unit levels	A value-adding investment, essential to the future of the business	Member of board, specialists/managers, teams and individuals	Shared by the parties	Continuous improvement of performance, and continuous development of organisations, teams and individuals. Purpose also to build a general climate of self-initiated learning and development	Planned and experiential learning to develop skills, knowledge and attitudes, and to aid development of learning skills

T&D = Training and Development

Source: HARRISON, R. (1999) *The training and development audit*. Cambridge: Cambridge Strategy Publications. p8. Reproduced with kind permission of the publisher.

intended. That link gives the essential focus to appraisal discussions and to recommendations for training, learning and development activity flowing from that discussion. The balanced scorecard can thus become 'the framework for linking employees' everyday actions to company-wide strategic objectives' providing that the organisation's management communicates with and educates employees about business strategy (Kaplan and Norton 2001, p57).

To summarise this section: L&D activity can help to point people in the right direction in an organisation by:

- Communicating the organisation's business strategy and goals through a variety of formal and informal learning processes.
- Identifying critical proficiency gaps in the organisation's workforce and proposing and organising measures to tackle them.
- Identifying barriers that are preventing people from applying their skills and knowledge in ways that could enhance organisational performance.
- Raising awareness in senior executives, team leaders and managers of the value of the balanced scorecard approach in helping employees to understand how to relate their performance to organisational objectives, and in linking to the performance management process.
- Equipping people across the organisation with the competence to use the balanced scorecard approach effectively.

ENGAGING THE PEOPLE

L&D: building commitment

It will be evident by this point in the book that building human and social capital has become a pressing task for today's organisations. To achieve it, organisational leaders must work to ensure that employees have a strong belief in their organisation's espoused values and a commitment to work towards a shared purpose. This short case illustrates how this realisation is changing the focus of some organisations' HR activity.

CASE EXAMPLE

Promoting organisational values

At the Britannia Building Society a new recruitment scheme focuses on candidates' attitudes and behaviour rather than on their job skills. The change manager, Mark Farmer, has emphasised that they want to attract people 'who are aligned with the basic values we're looking for'. Traditionally the Britannia has focused in their selection process on candidates' skills and abilities. Now, the emphasis is more on personal values and their fit with the values that underpin corporate strategy.

Clearly such a change in any company means new thinking on the part of the L&D function. Its activity from now on must ensure that induction, basic skills training, ongoing learning and development and career planning all promote the company's basic values and produce, develop and reinforce the behaviours needed to deliver its strategy.

Source: *People Management* (2004c)

Defining the notion of commitment and then measuring the extent to which it is being affected by L&D activity is complicated by the fact that commitment is a mix of attitudes and behaviour, different in every individual. It also varies in individuals through time, being particularly volatile when there are new pressures on the employment relationship and major changes in the operation of organisations (Swailes 2002).

Dave Ulrich, whose business partner model has had a profound influence on thinking in the HR profession, argues that 'organisation capabilities embedded inside a firm have intangible value to investors outside the firm' (Ulrich and Smallwood 2002, p43). The seven capabilities that he proposes suggest a framework that can guide L&D professionals in stimulating and enabling employees to work to a set of core values and to become committed to a common organisational purpose:

1. *Talent*: this capability is demonstrated in an organisation's success in attracting, motivating, retaining and developing the employees it needs for high performance. As we have already seen in Chapter 5, there is much that an L&D function can do to enhance the performance management process and thereby to assist in developing and motivating talented employees at all organisational levels.

2. *A shared mindset*: what is needed here is the kind of L&D activity that helps to raise awareness of the organisation's purpose, goals, strategic challenges and position in its environment, and that stimulates a conducive organisational culture together with strategic thinking across the business. L&D professionals are often already heavily involved in supporting culture change in their organisations. They also need to be proactive in stimulating strategic thinking – for example (as already mentioned in the previous section), through promoting the use of the balanced scorecard approach and equipping people with the techniques and understanding to apply it to their own area of work.

3. *Speed*: this capability enables an organisation to manage change, move quickly into new markets and regularly redeploy its resources (including people) and routines in ways that respond appropriately to new challenges and opportunities. In earlier chapters in Part 3 I have described the many challenges now facing the L&D function as it attempts itself to become more fast-adaptive and customer facing. In like manner L&D professionals also need to help employees to work faster and smarter in their jobs and become skilled at self-managed continuous learning. Unipart University, Buckman Laboratories' knowledge management programme, the PriceWaterhouseCooper shared professional services centre and the Westpac Bank Development Centre are at the leading edge of L&D practice but the principles of proactivity, strategic thinking and customer service that inform their work should also inform the work of any L&D function as it seeks to provide employees with the skills they need in order to respond quickly and confidently to new challenges.

4. *Learning and knowledge*: we have already seen in Chapter 8 how tapping into the learning and knowledge of all its employees can enable an organisation to continuously improve and radically innovate in products, processes and services, but how this requires a learning culture in the workplace and communities of practice that are willing to put their knowledge at the service of the business. As I have explained in that chapter, across Europe there is little evidence to indicate that L&D professionals are taking a lead in building learning cultures, or that most are even truly aware of the need to do so. The gap between what is needed and what is actually happening here is one that must be tackled with urgency by the profession (Tjepkema et al 2002b; CIPD 2004a).

5. *Accountability*: this concerns the organisation's ability to deliver what it promises. L&D activity here needs to help leaders, managers and HR professionals to set clear and interrelated goals, to translate goals into plans that can be implemented in the workplace, and to fully understand the consequences of failure in terms of reduced employee commitment and loss of mutual trust.

6. *Collaboration*: this capability is essential to an organisation's effective functioning in an environment characterised by structural forms that lay stress on co-operative arrangements, and in work environments that increasingly rely on effective teamwork and cross-functional working. To develop collaborative capability involves a wide range of L&D solutions, as will become clear in the next chapter.

7. *Leaders*: whether we look at the latest HR research findings, at the radical change agenda facing the public and not-for-profit sectors or at the highly competitive environment in which all private sector organisations now operate, there is an overwhelming need for effective leaders. At corporate level they are accountable for the results of an organisation and their brand has a major influence on shareholder confidence. At line manager level leaders play the key role in communicating and enacting the organisation's 'Big Idea' and in implementing HR strategies to raise employees' commitment to it. L&D activity that promotes and delivers effective leadership development in an organisation adds incalculable value to the business, and the ways in which it can do this will be discussed in some detail in Chapter 16.

Monitoring engagement

It should be evident at this point that L&D professionals have many opportunities to make a positive impact on employees' commitment to an organisation's goals and values. But their activity, no matter how carefully planned to form a coherent strategy, must be well implemented on the ground, and its progress needs to be monitored. Employee engagement is not something that many organisations review in any systematic way. A report produced in 2004 by consultancy firm Empower indicated that nearly half of FTSE 500 companies do not measure employee engagement, and those that do are failing to link it to business aims (Higginbottom 2004).

The L&D audit is one method to keep in touch with how far L&D activity is engaging people with the organisation's values and goals. It supplies a snapshot of a current situation across the organisation in order to compare what is happening with what should be happening, and to identify any action needed. Conducted through time, audits enable trends to be identified. They form part of a strategy to ensure continuous improvement of a function or of an area of activity (Harrison 1999). Every audit has its own focus. Once that has been determined, an audit framework can be devised and decisions taken on the areas of questioning that will produce the most relevant information. An audit can then be designed from scratch or, more usually, be bought off the shelf and tailored to context.

The diagnostic surveys used as an integral part of the *Investors in People* process provide one of the most familiar tools in the UK for assessing how far and in what ways L&D activity is engaging people with business goals. Their use involves working with expert external advisers and assessors, but they can provide uniquely valuable information and some at least of their cost can be offset by IIP funding.

MEASURING THE DATA

L&D: demonstrating improved results

Although measuring the outcomes of L&D activity is an important task, it must be kept in perspective. What matters most is to agree at the start with key stakeholders what L&D initiatives are likely to add the most value to the business and to individuals' capability, and to gain their commitment to helping to implement them on the ground. Methods of measurement should be agreed at that initial stage, and should focus on what is essential, affordable, and sensible.

The CIPD has produced a *Human capital external framework* (CIPD 2003i) that is adaptable to organisational context. The principles it sets out to guide the internal and external reporting process on L&D and three other areas relevant to the building of human capital are particularly helpful in suggesting how to approach the task of measuring L&D outcomes. The principles are:

- That whatever measuring framework is used it must avoid a single accounting formula or set of 'people numbers' and must contain indices that relate appropriately to organisational context.
- That the information gathered should be of value to its recipients and should bring benefits greater than the costs of obtaining it.
- That measurement should focus on factors material to the future performance of the organisation and so should include qualitative as well as quantitative information.
- That reporting should identify any barriers to the effective use of human capital within the firm – for example, a failure to reflect the diversity of its company base in its workforce.

Measuring what matters

Any push to closely measure the financial returns on the L&D investment should be resisted for a variety of compelling reasons:

- If agreement on how to spend the L&D investment has been reached at the start by key partners then no such detailed measurement should be needed. The important question should not be 'what did it cost?' but rather 'given what we agreed to do at the start, has it worked? If it has, let's move on. If it hasn't, what are the problems we need to tackle?' In the Black Box research it was found that measures of HR activity were not used to prove the value of HR or justify the existence of the function, since both were taken for granted. They were used to identify problems and monitor progress, as a guide to policy innovation and in some cases to predict downstream profit and performance (Purcell et al 2003).
- By definition 'learning and development' incorporates more activity focused on the

longer term than on the immediate, so measures restricted to identifying short-term financial returns will miss much of the value of L&D activity.

■ It is effectively impossible in any case to make a direct correlation between an organisation's financial performance and its L&D practice: L&D activity does not gain its most value-adding outcomes on its own, but by being incorporated in a cluster of HR practices. In the Black Box research it was found that (Purcell et al 2003, p72):

> (HR) measures which use profit or shareholder values are too remote from the practice of people management to be useful. What is important is operational measurement where a close link can be observed, and the regular collection of these measures covering people, operational, financial and customer areas is commonly done in the best firms, linking back to the logic of the balanced scorecard.

In L&D activity, what then should be measured to demonstrate improved results? In real life it is impossible to precisely measure all its outcomes, nor would it be worthwhile even if it could be done. This is not only because many of L&D's most valuable outcomes cannot be measured in quantitative terms, but because any such comprehensive measurement is far too time-consuming and costly to merit the effort. Measurement should be restricted to looking at what matters most, when it matters most. Without this common-sense approach, L&D initiatives and processes are likely to 'drown in a sea of quantitative and qualitative measures' (Lorenz 1994).

Using this pragmatic, selective approach, food company Geest includes an 'Our People' section in its annual report and accounts and in the L&D field this has to provide information on measures related to appraisal, career development, graduate and management development structures, analysed by sex and age and with case studies on the company's L&D initiatives that link them to its business strategy. These are the L&D areas that matter most to Geest, and where it invests heavily. They are therefore the areas where it makes sense to concentrate the measurement activity.

In organisations where enhanced product quality is the main way of adding value to the business, then an obvious way of measuring L&D's contribution would be to use ISO 9001:2000 quality management standard, which can be viewed on the ISO website (see end of chapter). Many thousands of organisations across the world are involved in attaining this organisational self-assessment standard. It is a process-based quality management system that highlights the various competencies that an organisation needs for work affecting product quality, requires the collection and evaluation of staff's and customer's views on quality standards and evidence that these are being acted on, and requires proof of a 'human resource development' policy that is in place and is resulting in the development of required competencies in everyone whose work affects product quality (Field 2001). Audits like the IIP's that monitor alignment and engagement of people with the business through L&D activity are also used to measure the impact of that activity.

However, the balanced scorecard approach discussed earlier in the chapter incorporates a uniquely powerful way of measuring L&D's results because it constitutes an ongoing strategic process, not a series of one-off diagnoses, and it concentrates on growth as well as learning, thus ensuring a pay-forward thrust for L&D activity. In the Black Box research (Purcell et al 2003) it was found to be in significant use in the organisations studied and to be regarded as a flexible and relevant tool. But what is meant by 'pay-forward'?

Pay-back and pay-forward assessments

An L&D function that is focused on providing 'value for money' is usually assessed by a pay-back approach, with attempts to measure return on training investment in financial or comparable quantitative terms (Lee 1996). A typical 'value for money' exercise would involve measuring the impact of past or current training outcomes on variables like turnover, profit, increase in sales, conversion of leads to sales – what accountants call the 'direct return' achieved.

However an L&D function that is focused on adding value needs to concentrate less on asking 'was it worth it?' and more on 'have we done what we agreed to do – and what should we do next?' In other words, there should be an emphasis on pay-forward. This means that once an agreed activity has been delivered and the situation that it was intended to affect seems satisfactory, then plans must be made for the next step. If the situation is not satisfactory, then of course reasons for that must be identified and tackled.

'Pay forward' assessment involves looking at any proposal to invest in future L&D activity and asking how far and in what ways it is likely to make a real and positive difference to future organisational performance (Lee 1996, p31). It requires the generation of options, so that partners can select those likely to achieve the greatest balance of benefits for the business and its employees. With pay-forward assessment far more than financial considerations alone are taken into account, as the following six pay-forward questions show:

- *Budgeting* – Which options are most affordable in terms of our L&D budgets?
- *L&D strategy* – Which of the options would be most consistent with the organisation's overall L&D strategy?
- *L&D needs* – How do options relate to needs? Have the needs been accurately identified, carefully analysed, and correctly prioritised? Are any needs in tension with each other? If so, what do we do about that?
- *L&D outcomes* – Which of the options is/are most likely to produce outcomes that give the most added value for the organisation and its employees? Which are most likely to increase organisational performance and employee commitment? What information can be obtained about the likely outcomes of each option, by reference both to past initiatives in the organisation and to external best practice?
- *Transfer of learning* – Which options are likely to ensure the most effective transfer of learning for individuals and teams?
- *Other options* – Are there any other ways in which the same kind and level of outcomes offered could be achieved, but at less cost? What about team-briefings, quality circles, project groups? What would be the costs of doing nothing? Or might that lead to reduced motivation of the learners, to lack of development of their ability and potential, to longer learning time for new techniques, or to poorer-quality work, and higher rates of absenteeism or sickness?

Guidelines for L&D practitioners

Putting all these various insights into perspective, L&D practitioners should therefore approach the task of 'measuring the data' by ensuring that:

- When business partners are agreeing on how best to 'spend' the L&D investment, they share a clear picture of the initial state of affairs and then envisage how various options would be likely to change that picture – again, scenario planning is of much value in generating and choosing options.

- They express desired outcomes in terms of clear and relevant goals. For example, a goal to do with 'improving managerial effectiveness' is too imprecise. In what ways do they want managers to improve? How would managers act and perform once training and development has taken place? What would they know and be able to do, and how would they behave then as distinct from now?
- There is agreement with partners on the path to follow in order to achieve agreed outcomes, and on how and when to measure progress along that path (making sensible use of strategic milestones and performance indicators).
- There is also agreement on what must happen in the workplace if that path is to be taken. For example, learning driven by new technology cannot achieve its aims in a workplace where there are no skills to use it, no infrastructure to support it, no willingness on management's side to exploit its full potential or a fear of new technology amongst the workforce.
- Measurement methods should be a pragmatic mix of quantitative for hard objectives, and for softer objectives a range of techniques to capture their essence – for example, behaviourally anchored rating-scales, surveys, benchmarking and observation to ensure cross-checks on value and outcomes.
- Measurement methods should be broad and flexible enough to capture the essence of L&D activity without interfering overmuch in operations by imposing excessive and time-consuming checks and balances. 'Measure everything' is not a natural law: it is a dangerous obsession.

Real life, of course, rarely follows the ideal path. However if the above principles are kept in mind when tackling a measurement task they can still suggest an approach that satisfies the key parties and points to a positive way forward. In the following real-life case an external consultant (myself, as it happens) was asked to undertake after the event the measurement of an organisation's four-year investment in a major programme of L&D activity. Much of the information that ideally should have been in place to aid this task had not been recorded at the time. Despite this, a mix of pay-back and pay-forward techniques made it possible to demonstrate results achieved by the activity and to propose a fruitful way ahead.

CASE EXAMPLE

Demonstrating L&D's added value at a prescription pricing authority

For a four-year period in the late 1980s a regional prescription pricing authority (PPA) in the National Health Service (NHS) had undergone profound organisational change involving restructuring, the advent of a new chief executive officer (CEO) and the introduction of new technology across all nine PPA divisional offices. PPA managers and team leaders had to quickly acquire the competence and the social skills to ensure the success of the change, and so the personnel department organised a four-year management development programme, using both internal and external resources to design, deliver and evaluate the initiative. Its purpose was to develop managers and team leaders to operate effectively in the new organisational structure and culture that had been spearheaded by the new CEO.

As an independent consultant, I was invited by the CEO to evaluate the PPA's Management of Change programme retrospectively, in order to assess whether the L&D investment had been worthwhile and to decide what to do next.

The first stage was to agree with the CEO on a process to tackle the project. This involved regular meetings with him where we would have a frank discussion of information emerging from the process and its implications for the authority. It also involved a guarantee of freedom of access for myself to anyone and to any kind of information that I judged necessary in order to complete my assessment.

The next stage was to collect whatever financial and non-financial data were available in order to assess the programme's true cost. In financial terms, it emerged that it had cost £47,400 over four years to put 210 officers through the programme and to provide some of them with the skills needed to facilitate the job-related training of a further 1,730 clerical officers. Part of that cost had been met by central NHS funding, the rest by the PPA itself. A great deal of the time and expertise of the PPA's small Personnel Department had been absorbed in the programme throughout its duration, and those costs too were incorporated in my financial calculations.

In parallel with this activity was the need to make contact with as many of the staff as possible in order to gain their views on the programme. This involved a desk review, a questionnaire survey, and follow-up face to face discussions with employees drawn from each staff sector covered by the survey, some of whom had taken part in the training, some of whom had not. The data from this stage of the evaluation process cast vital light on the workplace environment over the four years of the programme. It became evident that in many ways there had been a favourable context for the programme, because of:

- changes in top management personnel and a consequent change to a more flexible, team-centred, open style and culture at the top of the organisation, which was gradually making itself felt throughout the authority's structure
- changes in roles and job content due to computerisation, which also provided aids to greater efficiency
- a greater recognition of, and focus on, individual rates of productivity because of new control systems
- more delegated responsibility with the innovations in budgetary systems.

However, survey responses and face to face discussions made it clear that the climate of the workplace had also been unsettling because of the number and scale of changes that had taken place throughout the four-year period. The value of the programme here had been to provide staff with a supportive learning environment in which they could express their concerns about these changes openly. As these concerns emerged, the PPA's personnel director discussed them with top management and worked in a business partnership to tackle them constructively.

My evaluation report concluded that the programme had played a leading role in the successful and rapid introduction of radical change at the PPA. Specifically, the evidence provided through questionnaires and face to face discussions with participants, their line managers and also those who had been unable to take part indicated clearly that without the programme it would not have been possible to achieve the following outcomes:

- virtually no reduction in productivity during a time of fundamental change

- a positive approach to industrial relations issues
- increased motivation and commitment to organisational goals in the great majority of officers who went through the programme.

The programme was widely perceived to be constructive, motivating and energising. It was perceived to have helped newly promoted staff to establish themselves with more certainty in their managerial or supervisory roles. It had given longer-serving staff the opportunity to sit back, away from their pressurised routine, and reflect on their own performance and approach to work, while learning from tutors and colleagues in a trusting and team-centred atmosphere. Comments by one supervisor typified the views of many about what the programme had achieved at her level:

> All aspects of the course are in my mind daily. The week flies by, and I look forward to any further training

These comments were particularly significant because they came from someone working in a division that originally had a persistently poor industrial relations record. Her reactions were echoed by both the administrative assistants in that division, and it was at their initiative that, after the programme, weekly team meetings were introduced there.

My report concluded that the four-year L&D investment had produced outcomes, quantitative and non-quantitative, that significantly exceeded its financial and non-financial costs. Had it not been made there was no doubt that the success of the whole organisational change programme could not have been achieved. I therefore recommended that the management development programme be taken forward and expanded, with further financial underpinning, in order that the benefit of its 'added value' could be spread more widely across the authority and that the PPA's personnel function could be strengthened by the addition of a permanent training officer position. These recommendations were accepted and implemented, demonstrating the PPA board's active commitment to a 'pay-forward' approach to investing in learning and development activity.

CONCLUSION

By now you should have a sound understanding of the concept of adding value, and should be able to use an 'align, engage and measure' framework to assess the kind of added value that L&D activity is adding to an organisation and its human and social capital. You should also feel confident to tackle the review questions contained in Appendix 3.

The main ground covered by the chapter's four sections has been:

- The distinction between providing 'best value' and adding value, and three conditions which must be met if an L&D function is to achieve the latter.
- *Aligning the people*: the ways in which a business-led and proactive L&D function can help to point people in the right direction in an organisation, focused on its core goals; the value of the balanced scorecard approach as a way of directing people's attention to what matters most and stimulating strategic thinking and action.

■ *Engaging the people*: the importance of L&D activity that helps to build a culture of commitment to organisational beliefs and goals, and a framework to guide L&D's aligning activity in this sense, based on Ulrich's seven organisational capabilities that add value; taking the temperature of the workplace through surveys and audits to check on progress.

■ *Measuring the data*: the importance of measuring only what matters and of distinguishing between pay-back and pay-forward assessments; some frameworks of particular relevance in collecting and measuring data on L&D value-adding activity; and six points to guide a partnership approach to the measurement process.

Further information sources

HARRISON, R. (1999) *The training and development audit: An eight-step audit to measure, assess and enhance the performance of your organisation's training and development.* Cambridge: Cambridge Strategy Publications. See also http://www.cambridgestrategy.com [accessed 24 September 2004].

CHARTERED INSTITUTE OF PERSONNEL AND DEVELOPMENT. (2003i) *Human capital external reporting framework: change agenda.* London: Chartered Institute of Personnel and Development. Online version also available at: http://www.cipd.co.uk/changeagenda [accessed 24 September 2004].

Also:

■ The DTI's Benchmark project. Its Index covers a wide range of businesses, and is structured so that it is easy to compare your own business on a number of parameters (including spending on training) against those in your region, those of similar size, operations in the same industry and so on: http://www.dti.gov.uk/bestpractice/ [accessed 24 September 2004].

■ Investors in People website: http://www.iipuk.co.uk/ [accessed 24 September 2004].

■ A website explaining the balanced scorecard approach http://www.balancedscore card.org/basics/bsc1.html [accessed 25 September 2004].

■ ISO 9001-2000 website: http://www.iso.org/ [accessed 24 September 2004].

Developing L&D Business Partnerships

INTRODUCTION

The purpose of this chapter is to explore the concept of 'business partnership' applied to L&D professionals, and to examine what is involved in its practice. Keeping the big picture in mind through strategic thinking and business partnerships is essential if L&D activity is to make its best contribution to organisational as well as to individual performance.

The idea of partnership to raise commitment between stakeholders in organisations is being given active support by Government, the Trades Union Congress and the Confederation of British Industry. In 2001 the TUC launched a Partnership Institute to offer advice, support and training to unions and managers on partnership, with clients in large and small businesses, the National Health Service and local government (www.tuc.org.uk/pi). The Department of Trade and Industry has a partnership fund that meets up to half the cost of projects seeking to adopt partnership approaches. By April 2004 160 schemes across private, public and voluntary sectors had received a total of £5 million, with a further £9 million earmarked for future applications (http://.dti.gov.uk/partnershipfund). The aim in all this activity is to build mutual trust and commitment through shared goals, whether in a unionised or non-unionised setting (White 2004).

Although such initiatives are aimed at the macro level, the principles informing them explain the importance that the HR profession now attaches to its own business partnership role. Half the respondents to the CIPD's 2003 HR survey claimed to have that as a primary role (CIPD 2003h). In fact the title is in such common use there that it has almost lost meaning. It also drifts across all organisational levels. At the Royal Bank of Scotland it is reserved for the most senior HR position, at the Prudential the HR business partners work in business units, and in many other organisations the title is applied to middle-ranking HR professionals.

The chapter has three sections. The first identifies key partners for L&D practitioners in their professional activity. The second explores meanings and metaphors related to the concept of partnership and applies these to an L&D context, highlighting issues of culture, power, the management of conflict, and ways of building trust. The third section identifies core skills that L&D practitioners need in order to build and maintain effective business partnerships, and concludes with an illustrative case.

WHO ARE THE PARTNERS?

The external players

To appreciate the true meaning of partnership we must go back to basics (Pearsall and Trumble 1996):

> **'*Partner*: a person who shares or takes part with another or others, especially in a business firm with shared risks and profits.'**

So a business partnership is not merely about working to shared ends. It is about working with those who share in the risks and gains of an undertaking. Seen in this light, such partnerships must extend beyond the organisation. Who, for example, in a limited company takes some of the biggest risks in return for some of the biggest gains? Shareholders would say that they do, since they own the company and will ultimately determine its fate. Even if the extent of their risk-taking may be often be arguable, the gains that they can achieve are certainly great and their power is unquestionable. The ousting from Carlton Communications in 2003 of Michael Green, the company's founder who was set to become chairman of a merged ITV has been described as 'the most public example yet of a sea change in the relationship between big shareholders and company boards' (Durman 2003). Anthony Bolton's successful bid for power was backed by several leading investment firms, acting in defiance of heavyweight directors on Carlton's board.

Commentators like Durman see 'a rising tide of shareholder militancy' that bodes ill for the legitimate practice of management in many companies. Although L&D professionals may never deal directly with shareholders, the latter's influence over the performance measures by which a company's success is assessed can directly affect the company's L&D investment and agenda. Often it forces a focus on early payback, to the detriment of all but short-term training for proficiency. This is where the politics of L&D's bottom line begin.

However, as I noted early in Chapter 9, Government and customers are amongst other powerful external parties who are now significant organisational stakeholders. They too have a vested interest in the L&D strategies and initiatives pursued in an organisation. We have seen in Part 1 of the book the Labour Government's emphasis on a demand-led approach to meeting skills needs, the many implications of this for L&D professionals and the variety of funding now available for L&D initiatives.

Players within the organisation

Looking inside the organisation who, by the same kind of reasoning, are L&D's business partners there? Clearly the directors of the business, because they set the goals and strategy for the business and are held ultimately accountable for results. Clearly too managers. They carry the formal responsibility of ensuring that business targets are achieved at their organisational levels, and they receive rewards or penalties in line with the extent to which they discharge that responsibility effectively.

Our dictionary source, however, offers two further definitions of a partner (Pearsall and Trumble 1996):

- a player on the same side in a game
- a companion in dancing.

These definitions mean that we should expand our concept of the L&D business partnership to include yet more players. Externally, partners on the same side in the game include those agencies and individuals with whom L&D practitioners can collaborate to gain support – especially financial – for organisational L&D initiatives. Learning and Skills Councils are an obvious example here, providing not only funding but also a source of networking, local influence and support for L&D practitioners within their organisations. Educational institutions and consultancy firms are also frequently used as 'companions in dancing'.

Internally, other dancing partners include:

- team leaders
- teams and individuals with L&D needs
- learning champions in the business
- those occupying and managing L&D specialist positions
- other human resource professionals in the organisation, whose work impinges on L&D.

The implications of these varying interpretations of business partnership are wide-ranging. In this chapter I take as my major reference points the concept of a partner as 'player on the same side' and as 'companion in dancing'.

REFLECTION

Looking at your own organisation, who do you think should be the key business partners in the L&D process, and what kinds of L&D partnerships are actively being developed – or should be developed?

A GAME OR A DANCE?

Playing the game

One dictionary definition suggests that those holding major L&D responsibilities in an organisation should always play 'on the same side' as their business partners. If we believe that those who invest most heavily in the business and/or those who carry the major burden of accountability for its results are the key partners here, then coming on side means working in the interests of the shareholders (if any), the directors and the managers in the organisation. To play 'on side' with them, the L&D partner needs to:

- Aim for the same goals as those of the business. Setting up separate goal posts for L&D is a counterproductive exercise. There must be a clear even if loose-coupled alignment of L&D activity with business strategy.
- Show that the L&D process is about adding value for the business, as discussed in Chapter 13.
- Score wins for the business. Often, L&D staff are regarded as losers. If they are to become major players then they must not just preach 'added value'. They must get results.

At this point some reflection is needed. On the one hand it is surely fair to give the main consideration in a partnership to partners who carry most risk and invest much resource. This, however, is to ignore the fact that often within their ranks there can be conflict, dispute about ends and means. It also ignores the fact that, in L&D, other players are involved and their needs too must be considered. Key here are those whose learning and development management wishes to shape to business ends. Learning is a property of the individual. It cannot be bent to the purposes of others without the agreement of its owner. There are more sides than two in the L&D game. Employees must be convinced that they have something to win here, if they are to invest their own learning in a partnership with others whose interests they may not feel they share.

This view of the organisation as a pluralist, not a unitary system – a system where there are many and often conflicting values and interests – gives a new dimension to our concept of partnership in an L&D setting. It draws attention especially to the need for understanding organisational culture, since culture is strongly shaped as well as being shaped by the values of organisational members. It powerfully influences their reactions to any new policy, practice or initiative. It therefore needs some discussion at this point.

Issues of culture

We have seen throughout the book the importance in a new knowledge economy and an unpredictable business environment of building a core organisational identity around a coherent set of shared beliefs, values and language (Elfring and Volberda 2001, p273). What is at issue here is the building and sustaining of a conducive culture – something that has been highlighted in almost every chapter so far.

Culture affects behaviour by providing people with a 'tool kit' of material such as symbols, stories, procedures, habits and skills which become a set of general cultural 'capacities'. They draw on these capacities when making choices about which actions to take, which initiatives to support (Swidler 1986). Culture is dynamic. It is also different at different levels and locations, and indeed some claim that all cultures are local, being created by the behaviour of local managers and their teams (Buckingham 2001, p40). Yet running through all parts of an organisation there will be some common thread, some generalised sense of a common history and identity.

What counts is the strength and extent of that commonality. Often it can be built on by cross-functional L&D initiatives, but in some organisations such interventions do not work because the thread of commonality is too fragile and organisational identity is divided by more forces than those that unite it. For example, greater involvement of stakeholders in organisations' affairs and the blurring of boundaries between organisations whether through outsourcing, supply chain relationships or other causes can produce multiple organisational identities (Pratt and Foreman 2000). Where employees receive conflicting views about their organisation from different sources, they can become more influenced by the management of client companies to whom their employer provides services than by their own management.

Such considerations return us to the three fundamental influences on the context in which an organisation's members learn and perform from day to day: leadership, management and HR strategies. They need to interrelate in ways that engender a strong sense of collective identity and commitment (Purcell et al 2003). However that is no easy task, particularly where business strategies, management actions and HR practices differ across strategic business units. Differences in front-line managers' competence, use of discretionary power, and ability to balance local against corporate needs all have differentiating effects on workplace culture (Purcell et al 2003).

If L&D professionals are to achieve success in the implementation of L&D strategies in the workplace, then they need to work with managers to build a learning culture there – one where continuous learning is facilitated and accepted as an integral part of the everyday work process. However, where an unfavourable culture is already embedded it will be highly resistant to change, and no quick fix will be able to transform it. Only a long-haul approach in which the organisation's leadership and its HR strategies – particularly its performance management process and its management training and development initiatives – play a dominating part can offer real hope of change.

As I explained in Chapter 8, at present whether in the UK or more widely across Europe there are relatively few signs that L&D professionals, let alone line managers, are actively promoting learning cultures in their organisations. The European research detailed in that chapter showed that even in self-styled learning oriented organisations L&D professionals rarely appear to be taking a proactive stance and that few managers and their employees seem to be involved in the kind of new learning tasks and innovative learning processes that would typify such a culture (Tjepkema 2002, p172). Such findings are in line with earlier studies in suggesting that more often than not the true motive for changes in L&D orientation are to do with reducing training budgets and scaling down central training departments rather than with the emergence of any new learning philosophy (Raper et al 1997). That is an interesting thought to set against the claim that a shift in organisations today from trainers to learners represents a deliberate 'people development strategy' directed at 'the development of learning capabilities' (Sloman 2004).

To summarise: where learning cultures are concerned there seems to be a major gap between aspirations and reality. L&D professionals should be taking a lead in finding ways to tackle it if they are to ensure that they, managers and employees are all 'on side' in tackling the organisation's learning agenda.

Companions in the dance

If we interpret partnership not as a game but as a dance, that metaphor highlights themes of companionship, harmony and trust.

This underlines the fact that a business partnership is not just a matter of sharing risks and gains. It is also about sensitivity to needs and moving together. In the dance, individual differences can enrich the process. Each dancer can express themselves in their unique way, while responding with other dancers to the basic rhythm of the dance. There is thus a marriage of diversity. In responding both to the music and to each other, the dancers are companions in the dance. So too in the L&D business partnership, seen in its widest sense, diversity should be welcomed and built upon.

Dancing involves adjusting one's step to a partner's in order to move forward harmoniously. When discussing the organising of learning events earlier in the book I stressed the need to ensure 'external consistency' in L&D activity through engaging actively with partners at each stage of the L&D process. The partners must be companions in the dance, from its beginning to its conclusion. But harmony is a state that emerges from the resolution of tension, so the task is still a challenging one. A recent two-year study of management training and development in Britain and six major continental European countries, for example, found that management education in Britain has developed into an 'uneasy dance' between employers and employees, with both sides seeing the advantages in being partners but with each having a different dancing style (Mabey and Ramirez 2004).

You may find it helpful to identify some of the potential for tension in the new partnerships that have been developing between L&D professionals and union learning representatives in the following account. Feedback notes follow at its end.

CASE EXAMPLE

Dancing with a new partner

One example of a relatively new kind of L&D partnership is that between L&D practitioners, union learning representatives (ULRs, discussed in Chapter 2), individual employees and line managers.

ULRs are potentially valuable partners for the L&D function. They have a statutory right and indeed a requirement to be trained for their role and so will be competent partners. Their influence on adult workers who might not otherwise engage in learning is already well attested and can extend to the very types of employee and of minority groups who tend to receive the smallest (if any) slice of the training cake. In consequence they may have little experience of training and be fearful of undertaking any form of planned learning.

However ULRs' tasks are not the same as those of L&D practitioners. The ULR role is to promote and support the development of the individual, as distinct from any job-related training to achieve performance targets. Nevertheless ULRs can be valuable partners in organisational settings where there is a deliberate shift from a preoccupation with training to increasingly self-managed learning, a concern to enhance employees' basic skills, and a drive to build a workplace learning culture. Individuals who, for the first time perhaps, are supported in pursuing the kind of learning opportunities that can open up new horizons and interests for themselves are likely to find the experience stimulating, rewarding and confidence-building. Many are then more likely to become involved in business-focused training and some to take on new roles and tasks.

Comments

- The crucial issue here is the different interests and goals of two partners – L&D professionals working primarily for the business, ULRs working primarily for individual learners. However there is a shared purpose – in the desire to involve individuals actively in a meaningful learning process and, through its operation, to enhance their learning skills, competence and motivation. Although the ULRs' preoccupation with development for the individual will not always mesh well with the L&D function's preoccupation with set training and learning targets and with activity directly related to business goals, there is clear ground for collaboration, given mutual trust and a shared respect for learning and learners – as the progress of the whole ULR initiative is repeatedly demonstrating.
- There are other partners involved in this particular dance – line managers. They can be expected to be concerned about release of staff for training, about investing in the kind of learning that in the short term may not have an impact on individual or unit performance targets, and so on. In this kind of multiple partnership the inherent tensions are not to do with personalities or power (although in many situations they will complicate the relationship) but with structural arrangements in the workplace and with the performance management process (Rainbird 2003).
- As Rainbird (2003) explains, all of this highlights the importance of the learning agreement – requiring the parties to think through potential problems at the start, agree on how to tackle them, then formalise the commitment of line managers, ULRs and employees to training and development together with mechanisms for implementing it.

Dancing across boundaries

Extending the scope of the L&D dance beyond an organisation's boundaries is important for two reasons. First, it ensures that more of those on whom the organisation depends for the ultimate quality of its products and services become part of a mutually productive learning partnership. Second, it brings into the organisation skills, knowledge, networks and ways of perceiving and understanding the business environment that can add value for the business.

Supplier development programmes are a case in point. Many are driven purely by a training rationale, focusing on the improvement of skills to perform given tasks and carry out prescribed processes. Some, however, go deeper and seek through a partnership dance to produce double-loop learning – the kind of learning that involves questioning why problems occur in the first place and challenging the continued utility of long-standing systems and processes. Such programmes encourage participants to identify underlying causes instead of only their surface symptoms. They are therefore based on an adult-to-adult relationship. Questioning by suppliers of the client firm's way of doing things is a risky venture, but where there is sufficient trust and openness it can produce great gains for both sides. Innovations in both the client and supplier organisations can emerge from new ways of thinking and learning together (Batchelor et al 1995).

There are other kinds of boundaries across which L&D partnership should extend, including the contractual. Here is one example of an imaginative partnership involving players who are often disadvantaged in L&D strategies: part-time and temporary workers. Failure to integrate them into organisations' L&D systems has given rise to concern at government level (White 1996). Often, such workers have less access than permanent full-time workers to:

- upskilling through training, growth in the job and increased responsibility
- performance management processes that combine appraisal reviews, target-setting, performance feedback and merit pay
- increasing personal discretion in tasks.

CASE EXAMPLE

Developing a flexible workforce at Beeton Rumford

In the late 1990s the Earl's Court Olympia catering company Beeton Rumford employed around 200 temporary workers. It was unusual in the catering trade for its promise of a good benefits package and equal commitment to the development of all its workers, not only those occupying full-time positions. The determination of the managing director, Richard Tate, to have an integrated workforce was so great that he banned the term 'casual' as a description of temporary employees. He first developed his philosophy in an earlier career with Trust House Forte.

At Beeton Rumford the role of temporary employees was crucial but had in the past been undervalued. After 1991 the company was restructured from a functional to a customer-focused business, and a separate staff department was established to recruit, train and manage temporary personnel. The aim from then on was to ensure that temporary staff were recognised by themselves and others as the backbone of the organisation, supported by rather than supporting full-time staff. This was achieved through focused recruitment aimed at attracting and retaining high-calibre staff, and through eradicating from the company the previous 'casual labour' ethos.

At first, a large and relatively unproductive effort went into improving the status and training of temporary staff. Operational managers found it hard to support such a change in focus, given the stop-start nature of the business. Despite their efforts, the sizeable pool of expensively recruited and trained temporary talent would disappear at the end of every catering event.

Further HR policy change took place, and this brought the improvements sought. By the late 1990s, temporary staff were no longer laid off at 24 hours' notice but were treated as full-time in terms of the focus of their jobs, being given information about events scheduled over the coming year in order to aid their own planning activity. L&D strategy now incorporated a six-tier career structure based on core competencies, with appraisals carried out regularly.

Source: PICKARD, J. (1995)

In the partnership approach described in this case the firm's leaders and HR practitioners worked together to raise the status of hitherto undervalued stakeholders in the business. The whole L&D agenda of the firm gradually changed as these new partners joined the L&D dance.

BUSINESS PARTNER SKILLS

Demands on the role

As already discussed in the section about partnerships as game playing, if the term 'partner' seems to imply a cosy relationship this is far from the reality. Partnership involves resolving differences and reconciling diverse interests and values. It is about challenge as much as it is about agreement. It requires unlearning in order that new, mutual learning can develop. It calls for the skill, confidence and professional expertise to challenge assumptions about the nature of business and organisational problems, helping others to question their own ways of thinking and doing. It cannot prosper without the patient building of trust, and of commitment to shared tasks.

A study of HR in globalising firms showed that effective international HR executives working in situations across countries where they have to increasingly share information and work in virtual teams need process and political skills as much as technical knowledge. They have to be strong personal networkers with a capacity for and tolerance of the ambiguities and uncertainties inherent in new business situations, resource negotiators, appreciative of cultural differences and showing respect for them. Such skills are as important as being 'strategic thinkers' (Brewster et al 2002, p18).

However, it seems that in more typical organisational settings business partnership skills pose a problem for many in the HR area. The 2003 CIPD survey referred to earlier in the chapter found that large numbers of senior HR professionals are now engaged in strategy, where they must have credibility as business partners, yet that many felt poorly equipped for their roles. They identified a particular lack of business knowledge and strategy tools (CIPD 2003h). A similar lack of competence and confidence seems to apply at all organisational levels. One survey based on 360-degree questionnaire results for 250 people showed that HR professionals appeared to have fewer people management skills than some other managers and that their weakest areas were openness to others, assertiveness and self-belief (Katsen Consulting, referred to in Pickard 2004).

That last point moves partnerships skills into the territory of the emotional, the social and the personal. It highlights in particular the need for L&D practitioners to be skilled in striking a healthy balance between assertiveness and conflict, so that when disagreements occur both those processes are put to productive instead of destructive use.

Issues of power and politics

Within any organisation issues of power and conflict are bound to complicate the task of collaboration. Power is a property that exists in any human society, and politics is the way it is commonly expressed (Torrington and Weightman 1985). In any organisation there are three sources of power that an L&D practitioner needs to take into account when seeking to develop effective business partnerships. They can act as constraints or as opportunities depending largely on the practitioner's skills in achieving conflict resolution.

- *Resource*: 'Power accrues to those parts of the organization that can control the flow of resources, especially if these are scarce and critical for organizational functioning' (Miller et al 1999, p46). Resources in this sense can be of any kind – financial and non-financial, material and intangible, resources of time, space and expertise. They constitute the means to enable the achieving of an end. Resource management is not simply a set of tasks. It is a political process. Resource starvation in the L&D field is common. It is one of the many reasons why political and partnership skills must be a crucial part of any L&D professional's armoury.
- *Position*: the power derived from formal position, its accompanying status and the knowledge and information to which it gives access. Since knowledge is vital to decision-making at all levels, positions that act as gateways to information and to knowledge networks constitute a formidable power source. The formal positions bestowed on those who carry the main responsibility for the L&D function in an organisation will always be a primary indicator of the value that key players place on the L&D investment.
- *Expertise*: the power derived from a uniquely valued area of knowledge or competence. One well-known study of a French tobacco company revealed that maintenance workers, despite their lowly position, had exclusive possession of expert and essential knowledge. Through this power source they were able to gain and maintain control over production processes and so negotiate to their advantage (Crozier 1964). The parallels with L&D professionals working in or for an organisation may not at first sight be obvious but reflection should make them so.

When strains arise in an L&D partnership for whatever reason the players will tend to use their power in order to protect or pursue their interests. Conflict is natural in any pluralist society. Used effectively it can bring new ideas, innovation and progress. Handled without skill, it can lead to the breakdown of relationships. Morgan (1997, pp205–209) identifies the following typical responses to conflict situations:

- *Avoidance*: tries to avoid conflict, but when it arises tries to stifle or postpone it, or at least ensure that there is no direct confrontation.
- *Compromise*: seeks compromise by negotiation and by making deals.
- *Competition*: tries to win, either by exploiting rivalries or by exercise of power.
- *Submission*: usually gives way, either because of a belief that conflict is counter-productive or because it is clear from the start that winning is impossible.
- *Accommodation*: encourages the other party/parties to put the reasons for conflict on the table, so that it can be resolved.
- *Collaboration*: seeks to work together to find solutions that build on differences and that help each of the parties involved to win something.

The first instinct of most HR professionals new to their roles would probably be to favour the collaborative approach. Such professionals have been educated to espouse values of collaboration, of openness and of mutual benefit. These are the values that they have been taught underpin the concept of business partnership. However, the more experienced could not be blamed for responding more cautiously. Collaboration is not easy to achieve in some organisational contexts, and the more powerful the players the more politicised the game becomes. Politics is the art of achieving the possible. In an L&D partnership power should be used to achieve a positive outcome in L&D terms that also ensures the continuance of the healthy working relationships. Style cannot be prescribed, because it must respond sensitively to situation. Sometimes collaboration will not work: it may be better to go for compromise through negotiation in order to preserve all players' commitment and to move the game forward. Sometimes it will be wiser to abandon a chosen course in the interests of making progress on another front.

However, if ethics enters into the matter the metaphor of the L&D business partnership as 'a game' breaks down. Professionals must work to a basic code of conduct that they apply to all situations in which they become involved. Thus there is no context in which a L&D professional should behave in ways that seek to exploit or undermine any of the players. Vulnerabilities in individuals or groups must never be used by L&D partners to gain advantage for themselves or for more powerful players. That is why for them the metaphor of partnership as game is less appropriate than the metaphor of partnership as dance.

REFLECTION

Imagine that you are a training specialist, working with a line manager to identify training needs in his unit of the business. You have agreed together on a range of needs in members of his team, but his perception of the causes of poor performance in three of his staff differs significantly from yours. In consequence his ideas about how that performance should be improved – through sending them away on a short training course so that 'they can get themselves sorted out and then get back on the job' – differ greatly from yours, which for various valid reasons favour a more work-based coaching process. It is essential that the conflict that is developing between you is resolved. What do you think you would do to achieve that?

Good citizenship

In previous chapters there has been a consistent emphasis on the need for visionary leadership and facilitative, ethical management if organisational members are to work together in pursuit of a common business purpose. Lynda Gratton (2003a) takes these points further. In her concern with the balance that needs to be struck in an organisation between account-abilities, obligations and trust she argues the need for a truly democratic enterprise, and as noted in Chapter 9, proposes four tenets that go to the heart of any L&D partnership:

- There is an adult relationship between the parties.
- Individuals are able to develop their natures and express their diverse qualities.
- The freedom of some is not gained at the expense of others.
- Individuals acknowledge accountabilities and obligations both to themselves and to their community.

What is at issue here is strategies and behaviour that are informed by principles of good citizenship (Hosmer 1994). Harrison and Smith (2001) have described the kind of behaviour that this involves as the exercise of *practical judgement*, a term suggested by Aristotle's concept of 'phronesis' and one that is most easily explained as being to do with applying the wisdom born of experience in ways appropriate to the particular situation and respectful of the values of others. Two other concepts also have relevance here: those of *emotional intelligence* (EI) and of *spiritual intelligence* (SI).

EI has been explained in basic terms as (Jack Mayer, quoted by Pickard 1999, p495):

> **'the understanding of emotion. The ability to perceive, to integrate, to understand and reflectively manage one's own and other people's feelings.'**

EI is expressed through abilities related to (Goleman 1998):

- knowing one's emotions
- managing these emotions
- motivating oneself
- recognising emotions in others
- handling relationships.

Some are scathing about Goleman's claims, seeing them as no more than old wine dressed up in new bottles (Woodruffe 2001). Others express concern about how EI can be clarified sufficiently to enable it to be assessed in some meaningful way, especially when so much depends either on self-reporting or on the uncertainties of 360-degree feedback (Smewing 2004). Despite such problems, many do find that EI abilities have a unique significance in today's pressured and fragmented organisations, while others again go a stage further, proposing the concept of 'spiritual intelligence'. Zohar and Drake (2000) explain SI as the ultimate intelligence, because it represents an individual's deep, intuitive sense of meaning. They observe that when the immediate environment is uncertain, people need an inner security in order to be flexible, adaptable, imaginative, spontaneous, innovative, inspirational. SI can supply that security.

What is the difference between these three concepts, and how do they relate to the work of L&D professionals as business partners? EI and SI are essentially inwardly focused, being about how the individual uses emotional and spiritual intelligence to deal effectively with their environment and with others. Practical judgement concerns the manner in which the individual can make a contribution to their community, helping its members to move forward together. The concepts may resist close definition (although Dulewicz and Higgs (1999) have developed an EI competency framework based on Goleman's five EI domains). What matters, however, is that they draw attention to partnership as a process calling for more than technical and strategic skills. Learning is the most intimate and individualised of human processes that organisational leaders, managers and L&D specialists try to shape to their purposes. The oft-declared shift from a preoccupation with training to a concern that learners take charge of their own learning is born at least in part from the realisation that all employees are adults. They have their personal sensitivities, emotions, needs and insecurities that require care in the handling if they are to become committed to any wider learning agenda than their own.

For L&D professionals the skills and styles needed in business partnerships are not skin deep or easily acquired. Reflecting on the concepts of practical judgement, emotional and spiritual intelligence is not sentimentalism or wacky thinking. It is a valuable way of probing the nature of some essential but hard to express dimensions of partnership in a democratic community.

Practising the steps

The various elements of establishing and maintaining effective business partnerships in L&D can be summarised by identifying the major steps in the process. In real life, of course, these steps are rarely taken one after the other. They constitute a set of movements partners may have to perform almost simultaneously so that the dance can progress:

- **P**artner others: build effective working relationships inside and outside the business so that L&D strategies work on the ground and new initiatives gain the support they need.
- **A**chieve results: promote L&D activity that supports the business and the learners, work with others to monitor and evaluate its outcomes, and spread awareness of the value-adding contribution that the L&D function provides.
- **R**emember the People–Performance framework: without the right organisational context people cannot or will not use their learning and skills for the benefit of the business. Help to build commitment and a learning culture in the workplace through your partnerships and expertise.
- **T**ravel around: move about the organisation, establishing a live and proactive presence in the business, expanding and deepening your business knowledge and cementing valuable relationships.
- **N**ever be complacent: use partnerships as a vehicle for your own learning as well as that of others, stimulating your professional development and generating new knowledge to make the L&D function leading edge.
- **E**nsure professional and ethical practice. Respect the values of others, building on diversity of whatever kind in order to produce rich learning experiences, with access for all employees to opportunities to develop their performance and potential.
- **R**aise awareness: ensure that managers and all employees know about the big L&D issues facing the organisation and the part they can play in tackling them.

Finally, here is a case example to incorporate many of the principles discussed in this chapter. It is about a programme called (appropriately) 'Stepping Out' to reflect a philosophy of what one of the key partners, Egg plc, calls 'dancing with the customer'.

CASE EXAMPLE

The dancing companions

The dance

In 1999 Egg, Britain's first Internet bank, formed a business partnership with Harris Associates, a Birmingham-based training and organisational development company, to design a framework of training and development activity to complement current training provision at Egg. The aim was to recognise and accredit competence to national standards, without compromising the overriding purpose of the programme. A pilot was designed to cover around 500 call centre staff (called 'Associates') working across two of Egg's UK sites, at Dudley and Derby.

The rationale

When Egg launched in October 1998, much thought had been given as to how best to train and develop its people. Retention of staff was from the start a major target for the company, and a strong training programme was considered to be vital in achieving this. By April 1999 there was already internal training in place, and national vocational qualifications (NVQs) were an additional option for staff. Egg now sought an external partner who could work closely with Egg's training staff to devise such a programme – a dancing companion sensitive to the organisation's needs. Harris Associates was chosen.

The development process

Harris Associates developed a programme framework over three months designed to address some of the human resources challenges faced by Egg. These included the need to ensure adequate personal and professional support for sales centre staff working in a high-pressure environment. During that period, three processes were involved:

Research: Harris' staff collected data to enable them to understand Egg's values and culture, its people and the pressures on them, and the competitive environment in which Egg operates.

Design and develop: Harris' staff drafted a programme, delivery processes and materials to meet agreed objectives. Based on the outcomes of the research and analysis of the challenges facing Egg staff, they proposed a framework that was designed as a competency-based training programme. Through on-the-job training linked directly to customer service requirements, it would provide staff with the competencies they need, and would offer them the opportunity to gain national vocational qualifications. The programme was titled 'Stepping Out'. Its purpose was to provide staff with the skills, competencies and confidence to be able to deliver outstanding, customer-led servicing.

The 'Stepping Out' programme linked in to current training at Egg, and was designed to overcome the challenges facing the business in promoting skills development. These business improvement projects developed participants' understanding of the challenges facing Egg, and encouraged their proactive involvement with their teams and within the company. Internal champions were identified to act as coaches (who later became NVQ-accredited) and mentors.

The programme (including NVQ work) was designed to take 12 to 16 months to complete, in order to fit in with Egg's business cycle. It was pitched at NVQ level 3 as that best reflected Associates' job levels, and incorporated a more developmental process than levels below. For Egg, that process was one of the most important features of the programme.

Implement: Once the programme had been approved, the partnership of Egg and Harris Associates agreed on a structured project plan to ensure achievement, ongoing evaluation, quality assurance and performance review. The review focused on the achievement of quality standards, business benefits, and key performance indicators.

The outcomes

During the first stage of the pilot programme, which came to an end in June 2001, 504 Egg associates participated in the programme, including nearly the entire workforce of 300 at the Dudley site. 250 associates completed the initial programme and 18 months on 212 were still with the company – an exceptional retention rate for call centre staff in any organisation.

Specific results included the following:

- 77 per cent of associates recorded improvement in customer service through the use of proactive techniques and a focus on national customer service training standards.
- 72 per cent noticed an improvement in their confidence and ability to handle difficult calls.
- 74 per cent experienced an improvement in morale and motivation within teams.
- 66 per cent showed an improved relationship between colleagues/teams.
- 57 per cent of managers/team leaders noted improvements within their teams.
- 30 per cent had already achieved promotion or identified a new opportunity for development.
- In each group, the top performers in the team had all completed the 'Stepping Out' programme.
- All training being undertaken was accredited.
- Over 180 business improvement projects had been successfully implemented, producing significant savings in terms of costs and time. Many of these had a direct impact on customers, thereby also improving customer retention rates.

Harris Associates was then asked to extend the framework to cover seven more areas of the business. The (now renamed) 'Stepping Up' framework that was developed for this purpose also stretched to support organisational competencies. Again, it identified recommended internal training programmes to support staff development within the business.

Sue Savage, People Manager at Egg plc, commented: 'One of the key benefits of working with Harris Associates was their ability to adapt the programme to reflect the Egg culture and, through its project management, to avoid the bureaucracy usually associated with such a large internal qualifications framework. Egg is now looking at widening the programme to incorporate managers within the company as well as associates and team leaders.'

With acknowledgements to Egg plc and to Harris Associates, Birmingham

CONCLUSION

You should by now have a clear understanding of what an L&D business partnership involves, in terms of its purpose, its partnerships and its skills. You should also be able to tackle competently the review questions contained in Appendix 3.

Main themes in the chapter's three sections have been:

- The importance of understanding partnership as a process that involves both external and internal partners, whose aims and interests will not naturally be the same but whose agenda the L&D professionals must understand in order to gain the support needed for their activity.
- The value of applying to business partnerships the metaphors of both the game and the dance, since together they highlight issues of power and politics, together with issues of trust, mutual commitment and sensitivity to partners' diverse needs and concerns; the importance of L&D practitioners working with managers to build a learning culture in the workplace and evidence of insufficient progress being made as yet to do this.
- With many L&D partnerships stretching across organisational boundaries, the need for skilful management of conflict and diversity in order to produce commitment to an overarching shared purpose.
- The many demands on L&D practitioners made by their business partner role, both in terms of technical and managerial ability and of emotional intelligence and practical judgement. The need for L&D practitioners to develop seven major kinds of capability if they are to be effective in their performance of the role.

Further information sources

CHARTERED INSTITUTE OF PERSONNEL AND DEVELOPMENT. (2004e) *A guide: business partnering: a new direction for HR*. London: CIPD. (Looks at models proposed, based on case studies from the Department of Work and Pensions, and Royal Mail Letters). Available to download from http://www.cipd.co.uk/subjects/corpstrtgy/general/busprtnrnewdir.htm [accessed 8 November 2004].

JOHNSTON, R. (1996) Power and influence and the L&D function. In: J. STEWART and J. MCGOLDRICK (eds) *Human resource development: perspectives, strategies and practice*. London: Pitman. pp180–195.

MOYNAGH, M and WORSLEY, R. (2001) *Tomorrow's workplace: fulfilment or stress?* The Tomorrow Project, tel. 0115 925 1114. See also http://www.tomorrowproject.net [accessed 21 September 2004].

Building for the Future

PART

4

Developing Careers

CHAPTER 15

INTRODUCTION

In Part 4 of the book the focus is on building organisational capacity for the future. Since career development and management development play a central role here, they provide the subject matter for this chapter and the next. The final chapter reviews main themes that have emerged from the book to see what lessons they may signal for the L&D process and its professionals.

The purpose of this chapter is to explain what is involved in career development in organisations, and to explore some of the ways in which an organisation, through its career management system, can strengthen the link between people and organisational performance. Schein (1978, pvii) observed that career development marks the point at which the shifting needs of an organisation's people confront the shifting nature of its work. The challenge it embodies is one of matching the needs of the organisation with those of the people who work for it, from their entry into the organisation to their departure. The concept of mutual commitment lies at its heart.

The chapter has four sections. In the first I look at the concept of 'career' in changing times, at the increased investment that most organisations now seem to be making in career management and at the business case for this. In the second section principles are suggested to ensure that career management is effectively integrated into HR policies and practices and that the system is inclusive and well balanced in its attention to organisational and individual needs. The third section examines how support can be given to individuals at critical points in their career path while encouraging their self-management of the career development process. The final brief section identifies a career development agenda for L&D professionals both in their organisations and in the local community.

CAREERS IN CHANGING TIMES

The shifting concept of 'career'

Traditionally, the concept of 'career' has been one of upward movement involving (Sparrow and Hiltrop 1994, p427):

- entry criteria linked to educational attainment or vocational training
- a planned structure of job experiences and promotional steps
- progressive status and/or salary
- membership of an external professional or occupational body with its own codes and culture.

This concept is now shifting. Organisations are rarely able to guarantee lifetime job security. In many, waves of de-layering have produced flatter structures. The concept of the 'portfolio career' is increasingly common, and in the emerging knowledge economy many organisations find it more difficult to attract and retain valued knowledge workers, leading to the so-called 'war for talent'.

However there is little evidence that the traditional career is in the throes of collapse. Research carried out on a major scale in the ESRC's *Future of Work Programme* (White et al 2004) shows that the trend to flatten organisations seems at last to have slowed down and to an extent even been reversed, and many organisations are increasing the number of management and non-management grades. Two out of three have opened career ladders to most employees, and sectors that historically have not done so are now becoming involved in organisational career management, opening up new career routes for their employees. There is a widespread use of flexible patterns of working, including temporary and part-time labour and outsourcing, but again the trends seem to be stabilising, not increasing. HR strategies such as appraisal, performance-related pay, involvement through communications are increasing, and in one in five workplaces there is a high benefits strategy. All of this indicates that most organisations are now trying to offer internal career paths with associated inducements to their employees, and are not restricting these opportunities to the management level. Emmott (2004) in his review of the ESRC research concluded that most employees below management/professional level now see their best chances for the future in staying with their present employer.

Here is an example of the care that some organisations are putting into their career management strategy to ensure it is flexible to local as well as central needs, even when 'local' refers to an offshore facility. You may find it helpful to identify the key features of the Prudential's approach. Comments follow at the end.

CASE EXAMPLE

The Prudential's call centre, India

In 2003 the Prudential (the Pru) opened a call centre with 900 staff in Mumbai, India. Unlike many such operations, the centre is an integral part of the UK operation and is treated as one of the company's five UK sites. The industrial relations policies, HR practices and training that are applied are consistent with those provided at the Pru's UK and US sites, making Indian staff feel a core part of the company.

The employee profile at Mumbai is very different both from call centre workers generally and from Pru employees' profile in the UK and the USA. The Indian employees are far younger than the average, with 90 per cent being between 21 and 24, and they are far better educated, with over 95 per cent having a degree and a further 3 per cent having two degrees. So far, the Mumbai centre has achieved an exemplary record of success, and has half the employee turnover that is common in call centres.

The company pays particular attention to understanding Indian culture. It has invested in voice and accent training and cultural awareness so that Indian employees can establish empathy and good relationships with their overseas customers. Recognising that in India a heavy premium is placed on career paths, further education and job titles, the Pru provides for all its call centre workers at Mumbai structured career progression and opportunities to study for an MBA. The local management team is made up of Indians and reports through UK functional lines, using the same HR business model as in the UK.

Source: SIMMS, J. (2004)

Comments

- The Pru has integrated its career management practices at Mumbai with its other HR practices there, and has ensured that common HR strategies are in place across the whole company wherever it is located worldwide. This consistent approach helps to make all Pru employees feel a close identification with the Pru brand and values.
- However local detail matters. At Mumbai the career development package has been planned to fit local culture and value systems. It offers to the Indian employees the kind of rewards that are likely to have the most appeal for them.

The impact of a new knowledge economy

In their survey of the changing employment relationship Sparrow and Cooper (2003) identify that while the psychological contract between employers and employees is not being breached in the dramatic way that many suppose, there is a clear switch in emphasis from organisations to individuals as drivers of change in the employment relationship and that a process of negotiation lies at the heart of modern careers. Some may want a relational type of psychological contract, others a more transactional type, but one way and another individuals appear to be taking more control in that negotiating process.

Of particular significance here is the impact of the emerging new knowledge economy, and of the importance within it of specialist knowledge workers. A study of six UK-based research and technology organisations has confirmed that knowledge-intensive work poses major challenges to widely held beliefs about how organisations in an emergent knowledge-based economy should be managed. Three needs are especially critical in the case of knowledge workers (Swart et al 2003, pix):

- the development of their individual knowledge and skills
- the sharing and development of their knowledge within their organisations
- the sharing and development of their knowledge with clients and other parties in their external networks.

Knowledge workers formed a high proportion of employees in the six firms studied and they were uniquely important to the success of those firms. However, there was considerable tension between those workers' individual needs and the requirement to share their knowledge within and beyond the organisation. Knowledge workers want to work on interesting projects that make good use of their high-level knowledge and skills (ibid. p69). Given their importance to knowledge-intensive firms (KIFs), care must be devoted to crafting HR policies to do with their recruitment, development, reward and retention. But it is also essential to find ways of ensuring the transfer of knowledge between separate project teams, and of resolving the potential tension between knowledge workers' competing loyalties – to the team, the organisation, the client and the profession (ibid. p71).

People management practices are key to the overcoming of knowledge barriers in KIFs, but the research findings suggest that they are likely to work best when they evolve naturally from the organisation's culture and its structural arrangements, rather than when they are imposed from the top down (ibid. p7). This, of course, goes much further than considering what approach to take to career management for scarce talent. It strikes at the heart of the management process, raising a question mark over the relevance and value of formal management roles in such organisations. As Harrison and Kessels observe (2003a, p49):

'Such an approach is of course far easier for small than for larger firms, but it does underline the need to consider with particular care the form the management process should take in organisations operating in a knowledge economy. Management, after all, was the product of the Industrial Revolution. In a new kind of economy where knowledge is the key asset, we have to ask whether some new conceptualisation should replace the old.'

The business case for investing in a career management system

Another factor arguing for a significant investment by any organisation in inclusive career management is the evidence that has accumulated from HR research studies concerning the part it can play in enhancing organisational performance. As *Career management: a CIPD guide* (King 2004) explains, it is a powerful way of activating the potential contained in the AMO model (described in Chapter 5) and thereby of strengthening the people–performance link:

'By developing able and motivated employees and giving them an environment in which they can excel, effective career management should, in conjunction with other factors, enable the business to achieve superior performance in terms of labour productivity, cost-effective investment in HR, quality, innovation and customer satisfaction.'

The Guide stresses the need for career management in today's organisations to be inclusive, covering all employees, even non-core workers, through a variety of relevant opportunities. Such activity should involve (King 2004, p11):

- Drawing from and developing the widest possible pool of talent and ability, including employees on non-conventional career paths.
- Reconciling individual and organisational objectives for the development of relevant skills and abilities over time, increasing the likelihood of return on investment in career development.
- Engaging employees' with their work, making them feel valued, and fostering commitment to the organisation.
- Promoting self-responsibility and initiative, and facilitating adaptation to new challenges and change.
- Accommodating and supporting employees' obligations to their home lives such that they are productive and effective while they are at work.

Two approaches to career management

Organisations now tend to follow one of two approaches in their career management strategies, although some use both across a differentiated workforce: an 'organisational career management' approach, and a 'career self-management' approach. Sturges et al (2002) explain these as follows:

Organisational career management refers to a planned approach to career development for some or all of an organisation's employees. Its aim is to raise levels of 'affective commitment' – meaning the extent to which an individual identifies with, and is actively involved in, an organisation.

This approach is likely to be valued by employees who need help in managing their careers and look to the organisation for a strategy that tackles career management in an integrative way, with line managers who are committed to its implementation and access to a variety of clear career paths together with L&D support in moving along them.

Career self-management involves putting career planning largely into the hands of the individual but providing support for their continuous improvement in a current role, using HR strategies that help employees acquire a portfolio of skills and experience to increase their general employability. This approach is likely to be attractive to the kind of knowledge workers studied by Swart et al (2003), but in dealing with these and other 'talent', certain dilemmas have to be resolved by the organisation, as will be seen in the next section.

REFLECTION

Looking at your own career aspirations, to what extent do you find that your organisation offers support in realising them, and how far does its approach to career management resemble either of the two just identified?

PRINCIPLES FOR EFFECTIVE CAREER MANAGEMENT

Strategic integration

If an organisation is to have a successful career management system there must be strong direction from the top and effective integration of career development policy with business and HR policies. It must be a coherent process rather than simply a knee-jerk response to each changing situation. Therefore it needs to be an integral part of strategy, planning and action at corporate, business unit and individual levels of the organisation.

At *corporate level* it should be part of business strategy and planning and the direct responsibility of senior management. Only in this way can there be full commitment to developing objectives and a policy for career development throughout the organisation, and to ensuring that policy is implemented. At this level the framework for career development is set by the decisions made about work to be done, the structure required for the organisation, the roles needed within the structure and the goals to be achieved across the organisation.

In larger organisations a central integrative body is usually needed in order to develop company-wide policy, systems and procedures for career development. Evaluation of career development activity can then reveal whether the system is achieving its success criteria, and whether chosen development programmes and other activities are providing the most mutually beneficial growth paths for individuals and for the organisation. This is particularly important when the organisation is undergoing fundamental restructuring leading to changed employment policies.

At *business unit level* it should be a formal part of the managerial role to carry responsibility for career development of employees. This responsibility should be a key result area on which managers are appraised, and for which they are trained and recognised. The skills they need to acquire are those related to job design, career coaching and counselling, succession planning, the giving of feedback and the assessment of potential. Managers can enhance career development by arranging job movements, including inter-unit co-operative arrangements such as transfers, secondments, special projects and other assignments.

At *individual level* there should be a process of joint career planning that involves individual and manager in exchanging information about wants and expectations, and in negotiating ways in which the individual's career can be progressed to meet their and the organisation's needs.

Dealing with diversity

Some of the most intractable problems in developing career paths in an organisation are to do with achieving consistency from one occupational or professional group to the next. In the public sector the complexity of the occupational structure makes integration in this sense very difficult. Each group has its own historical patterns of recruitment, training, pay, and terms and conditions of service. Many have their own negotiating rights. In Chapter 10 I have explained the radical modernisation agenda facing all public sector organisations. One of the central planks of HR strategy in the NHS relates to a quite new approach to career planning, with the Skills Escalator playing a crucial role in opening up career pathways for all staff at every level. That model could usefully be applied in many other organisational settings.

The problem of managing talent is the one that tends to receive the most publicity. Here, it is sufficient to identify some of the issues that relate to career management for individuals or groups of unique value to an employer. Opportunities for career development are used to attract and retain scarce talent, but as I have explained already in relation to specialist knowledge workers, they raise a number of dilemmas for HR strategies (Baron 2004):

- 'Talented' individuals want up to date skills that will enable them to move easily out of one firm into another in pursuit of attractive career moves. The employer, on the other hand, does not wish to lose them by investing heavily in their self-managed strategy only to see competitors poach them at a critical point.
- Valued specialist workers want to hang on to their unique knowledge, since it is their negotiating tool and key source of employability. The employer, on the other hand, needs to find ways of inducing them to share their knowledge so that it can be put to the organisation's use.
- 'Talent' is highly mobile. In giving it a special consideration there is a risk of alienating other employees who do not have the same rewarding career trajectory to look forward to, yet who provide the organisation's bedrock of capability. The CIPD's careers survey in 2003 showed that whilst HR professionals wanted to improve career development for all employees in their organisations, only a third believed that senior managers were fully committed to this. In practice most effort was perceived to be focused on relatively small groups of senior or high-potential employees. The

findings appear to contradict those produced by White et al (2004) from their analysis of data from the far larger ESRC's *Future of Work* research programme, but whatever the reality the fact remains that a preoccupation in career management with favoured groups who are also highly mobile runs a real risk of reducing affective organisational commitment elsewhere in the workforce.

What, then, is the way forward here? First, there must be clarity about what the organisation wants from its 'talent', and a sound understanding of what such employees can contribute to the business as well as of what they want from their employment there. Wants and needs must then be carefully balanced in order to find an approach to career management that works in the interest of the parties without creating damaging effects elsewhere in the organisation. The kind of package that contains a balance of benefits for both sides is:

Development activity to build internal and external employability, offering transferable core skills:

- training courses
- networking
- challenging assignments
- mentoring support
- involvement in change management
- involvement in teamwork and in team management
- opportunities for lateral development.

Processes to give structure and flexibility to the career development system:

- clear career paths through the organisation
- management support for imaginative career practices including career breaks, secondments or placements to other organisations or divisions
- effective assessment of learners' needs, goals and opportunities, with personal development plans that are regularly updated.

Just as important as the management of talent is the opening up of career paths to those for whom, traditionally, access has either been barred or has been very difficult to achieve – for example, minority groups in the organisation, whether in full-time or part-time positions, those with low levels of educational attainment and poor basic skills, and those who need to take career breaks at crucial points in their career development. European companies tend to be more progressive in career break policies that are sensitive to the stress factors involved in combining a full-time career with childbearing or eldercare, for example, and to the adverse effects on productivity and performance that can result. The Labour Government in the UK is now pushing hard for an increase in such policies in all UK organisations.

The integration of international career development planning into a company's career management process is another major HR challenge and a field of study in its own right, with international careers becoming a common feature for middle as well as senior managers. There is no space to consider this topic here but many specialist texts now provide for its in-depth study.

To summarise: without strategic integration that starts at corporate level, all that will result from career planning at unit or operational levels of the organisation is a proliferation of initiatives without any overall coherence. Employees are likely to find their expectations frustrated as action that has been promised fails to materialise or does not deliver the expected outcomes. Many may find that access to career development opportunities becomes effectively impossible.

Figure 14 taken from *Career management: a CIPD guide* (King 2004) shows how integration of organisational career management with wider people management activities can be achieved. The inner oval depicts five key components of career management. The outer oval shows the three other sets of HR activities that interact loosely with the career management system. The diagram highlights areas that any HR professional, including those in the L&D field, should analyse in order to assess the integration and likely effectiveness of their organisation's CM processes.

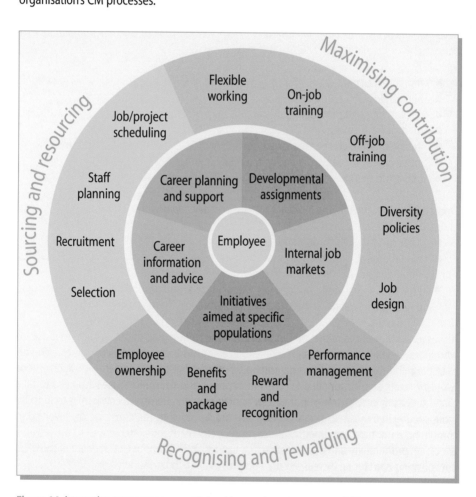

Figure 14 *Integrating career management into wider people management activities*
Source: KING, Z. (2004) *Career management: a CIPD guide*. London: Chartered Institute of Personnel and Development, p28. Reproduced with kind permission of the publisher.

Principles to guide the career management process

In the CIPD guide four principles are identified as critical to any career management process (King 2004, p8):

- *Consistency.* In all situations, whether involving an HR department or their line managers, employees should pick up a clear and consistent message about career development opportunities and about where career management strategy fits in the overall organisational picture.
- *Proactivity.* Effective career management should 'maintain the current capabilities of the organisation while building flexibility and agility for the future'.
- *Collaboration.* Effective career management requires partnership, between employer and employee and between HR professionals and line managers, in order to find career development solutions that strengthen the employee's affective commitment to the organisation.
- *Dynamism.* Career management must be dynamic, reflecting changing external and internal conditions and consequent changes to wants and needs of employer and employee.

Here is an example, taken from a different source, of an organisation whose career management practice was clearly informed by those principles during a difficult period in its growth.

CASE EXAMPLE
SCO's approach to career development

SCO, a computer software company founded in the USA, was typical in the late 1990s of many young, fast-growing firms whose rapid rise depended on a judicious mix of acquisition strategy and restructuring in order to develop new skills and products. Career development in such firms is inevitably an uncertain process. Yet the type of employees needed – with rare and high-level technical skills – have to be attracted and then motivated to stay long enough to make an impact on the firm's growth that repays the investment in recruiting them.

Macaulay and Harding's (1996) account identified the trigger to change in SCO's approach to career development as the recognition by the company of the need to change traditional employee expectations about career development to one more consistent with that which SCO could offer. Internal surveys and focus groups revealed widespread employee discontent with the gap between expectations and reality: 'loyalty no longer guaranteed security or promotion' (ibid. p34). Employees were also critical of the HR department which, they felt, did not offer the expected level of support or expertise in relation to personal development.

A 'best practice' review of other world-class organisations showed the need for a career development system that was closely aligned with the company's vision and direction, that attracted, motivated and rewarded high-performing people, and that communicated well. This led to a plan of action focusing on four parameters:

- building a learning culture through emphasising self-development and career management driven by the individual
- improved feedback and communication
- a more effective performance management system (PMS)
- increasing the ability of individuals to bring about change.

The following type of practical interventions were involved in this plan:

- the production and distribution to all employees of a self-development guide containing a variety of inventories and activities, and stressing the joint nature of development in the company
- career management workshops
- project teams for specific business issues, incorporating technical problem-solving workshops
- lunchtime training sessions on key company issues
- a move towards total quality and continuous improvement
- workshops on managing transition
- a review of the PMS.

These interventions were not trouble-free, and the company was only at the start of a complex process requiring management's sustained commitment to investing heavily in time and effort over the long term in order to achieve the desired outcomes. It was willing to give that investment, however, because of its crucial need to achieve growth in a tough market environment.

Source: MACAULAY, S. and HARDING, M. (1996)

HELPING THE INDIVIDUAL

Tensions points in the career life-cycle

The aim of an integrated career management system of the kind described in the previous section is to stimulate a process of continuous development during which all employees have the opportunity to acquire new skills, expand their experience and develop their potential. However at the individual level many will need help in order to obtain the full benefit of that process.

Gilley and Eggland (1989, p72) identified four questions on which each individual continuously seeks information during their career:

- Who am I (in terms of abilities and potential)?
- How am I viewed by others?
- What are my career options?
- How can I achieve my career goals?

These questions are of particular importance at key transition points in an individual's career progress. Such points vary with individuals, but three are very common:

- The first point at which meaningful career development opportunities become accessible.
- The plateau reached when little if any further upward career movement is likely.
- The point when exit from the organisation is approaching.

It is at these transition points that helping activity provided by the organisation can be uniquely valuable, enabling individuals to find answers to the four questions that are of such importance to them, and enhancing their affective commitment to the organisation.

Opening up a career path for individuals

This first transition point is one with which Government Skills Strategy has now a particular concern, as I have explained in Chapters 2 and 3. The push to improve basic skills levels across the economy, raise levels of educational participation, reduce wastage rates during educational programmes, and lower barriers that have traditionally prevented many groups and individuals in society from gaining access to meaningful career paths – all of these factors are now helping to put career development on the map for the hitherto disadvantaged.

Organisations' increasing preoccupation with how to tackle career development of 'talent' has already been discussed. At the other end of the spectrum are those who in the past have been overlooked in career management systems, but who are now beginning to see hope of a more promising future. One early example of opening up access for such employees was BP's career development scheme for petrol station attendants, which received a National Training Award in 2001. Using that as a template, the kind of L&D activity that can open career doors for many such individuals and groups would include:

- A sound and motivating induction process, supported perhaps by mentors, and involving basic training and agreement on personal development plans that are feasible for the staff in question and for the nature of their work. The induction period would represent the first stage in the new recruit's career development with the company and should aim to develop affective commitment to the organisation and the development of learning skills relevant to the next stage, which could be...
- A learning programme comprising a short period of core competence training followed by an extended period of exercises on the basics of the particular business of the organisation. At BP, the basics of retail work were covered and the programme was followed by distance learning.
- The support of front-line managers who act as trainers and sign off employees' workbook modules (at BP the modules were designed to go online and to be supported by an electronic database that could monitor learners' progress).
- Pay rises linked to the acquisition of trained competencies/national vocational qualifications that are relevant to the business and add to the individual's broader employability.

What is crucial to any such scheme is active support from the organisation, its managers and its HR practitioners.

Motivating employees who have reached a career plateau

For employees who are in the later stages of their career development with the organisation the availability of career counselling, joint planning, job redesign may all be helpful forms of keeping their commitment to the organisation high and also of reorientating them either to expanded or different tasks or to opportunities outside the organisation. Offering employees the opportunity and training to become coaches or mentors is another positive way of utilising their skills and accumulated experience to the benefit of others and of giving them additional roles that they can find rewarding.

Supporting employees at the exit point

When restructuring, downsizing or mergers lead to the loss of sections of a workforce, and also when individuals reach the time when they are likely to retire from the organisation, it is vital to have positive career planning strategies in place to ease their exit and to keep the organisational commitment of those who are staying on. Too often in such situations it is the competent people on whom much of the firm's future depends who leave, while those who stay fall prey to loss of focus, reduced commitment and ultimately loss of performance. Career management strategies should incorporate plans for dealing with such contingencies, since random initiatives only thought of at the time are of no value. What is needed is a comprehensive strategy that embraces those who leave, those who stay and those who have to manage the change process. Helpful L&D activity should be of four kinds, in an integrated bundle of practices:

- activity before the changes take place, to ease its path
- support and opportunities for those leaving the organisation
- initiatives to equip those staying in the organisation to handle new roles and tasks
- activity to sustain organisational commitment and continuing development in those who are staying on.

All activity related to easing the passage of critical career transition points should be incorporated into an organisation's career management strategy from the start, providing a framework with guidelines on blending on-the-job development and other developmental methods with formal development experiences. It should identify what approaches should be used for what purposes at each career phase.

Using development centre methodology

At the heart of any career management system there should be a process, accessible to all employees, that will aid the identification of career needs and potential of individuals. Such assessment can be carried out in a variety of ways, through systems established by the organisation or processes initiated by the individual. In the former category, the appraisal process has an important role to play, but the appraisal discussion is not an adequate or appropriate occasion for comprehensive assessment of potential. Development centre methodology has an important part to play here.

Development centres should not be confused with assessment centres, although both share a similar methodology. With both approaches (which are sometimes incorporated in a physical assessment or development centre) groups of participants take part in a variety of job simulations, tests and exercises with observers who assess their performance against a number of pre-determined, job-related dimensions. When the collected data are used to diagnose individual training needs, facilitate self-development or form part of an organisational career management system, then the most appropriate description is a *development centre* (Rodger and Mabey 1987). When the data are used primarily to feed into decisions about selection, promotion or some other form of employee redeployment, then the most appropriate description is *assessment centre*. It is essential that employees and others who may become participants do not confuse the two.

Development centres offer a particularly valuable opportunity for individuals to clarify what kind of career paths they want and seem equipped to follow, since they bring not only current and potential skills to the surface, but also personal values and motivation. Here is an example of how one company used development centres and the outcomes.

CASE EXAMPLE

Career planning at Allied Domecq Spirits and Wine

John Refausse, HR director (customer services and development) at Allied Domecq Spirits and Wine, described a career planning workshop introduced in 1995 as part of a much wider programme of organisational change following some years of re-engineering and far-reaching strategic change in an international company formed by the acquisition of Allied Lyons – the mainly UK-based firm – and the Domecq group. Flatter management structures, significant job changes and movement into new markets all meant that there was a mismatch between organisational needs and expectations and those of individuals. In a climate of uncertainty for the business as well as for its workforce it was seen in the mid-1990s to be essential to help people adjust to the changes and become less focused on job security, more capable of planning their own future careers.

The workshop was piloted in 1995 for senior middle managers who confronted such uncertainties. Its aims were to help them 'take stock of their own achievements, identify the factors that had contributed to their past successes and understand how they matched up against the core competencies of the business' (Refausse 1996, p34).

Development centre methodology helped participants to generate and handle a wealth of information that enabled them to gain insights into their fundamental motivation and talents, and into the past career choices they had made. This in turn 'helped them to look at their current roles and consider how these might be made to fit their aspirations and needs more closely' (ibid. p35).

Refausse described motivational outcomes for most of the eight participants. Two negotiated major career moves shortly afterwards: one, managing director of a wine subsidiary, achieved greater autonomy from her line manager; another applied successfully for promotion from a specialist to a general managerial post, having discovered during the workshop a 'creative professional' career possibility that he had never previously identified or considered.

Source: REFAUSSE, J. (1996)

Ensuring value from development centres

Accounts of innovative and apparently successful development centres abound. To assess their true value, however, they need to be followed up through time, and the views of participants as well as of observers and organisation must be obtained. Iles and Mabey (1993), commenting on a range of empirical studies, found that development centres, psychometric tests with feedback, and career review with superiors were particularly well viewed. The reasons were revealing:

- focus on the future as much as on the past and present
- promotion of reflection and insight as well as measurement of skills or competencies

- two-way, collaborative processes
- transparent, with participants able to see clear evidence for assessments
- realistic, not only on account of the methodology used but also because managers were involved as assessors and because of the focus on the actual career criteria and activities used in the organisation.

Supporting self-development

Self-development encourages active ownership of their career development by the individual, whether or not they opt for an entirely self-managed career process. Self-development, however, is not easy. It requires an informed and objective assessment of the kind of skills and experience that will be relevant for the future, together with access to opportunities to develop those skills and acquire that experience. Many organisations now provide specific resources and facilities to aid self-development, and some have been included in earlier chapters, notably Unipart's corporate university in Chapter 8. Typical support systems include:

- Personal and career development workshops and seminars to encourage individuals to take responsibility for their careers.
- Resource centres giving access to a variety of facilities for self-directed and e-based learning at the company's expense, although in the employee's time. Such centres can offer occupational guides, educational references, e-based self-assessment questionnaires and other diagnostic instruments to help people consider their career interests, values and competence, together with e-based educational and training programmes.
- Provision of access to career and counselling services of local colleges and universities and to their vocational and non-vocational courses.

L&D practitioners have a range of tasks to perform in promoting and gaining support for employees' self-development:

- *Raising awareness of the centrality of self-development to the career development process.* This is the vital link to make, and it needs to be identified during the career development planning cycle. Self-development should from the start form an integral part of the career development process.
- *Promoting awareness about the links between continuous improvement and the self-development process.* L&D practitioners should use formal as well as informal situations in order to raise managers' awareness of these important links.
- *Utilising the personal development planning process.* Personal development plans as outcomes of appraisal discussions are now widely used in organisations. When training appraisers and appraisees, L&D practitioners should explain why self-development matters and how it can be achieved
- *Introducing a focus on learning styles and skills.* While bearing in mind that learning styles inventories are not scientific instruments but are best used as aids to discussion about ways in which individuals feel they learn best, L&D practitioners should raise awareness across the organisation of the ways in which individual learning style and skills influence the effectiveness of the self-development process. Raising managers' awareness is particularly important, and one way in which this can be done is to draw attention to learning styles when discussing with them the learning needs of members of their units or teams.

■ *Resourcing the self-development process.* L&D practitioners should advise their organisations on the affordability, feasibility and benefits of resources that can encourage and support employees' self-development, whether through a learning resource centre, the introduction of coaching or mentoring, or encouraging managers to achieve NVQs at Level 4 related to learning and development.

REFLECTION

Imagine that you had a free hand to change the career management system in your organisation, or to introduce one if it does not already exist there. What major changes do you think you would make, or what kind of new system might you propose?

CAREER DEVELOPMENT: THE L&D AGENDA

Throughout the chapter a clear career development agenda has opened up for L&D professionals. It can be summarised as:

■ Promoting the business case and individual benefits of an organisational career management system and of support for self development.
■ Producing and working with management to introduce innovative, value-adding initiatives to help drive the career development process.
■ Working to achieve access to meaningful career development for all employees, achieving an inclusive approach instead of one that provides opportunities only for the organisation's perceived 'talent' and its senior personnel.
■ Taking a lead in building learning cultures that can encourage and support an essentially self-managed approach to career development.

There is another L&D agenda whose reach goes beyond the organisation into wider society. Chapter 3 explained the Government's vision of lifelong learning, and the strategy and types of educational and training initiatives that it is attempting to implement in line with that vision. There is an important task here for L&D professionals not only in promoting equality of opportunity and access to career development for all employees in their organisations – especially by helping to build learning cultures in the workplace and to enhance basic skills of those who lack educational qualifications and attainment – but also in promoting similar activity in the local community. Many organisations' L&D professionals are now also working alongside business, community and educational and training providers to find new ways of aiding career development for young people and for those currently not in employment for whatever reason. A number, for example, have a key role in consortia that are developing foundation degrees to open up career routes for those who currently have little hope of gaining access to them. Many act as mentors to young people or to disadvantaged individuals and groups in a variety of social settings.

In concluding this chapter it is appropriate to emphasise that the development of a meaningful career – in the broad sense of a rewarding and stimulating path of continuous development for every individual – is something to which all members of society should be able to aspire, and should have support in trying to achieve. Within their organisations HR professionals can now produce a solid, well-researched business case for an inclusive career management system and suggest strategies and initiatives to drive it forward. Outside their organisations there are further challenging tasks for those who seek to apply their expertise and knowledge to a wider lifelong learning agenda.

CONCLUSION

You should by now have a clear understanding of principles that underpin an effective career management system in an organisation, and how through focusing on career development an increasing proportion of organisations now hope to raise employees' commitment to the organisation, engage them actively in their jobs and motivate them in ways that will ultimately improve organisational as well as individual performance. You should also be able to tackle competently the review questions in Appendix 3.

In the four sections of the chapter the following have been the main issues covered:

- What research reveals about the concept of 'career' in today's organisations, and evidence to indicate that most organisations are trying to offer internal career paths to their employees, but are in many cases breaking new ground by opening these up to those below the management level; the impact of the new knowledge economy and the importance of motivating developmental opportunities for specialist knowledge workers.
- The business case for organisational career management: a reminder of the People Performance framework and the AMO model, and how career management activity can link positively to both; two different approaches to career management in organisations.
- Four principles to produce an effective career management process, and ways of ensuring a strategic approach to career management at all organisational levels; problems of diversity and ways of achieving a balanced and inclusive career management system.
- Processes and practices to aid individuals in their career path through an organisation, sustaining organisational commitment at key tension points and supporting and encouraging control by the individual over their own career development.
- The business and wider social career development agenda for L&D professionals; setting career management in the context of lifelong learning for all.

Further information sources

CHARTERED INSTITUTE OF PERSONNEL AND DEVELOPMENT (2003j) *Managing employee careers: issues, trends and prospects. Survey report.* London: Chartered Institute of Personnel and Development. Online version also available at: http://www.cipd.co.uk/surveys [accessed 29 September 2004].

JACKSON, C., ARNOLD, J., NICHOLSON, N., WATTS, A.G. (1996) Managing careers in 2000 and beyond. *Institute for Employment Studies Report 304.* Brighton: IES. Summary available online at http://www.employment-studies.co.uk [accessed 29 September 2004].

KING, Z. (2004) *Career management: a CIPD guide.* London: Chartered Institute of Personnel and Development.

Developing Leaders and Managers

INTRODUCTION

The purpose of this chapter is to explore how an organisation's strategy for leadership and management development can help to build its future capability as well as aiding the achievement of excellent performance in a current situation.

For John Kotter, professor of leadership at Harvard Business School, leaders and managers are quite distinct in their roles and functions (Kotter 1996). Management is to do with planning and organising, leadership to do with creating, coping with change and helping to adapt to a turbulent world. In Kotter's view the biggest leadership challenge in an organisation is that of transforming people's behaviour through changing their feelings. That is why emotional intelligence plays such an important part in the successful performance of leadership roles. Boydell and his colleagues (2004) have carried out research for many years in the management development field and take a similar view: management is about implementation, order, efficiency and effectiveness, whereas leadership is more concerned with future direction in uncertain conditions. Management may be sufficient in conditions of relative stability. It is not enough in conditions of 'complexity, unpredictability and rapid rates of change'.

Yet while the two functions are distinct there is an overlap between them. The development of leaders and managers therefore needs to be an integrated process, set in its organisational context and shaped by the particular challenges facing an organisation. Because of its strategic importance, such development should be a core component of any corporate HR strategy (CIPD 2001b).

In the space of one chapter it is only possible to provide an overview of some key issues related to the leadership and management development process (LMDP). The chapter has four sections. In the first two I explore the roles and key tasks of corporate leaders, managers and first-line team leaders. The third section looks at the present state of management development in the UK. It reviews issues to do with the appropriate focus for the LMDP, and with who it should be developed and through what kind of learning approaches. The chapter concludes with an identification of principles to follow in order to gain active ownership of the LMDP by all organisational members.

CORPORATE LEADERSHIP

The role of corporate leaders

'Purposing'

As far back as 1938 Chester Barnard described the essential task of an organisation's formal or corporate leadership as one of inculcating in all organisational members a belief in a common purpose. Vaill (1996) described this process as 'purposing', involving a continuous stream of actions that result in inducing clarity, consensus and commitment regarding the organisation's basic purposes.

Corporate leadership thus provides the overall vision and co-ordination that drives the organisation forward. It has the prime responsibility for developing a language and organisational identity that binds everything together, directing people's attention to 'what really matters here' and inspiring them to move forward collectively. In firms with this capability, every member feels a strong loyalty to the goal of preserving, extending or perfecting the organisation's mission. All employees can therefore be trusted to make decisions in the organisation's interests (Elfring and Volberda 2001, p273). As we have seen in earlier chapters, Purcell et al (2003) refer to the power of the 'Big Idea,' developed, communicated and exemplified in the behaviour of organisational leaders, supported by management actions and by HR strategies and practices, and brought to life at the front line by team leaders.

Shaping context

In the new knowledge economy all organisations need to be knowledge-productive, with a capability not only for continuous improvement but also for radical innovation that can be applied to products, processes and services. Therefore corporate leaders must build a culture of working with customers, forming teams, solving problems creatively, applying technical potential to market needs, appreciating the relationships among functions and businesses well enough to shift them as necessary, and develop an ongoing sense of how well they are doing. Dougherty (1999, p186) calls this 'high cross-value development' because it is about cutting across all internal boundaries, as well as reaching out across external ones, in order to co-create value throughout the value chain of the business. Prahalad and Ramaswamy (2002) described the case of the Saturn Corporation, launched by General Motors in 1985 as not just a new car company, but as a community working with its customers in its design, manufacturing and sales processes and engaging Saturn owners to help continuously innovate and improve its cars.

Strategising

Senge (1996) saw corporate leaders as the social architects of their organisations, designing purpose, vision and core values and working with a broad-based group whose membership stretches beyond the traditional elite of senior managers, in order to design policies, strategies and structures that can translate ideas into business decisions. The key is not 'getting the right strategy' but fostering strategic thinking to gain insights into the nature of the complexity facing the organisation and to formulate concepts and world views for coping with it (Mason and Mitroff 1981, p16).

As we have seen in Chapter 11, for organisations in a knowledge economy what matters most is not strategy but continuous strategising, and this applies to the HR area also. HR leaders, including those in the L&D field, must make sure that they continuously innovate in their practices in order to meet changing organisational challenges, the needs of a shifting array of workforces and new customer demands.

Promoting collective learning and innovation

A recurring theme in the scholarly literature is the changing demands placed on an organisation's strategy and knowledge processes when the business environment becomes more turbulent. Ansoff and Sullivan (1993, p13) explained turbulence by reference to four variables:

- complexity of events in the environment
- familiarity of the successive events
- rapidity with which the events evolve after they are first perceived
- visibility of the consequence of these events.

At the more stable end of the spectrum, the past can act as a good guide for the present, so strategic decision-makers need formal strategic planning skills, together with competence in financial and human resource management and a focus on continuous improvement. At the unstable end, however, they need to rely increasingly on entrepreneurial skills, collective learning and innovation. If what an organisation needs in order to make progress towards its strategic goals is, essentially, continuous improvement, then this will put a premium on the generation of adaptive knowledge (Senge 1990). This is the kind of knowledge that, by producing understanding of the gaps with competitors that relate to productivity, quality or operational flexibility and cost, enables the steady closing of those gaps. When, on the other hand, new classes of assets and strategies are needed and corporate character may need to be radically changed, this calls for learning that will produce, and sustain, discontinuous change. Argyris and Schon (1996) described this as double-loop learning, where the very goals, norms and assumptions of the organisation itself have to be questioned.

Thus in the new knowledge economy it is a primary task for organisational and HR leaders to promote the kind of workplace and collective learning that enables new knowledge to be generated, shared and applied in uniquely valuable ways.

Organising

Again as discussed in Chapter 11, corporate leaders in today's organisations must engage increasingly in a continuous organising process so that structural arrangements are flexible enough to allow a balance between 'getting on with the business' and 'creating new business'. The task is a complex one (Kirjavainen 2001, p189) but organisations have only short periods in which they can maintain competitive advantage before strategic assets lose their relevance. Regular structural reconfiguration of the firm must be integrated with continuing changes in strategy as current stocks and resources within the firm are redeployed and/or new ones are acquired (Whittington and Mayer 2002).

Here is a famous case study that has many lessons to teach about corporate leadership. You may find it helpful to identify the insights you gain from reading it. Comments follow at its end.

CASE EXAMPLE

Strategic leadership in Ford Motor Company, US and Europe, 1980s and 1990s

Success in Ford US

Pascale (1990, pp119–121) studied a range of American companies during the 1980s and concluded that Ford US stood alone in appearing to have truly transformed itself. Between 1980 and 1982 it lost $3.3 billion. In 1986 it surpassed GM in profits for the first time since 1924. In 1987 it broke all previous industry records for profitability.

The process started when, seeking ways of turning the company around, a Ford task force examined outstanding American companies and their characteristics. Top management decided that Ford's core values were people, products and profits and developed a new statement of Ford's mission and guiding principles of behaviour. The major organisational challenges to support the strategic agenda were employee involvement (EI) and participative management (PM). The latter at Ford US was used:

- to complement EI by developing managerial skills needed to provide employees and fellow managers with opportunities to participate in the managerial processes of planning, goal setting, problem-solving and decision-making
- to integrate managerial effort across rigid functional barriers.

In Ford US, functional groups formed 'organisational chimneys' – an organisation structured for vertical relationships within functions, and that in so doing put up barriers that prevented effective horizontal linkages. PM sought to change managerial attitudes and to dismantle dysfunctional structures by simplifying managerial control, devolving authority and breaking down barriers between managerial groups. This was of crucial strategic significance, since the success of Ford's shift towards innovation hinged on the integration of design, manufacture and sales and marketing – as in Japanese companies operating in the same kind of increasingly turbulent market conditions. PM and product development came together for Ford in a new strategic vision of the company as design leader, and its turnaround in the USA was design-led with the new Taurus/Sable range.

Pascale (1990) attributed Ford US' transformation to the role of top management and the top team dynamic – notably the relationship of Don Petersen, president from 1980–1985 and chairman from 1985–1990, and Harold 'Red' Poling, vice president, Ford North American Automotive Operations, then president from 1984 and chairman of Ford US in 1989. Their partnership was perfectly balanced. Petersen gave the visionary leadership, engaging with people's feelings, exciting them and reshaping their goals, needs and aspirations through redefining Ford's mission and values. Poling made sure that behaviour corresponded to the new goals. He concentrated on the quantifiable, getting quality and numbers right and benchmarking against key competitors. He saw to the cost structure, Petersen to EI and PM. Taken together, their leadership and managerial skills were instrumental in tipping Ford into a new era (Starkey 1996).

Petersen deliberately disrupted conventional mindsets at Ford by setting up a participative approach to top decision-making that broadened, deepened and enriched the company's strategic decision-making'. He shifted management's focus from the functional to the strategic and ensured a balanced management team where difference was valued, using the Myers–Briggs teambuilding process to help Ford managers powerfully learn for themselves how the nature of the strategy process is a dynamic outcome of team interactions and also of individual personality characteristics. He 'brought to Ford's top team an intuitive and feeling approach to decision-making, something which is rarely found at that level' (ibid. p371, 379).

Failure in Ford Europe

Ford Europe, however, failed to pull off a similar transformation in the 1990s. The reasons were many, but a major problem was that although Bill Hayden, Europe's Vice President of Manufacturing, said in 1992 that the Japanese had caused Ford to completely rethink their policies and behaviour patterns, in fact mindsets had not changed. The primary focus was still on cost differences, and the belief remained that the old Ford system, if intensified, could still match the Japanese. Leadership failed to diagnose that the fundamental problem was in Ford Europe's backward-looking and finance-dominated culture. The whole drive was one of cost reduction. An 'After Japan' change management initiative strengthened, not reduced, the managerial emphasis on control, doing nothing to stimulate a culture change. In meetings, functional heads would arrive in a defensive stance, using figures not to improve the quality of decision-making but to improve political advantage of sectional groups.

When, eventually, the same American change initiative that had been introduced successfully in the USA was attempted in Europe, with a new company mission, values, guiding principles and a new managerial emphasis on teamwork, the barriers had become too great. In particular 'top management endorsement and leadership in getting the whole organization aligned and working towards the same goal was felt to be lacking' (ibid. p374). There was no creative tension, no balance of top champions.

Bill Hayden was VP of Manufacturing in Europe from 1974 to 1991 when he became the first Ford chairman of Jaguar after its acquisition. Given the steady turnover in Ford's European top management cadres he exerted a disproportionate influence, particularly because of the force of his personality and the iron control he exercised over Manufacturing.'He was quite willing to innovate in search of cost-reduction, as with the 'After Japan' initiative, but was more wary of other kinds of innovation' (ibid. p375). His role was comparable to that of Poling's in the USA, but there was no strong counter-balance to him or to his urge to centralise control. The result was that 'commitment to the implications of Ford's new mission and the values and principles of behaviour necessary to support it such as PM, was only skin deep' (ibid. p376).

Source: STARKEY, K. (1996)

Comments

Many messages come across from this study, including the following:

- Corporate leaders must create the right organisational context for unlearning and new learning to occur. That was achieved in Ford US, but not in Ford Europe.
- Creating that context across boundaries – whether internal, local or international – depends on developing managers with broadly based perspectives and relation-ships and fostering supportive organisational norms and values. Petersen in Ford US realised this. Hayden in Ford Europe had no similar understanding. Because he and co-leaders made no real attempt to change the culture of the organisation at any level, mindsets became rigid. In consequence 'skilled incompetence' (Argyris 1996) became so deeply entrenched across the organisation that the subsequent American change management initiative could not take root.
- Corporate leadership is not achieved through any one individual, but through collaborative relationships and complementary skills. In Petersen and Poling Ford US had the perfect combination at the helm. There was no such partnership in Ford Europe. In Ford US strategic decision-making was deliberately vested in the hands of a broad-based group in which diversity of opinion, knowledge and background allowed a thorough voicing of alternatives. Such heterogeneity (as it is called) is essential in a turbulent environment. It was not present in Ford Europe – any more, in fact, than it was at Marks and Spencer in the late 1990s when for the first time the company began to lose its way under the dominating but outmoded leadership of Sir Richard Greenbury.
- A firm's ability to develop managers to implement strategy effectively is crucial to its

capacity to adapt to changing conditions. Petersen saw and acted on this at Ford US. The story at Ford Europe was very different.

■ The vision, goals and culture that are transmitted by corporate leadership provide the framework for leaders elsewhere in the organisation. But that framework can act as a constraint – as it did in Ford Europe – rather than as a liberator, as in Ford US.

■ What is memorably illustrated in the Ford US story is leadership's role and contribution related to the development of strategic capability, defined as (Harrison and Miller 1999, p27):

> A capability that is based on a profound understanding of the competitive environment, the resource base and potential of the organization, and the values that engender commitment from stakeholders to corporate goals. It provides the strategic vision, the rich and sustained knowledge development, the integrity of common purpose and the durable, coherent direction and scope to the activities of the firm that are needed to secure long-term survival and advancement.

Key tasks of corporate leaders

Research such as that just outlined suggests the following as key tasks for corporate leaders:

■ The building and sustaining of a shared vision and high ethical values that provide a compelling, engaging picture of a desired future, while also communicating an accurate picture of current reality.

■ Working with a broad-based inclusive group in a continuous strategising process to identify and communicate long-term goals and strategic direction for the organisation.

■ Determining and overseeing the courses of action and the allocation of resources necessary for achieving strategic goals.

■ Leading a continuous organising process that enables the organisation to be flexible, fast-moving, knowledge-productive and proactive in its environment.

■ Promoting and managing the development of strategically valuable knowledge, and continuously bringing to the surface and challenging prevailing mental models in order that the necessary unlearning can occur and new ways forward can be found.

■ Achieving a quality of life in the organisation that will generate the sustained commitment of internal and external stakeholders to the organisation's corporate goals.

Responsibility for learning and knowledge productivity is one of the most difficult but essential of leadership tasks not only at corporate level but at other leadership levels also, including within the HR area. It is no longer possible for the CEO to 'learn for the organisation'. Leaders must ensure integrated thinking and action at all levels, given the dynamic and turbulent nature of the business environment today. The focus should be on generative learning – which is about creating new ideas, new assets for the organisation – as well as adaptive learning, which is about coping with current tasks and workloads.

REFLECTION

To what extent does corporate leadership in your own organisation successfully tackle the tasks discussed in this section? Where do you see the greatest barriers and aids to effective corporate leadership to lie, and what kind of L&D activity do you think could tackle areas of ineffectiveness (remember that non-executive directors are a part of corporate leadership and that the Higgs report has been instrumental in directing attention to their need for appraisal, development and effective leadership)?

MANAGEMENT ROLES AND TASKS

The world of the manager

In a turbulent environment and a developing knowledge economy it is unsurprising that the meaning and parameters of 'management' are changing. Over a decade ago Brewster and Tyson (1991, p218) pointed to the blurring effects of technology on the lines of distinction between managerial tasks and the work of other occupations. De-layering and decentralisation involve devolution of problem-solving and decision-making. They often result in supervisors having to take on new team leadership roles, while an increasing number of those occupying traditional middle management positions find themselves in charge of semi-autonomous business units and therefore involved for the first time in the strategy process. Their strategic role can have a direct impact on the performance of the organisation, especially in those de-layered structures where innovation and market-sensitivity are essential to innovation and the advancement of the business in its competitive environment (Floyd and Wooldridge 1994b; Hedlund 1994). Professionals like the clinical directors in the case example in Chapter 7 are frequently having to take on expanded managerial responsibilities, some of a strategic nature.

All these managers use a range of skills that cannot easily be categorised and that must be integrated in their practice. This integrative task involves achieving synergy, balance and perspective. Such skills have been termed 'overarching competences' since by their nature they go far beyond the functional, explaining why effective management is more than just the sum of its parts (Burgoyne 1989).

Partridge in his research observed (1989, p205)

> '**Managerial work across all levels ... is characterized by pace, brevity, variety and fragmentation.... It is hectic and fragmented, requiring the ability to shift continuously from relationship to relationship, from topic to topic, from problem to problem.**'

Most management activity is undertaken through complex webs of social and political interaction. It involves a continuous process of adaptation to changing pressures and opportunities, and has to operate across many internal boundaries and – for leaders at least – across many external boundaries also. With a new emphasis on partnership rather than control and on processes that will add value, managers still have to manage, but anyone planning their development has to answer searching questions concerning how they should manage, with whom they should collaborate as they manage, and how they should behave in order to achieve desired outcome.

In their major report on management training and development across Europe, Mabey and Ramirez (2004) confirmed the vital role performed by managers in creating high-performing workplaces, with their importance most marked in the following respects:

- making critical decisions about opportunities afforded by communication and information technology
- ensuring the success of organisational change
- creating a culture of lifelong learning for all employees, particularly those traditionally disadvantaged.

Front-line leadership

The Black Box research carried out at Bath University by Purcell and colleagues (2003) has produced important insights into the leadership tasks of front-line managers. Their reports contain many cases illustrating aids and constraints on the effective performance of those tasks, and showing these leaders' direct influence over the amount and exercise of employees' discretionary power. But long before these and other studies into characteristics of high-commitment, high performance organisations Bartlett and Ghoshal (1993, p45) had memorably identified the extent to which human behaviour, while partly determined by individuals' own prior disposition, is powerfully influenced by the actions of their leaders, especially those at the front line. I conclude this section with a brief outline of their study, based on research they carried out in the USA in the 1980s–1990s. It concerns a multi-national company, still a leader today, and how it formed at its inception a structure and strategy that ensured the development of excellence in its leaders and managers. This is only a brief outline of an engrossing account.

CASE EXAMPLE

Asea Brown Boveri

Asea Brown Boveri (ABB) was formed in 1988 from a merger between the Swedish Asea AB and the Swiss firm, BBC Brown Boveri. It was an international electrical engineering company manufacturing machinery and composite plants. In its early years it confronted challenges arising from slow growth and overcapacity, and also from the newness and fragility of its organisational structure and management processes.

Percy Barnevik, formerly the Swedish company's highly successful CEO, articulated ABB's core value as:

individuals and groups interacting with mutual confidence, respect and trust ... to eliminate the we/they attitude ... and to remain flexible, open and generous.

Barnevik introduced a decentralised matrix organisation designed as a federation of 1,300 companies. Each on average employed 200 people and in 1993 ABB's total work-force numbered around 200,000. Barnevik and his management did not hold the traditional view of an organisation. They saw it as 'a cluster of roles and their interrelationships whereby to generate, link and leverage unique capabilities'. Barnevik saw their role as one of translating this core value into action through selecting and promoting those who reflect such behaviours, imposing sanctions against those violating the values, and through their own role modelling actions.

Resources were decentralised to the front-line units that operated with limited dependence on the corporate parent for technological, financial or human resources, but with considerable interdependence among themselves. In 1993 there was only one intermediate level between the small ABB corporate executive committee and the managers of these companies. At ABB both middle and top managements remained involved in the operational realities of the business and contributed directly to the entrepreneurial process. Human resources were recruited and developed at the level of the front-line companies, who also carried out most of the technology development and had responsibility for their own balance sheets. Middle-level managers coached and supported the front-line manager while top management developed a set of objectives.

Source: BARTLETT, C.A. and GHOSHAL, S. (1993).
See also HARRISON, R. and KESSELS, J. (2003a, pp55–59)

LEADERSHIP AND MANAGEMENT DEVELOPMENT IN CONTEXT

Some international comparisons

A report in 2002 from the newly established Council for Excellence in Management and Leadership showed that 36 per cent of organisations believe their managers are not proficient (CEML 2002). In 2004 a report by Mabey and Ramirez, who had conducted a two-year study of management development across Europe, produced further and even more worrying findings.

Mabey and Ramirez found strong statistical evidence that management development leads to superior organisational performance across companies of all sizes, sectors and national location, with three factors being key here:

- the extent to which HR is integrated with business strategy
- the degree to which the firm takes a thoughtful, long-term approach to developing managerial capability
- the belief by line managers that their employer is taking management development seriously.

Their research showed that on all three criteria the UK performs poorly, and that it is falling significantly behind other countries in developing its managers despite progress made since the mid-1980s in national policy and qualification frameworks. It relies far more than any European country except Denmark on a qualifications-based approach to management development, and like most countries is making little use of e-learning.

Less than half the organisations surveyed appeared to have a management development policy statement, but most had a clear business strategy. On average the HR contribution to that was 'moderate at best', but the UK, along with France, has the least faith in human resource management as delivering competitive advantage and is much less likely than other countries to adopt a strategic approach to HR management. It is therefore unsurprising that firms in the UK were found to be comparatively weak in taking a thoughtful, long-term and consistent approach to the creation of a management cadre, and to be often following a short-term, 'tokenistic' and non-strategic approach, paying too little attention to management development. Management training suffered from similar weaknesses, being often non-strategic, piecemeal and rarely evaluated.

In 2003 a new government-backed professional hallmark for managers had already been launched in an effort to improve management skills in the UK and boost productivity. Drawn up by the Chartered Management Institute, it enables employers to benchmark individual performance in the workplace, with managers required to provide evidence of how they are meeting their organisation's objectives and being assessed by their peers in six areas of their performance: leading people, meeting customer needs, managing change, managing information and knowledge, managing activities and resource, and managing yourself. The CM is a national vocational qualification and once awarded it involves undergoing re-assessment in order to be retained through time.

Putting the LMDP into context

Although the UK strongly favours a qualification-led approach to management development typified by the CMI initiative, this is often not the most relevant way for an organisation to tackle its leadership and management development needs. In their extensive research into the development of directors Mumford et al have concluded that the possession of a management qualification is of little relevance – what promotes the most effective learning is day to day work-based experience and role models (Mumford et al 1987).

Where should an organisation begin, then, with its LMDP? Boydell et al (2004) urge that the first priority should not be on selecting individuals with potential and deciding how best to develop them, but on identifying the situation in which enhanced leadership and management is needed – in other words, by looking at context. The first step should be to identify:

- challenges – that require action involving leadership and management development
- context – the setting in which the challenges arise and in which action and learning must take place
- characteristics – the qualities, abilities, skills and competencies of all the people involved in the situation.

A decade earlier Ghoshal and Bartlett (1994, p91) made a similar point, and their explanation suggests one possible kind of focus for an LMDP. They argued that it is a primary task of leaders and managers to create a context in which their organisation can collectively achieve high performance. They proposed that such a context should have as its key dimensions discipline, stretch, trust and support, since a focus on these qualities would release the skills, motivation and commitment of all employees and direct them to achieving organisational goals. They saw the task of organisational leaders and front-line managers as especially vital in turn-round situations where fundamental organisational changes must be achieved and where there must be entrepreneurial behaviour at all levels in order to achieve excellent performance. Although the methodology behind their research has been questioned, their findings and proposals bear a striking resemblance to the current widely publicised People–Performance framework (Purcell et al 2003).

In its new leadership and management standards the CIPD too stresses the central role of leaders and managers in creating conditions conducive to excellent performance. It urges a strong focus on understanding organisational context and the challenges the particular organisation faces in order to set an appropriate direction for the LMDP. It sees 'outstanding organisational performance' as resting on two things (Whittaker and Johns 2004):

- *Organisational infrastructure*: an organisation's basic systems, processes, procedures and ethical/legal compliance features. Once infrastructure is in place 'it yields returns only in incremental improvements or through remedial action. By contrast the benefits available from focusing on the differentiators are infinite'.
- *Organisational differentiators*: the practices that make one organisation uniquely different from any other. These are the organisation's critical success factors that stimulate employees to engage in discretionary behaviour that results in exceptional organisational performance.

This concept of infrastructure and differentiators is used also by Mabey and Ramirez (2004), who apply it to management development systems. They found in their European research that while it is important for management development systems to be put into place, an infrastructure of formal policies and budgets is necessary but not of itself sufficient to improve management performance. What is then needed is for top management and HR professionals to work as partners in cultivating managerial talent at all levels in the organisation and in developing future potential rather than just looking to meet immediate requirements. They found that performance and productivity are enhanced when line managers see their senior management team giving management development sustained priority and when they see it linking to a consistent set of organisational skills and competencies.

At this point it is relevant to query the meaning of terms like 'outstanding' and 'excellent' organisational performance. Such terms, like many in the HR literature, are in common use but are rarely given any meaningful definition. Vaill (1996) found eight criteria in his research and these are of considerable practical value when seeking to clarify exactly what kind of outstanding performance an organisation requires its leaders and managers to be developed to achieve:

- excellent performance as judged against an accepted external standard
- excellent performance as judged by informed observers
- excellent performance against the assumed potential level of performance for that type of organisation
- excellent performance compared with the organisation's original performance
- performance achieved with significantly less resources than are normally assumed to be necessary
- performance that is perceived to make the organisation an exemplar to others
- performance that is perceived to fulfil at a high level ethical values and cultural ideals that are espoused by the organisation
- performance achieved by organisations that are the only ones to be able to do what they do.

Leadership as a collective capacity

Conventional leadership development programmes and competency frameworks concentrate on developing so-called leadership characteristics in individuals or groups, but this is a limited approach because (Boydell et al 2004):

- It carries the message that leadership is about the personal qualities of outstanding individuals.
- It carries the assumption that selected individuals can be 'trained' into leadership and will then provide good leadership for others.

Tesco has traditionally sought to grow its own leaders, always rejecting the idea of selecting senior managers purely from an elite group. It believes in talent spotting, with lists of people with potential for promotion being drawn up regularly from store level upwards and a senior team at that level selecting on the basis of three criteria:

- those who always improve the business for customers
- those who take people with them
- those who live the company's values.

Such examples carry the message that what should be the priority is collective leadership development since only collectively can challenges that require action be tackled, and ways forward that fit with context can be found. The skills and impact of the individual do count, of course, but it is also essential to develop leadership as a collective capacity to move forward in difficult times. This is illustrated perfectly in the cases of Ford US – where there was such development – and of Ford Europe – where there was not. The LMDP should not be seen as a one-off training process or as 'development for the few' but as a continuous activity that helps all organisational members to learn from their actions and to move in concert as they tackle challenges to the business.

Arguably the most effective form of developing leaders is organisation-based and grounded in their ongoing tasks. New approaches can be reinforced, and sometimes activated, by changes in business processes and unlearning and relearning can take root when supported by organisational systems. But again it is essential to focus not just on tasks and processes, but on values, attitudes and behaviour change (Lippitt 1983, p38):

> **'The most meaningful aspect of personal change resulting from a management development process is the examination and alteration of attitudes within the organisation. Reinforcement will need to be related to meaningful renewal systems.'**

Lippitt's observation underlines the need for there to be a real willingness in the organisation to accept the changed managerial values and attitudes that an LMDP should produce. Wherever relevant cultural changes should be introduced to support LDMP's outcomes in this respect (Mabey and Ramirez 2004). If the 'renewal' offered by such development is resisted by those who hold the most powerful positions in the organisation, it can only indicate that the true agenda for the LMDP is a political one: the process is not intended to produce fundamental changes in the status quo. It is not uncommon for development programmes to be used to reinforce, not challenge, the existing order of things. This is compounded when opportunities for development are offered fundamentally as a reward to secure 'loyalty' rather than running the risk of any upsetting of the current applecart.

What kind of development should it be?

Work-based learning

When relying primarily or entirely on work-based learning to develop the organisation's current leaders and managers and secure its stock for the future, careful thought must be given to how that learning can be achieved and evaluated.

As one important example, to enhance the quality of strategic capability those with L&D responsibilities can help with:

- initiatives to raise awareness of the variety of strategy process modes that can be used to ensure that there is broad-based knowledge and experience informing the strategy process, and that set ways of thinking and of decision-making are challenged (Hart and Banbury 1994; Ginsberg 1994).
- Processes and initiatives to develop 'thinking performers' at all levels and to ensure skilled use of the organisation's strategic processes and routines (for example, through informational processes to do with environmental scanning, scenario-building, the identification of strategic issues, and the generation of wide-ranging strategic options).
- Processes and initiatives to continuously improve the cognitive abilities and emotional intelligence of strategic managers and teams. This is particularly important at middle management level where strategic orientation may be critical for organisational performance yet where many feel ill-equipped to deal with their newly acquired strategic roles (Floyd and Wooldridge 1994b).
- Processes and initiatives to improve skills related to the implementation of strategy – for example, skills in setting and monitoring plans and targets, and in evaluating their impact in the workplace.
- The stimulation of a search for strategically valuable knowledge throughout the organisation through work-based learning processes.

And as another example, L&D processes to aid the development of front-line leaders should include:

- Learning activity that incorporates and helps to embed strong organisational values that show clearly those leadership behaviours expected and those not permitted.
- Skills training related to team leadership and team management.
- Career development and access to meaningful career paths. Without that, their commitment levels drop, especially if coupled with little or no sense of support from their managers.
- Learning activity that induces and reinforces good working relationships with their managers – this emerged from Hutchinson and Purcell's report (2003) as the most important factor in influencing their levels of commitment to the organisation. 360-degree appraisal was particularly important here.

Work-based learning can be stimulated in many ways, including project work, self-development, action learning, coaching and mentoring. Such methods can also provide a powerful bridge between externally based programmes and work-based learning (see, for example, the clinical directors' programme described in Chapter 7).

Competency frameworks

Development centres, a methodology described in the previous chapter, are widely used in LMD programmes. So too are competency frameworks which are often used as the basis for such centres on the grounds that they provide a clear set of performance criteria at all organisational levels, and express in measurable ways the expected outcomes of achieving those criteria, thereby offering an inclusive and objective approach to assessment and development. Competencies in this sense are a set of character features, knowledge and skills, attitudes, motives and traits that comprise the profile of a leader or of a manager and enable an individual to perform effectively in the role. A competency framework provides a template against which teams as well as individuals can be developed, since no individual will have more than a few of the competencies needed for superior organisational performance (Miller et al 2001).

However competency frameworks are expensive to design, install and monitor and need to be expertly conceived and administered. Many are critical of their use as part of an LMDP, finding that such a framework rarely discriminates enough between leadership and management roles and needs. Instead it is based on the assumption that a number of discrete components can adequately describe critical features of a role, and that those components will remain relatively constant and standardised through time.

Mintzberg (1973) provided a mass of evidence to show the high level of variability in management roles, emphasising managers' often simultaneous pursuit of a variety of objectives in changing ways according to their judgement in the particular situation. He has repeatedly portrayed managers' work as highly contextualised and as requiring managers to have significant discretion in deciding how best to operate, what tasks to tackle and how. In his latest book (2004) he launches a swingeing attack on MBAs for propagating a view of management that he claims is completely out of touch with the reality of the manager's world and shows no real understanding of the basis of skilled managerial performance.

Finally, to stand the argument about context somewhat on its head, Alvarez (1996) was concerned about the danger of competency frameworks that are too tightly coupled with current organisational context. In his research he noted many attempts to formalise and link both individual and organisational competencies to strategic priorities and to human resource systems, but doubted their ability to do this successfully. Tight coupling can simply reinforce any given strategy, regardless of its quality, resulting in dangerously narrow managerial perspectives that stifle questioning and so can hinder change and progress. The same criticism can, of course, be made of any LMDP that is grounded purely in the context of everyday organisational life.

These varied views and findings on competency-based approaches to LMD suggest four conclusions:

- Leaders and managers do need training and development in their many functional tasks, but there is a danger that reliance on functional frameworks as the basis for the LMDP may ignore the higher level capacities and holistic skills that are crucial to success in their roles.
- In the short term, and in the more stable organisations, a competency-based approach to management development can produce useful results, enabling the linking of performance criteria, development activity and performance outcomes at individual and organisational levels.
- However an alternative approach to LMD should be considered in those organisations where the future is highly uncertain, where leaders and managers are already

facing complex, unfamiliar problems, and where there can be no certainty as to the exact nature and interrelationship of the competencies needed to deal with them.

■ Where a competency-based approach is used, competencies should always be analysed in the context of the particular organisation and agreed as meaningful and relevant by the key parties involved in and affected by the MDP. The IIP Leadership and Management framework (Appendix 4) and the CIPD's new Leadership and Management standards are useful here because they are flexible in allowing for full adjustment to context and the particular challenges facing the organisation, while also attempting to make an adequate distinction between leadership and management roles.

The role of formal programmes

When considering what part formal training and education programmes should play in an LMDP, the real question to ask is not 'Why do we not have enough qualified managers?' but 'will qualification make our managers more effective?' (Chambers 1990). The Japanese and the Germans virtually ignore the Master of Business Administration route to management development, yet as a sector their managers are highly regarded. However in both those countries recruits have a high standard of educational attainment by the time they enter employment. Most well-educated Germans do not join a large company until 27 years of age because they tend to have followed an apprenticeship after school and then pursued a degree and often a higher degree in subjects such as engineering, law or economics. In Japan and in Britain, the average age for joining such a company is 22, but in Japan the potential manager will study law or engineering at a top university, and, after entry to a large firm, will go through a rigorous process of job rotation, private study and classroom learning which can last for up to 15 years before being promoted to the first level of management.

In France, the route to management in a larger organisation is either through business or engineering at one of the Grandes Ecoles, or through some other educational pathway leading to the same kind of functional qualifications as in Japan and Germany. In France, too, the law requires all firms to spend 1.1 per cent of the wage bill on continuing education and training, and corporations with more than about 2,000 employees spend three times that amount, about one third going on management training. Such investment is common across most of mainland Europe and the USA, but not in the UK.

Where managers are poorly educated this can lead to low levels of ability to cope with new technologies, to manage and develop people, and to think and act strategically. Given that the average new recruit to supervisory roles is far less well educated in the UK than in most competitor countries, and that most managers still lack the strong all-round base of education and relevant work experience that is common in countries like Germany, France and Japan, there is a clear place for educational programmes to supplement ongoing work-based learning in an LMDP. Such programmes can incorporate a variety of work-based scenarios in their design. Precisely because they take participants out of their daily work environment they can broaden their vision, challenge their customary ways of thinking and behaving in the organisation, and expand their intellectual capacity. They offer a safe environment in which individuals can identify and reflect on their personal weaknesses and strengths and explore problematic scenarios in a variety of organisational settings. They have an important role in stimulating and aiding the unlearning that is essential to enable new mindsets and behaviours to develop (Harrison and Miller 1999).

REFLECTION

Imagine that a manager who has been converted by the works of Alan Mumford says to you forcefully:

> Management development? No two ways about it – learning from the job, in the workplace is the only real way. Give us a good job pathway and plenty of role models and mentoring – and you'll find our development takes care of itself.

How do you think you should reply?

OWNERSHIP OF LEADERSHIP AND MANAGEMENT DEVELOPMENT

Principles to gain stakeholders' active ownership of the LMDP

In reflecting on what he saw to be the continuing problem of British management, Adrian Hamilton observed that the British business culture puts far too little emphasis on the skills and qualities needed to grow a business rather than merely stripping it down (Hamilton 2004). In his view, much of the blame for this lies in management reward systems that have focused excessively on cost cutting and other 'easily measurable targets'.

From such reflections and from findings reviewed in this chapter it can be concluded that if leadership and management development is to be effective in expanding organisational capacity for the future as well as improving current financial performance, then:

- The LMDP must have a vision and strategy that are relevant to the business and that enable the continuous identification, assessment and development of potential.
- Those representing HR and management development in their organisations must be assertive in interpreting business priorities and in translating these into well resourced and well understood policies and practices (Mabey and Ramirez 2004). HR professionals (including those in the L&D field) therefore need a thorough knowledge of the business, its goals and strategy in order to advise on the design, delivery and evaluation of leadership and management development strategy, processes and learning methods
- The LMDP must be owned by managers and achieve strong external consistency. Executive leadership, managers and HR professionals must work as business partners in this, and be clear as to their respective roles and responsibilities. The views and experience of those involved as learners in the LMDP should also inform LMDP planning and its implementation.
- The LMDP must be integrated with other HR strategies and practices in order to achieve consistency across the processes of planning, recruitment, selection, appraisal, rewards and development. This argues for the HR function to have a central involvement in planning and managing the MDP. However, such specialists must not dominate the MDP, or it will not achieve management ownership.
- Managers must be trained in how to train and develop others and in how to implement the LMDP across the organisation. This may involve the need for cultural change if they are to have the active commitment that these activities involve, and if the outcomes of the LMDP are to be transferred into workplace practice.

- Where an organisation is decentralised, the units as well as the centre must be actively involved in planning, operating and evaluating the LMDP. It must be 'owned' by units but also be well integrated across the whole organisation. The danger of loosening central control is that divisions/units will take too much power into their own hands, and end by doing things their own way according to their own cultures. The danger of putting central control into the hands of a personnel function is that its specialists may hold insufficient power, and be seen as 'outside' the real management system of the organisation.
- For any formal leadership and management development programme to make an impact on organisational performance, the LMDP must encompass a critical mass and be founded on transparent, relevant and fair principles.

CONCLUSION

You should by now have a sound basic understanding of the differences and overlaps between leadership and management roles in an organisation, and have developed useful insights at a practical level into different approaches to the LMDP that are common across organisations. You should be able to tackle the review questions for this chapter, found in Appendix 3.

In the chapter's four sections the following main issues have been discussed:

- The nature of the corporate leadership role and key tasks that it involves.
- The complex and dynamic world of the manager, and the front-line leadership roles that are of critical importance in the pursuit of excellent organisational performance.
- The weak, non-strategic and tokenist investment made by the UK in management development compared with most European countries, and an excessive reliance by UK-based firms generally on a qualifications-based instead of contextualised approach to leadership and management development.
- The importance of grounding any LMDP in an organisation's specific needs and challenges; the need to develop leadership as a collective capacity, and to choose a relevant mix of learning approaches and methods to use in the LMDP.
- Seven principles for ensuring that ownership of the LMDP in an organisation is shared by all stakeholders and has their active commitment and involvement.

Further information sources

HUTCHINSON, S. and PURCELL, J. (2003) *Bringing policies to life: the vital role of front line managers in people management.* London: Chartered Institute of Personnel and Development.

MABEY, C. and RAMIREZ, M. (2004) *Developing managers: a European perspective: a survey of management training & development in the United Kingdom, France, Germany, Spain, Denmark, Norway & Romania.* London: Chartered Management Institute. Online version of report's summary also available at: http://www.managers.org.uk/institute/content_toc_description_1.asp?category=3&id=234&id=211&id=44 [accessed 1 October 2004].

SENGE, P.M. (1996) The leader's new work: building learning organizations. In K. STARKEY (ed) *How organizations learn.* London: International Thomson Business Press. pp288–315.

Also:

Information about the IiP's Leadership and Management model: http://www.investorsin people.co.uk/leadership/about/about.asp [accessed 30 September 2004].

CHAPTER 17

Conclusion: Pulling the Threads Together

SURVEYING THE LEARNING AND DEVELOPMENT FIELD

Have we made progress?

It is difficult to know how to end a book of this kind. No point in summarising the summaries that have already appeared at the end of each chapter, but too late to introduce anything startlingly new. And that is the prompt for this final chapter – what *is* new in the field of learning and development? What, really, are the compelling challenges we face now that we have not faced many times in the past?

Consider these two quotations:

> 'To discuss training in industry without considering the learning process is meaningless. And yet, after reviewing the literature on the two processes, one can easily get the impression that they are only remotely related.... We believe there is a considerable body of knowledge concerning the learning process that can be applied in training programs now. We believe learning can be exciting and rewarding, in and of itself. We believe training programs that do not take account of significant factors in the learning process are extremely wasteful of human resources.'

> 'Why is it that education and training in industry receive such scant attention? When a firm decides to reduce its staff, the training department is often the first to go. ... Conversely but quite illogically, when a firm wishes to expand its production it will often push trainees into the production line before they are fully skilled.... Even race-horses receive more training than many non-apprenticed industrial workers. But then animals tend to get favoured treatment in the United Kingdom.'

No, the first quotation has not been taken from a CIPD research report or from an article by Martyn Sloman and colleagues, nor does the second come from the November 2001 *In demand* report to government that was so fundamental in changing official views on national skills strategy (PIU 2001). The first was written in 1967 by Bass and Vaughan, the American industrial psychologists, and the second by David King, a UK social scientist who in 1964 produced a small book that has since become a classic on training in organisations.

Taken together, their reflections represent a salutary reminder of how very long it has taken the UK to get to its present point in the L&D field. Only in the past few years has Bass and Vaughan's opening line started to become redundant. As we have seen in the book's first four chapters and in its tenth, from government down to organisational levels there is now a concern to move away from an excessive preoccupation with training to give more attention to the whole learning process, especially as it operates in communities of practice in the workplace. The considerable body of knowledge that was built up steadily in the USA and UK from the earliest years of the twentieth century is at last beginning to make an impact on those outside academia and the education profession, thanks not least to the work of the CIPD's research function, with its constant flow of widely publicised, easily accessible research reports that contain both old wisdom and new findings. With the advance of information and communication technology, coupled with an increased awareness of one simple fact – that learning cannot be forced out of anyone – more attention is at last being paid to the learners, and to the intrinsic as well as business-focused rewards that they can obtain from the learning process.

In the past three years since the third edition of this book was written, there has been an extraordinary expansion of government strategies, plans and initiatives to open up the whole field of training, learning and development. Chapters 2, 3 and 10 have only been able to provide the briefest account of its scale, its breadth, and the extent of its radical break with the past. There is a clear if not entirely compelling focus on a demand-driven route to upskilling and on opening up access to lifelong learning opportunities to everyone, whether in or out of employment. Certainly the opening line in my quotation from David King's book no longer holds true. Indeed within 20 years of its appearance King would have been the first to welcome the major overhaul of the national training system that then began, as government struggled to do what government now still hopes to achieve – complete transformation of learning and educational provision, an economy that is a world leader, and a society in which every individual has regular and meaningful opportunities to develop their abilities and apply their intelligence, energy and initiative to meaningful work.

From intent to reality

Yet behind the intent there is always the reality – and that is another major theme of the book. One issue that is involved here is how to establish 'reality'. How can we be sure that we know the intentions behind L&D activity, or that we understand what is actually going on in the workplace where that activity is supposed to be making an impact? In the Preface to this book I referred to the 'major disconnect' that HR researchers often find between the espoused and the real. One reason for this may be that it is their intended HR or L&D strategy that management attempts to relate to business strategy, not their realised strategy – that is to say, strategy as it is implemented from day to day in the workplace (Truss and Gratton 1994, p681). Another is that HR strategies, like business strategies, can sometimes be an illusion. Action may have preceded thought, rather than the reverse, so that what are claimed after the event to be 'strategies' are in fact little more than accidents – what have been called 'reconstructions after the fact' (Pettigrew et al 2002, p12).

Such observations have a unique importance when related to the study of learning and knowledge processes in changing organisational forms. In the new knowledge economy competitive advantage is 'a function of an organisation's ability to continually navigate its way into realms of the unknown' (Venkatraman and Subramaniam 2002, p471). This creates a special need for a tentative and broad-based research approach. It is true that a substantial body of studies now throws light on the part played by practical, social and emotional factors as well as by individual cognitive process in the operation of the knowledge process. However, under the impact of radical external and organisational changes non-traditional notions of learning and knowledge are gaining ground, as this book has explained. These require a fresh conceptual research framework that can relate knowledge creation, gradual improvement and radical innovation to characteristics of the daily work environment perceived as a powerful arena for learning (Harrison and Kessels 2003b).

There are no clear guidelines as yet on quite how that framework might be constructed. What is clear is that in seeking to expand the theoretical and empirical base of 'knowing' in organisations 'honest probing is needed now, rather than glib answers' (Bertels and Savage 1998, pp7–25). Probing beneath the surface is essential, since even apparently conventional structures can mask what is in reality unconventional. It is vital to find research methodologies that can reveal what is really happening within the firm through time and its effects on firm performance. It is as important for L&D practitioners as it is for L&D academics to give careful thought to how best to identify and understand the intention, the appearance and the reality of the L&D process in the workplace. Without this, L&D policies run the risk of irrelevancy and practice. They may turn out to be inappropriate, insufficient and sometimes plain dangerous.

In raising the theme of intent and reality the other major issue is that the gap between strategy and its delivery, between what is espoused at the top and what is experienced lower down, is disturbingly wide at every level of society. Reducing that gap is an enduring problem and challenge in organisations. There, the crucial determinant of 'what really goes on here' is organisation context, shaped powerfully by top management's vision and values, goals and leadership, by management – especially front-line management – style and actions, and by human resource strategies and practices. Context is shaped just as powerfully, however, by its past. The history of human resource development alone should show how great a part the past plays in determining what can be achieved in the present. In Chapter 1 we saw a function – L&D – whose complex roots contained from the start the sources of all the tensions that it still faces as it struggles to satisfy both the demands of management and the needs and expectations of individuals, while also trying to respond to government pressures to support its many educational and training initiatives.

The hand of history

For the organisation too, as again we have seen throughout the book, history plays a major but often unacknowledged part in enabling or constraining present progress. Embedded structures, routines and procedures, a culture and organisational identity forged often over many decades, myths, stories and symbols that reinforce it, learning and knowledge that have either produced thinking performers or skilled incompetence – all come together either to pull an organisation back as it attempts to come to grips with new challenges (and we have only to look at the sorry story of Marks and Spencer since the late 1990s to see the truth of that) or to provide the impetus it needs to move forward yet again.

Looking once again at David King's reflections and at those of Bass and Vaughan, it becomes clear that in too many ways progress in the L&D field has been painfully slow over the past 40 years. As has been shown in Parts 2 and 3 of the book, basic L&D practice and its management is often surprisingly poor, while the L&D function in many organisations, like HR functions more widely, is often embattled, criticised for its past failures to add value, rigidly structured and inward looking, sometimes unable even to clarify what has been spent on its operations and to what point. Processes like coaching and mentoring suddenly expand remarkably, yet when asked for their business rationale or for evaluation of their outcomes, few L&D staff can provide a convincing reply. Much money is invested in training programmes covering critically important skills, yet, just as Bass and Vaughan noted with concern, the organisation will still too often put unprepared trainees out on the road – or on the rail tracks – with no apparent thought to the consequences of their actions. Sometimes those consequences have been devastating. Management and leadership development, although now the focus of much government attention and funded initiatives especially across the public sector, has emerged this year just as did in the 1980s as an area woefully in need of greater investment by UK organisations. At the same time human resource management in the public sector received a swingeing verdict of incompetence in the 2002 Audit Commission's survey of local government.

Yet in survey after survey it is leaders, managers and other 'key' workers who in the UK receive the lion's share of the L&D investment – another theme that has surfaced in the book. So if even with that investment they are not adequately trained and developed, then who is? What of the much-hyped 'management of diversity', of the espoused ethical approach to human resource management and development, of the needs, rights and concerns of all those who still labour in unfulfilling jobs, without any prospect of advancement and for little extrinsic reward? We have seen in Chapter 5 of the book how simply sending such employees on a course to give them basic skill qualifications (and thereby attract some government funding) may achieve nothing, may in fact make the last position worse than the first because, with no way of using such qualifications and no way out of dead-end jobs, what is the point of qualifications anyway?

Innovation and change

But despite so much that remains negative, there is of course a positive side. Bass and Vaughan, nearly 40 years ago, were right in balancing out concern with a message of hope and of excitement. Much is still disturbing in the field of L&D practice. It has to be accepted that between the hype and the reality there is still a dauntingly wide gap in many organisations. The aspirations of government and the enormous effort being put into changing the face of training, education and learning across the UK may in the end come to little, pulled down by collapse of collaboration where it matters most, by failure of the voluntary approach that has never thus far worked, by the sheer scale of what has to be done. But there is undeniable progress too. Not, perhaps, at the macro level where intent has yet to be matched by reality, but within particular organisations and due to the efforts of particular leaders, managers, learners and HR professionals.

This more hopeful side of the story is another major theme that should by now have emerged quite strongly from the book: that even since the third edition was written in 2002 some remarkable and positive changes have occurred on the L&D front in many organisations. They show what can be done by taking a proactive stance, by expert and innovative thinking and by a careful integration of L&D activity with HR practices linked to organisational goals. They demonstrate the value of carefully preparing the culture and management of the organisation for new L&D initiatives and processes, of ensuring the skills and resource that will support and embed them, and above all of working constantly to build mutual commitment and trust between employees and their organisations that is essential if individuals are to apply their skills, energy and inventiveness in ways that benefit the business as well as themselves.

Linking people and organisational performance

That, of course, leads to another key theme in the book: the importance of the People Performance framework and, within it, of the Ability, Motivation and Opportunity model, both produced by the Bath University research team recently under the leadership of John Purcell (Purcell et al 2003). It has been mentioned in almost every chapter of the book and formed a centre point of attention in Chapter 5. This is not so much because of the novelty of the concepts that underpin the framework, since in truth there is little that is new about them – as again the book has shown when drawing attention at various points to a range of other and much earlier research both in the UK and the USA that has heralded virtually all its themes. It is because of the framework's striking presentation, its grounding in the practices of familiar British organisations across all sectors and of varying types and sizes, and because of its research methodology that is more rigorous and therefore more reliable than the methodology used in many earlier studies. L&D activity has a central place in the People Performance framework. Its role there is not just one of helping people to acquire skills and knowledge. It is one of enhancing their commitment to the organisation through development that is rewarding in itself and a gateway for many employees to a more promising and exciting future. L&D as an organisational process thus emerges from the Bath University and much other HR research as a key vehicle for forging a relational psychological contract between employees and employers: one that is cemented by mutual trust and shared purpose, not simply by mutual convenience.

Learning and development in a new knowledge economy

One final theme of great importance in the book is the significance for L&D and its practitioners of the emergence of a new knowledge economy, where adding value by means of knowledge creation and knowledge application is more important than the availability of the traditional factors of capital, material and labour. As has been emphasised in various chapters, to achieve this added value calls not only for the acquisition and development of superior human capital, but also for social capital to be skilfully organised, developed and sustained through time and space. At organisational level, an emphasis on process rather than on product in relation to both strategy and structure can only increase in a world that is no longer 'firm-centred' but where organisation and customers must collaborate in the value-creation process and where a turbulent environment is regularly generating unfamiliar and complex challenges. Where top management's vision and values focus convincingly on knowledge productivity as an organisational capability, and where management actions, work practices and HR processes support that focus, then L&D activity can make a powerful contribution to value creation. But where context is unfavourable and/or where L&D and other HR professionals are passive, uninformed or both, the necessary culture change interventions are unlikely to take root.

In a knowledge economy there is a need not only for visionary leadership and facilitative management but also for 'good' leadership and management that goes about its business in a manner respectful of certain values (Harrison and Smith 2001). Knowledge-productive organisations, where 'work has become the new classroom', depend on a sense of community and an inclusive approach to learning (Rana 2002). This calls for workplace training and learning processes that are informed by concern for an ethical approach and that respect and build on diverse value systems.

FOUR CHALLENGES FOR THE LEARNING AND DEVELOPMENT PROFESSION

Elsewhere, my colleague Professor Joseph Kessels and I (2003a, p225) have identified from an extensive review of practice and research that four major challenges face organisationally based L&D in the new knowledge economy. We have discussed them at length in an international context. Here, it is relevant to observe that the same challenges have emerged repeatedly throughout this book as confronting L&D functions and L&D professionals in UK-based organisations.

Challenge 1: to achieve strategic thrust through integration of L&D strategies with current business and HR strategies, coupled with a focus on building future organisational capacity for superior speed, flexibility and knowledge creation

The real issue when considering the relationship between human resource management and L&D is not to do with structural positioning, or with the subordination of any one specialist function to another. It is to do with integration. If L&D is not to be impeded by barriers of HR practice and policy as it strives to provide a strategically focused response at all organisational levels to the challenges of a more knowledge-based economy, then L&D practitioners must work in close partnership with their other HR colleagues. Furthermore while short-term training interventions have their part to play in building future organisational capacity, it is only a part. The greater need is for durable L&D strategies that are focused on developing and embedding a fast-responsive learning culture.

Challenge 2: to facilitate culture change and build a knowledge-productive learning culture

The effectiveness of L&D in contributing to culture change rests on its practitioners' alertness and responsiveness to new needs in the workplace, on their ability to raise awareness of the importance of a culture of learning and what that means in practice for managers and other employees, and on their production of relevant interventions that can form part of culture's new context. To do this, they require a deep knowledge of culture, of its historical roots, and of its typical impact on workplace behaviours and performance. They must be able to identify aspects of organisational context that may interact negatively with L&D interventions aimed at changing culture. They must be effective business partners, skilled communicators, and proposers of strategies to increase motivation to share and apply new knowledge across the organisation.

Challenge 3: to promote high quality workplace learning processes that will enhance the value of social as well as of human capital

Workplace learning has a long history, but what is new is the extent to which it is becoming recognised as a crucial source of competitive advantage that can produce the higher levels of innovation and customisation needed as customers become more discriminating and as competition becomes increasingly globalised (Stevens 2001). L&D professionals should place particular emphasis on technical competence and closeness to the customers in organisational scenarios where computerisation facilitates large increases in productivity, autonomous team working, flatter structures and more accessible knowledge management and learning systems (ibid.). However, research across countries reveals that much of the attention of funding providers, managers and trainers is on formally planned learning (Stern and Sommerlad 1999; Ashton et al 2001). There is also evidence to show that trainers, for whatever reasons, are proving slow to maximise the potential of e-technology to transform training and learning. L&D professionals need to take a lead in ensuring a stronger focus on informal learning processes and outcomes, and in integrating informal learning with planned training and off-the-job vocational education creatively and effectively.

Challenge 4: to develop managerial and leadership capability that will aid processes of strategising, organising and L&D

In a knowledge economy managers and team leaders increasingly have to master strategising, organising and L&D processes relevant to innovative organisational forms. L&D professionals should be designing and helping to implement leadership and management development strategies to build three interacting types of core competence:

Strategic capability

- An understanding of the strategy process that will produce challenges to dominant mindsets in the organisation that have begun to stifle innovation and organisational progress.
- Skills to introduce and operate strategy process modes that are most relevant for the particular organisation, and to monitor utilisation and outcomes.
- A deep knowledge base and variety of expertise in order to devise appropriate responses to new challenges and opportunities 'out there'.

Flexibility

- A high 'absorptive capacity' (Cohen and Levinthal 1990) for recognising the need to change. This involves recognising the value of new external information, assimilating it, and applying it to improvement and innovation in processes, products and services. This capacity can be developed particularly through social networks and boundary spanning and calls for high-level skills in those areas.
- The ability to work with others within and increasingly across organisations to increase the variety of their firm's dynamic capabilities by identifying and supporting new ideas rather than just exploiting existing routines. This involves double-loop learning skills and political ability to successfully challenge current operating assumptions.

Learning orientation

- The motivation and ability to develop in the workplace a learning culture that will stimulate and support teams and individuals in providing the knowledge needed to achieve continuous improvement and radical innovation in goods, products, services and processes.
- The motivation and ability to handle effectively decentralised L&D responsibilities, especially in new organisational forms.

Confronting the challenges

These, then, are the four fundamental challenges that now confront L&D professionals in an emergent knowledge economy. Yet as this book has made clear at various points there is little to show that at present they are being recognised or tackled. European research studies and UK surveys provide significant evidence that, despite considerable innovation in L&D practice, there is a generalised failure to promote and support a true learning culture in the workplace, to achieve full strategic integration for L&D and evaluation of its organisational impact, and to promote high-quality workplace learning both in informal and formal modes (Stern and Sommerlad 1999; Ashton et al 2001; Stewart and Tansley 2002; Tjepkema et al 2002b). The dominant L&D paradigm even in organisations styling themselves as 'learning oriented' appears too often to be that of 'training', not of learning in any broader sense.

To rise to the challenges that confront them, L&D professionals schooled in 'training' and familiar in their organisation for their training role need to begin to promote a different perspective: one of learning and actions that facilitate the sharing, production and utilisation of knowledge in the day to day work environment. When an organisation is understood as an evolving system of knowledge production and application, L&D professionals have the opportunity to become strategic players. To do that, they will need mastery of expertise similar to that possessed by the HR professionals identified in recent research who are carrying strategic roles in globalising organisations. That expertise incorporates (Brewster et al 2002):

- The ability to deal with social and cultural factors of learning situated in workplace communities of practice.
- Skills in coaching, counselling and mentoring individuals and teams in knowledge work.
- The ability to think strategically, to work in virtual contexts and to tolerate ambiguities in new business situations.
- The ability to work in many overlapping partnerships to create and sustain an organisational culture favourable to learning that can drive improvement and innovation.

In the paper on which this part of my concluding chapter is based (Harrison and Kessels 2003b), Joseph Kessels and I concluded that while the emergence of a knowledge economy presents some daunting challenges to those in the L&D profession, it also offers real and exciting opportunities. At the end of this book, I want to reiterate that conclusion. I believe that the primary task of the L&D profession is to work with organisational stakeholders to create a synergy between the learning, development and knowledge-creating capability of all organisational members, the thrust of strategising and organising, and the progress of the organisation as its boundaries grow ever more fluid in a turbulent world.

CONCLUSION

Throughout this book themes of challenge, business partnership, strategic alignment, professionalism, and the contribution that the L&D process can make to improving human performance and aiding strategic progress have all been pursued. Theories, frameworks and prescriptions have jostled for place in an attempt to express both the intellectual rigour involved in the study of L&D and the need for it to achieve outcomes that will substantiate its claim as a value-adding process.

There are, however, two words that have appeared little if at all in the book so far, yet they go to the heart of its matter. The words are wisdom and humility: the wisdom to search for the fundamental questions to ask, and the humility to realise that some may never be possible to answer. In a book characterised by themes of turbulence, of uncertainty, of irrelevant logics and of human fallibility it is appropriate at this last point to recall the difference between learning and knowledge. This book began with a quotation from Dickens. Now, an author from quite a different age and country (Australia) offers a crucial insight at its close (Janette Turner Hospital 2001):

> **'When we learn that we are too ignorant to formulate intelligible questions we learn a great deal. We begin to cross the divide, to think with 'forked brain', to become a different self, one which is no longer at ease in the old dispensation. From that moment, we understand how very strange our own unexamined assumptions are and, like T.S. Eliot's Magi, we begin to feel foreign in our own country.'**

Wisdom and humility are the trademarks of the true professional. The acknowledgement of the need to 'think with forked brain', the realisation of how little we know, how much more we need to discover, and the determination to constantly unlearn in order to learn – these are the human qualities that offer to the profession its best hope of moving forward with its partners both in and beyond the organisation.

This book has involved a long journey across the corporate landscape of learning and knowledge. Sometimes that landscape has seemed barren, sometimes rich, and always the way ahead has seemed uncertain. This, however, is no new experience in the long history of learning and development. At the end of the First World War, a war more terrible in the face to face ferocity of its fighting and in its toll on human life than any since, a distinguished educationalist spelt out a warning that still has relevance today (Bobbitt 1918, p14):

> **'The controlling purposes of education have not been sufficiently particularized. We have aimed at a vague culture, an ill-defined discipline, a nebulous harmonious development of the individual, an indefinite moral character-building, an unparticularized social efficiency, or, often enough, nothing more than escape from a life of work.'**

This is more than a commentary on dilemmas that still face our educational system, but within it there is a kind of promise. For those in the field of learning and development there is particular resonance in the phrases 'nebulous harmonious development' and 'escape from a life of work'. The seventeenth-century mystic, Henry Vaughan wrote of how 'the liberated soul ascends, looking at the sunset towards the west wind, and hearing secret harmonies'. But Bobbitt spoke of 'nebulous' harmonies, and that is the most telling observation. In learning and development it is indeed a constant struggle to reconcile the business imperative with the noble aspiration to transform individuals through the realisation of their human potential. Yet harmony can emerge. It is produced by the resolution of tensions, so it should not unduly dismay that the history of learning and development is one of a continuing search for a balance that can satisfactorily respond to the needs of the economy, of the organisation and of the individual. The search should be viewed as a challenge, not as a fruitless endeavour. Bobbitt's commentary must not become an epitaph for human resource professionals. The last message should rather be one of hope, like Vaughan the mystic who journeyed on 'looking towards the west wind and hearing secret harmonies' ...

Appendices

The CIPD's Learning and Development Generalist Standard (CIPD 2001a): Performance Indicators and Links to the Core Text

Performance Indicator 1. Integrating learning and development activity and organisational needs

Practitioners must be able to co-operate with learning and development stakeholders in producing and integrating learning and development policy, strategy and plans, in order to integrate their activity with wider personnel and business policy. (All chapters)

Performance Indicator 2. Providing a value-adding learning and development function

Practitioners must be able to advise on how to achieve a well-managed, appropriately staffed and value-adding learning and development function. (Chapters 11, 12, 13, 14)

Performance Indicator 3. Contributing to the recruitment and performance management processes

Practitioners must be able to contribute to learning and development that will aid the processes of recruitment and performance management. (Chapters 5, 8, 13)

Performance Indicator 4. Contributing to the retention of employees

Practitioners must be able to contribute to learning and development that will help the organisation retain the people it needs for the future. (Chapters 5, 15, 16)

Performance Indicator 5. Contributing to building organisational capacity and facilitating change

Practitioners must be able to contribute to learning and development that will expand the organisation's overall capacity and competence, and will help to introduce and embed organisational change. (Chapters 1, 2, 3, 5, 8, 9, 10, 12, 15, 16)

Performance Indicator 6. Stimulating strategic awareness and the development of knowledge

Practitioners must be able to promote learning that will stimulate strategic awareness, and will develop and help to disseminate organisationally valuable knowledge. (Chapters 4, 8, 9, 16)

Performance Indicator 7. Designing and delivering learning processes and activity

Practitioners must be able to contribute to the design and provision of effective learning processes and activity, using new technology as appropriate. (Chapters 4, 6, 7, 8)

Performance Indicator 8. Evaluating and assessing learning and development outcomes and investment

Practitioners must be able to evaluate learning outcomes, and help to assess the returns on the organisation's past and planned investment in learning and development. (Chapters 7,10,13,14)

Performance Indicator 9. Achieving ethical practice

Practitioners must be able to identify and promote learning and development processes and practices that meet or exceed legal, mandatory and ethical requirements. (Chapters 9,10)

Performance Indicator 10. Ensuring continuing professional self-development

Practitioners must be able to continuously develop their own expertise, professionalism and credibility in the Learning and Development field. (All chapters)

Useful CIPD Websites

CIPD annual Training and Development survey and many other CIPD surveys of relevance to the L&D field can be found at http://www.cipd.co.uk/surveys.

CIPD research reports. These are invaluable but quite expensive products and may not always be stocked in college or university libraries. Summaries are available on http://www.cipd.co.uk/researchsummaries.

The quarterly publication *Impact* updates CIPD policy and research activities (http://www.cipd.co.uk/impact).

'Change Agendas' are forward-thinking essays by leading authorities on a variety of key topics such as people and public sector reform. They are available at http:// www.cipd.co.uk/changeagendas.

http://www.cipd.co.uk/research advises when articles on the details of CIPD-sponsored research have appeared in *People Management* and when press releases have come out. It also provides links to presentations that CIPD's professional knowledge advisers have given around the country.

The 'training community' area of CIPD's website is a useful way to network, find out information and exchange views, ideas and experiences. See http://www.cipd.co.uk/communities.

Finally, the CIPD provides new online, downloadable tools that help to turn its research findings into practical, relevant material for its members. http://www.cipd.co.uk/tools gives access to downloadable checklists, diagnostics and good-practice frameworks like 'Planning the implementation of e-learning'.

Chapter Review Questions

Chapter 1. Main themes and issues in Learning and Development

It is claimed that organisations operating in a knowledge economy need to build social capital. What is social capital, and why is it so important in that kind of economy?

Why is so much importance attached to the 'integration' of L&D, and how far in your own organisation do you think that integration is achieved?

Chapter 2. The national framework for workforce development

Identify the main ways in which the Labour Government's national skills strategy announced in 2003 made a radical break with the past, and assess the value of <u>one</u> workforce development initiative related to it that is, or you think should be, taken up by your organisation.

National Skills Strategy is claimed to be 'demand-driven'. Explain what that term means, and identify and justify <u>up to three</u> tasks that it presents for an organisation's training/learning and development professionals.

Chapter 3. The education system and lifelong learning opportunities

Identify and justify reasons why your own organisation should, or should not at present, get involved in the development of a foundation degree within its sector.

The provision and management of LSC-funded work-based learning has been severely criticised in recent years. Looking at one example of such learning in your own organisation, to what extent do you feel that such criticisms apply? Provide reasons for your answer.

Chapter 4. Understanding learning and the learners

Much attention is currently being paid by commentators on training and development to a shift from trainers to learners. Drawing on published research, assess the main implications of such a shift for trainers.

As Training Manager in an organisation with around 250 employees, many of whom are only familiar with traditional learning methods, what are <u>three</u> things that you would do in order to ensure that e-learning technology can begin to make a real contribution to learning?

Chapter 5. Linking learning and development to performance

Despite commitment by an organisation's top management to mentoring for new employees, the company's mentoring scheme is unsuccessful. Drawing on good practice, what steps will you, as the organisation's L&D professional, do to put things right – and why?

Drawing on published research to support your proposal, if as a learning and development professional you could introduce <u>one</u> feasible activity or process to improve performance management in your organisation, what would it be?

Chapter 6. Organising learning events: stages 1 to 4

As training manager, you are preparing to submit to management a business case for a particular new training course that you have in mind. Outline and justify essential points that you must cover in your proposal.

A course tutor complains: 'I can't do anything with these students – they just don't seem to want to learn!' Drawing on published research or wider organisation practice, outline and justify some advice for the tutor.

Chapter 7. Organising learning events: stages 5 to 8

As a training consultant, identify and justify final learning objectives and major topics for a short (two or three day) course on any learning and development subject you wish that would be relevant for a small group of human resource generalists from a range of organisations, who have not covered Learning and Development in any detail in their professional studies.

Suggest and justify a realistic evaluation process for a major modular training programme for newly appointed team leaders in an organisation.

Chapter 8. Promoting workplace learning and knowledge

Identify and explain <u>up to three</u> ways in which to develop the workplace as a learning environment.

Drawing on wider organisational practice, how far do you believe that the concept of the 'learning organisation' has practical value?

Chapter 9. Achieving ethical practice

A check of training records going back over the past three years in an organisation has revealed that members of one particular ethnic group in the workforce have consistently lacked the training to enable them to gain promotion to certain posts in the organisation. They have thus been regularly disadvantaged in their attempts at career progression. What should the L&D staff do now?

An external trainer has been delivering in-house bespoke sessions on themes like stress and well being. Both during the sessions and at coffee breaks afterwards he meets with the following typical comment: 'I agree with what you are saying and I am really enjoying the session but there's no way we can get that accepted in our department because the manager simply wouldn't hear a word of it'. Justify your advice as to how he should respond.

Chapter 10. The L&D agenda in different sectoral settings

You are a human resource consultant, asked by the owner-manager of a small but growing firm to advise her on how best to organise training and development in the firm. Identify and justify <u>up to three</u> contextual factors that you will examine before giving her your advice.

Outline and justify advice you would give to an HR professional who wants to work in the L&D field in the public sector.

Chapter 11. Shaping and managing the L&D function

Draw on research or wider organisational practice to assess whether an L&D function substantially devolved to line management might be appropriate for a fast-moving, fairly large organisation, operating in a tough business environment.

An organisation advertises for a L&D manager post, and refers to the need for applicants with team management skills and 'the ability to lead, train and motivate staff'. Identify and briefly justify some key tasks that such a post is likely to involve.

Chapter 12. Producing and implementing L&D strategy

One of your L&D colleagues says to you, rather cynically, 'We're always being told "get strategic" with the L&D process. Just give me a few basic tips here...' Provide those tips.

On what grounds would you recommend the use of scenario planning to develop an organisation's L&D strategy, and what might cause its use to fail?

Chapter 13. Adding value

A manager says 'All you L&D people do is produce knee-jerk reactions. You don't contribute any added value to the business.' What might you do to avoid this criticism?

Reflecting on your own organisation, or one known to you that has a specialist L&D function, what are the main performance indicators against which L&D activity is measured, and to what extent do they focus on adding value?

Chapter 14. Developing L&D business partnerships

Someone has said to you that the art of being a 'business partner' lies in power and politics. How would you reply, and with what reasoning?

Produce a short practical example from your own organisation to illustrate and evaluate the operation of an L&D business partnership.

Chapter 15. Developing careers

What is meant by an 'inclusive' career management process, and how far does it seem to be inclusive in your own organisation?

Your senior management is interested in using development centre methodology in order to improve the career development process. Why should it want to do so, and what advice would you offer?

Chapter 16. Developing leaders and managers

The six members of the top management group in an organisation do not work well together as a corporate team, and strategic direction is suffering in consequence. Identify possible causes of this failure, and as a learning and development professional suggest an approach to tackle the problem.

Why is there so much concern currently about management development in UK organisations, and to what extent does practice in your own organisation justify such concern?

The Investors in People
Standard

Investors in People (IIP) is a national Standard, established in 1991, that aims to establish good practice in linking an organisation's investment in the development of its employees to its business goals. It provides a national framework whose purpose is to improve business performance and competitiveness through a planned approach to setting and communicating business goals and to managing and developing people in line with those goals. The aim in following the cyclical IIP process is to produce a culture of continuous improvement.

The IIP Standard therefore provides a valuable tool for any organisation wishing to maximise the performance of its people. It has evolved as a result of three-yearly reviews to ensure that it continues to meet the needs of its customers. During 2003–2004 those needs were reviewed, challenging existing assumptions about how best to meet them and identifying ways of delivering continuous improvement. Following extensive consultation the Standard was then revised, and is now based on the following principles:

- *Developing strategies* to improve the performance of the organisation.
- *Taking action* to improve the performance of the organisation.
- *Evaluating the impact* on the performance of the organisation.

The principles are underpinned by 10 indicators of good practice, each with a central theme. Every indicator has a number of evidence requirements, all of which need to be met in order to gain IIP accreditation.

'Profile' was introduced in 2002 as a continuous improvement tool for organisations wishing to see if they exceed the requirements of the Standard and if so by how much. It provides a more in-depth assessment tool than before, comprising four levels of attainment and has been developed in line with the revised IIP Standard so that the scope and content of Profile level 1 is exactly the same as the Standard. The scope of Profile levels 2–4, on the other hand, provides greater depth and breadth based on the indicator theme.

For each indicator, a level of good practice has been identified as follows:

- Level 1 represents an organisation meeting the evidence requirements of the Standard and demonstrating good practice.
- Level 2 represents an organisation exceeding the requirements of the Standard by achieving at least 50 per cent of level 2 and 3 statements in addition to level 1 requirements.
- Level 3 represents an organisation significantly exceeding the requirements of the Standard by achieving 100 per cent of level 2 and 3 statements in addition to level 1 requirements.
- Level 4 represents an organisation demonstrating excellent practice by achieving all of the level 1, 2, 3 and 4 requirements.

The levels are therefore cumulative and it is not possible to achieve a higher level without having first achieved the standards required in the lower level.

Following these revisions, organisations can now choose whether they wish to be assessed against the IIP Standard (ie level 1) or against the IIP Profile. The latter involves an organisation being assigned one of the four levels for each indicator based on the evidence that the IIP assessor finds when conducting the assessment/review. Should the organisation not meet the necessary requirements a level 0 is assigned.

A number of stand-alone Investors in People models now complement the IIP standard, providing advice for good practice and additional accreditation against set criteria across key disciplines of:

- recruitment and selection
- work–life balance – seen to be a key recruitment and retention tool
- leadership and management.

The Leadership and Management Model, for example, explains how an organisation can take the IIP principles forward. It is a flexible business tool that has been piloted on businesses across a range of sectors. The IIP's website explains it as a 'straightforward framework you use as you want – either for your own internal purposes, or for a more formal external assessment'.

Visit the CIPD's website at http://cipd.co.uk/quickfacts and the IIP website at http://investorsinpeople.co.uk for further information.

© Investors in People UK 2005

The Cabinet Office Code of Ethics and Practice for Developers, Trainers & Training Managers (CMPS, Cabinet Office 2002)

Reproduced with the permission of CMPS

CODE OF ETHICS AND PRACTICE

Introduction

The purpose of this Code of Ethics and Practice is to establish and maintain standards for all developers, trainers and training managers for the delivery of professional training and development services. It gives a frame of reference within which to manage their responsibilities to clients, colleagues and trainees. Whilst this code cannot resolve all ethical and practice related issues, it aims to provide a framework for addressing ethical issues and to encourage optimum levels of training practice. Training managers, trainers and developers will need to judge which parts of this code apply to particular situations.

CODE OF ETHICS

Values

Training is a non-exploitative activity. Its basic values are integrity, impartiality and respect.

Anti-discrimination

Developers, trainers and training managers must promote and comply with Equal Opportunities policies and legislation and should model good practices in managing diversity issues. They must ensure that an antidiscriminatory approach is integral to all the training and development they provide.

Safety

All reasonable steps shall be taken to ensure the safety of trainees during all forms of training and development activities. They should take care to comply with Health and Safety policies and legislation.

Competence

They must take all reasonable steps to monitor and develop their own levels of competence and ensure that they work within the limits of that competence. They should adapt their own practice to reflect continual changes in training and development and their own knowledge base.

Confidentiality

Legitimate needs and requirements for confidentiality must be respected at all times. As well as personal confidentiality, Political, Governmental and Commercial confidentiality should also be respected.

Contracts

The terms and conditions on which the training is offered must be made clear to trainees and/or clients before the start of the training programme. Subsequent revision of these terms must be agreed in advance of any changes.

Boundaries

Within the working environment, trainers and training managers must establish and maintain appropriate boundaries between themselves and their colleagues, trainees and any outside consultants or guest speakers. There may be occasions on which one has to work with people with whom there is a relationship outside the working environment. When this occurs it is important to remember that working relationships should not be confused with friendship or other relationships.

CODE OF PRACTICE

This code applies the ethical principles to more specific situations which may arise in the practice of training and development. Most of the situations are equally applicable to all roles in the training and development profession.

Issues of Responsibility

Your responsibility covers the entire time that you are with trainees and/or clients in the course of your work, including residential training.

- You should demonstrate a commitment to professional and ethical practice.
- You should ensure that your relationships with learners are not exploitative or a misuse of your role or power.
- You should behave with sensitivity and professionalism, being an ambassador for your organisation and your profession.
- You should at all times make every effort to avoid bringing the profession into disrepute.
- You should demonstrate a respect for individuals and their needs.
- You should deal with trainees fairly, consistently and with impartiality.
- You should avoid language that could be regarded as offensive, suggestive or discriminatory.
- You should avoid behaviour that could be regarded as harassment, bullying, exploitation or intimidation.
- You should avoid situations that could be construed as sexual harassment, eg unwanted bodily contact.
- You should not embark on intimate relationships or sexual liaisons with trainees or clients.
- You should seek to become aware of and address your own prejudices and avoid stereotyping.

- You should challenge any behaviour by your trainees that could be regarded as harassment, bullying or intimidation.
- You should support learners, promote access to learning and promote anti-discriminatory practice.
- You should avoid the use of alcohol or other substances that might affect your ability to perform effectively.
- You should not use your professional position to obtain information to influence a trainee or client for personal gain.
- You should carry out your professional responsibilities totally without prejudice on the grounds of ethnic origin, gender, sexual orientation, disability, age, nationality, colour, religion or status.
- You should aspire to give access to learning opportunities to all relevant people irrespective of age, disability, employable hours or geographical location.
- You should, within your own or any client organisation and in whatever capacity you are working, seek to achieve the fullest possible development of people for present and future organisational needs and encourage self-development by individuals.
- You should, within your own or any client organisation and in whatever capacity you are working, seek to adopt the most appropriate people management processes and structures to enable the organisation to best achieve its present and future objectives.
- You should act within the law and must not encourage, assist or act in collusion with employers, employees or others who may be engaged in unlawful conduct.
- You should observe the principles embodied in other codes of practice for any professional bodies to which you belong. On any matter of doubt of ethical propriety, you should seek expert guidance.
- You should observe this code of practice irrespective of the methods or technology used for learning.
- You should ensure that any form of assessment, test or measurement of performance is fair and valid.
- You should ensure that information is acquired and disseminated through ethical and responsible means. In particular, respect for privacy and confidentiality should be ensured in both administrative and training practices.

Competence

- You should regularly evaluate your own competence and practice.
- You should seek continually to improve your performance and to update and refresh your skills and knowledge.
- You have a responsibility to yourself, to your trainees and your clients to maintain your own effectiveness, resilience and ability to work with others.
- You should recognise the limitations of your own knowledge and ability and should not undertake activity for which you are not yet appropriately prepared or, where applicable, qualified.

Confidentiality

- Confidentiality within the training process must be clarified at the beginning of a training programme or any other training and development activity.
- You should establish a contract for confidential working which makes explicit the responsibilities of both trainer and trainees throughout a programme.
- You should inform trainees at the beginning of the training programme of all

reasonably foreseeable circumstances under which confidentiality may be breached during the programme.

■ You should not reveal confidential information about trainees, or former trainees, without the permission of the trainee, unless the trainee has committed an illegal or disciplinary act.

Management of the Training Process

■ You should seek to ensure that differences of opinion are dealt with in ways which minimise offence, and conflicts are resolved in ways that maintain respect.

■ You should ensure that trainees receive regular feedback on their work and that self and peer assessment are encouraged at regular intervals, as appropriate.

■ Trainee requests which conflict with the professional code should be refused; clear reasons should be given and alternative measures proposed to prevent conflicts recurring.

■ You should be alert to any prejudices and assumptions that trainees reveal and raise their awareness of these issues so that trainees are encouraged to recognise and value difference.

■ You should take responsibility for vetting all training designs and learning materials for their suitability before using them.

■ You should comply with copyright legislation and give credit to others where you are using materials, or extracts from materials, that they have originated.

Acknowledgments

Thanks to Christopher Mallett (CMPS Librarian) for his help in researching other professional codes and to colleagues in the Development & Training Consultancy team for their contributions to this booklet. Original devised by David Jameson. Adapted and updated by Graham O'Connell. Revised and Reprinted June 2002.

CMPS
Sunningdale Park
Larch Avenue
ASCOT
SL5 0QE
www.cmps.gov.uk
© Crown Copyright June 2002

The Corporate Training/
Learning and Development Plan

A typical corporate T&D plan might comprise:

1. Staffing plan for the whole organisation, including a breakdown by departments and/or business units showing:
   - staff currently in post
   - movements anticipated in coming year through retirements and other unavoidable departures, likely rate of resignations, transfers in and out, and authorised T&D new recruitment
   - staff anticipated in post at year-end
   - staffing gaps, taking into account the goals and specific targets to be met by departments/business units.

2. General T&D implications of the staffing plan – ie priority to give investment in T&D in the coming year given the above information and identification of likely skills gaps.

3. T&D activity agreed to meet business needs at corporate and unit levels in the coming period and to support longer-term strategic goals:

   Short-term: focus on proficiency
   - training to close current key skills gaps
   - training to meet policy or systems changes
   - training to support new business goals or strategies
   - training to meet mandatory requirements (health and safety, equal opps and so on).

   Longer term: focus on building for the future through policies in three key areas:
   - leadership development
   - management development
   - workforce T&D initiatives to facilitate restructuring or other major business changes likely in next two or three years.

4. For each area of the plan, detailed information to show:
   - planned content of training
   - performance standards to be achieved through training
   - where and how training will be given
   - who is responsible for making arrangements and for the training
   - timing and sequence of training events, bearing in mind priorities
   - method and personnel to be used in evaluating results.

References

ACTIVE COMMUNITY UNIT (2004) *ChangeUp: Capacity building and infrastructure framework for the voluntary and community sector*. London: HO Distribution Unit, email: home office@prolog.ul.com. Online version also available at: http://www.homeoffice.gov.uk/comrace/active/developing/ [accessed 17 September 2004].

ADULT LEARNING INSPECTORATE (2004) *Annual Report of the Chief Inspector, 2003–04*. Coventry: ALI or email publications@ali.gov.uk. Online version also available at: http://docs.ali.gov.uk/ciar/0304/index.htm [accessed 25 November 2004].

ALLEN, R. E. (1990) *The concise Oxford dictionary of current English*. 8th edn. Oxford: Clarendon Press.

ALLINSON, C. and HAYES, J. (1996) The cognitive style index. *Journal of Management Studies*. Vol. 33. 119–135.

ALRED, G., GARVEY, B. and SMITH, R. (1998) *The mentoring pocket book*. Arlesford, UK: Management Pocket Books Series.

ALVAREZ, J. L. (1996) Are we asking too much of managers? *Financial Times*. 12 July. 13.

ANSOFF, H. I. and SULLIVAN, P.A. (1993) Optimizing profitability in turbulent environments: a formula for strategic success. *Long Range Planning*. Vol 26, No. 5. 11–23.

ARGYRIS, C. (1957) *Personality and organization*. New York: Harper and Row.

ARGYRIS, C. (1977) Double loop learning in organizations. *Harvard Business Review*. September–October. 115–124.

ARGYRIS, C. (1982) *Reasoning, learning and action*. San Francisco, CA: Jossey-Bass.

ARGYRIS, C. (1996) Skilled incompetence. In K. STARKEY (ed) *How organizations learn*. London: International Thomson Business Press. 82–91.

ARGYRIS, C. and D.A. SCHON. (1996) *Organizational learning II: theory, methods and practice*. Reading, MA: Addison Wesley.

ARKIN, A. (1995) Breaking down skills barriers. *People Management*. Vol. 1, No. 3, 9 February. 34–35.

ARKIN, A. (2001) Central Intelligence. *People Management*. Vol. 7, No. 23, 2 November. 38–41.

ARMSTRONG, M. and BARON, A. (2004) *Performance management: action and impact*. London: Chartered Institute of Personnel and Development.

ASHTON, D., SUNG, J., RADDON, A. and POWELL, M. (2001) National frameworks for workplace learning. In *Workplace learning in Europe* [summary of the European Workplace Learning Seminar, London. 2 April]. London: Chartered Institute of Personnel and Development. 35–60.

AUGUSTINE. *Confessions*. Trans. R. S. Pine-Coffin (1964). London: Penguin Classics.

BAJER, J. (2001) Same old seasoned greetings. *People Management*. Vol. 7, No. 24, 6 December. 27.

BARNARD, C.I. (1938) *The functions of the executive*. Cambridge, MA: Harvard University Press.

BARON, A. (2000) Advance beyond intuition. *People Management*. Vol. 6, No. 15, 20 July. 30–31.

BARON, A. (2004) Get to know those in the know. *People Management*. Vol. 10, No. 14, 15 July. 25.

BARTEL, A. (2000) Human resource management and performance in the service sector: the case of bank branches. *NBER Working Paper Series*. Cambridge, MA: National Bureau of Economic Research.

BARTLETT, C.A. and GHOSHAL, S. (1993) Beyond the M-form: toward a managerial theory of the firm. *Strategic Management Journal*, Winter Special Issue. Vol. 14. 23–46.

BASS, B.M. and VAUGHAN, J.A. (1967) *Training in industry: the management of learning*. London: Tavistock Publications.

BATCHELOR, J., DONNELLY, R. and MORRIS, D. (1995) Learning networks within supply chains. *Working paper, Coventry Business School*. Coventry: Coventry University.

BECKER, B. and GERHART, B. (1996) The impact of human resource practices on organizational performance: progress and prospects. *Academy of Management Journal*. Vol. 39. 779–801.

BECKER, G. (1975) *Human Capital: A theoretical and empirical analysis with special reference to education*. 2nd edn. New York: Columbia University Press.

BEE, F. and BEE, R. (2003) *Learning needs analysis and evaluation*. 2nd edn. London: Chartered Institute of Personnel and Development.

BEE, F. and FARMER, P. (1995) HR projects on the right track. *People Management*. Vol. 1, No. 16, 10 August. 28–30.

BERTELS, T. and SAVAGE, C.M. (1998) Tough questions on knowledge management. In G. VON KROGH, J. ROOS and D. KLEINE (eds) *Knowing in firms: understanding, managing and measuring knowledge*. London: Sage. 7–25.

BETTIS, R.A. and HITT, M.A. (1995) The new competitive landscape. *Strategic Management Journal*, Summer Special Issue. Vol. 16. 7–19.

BIRCHENHOUGH, M. (2004) A change as good as the rest? *People Management*. Vol. 10, No. 16, 12 August. 28.

BOBBITT, F. (1918) *The curriculum*. Cambridge, MA: Riverside Press. Reprinted 1971. Boston, MA: Houghton Mifflin.

BOHN, R.E. (1994) Measuring and managing technological knowledge. *Sloan Management Review*. Vol. 36, No. 1. 61–73.

BOYDELL, T. (1971) *A guide to the identification of training needs*. London: BACIE.

BOYDELL, T., BURGOYNE, J. and PEDLER, M. (2004) Suggested development. *People Management*. Vol. 10, No. 4, 26 February. 32–34.

BRAMLEY, P. (2003) *Evaluating training*. 2nd edn. London: Chartered Institute of Personnel and Development.

BREWSTER, C., HARRIS, H. and SPARROW, P. (2002) *Globalising HR: executive briefing*. London: Chartered Institute of Personnel and Development.

BREWSTER, C. and TYSON, S. (eds) (1991) *International comparisons in human resource management*. London: Pitman.

BRICKLEY, J.A. and VAN DRUNEN, L. (1990) Internal corporate restructuring: an empirical analysis. *Journal of Accounting and Economics*. Vol. 12. 251–280.

BRITTAIN, S. and RYDER, P. (1999) Get complex. *People Management*. Vol. 5, No. 23, 25 November. 48–51.

BROMILEY, R., CONWAY, P., HARRISON, R. and HUDSON, R. (1999) *Developing local learning environments to aid regional regeneration: working paper produced for One NorthEast*, July. Available from m-rharrison@tiscali.co.uk.

BROWN, D. (2003) Orchestral manoeuvres in the dark. *People Management*. Vol. 9, No. 10, 15 May. 25.

BROWN, D. and EMMOTT, M. (2003) Happy days. *People Management*. Vol. 9, No. 21, 23 October. 16–17.

BROWN, J.S. and DUGUID, P. (1991) Organisational learning and communities-of-practice: towards a unified view of working, learning and innovation. *Organization Science*. Vol. 2, No. 1. 40–57.

BRUCE, I. (2004) Think tank. *Society Guardian*. 7 April. 9.

BUBB, S. (2004) Charities need to get tough. *The Times, Public Agenda*. 30 November. 5.

BUCKINGHAM, M. (2001) What a waste. *People Management*. Vol. 7, No. 20, 11 October. 36–40.

BURACK, E.H. (1991) Changing the company culture – the role of human resource development. *Long Range Planning*. Vol. 24, No. 1. 88–95.

BURDETT, J.O. (1994) To coach, or not to coach – that is the question! In C. MABEY and P. ILES (eds) *Managing learning*. London: Routledge and Open University. 133–145.

BURGOYNE, J. (1989) *Management development: context and strategies*. Aldershot: Gower.

BURGOYNE, J. (1999) *Develop yourself, your career and your organisation*. London: Lemos and Crane.

BUTLER, E. (1999) Technologising equity: the politics and practices of work-related learning. In D. BOUD and J. GARRICK (eds) *Understanding learning at work*. London: Routledge. 132–150.

CABINET OFFICE (1999) *Modernising government*. White Paper. London: The Stationery Office. Online version also available at http://www.archive.official-documents.co.uk/document/cm43/4310/4310.htm [accessed 16 September 2004].

CAMBRIDGE UNIVERSITY SMALL BUSINESS RESEARCH CENTRE (1992) *The state of British enterprise: growth, innovation and competitive advantage in small and medium-sized firms*. Cambridge: Small Business Research Centre.

CANNELL, M. (2002) The value of learning. *People Management*. Vol. 8, No. 4, 21 February. 51.

CANNELL, M. (2004) *Training – a short history*. Available online at: http://www.cipd.co.uk/subjects/training/general/thistory.htm [accessed 29 August 2004].

CAULKIN, S. (2003) *People and public services: why central targets miss the mark.* The Change Agenda. London: CIPD.

CHAMBERS, C. (1990) Self reliant. *Times Higher Education Supplement.* 6 April. 26.

CHARTERED INSTITUTE OF PERSONNEL AND DEVELOPMENT (2000) *Code of professional conduct and disciplinary procedures.* London: CIPD.

CHARTERED INSTITUTE OF PERSONNEL AND DEVELOPMENT (2001a) The learning and development generalist standard. In *CIPD practitioner-level professional standards.* London: CIPD. Online version also available at: http://www.cipd.co.uk/mandq/standards/prac/sgpd/lrndev.htm [accessed 22 August 2004].

CHARTERED INSTITUTE OF PERSONNEL AND DEVELOPMENT (2001b) *The change agenda: performance through people – the new people management.* London: CIPD. Online version also available at http://www.cipd.co.uk/changeagenda [accessed 25August 2004].

CHARTERED INSTITUTE OF PERSONNEL AND DEVELOPMENT (2002a) *How do people learn: change agenda.* London: CIPD. Online version also available at: http://www.cipd.co.uk/howdopeoplelearn [accessed 25August 2004].

CHARTERED INSTITUTE OF PERSONNEL AND DEVELOPMENT (2002b) *Perspectives: corporate social responsibility.* London: CIPD.

CHARTERED INSTITUTE OF PERSONNEL AND DEVELOPMENT (2002c) *Developing managers for business performance.* London: CIPD.

CHARTERED INSTITUTE OF PERSONNEL AND DEVELOPMENT (2003a) *Evaluating human capital. Research summary.* London: CIPD.

CHARTERED INSTITUTE OF PERSONNEL AND DEVELOPMENT (2003b) *Organising for success in 21C: a starting point for change. Research summary.* London: CIPD.

CHARTERED INSTITUTE OF PERSONNEL AND DEVELOPMENT (2003c) *Investors in people: quick facts.* London: Chartered Institute of Personnel and Development. Online version also available at: http://cipd.co.uk/quickfacts [accessed 29August 2004].

CHARTERED INSTITUTE OF PERSONNEL AND DEVELOPMENT (2003d) People and performance in knowledge-intensive firms. In *Impact.* London: CIPD. Issue 2. 12–13.

CHARTERED INSTITUTE OF PERSONNEL AND DEVELOPMENT (2003e) *Managing the psychological contract: quick facts.* London: Chartered Institute of Personnel and Development. Online version also available at: http://cipd.co.uk/quickfacts [accessed 29 August 2004].

CHARTERED INSTITUTE OF PERSONNEL AND DEVELOPMENT (2003f) *Training and development 2003. Survey Report.* London: CIPD. Online version also available at: http://www.cipd.co.uk/survey [accessed 20 August 2004].

CHARTERED INSTITUTE OF PERSONNEL AND DEVELOPMENT (2003g) *Reorganising for success: CEOs' and HR managers' perceptions. Survey Report.* London: CIPD. Online version also available at: http://www.cipd.co.uk/surveys [accessed 16 August 2004].

CHARTERED INSTITUTE OF PERSONNEL AND DEVELOPMENT (2003h) *Where we are, where we're heading. Survey Report.* London: CIPD. Online version also available at: http://www.cipd.co.uk/surveys [accessed 16 August 2004].

CHARTERED INSTITUTE OF PERSONNEL AND DEVELOPMENT (2003i) *Human capital external reporting framework: change agenda*. London: Chartered Institute of Personnel and Development. Online version also available at: http://www.cipd.co.uk/changeagenda [accessed 24 September 2004].

CHARTERED INSTITUTE OF PERSONNEL AND DEVELOPMENT (2003j) *Managing employee careers: issues, trends and prospects. Survey Report*. London: CIPD. Online version also available at: http://www.cipd.co.uk/surveys [accessed 29 September 2004].

CHARTERED INSTITUTE OF PERSONNEL AND DEVELOPMENT (2004a) *Training and development 2004. Survey Report*. London: CIPD. Online version also available at: http://www.cipd.co.uk/surveys [accessed 20 August 2004].

CHARTERED INSTITUTE OF PERSONNEL AND DEVELOPMENT (2004b) *Trade union learning representatives: a change agenda*. London: CIPD. Online version also available at http://www.cipd.co.uk/changeagendas [accessed 23 August 2004].

CHARTERED INSTITUTE OF PERSONNEL AND DEVELOPMENT (2004c) *Towards a unified e-learning strategy: CIPD response to the Department for Education and Skills*. London: CIPD. Online version also available at: http://www.cipd.co.uk/about/_unielrnstrg.htm [accessed 19 August 2004].

CHARTERED INSTITUTE OF PERSONNEL AND DEVELOPMENT (2004d) *Re-organising for success: a survey of HR's role in change*. London: CIPD. Online version also available at: http://www.cipd.co.uk/surveys [accessed 4 December 2004].

CHARTERED INSTITUTE OF PERSONNEL AND DEVELOPMENT (2004e) *A guide: business partnering: a new direction for HR*. London: CIPD. Online version also available at: http:// www.cipd.co.uk/subjects/corpstrtgy/general/busprtnrnewdir.htm [accessed 8 November 2004].

CHRISTIAN-CARTER, J. (2001) *Mastering instructional design in technology-based training*. London: Chartered Institute of Personnel and Development.

CLARE, J. (2001) Teaching profession 'cannot be sustained'. *Daily Telegraph*. 31 August. 2.

CLARE, J. (2004) Alarm over loss of vital college courses. *Daily Telegraph*. 2 December. 1.

COFFIELD, F. (2002) Britain's continuing failure to train: the birth pangs of a new policy. *Journal of Education Policy*. Vol. 17, No. 4. 483–497.

COFFIELD, F., MOSELEY, D., HALL, E. and ECCLESTONE, K. (2004) *Should we be using learning styles? What research has to say to practice*. London: Learning and Skills Research Centre. Online version also available at: http://www.lsda.org.uk/files/PDF/1540.pdf [accessed 25 August 2004].

COHEN, W.M. and LEVINTHAL, D.A. (1990) Absorptive capacity: a new perspective on learning and innovation. *Administrative Science Quarterly*. Vol. 35, No. 1. 28–52.

COLLIS, B. and MOONEN, J. (2001) *Flexible learning in a digital world*. London: Kogan Page.

CONFEDERATION OF BRITISH INDUSTRY IN ASSOCIATION WITH PERTEMPS (2003) *Measuring flexibility in the labour market: employment trends survey 2003*. London: CBI. Online summary available at http://www.cbi.org.uk/home.html [accessed 2 October 2004].

COOPER, C. (2000a) The Met fails inspection on race and recruitment. *People Management*. Vol. 6, No. 2, 20 January. 11.

COOPER, C. (2000b) Southall rail crash report orders review of training. *People Management*. Vol. 6, No. 5, 2 March. 17.

COOPER, C. (2003) Hooked on ethics. *People Management*. Vol. 9, No. 14, 10 July. 30–32.

COOTE, A., ALLEN, J. and WOODHEAD, D. (2004) *Finding out what works*. London: Kings Fund. Online version also available at: http://www.kingsfund.org.uk/news/news.cfm?contentID =265 [accessed 3 December 2004].

CORNEY, M. (2004) Opinion. *'Future' Guardian*. 18 May. 15.

COULSON-THOMAS, C. (2001) Fashion victim. *People Management*. Vol. 7, No. 17, 30 August. 51.

COUNCIL FOR EXCELLENCE IN MANAGEMENT AND LEADERSHIP (2002) *Managers and leadership: Raising our game. Final Report of the Council for Excellence in Management and Leadership*. London: CEML. Online version also available at: http://www.managementand leadershipcouncil.org/ [accessed 1 October 2004].

CROZIER, M. (1964) *The bureaucratic phenomenon*. London: Tavistock.

CULLY, M., WOODLAND, S., O'REILLY, A. and DIX, G. (1999) *Britain at work as depicted by the 1998 Workplace Employee Relations Survey*. London: Routledge.

CYERT, R.M. and MARCH, J.G. (1963) *A behavioural theory of the firm*. Englewood Cliffs, NJ: Prentice-Hall.

DARLING, J., DARLING, P. and ELLIOTT, J. (1999) *The changing role of the trainer*. London: Institute of Personnel and Development.

DEPARTMENT FOR EDUCATION AND EMPLOYMENT (1998) *The learning age*. Green Paper. London: HMSO.

DEPARTMENT FOR EDUCATION AND EMPLOYMENT (1999) *Learning to succeed*. White Paper. London: HMSO.

DEPARTMENT FOR EDUCATION AND EMPLOYMENT (2001) *Skills for life*. London: HMSO. Online version also available at: http:// www.dfes.gov.uk/readwriteplus/ [accessed 17 July 2004].

DEPARTMENT FOR EDUCATION AND SKILLS (2002a). *Success for all: reforming further education and training – our vision for the future*. Nottingham: DfES. Online version also available at http://www.dfes.gov.uk/learning&skills/pdf/successforallr.pdf [accessed 25 August 2004].

DEPARTMENT FOR EDUCATION AND SKILLS (2002b). *The future of higher education*. Norwich: The Stationery Office. email orders@tso.co.uk Online version also available at: http:// www.dfes.gov.uk/hegateway/hereform/ [accessed 25 August 2004].

DEPARTMENT FOR EDUCATION AND SKILLS (2003a) *21st century skills: realising our potential: individuals, employers, nation*. White Paper. Norwich: The Stationery Office. email orders@tso.co.uk. Online version also available at http://www.dfes.gov.uk/skillsstrategy [accessed 25 August 2004].

DEPARTMENT FOR EDUCATION AND SKILLS (2003b) *Towards a unified e-learning strategy*. Norwich: DfES. Online version only, available at: http://publications.teachernet.gov.uk/ then search for 'e-learning strategy' [accessed 25 August 2004].

DEPARTMENT FOR EDUCATION AND SKILLS (2004a) *Skills alliance: skills strategy progress report*. Nottingham: DfES Publications. email dfes@prolog.uk.com. Online version also available at http://www.dfefs.gov.uk/publications [accessed 17 July 2004].

DEPARTMENT FOR EDUCATION AND SKILLS (2004b). *DfES: five year strategy for children and learners – putting people at the heart of public services.* Norwich: The Stationery Office. email orders@tso.co.uk Online version also available at http://www.dfes.gov.uk/14-19/documents/5YearStrategy-14-19.d [accessed 25 August 2004].

DEPARTMENT OF HEALTH (2001) *Working together, learning together.* London: DoH. Online version also available at: http://www.dh.gov.uk/PublicationsAndStatistics/Publications [accessed 17 September 2004].

DEPARTMENT OF HEALTH (2003) *Delivering the HR in the NHS Plan 2003. Annual Report.* London: DoH. Online version also available at http://www.dh.gov.uk/PublicationsAnd Statistics/Publications [accessed 17 September 2004].

DEPARTMENT OF TRADE AND INDUSTRY (2004) *Government action plan for small businesses.* Order by email from: publications@dti.gsi.gov.uk. Online version also available at: http://www.sbs.gov.uk/ [accessed 15 September 2004].

DEPARTMENT OF TRANSPORT, LOCAL GOVERNMENT AND THE REGIONS (2001) *Strong local leadership – quality public services.* White Paper. London: Office of the Deputy Prime Minister. Online version available at http://www.odpm.gov.uk/stellent/groups/odpm_localgov/documents/page/odpm_locgov_605682.hcsp [accessed 14 September 2004].

DOLAN, S. (1995) A different use of natural resources. *People Management.* Vol.1, No. 20, 5 October. 36–40.

DOUGHERTY, D. (1999) Organizing for innovation. In S.R. CLEGG, C. HARDY and W.R. NORD (eds) *Managing organizations: current issues.* London: Sage. 174–189.

DRUCKER, P. (1993) *Post-capitalist society.* Oxford: Butterworth-Heinemann.

DRUMMOND, J. (2004) A matter of principle. *People Management.* Vol. 10, No. 12, 17 June. 42.

DULEWICZ, V. and HIGGS, M. (1999) *Making sense of emotional intelligence.* ASE (tel. UK: 01753 850333).

DURMAN, P. (2003) Tip of the iceberg. *Sunday Times.* 26 October. 3.5.

EISENHARDT, K.M. and SANTOS, F.M. (2002) Knowledge-based view: a new theory of strategy? In A. PETTIGREW, H. THOMAS and R. WHITTINGTON (eds) *Handbook of strategy and management.* London: Sage. 139–164.

ELFRING, T. and VOLBERDA, H.W. (2001) Multiple futures of strategy synthesis: shifting boundaries, dynamic capabilities and strategy configuration. In H.W. VOLBERDA and T. ELFRING (eds) *Rethinking strategy.* London: Sage. 245–285.

ELY, R. and THOMAS, D. (2001). Cultural diversity at work: the effects of diversity perspectives on work group processes and outcomes. *Administrative Science Quarterly.* Vol. 46, No. 2, June. 229–275.

EMMOTT, M. (2004) Britain's real working lives. *People Management.* Vol. 10, No. 13, 30 June. 14–15.

EMMOTT, M. and HARRIS, L. (2004) *Shared human resources pilots.* London: Chartered Institute of Personnel and Development.

EMPLOYERS' ORGANISATION FOR LOCAL GOVERNMENT (2003) *Guide to workforce planning in local authorities.* Available online at http://www.lg-employers.gov.uk/recruit/working_planning [accessed 25 September 2004].

EMPLOYMENT DEPARTMENT GROUP (1991) *A strategy for skills: Guidance from the Secretary of State for Employment on training, vocational education and enterprise.* London: Department of Employment.

ENGINEERING EMPLOYERS FEDERATION AND CIPD (2003). *Maximising employee potential and business performance: the role of high performance working.* London: Chartered Institute of Personnel and Development.

EVANS, T. (2004) Why Tomlinson is so depressing. *Independent: Education and Careers.* 21 October. 3.

FACTEAU, J.A., DOBBINS, G.H., RUSSELL, J.E.A., LADD, R.T. and KUDISCH, J.A. (1995) The influence of general perceptions of the training environment on pretraining motivation and perceived training transfer. *Journal of Management.* Vol. 21, No. 1. 1–25.

FAIRBAIRN, J. (1991) Plugging the gap in training needs analysis. *Personnel Management.* February. 43–45.

FIELD, A. (2001) How to work with the new ISO 9001. *People Management.* Vol 7, No. 24, 6 December. 48–49.

FIELD, J. (2000) *Lifelong learning and the new educational order.* Stoke on Trent: Trentham Books.

FLETCHER, C. (2004) *Appraisal and feedback: making performance review work.* London: Chartered Institute of Personnel and Development.

FLOYD, S.W. and WOOLDRIDGE, B. (1994a) Middle management behaviour, dynamic capability, and organizational performance. *Working Paper.* Amherst: Universities of Connecticut and Massachusetts.

FLOYD, S.W. and WOOLDRIDGE, B. (1994b) Dinosaurs or dynamos? Recognizing middle management's strategic role. *Academy of Management Executive.* Vol. 8, No. 4. 47–57.

FOMBRUN, C., TICHY, N.M. and DEVANNA, M.A. (eds) (1984) *Strategic human resource management.* New York: Wiley.

FOSTER, C. and HARRIS, L. (2004) *'Easy to say but difficult to do' – managerial perspectives on implementing diversity in retailing.* Ian Beardwell prizewinning research paper presented at the CIPD Professional Standards Conference, Keele University, 28–30 June. Nottingham: Nottingham Business School, Nottingham Trent University. (CD Rom).

FOWLER, A. (1996) *Employee induction: a good start.* 3rd edn. London: Institute of Personnel and Development.

FREEMAN, R. and GILBERT, D. (1988) *Corporate strategy and the search for ethics.* Englewood Cliffs, NJ: Prentice-Hall.

FULLAN, M. (2001) Reform and results: the miraculous turnaround of English public education. *(Canadian) Globe and Mail.* 4 September. Online version also available at http://www.saee.bc.ca/2002 [accessed 14 August 2004].

FULLER, A. and UNWIN, L. (2003) Learning as apprentices in the contemporary UK workplace: creating and managing expansive and restrictive participation. *Journal of Education and Work.* Vol. 16, No. 4.

GALBRAITH, J.R. and NATHANSON, D. (1978) *Strategy implementation.* St Paul, MN: West Publishing.

GARNETT, J. (1992) My biggest mistake. *Independent on Sunday.* 8 March.

GARROW, V. (1997) *A guide to the implementation of 360-degree feedbac*k. Horsham: Roffey Park Institute. Online ordering at http://www.roffeypark.com

GARROW, V. (2003) *Managing on the edge: psychological contracts in transition.* Horsham: Roffey Park Institute. Online ordering at http://www.roffeypark.com

GARVEY, B. (2004) Call a rose by any other name and perhaps it's a bramble? *International Journal of Development and Learning in Organizations.* Vol 18, No. 2. 6–8.

GARVEY, B. AND WILLIAMSON, B. (2002) *Beyond knowledge management: dialogue, creativity and the corporate curriculum.* Harlow: Financial Times & Prentice Hall.

GHOSHAL, S. and BARTLETT, C.A. (1994) Linking organizational context and managerial action: the dimension of quality of management. *Strategic Management Journal*, Special Summer Issue. Vol. 15. 91–112.

GILLEY, J. W. and EGGLAND, S. A. (1989) *Principles of human resource development.* Maidenhead: Addison Wesley.

GINSBERG, A. (1994) Minding the competition: from mapping to mastery. *Strategic Management Journal, Winter Special Issue.* Vol.15. 153–174.

GLOVER, C. (2002a) Good for the soul. *People Management.* Vol. 8, No. 14, 11 July. 29–31.

GLOVER, C. (2002b) A common good. *People Management.* Vol. 8, No. 20, 10 October. 38–9.

GOLEMAN, D. (1992) Leadership that gets results. *Harvard Business Review.* March–April.

GOLEMAN, D. (1998) *Working with emotional intelligence.* London: Bloomsbury.

GORMAN, T. (2000) C's the opportunity. *People Management.* Vol. 6, No. 7, 30 March. 57.

GRATTON, L. (2003a) Paradise Club. *People Management.* Vol. 9, No. 23, 20 November. 35–37.

GRATTON, L. (2003b) The Humpty Dumpty effect. *People Management.* Vol. 9, No. 9, 11 May. 18.

GRATTON, L. (2003c) The HR matrix reloaded. *People Management.* Vol. 9, No. 12, 1 June. 21.

GREEN, K. (1999) Offensive thinking. *People Managemen*t. Vol. 5, No. 8, 22 April. 27.

GREGORY, R.L. (ed) (1998) *The Oxford companion to the mind.* Oxford: Oxford University Press.

GRIBBEN, R. (2004) An investment in learning. *Daily Telegraph.* 25 June. 31.

GRIFFITHS, J. (2004a) NHS teamwork is called into question. *People Management.* Vol. 10, No. 13, 30 June. 12.

GRIFFITHS, J. (2004b) Civil unrest. *People Management.* Vol. 10, No. 15, 29 July. 26–30.

GRIFFITHS, W. (2002) Performance testing. *People Management.* Vol. 8, No. 8, 18 April. 65.

GRUGULIS, L., VINCENT, S. and HEBSON, G. (2003). The future of professional work: the rise of the 'network form' and the decline of discretion. *Human Resource Management Journal.* Vol. 13, No. 2. 45–60.

GUARDIAN (2004) Education reform: a new school consensus. *Guardian*, leader. 18 February. 23.

GUEST, D. and KING, Z. (2001) Personnel's paradox. *People Management.* Vol.7, No.19, 27 September. 24–29.

GUEST, D., KING, Z., CONWAY, N., MICHIE, J. and SHEEHAN-QUINN, M. (2001) *Voices from the boardroom*. London: CIPD.

HACKETT, G. and WOODS, R. (2004) Tomorrow this man will unveil a 10-year plan to revolutionise British schooling.... *The Sunday Times*. 17 October. 1.15.

HALL, D.T. (1984) Human resource development and organisational effectiveness. In D. FOMBRUN, N.M. TICHY and M.A. DEVANNA (eds) *Strategic human resource management*. New York: Wiley. pp159–181.

HALL, G. (2004) Work in progress. *People Management*. Vol. 10, No. 19, 30 September. 25.

HALL, R. (1993) A framework linking intangible resources and capabilities to sustainable competitive advantage. *Strategic Management Journal*. Vol.14. 607–618.

HALL, R. (1996) Supply chain management – the challenges for the 21st century. *Paper presented to the CIPS Conference at Durham University Business School*, 9 May. Durham: Durham University Business School.

HAMBLIN, A. C. (1974) *Evaluation and control of training*. Maidenhead: McGraw-Hill.

HAMEL, G. (1991) Competition for competence and inter-partner learning within international strategic alliances. *Strategic Management Journal*. Vol. 12. 83–103.

HAMES, T. (2004) A one-size exam won't pass. *The Times*. 19 October. 17.

HAMILTON, A. (2004) The continuing problem of British management. *Independent*. 21 October. 39.

HANDY, C. B. (1985) *Understanding organizations*. 3rd edn. Harmondsworth: Penguin.

HARLOW, T. and SMITH, A. (2003). Necessary measures. *People Management*. Vol.9, No. 23, 20 November. 48.

HARRISON, R. (1988) *Training and development*. London: Institute of Personnel Management.

HARRISON, R. (1996a) Action learning: route or barrier to the learning organization? *Employee Counselling Today, The Journal of Workplace Learning*. Vol. 8, No.6. 27–38.

HARRISON, R. (1996b) Developing human resources for productivity. In J. PROKOPENKO and K. NORTH (eds) *Productivity and quality management: a modular programme: part II*. Geneva: International Labour Office and Tokyo: Asian Productivity Association. 1–53.

HARRISON, R. (1999) *The training and development audit: an eight-step audit to measure, assess and enhance the performance of your organisation's training and development*. Cambridge: Cambridge Strategy Publications.

HARRISON, R. (2004) *Learning and development revision guide, 2005*. 2nd edn. London: Chartered Institute of Personnel and Development.

HARRISON, R. and KESSELS, J. (2003a) *Human resource development in a knowledge economy: an organisational view*. Basingstoke: Palgrave Macmillan.

HARRISON, R. and KESSELS, J. (2003b) Human resource development: key organisational process in a knowledge economy. In *Proceedings of the 4th Conference on HRD research and practice 2003: Groupe Esc Toulouse*. CD produced by The Andorra Group Limited.

HARRISON, R. and MILLER, S. (1993) Doctors in management: two into one won't go – or will it? *Journal of Executive Development*. Vol. 6, No. 2. 9–13.

HARRISON, R. and MILLER, S. (1999) The contribution of clinical directors to the strategic capability of the organisation. *British Journal of Management*. Vol. 10, No.1. 23–39.

HARRISON, R., MILLER, S. and GIBSON, A. (1993) Doctors in management, part II: getting into action. *Journal of Executive Development*. Vol. 6, No. 4. 3–7.

HARRISON, R. and SMITH, R. (2001) Practical Judgement: its implications for knowledge development and strategic capability. In B. HELLGREN and J. LOWSTEDT (eds) *Management in the thought-full enterprise. A socio-cognitive approach to the organization of human resources*. Bergen: Fagbokforlaget. 195–213.

HART, S. and BANBURY, C. (1994) How strategy-making processes can make a difference. *Strategic Management Journal*. Vol. 15. 251–269.

HEDLUND, G. (1994) A model of knowledge management and the N-Form corporation. *Strategic Management Journal, Summer Special Issue*. Vol. 15. 73–90.

HENDRY, C. (1995) *Human resource management: a strategic approach to employment*. London: Butterworth-Heinemann.

HENDRY, C., JONES, A., ARTHUR, M.B. and PETTIGREW, A.M. (1991) Human resource development in small to medium sized enterprises. *Research Paper No. 88*. Sheffield: Employment Department.

HERTZBERG, F. (1966) *Work and the nature of man*. London: Staples Press.

HEWITT, G. (2003) Come together. *People Management*. Vol. 9, No. 21, 23 October. 36–38.

HEWITT, P. (2004) On the up. *People Management*. Vol. 10, No.4, 26 February. 28–30.

HIGGINBOTTOM, K. (2003) HR in the spotlight. *People Management*. Vol. 9, No. 23, 20 November. 12–13.

HIGGINBOTTOM, K. (2004) Firms ignoring staff opinion. *People Management*. Vol. 10, No. 5, 11 March. 7.

HIGGINBOTTOM, K. and PICKARD, J. (2003) Smooth operations. *People Management*. Vol. 9, No. 21, 23 October. 41–47.

HILLS, H. and FRANCIS, P. (1999) Interaction learning. *People Management*. Vol. 5, No.14, 15 July. 48–49.

HISCOCK, D. (2004) The only way is up. *People Management*. Vol. 10, No. 14, 15 July. 37–39.

HOLBECHE, L. (2003) *High performance organisation checklist*. Horsham: Roffey Park Institute.

HONEY, P. and MUMFORD, A. (1992) *A manual of learning styles*. 3rd edn. Maidenhead: Honey.

HOPE, K. (2004a) Back to basics. *People Management*. Vol. 10, No.15, 29 July. 14–15.

HOPE, K. (2004b) NHS support staff get left on waiting list for training. *People Management*. Vol. 10, No. 9, 6 May. 13.

HOSMER, L.T. (1994) Strategic planning as if ethics mattered. *Strategic Management Journal, Summer Special Issue*. Vol. 15. 17–34.

HOSPITAL, J.T. (2001) *Strangers in a strange land.* Talk on Radio 4. 7.45–8.00 pm, 18 August.

HUSELID, M.A. (1995) The impact of human resource management: an agenda for the 1990s. *International Journal of Human Resource Management.* Vol. 1, No.1. 17–43.

HUTCHINSON, S. and PURCELL, J. (2003) *Bringing policies to life: the vital role of front line managers in people management.* London: Chartered Institute of Personnel and Development.

HUYSMAN, M. and DE WIT, D. (2002) *Knowledge sharing in practice.* Dordrecht: Kluwer Academic Publishers.

ILES, P. and MABEY, C. (1993) Managerial career development programmes: effectiveness, availability and acceptability. *British Journal of Management.* Vol. 4, No. 3. 103–111.

INTERNATIONAL SURVEY RESEARCH (2002) *UK plc: leader or follower?* London: ISR. Online version also available at: http://www.isrsurveys.com/en/pdf/insight/ukplc_leader_follower.pdf [accessed 29 August 2004].

JACKSON, C., ARNOLD, J., NICHOLSON, N. and WATTS, A.G. (1996) Managing careers in 2000 and beyond. *Institute for Employment Studies Report 304.* Brighton: IES. Summary available online at http://www.employment-studies.co.uk

JACKSON, L. (1989) Transforming managerial performance – a competency approach. In *Proceedings of Institute of Personnel Management National Conference, Harrogate.* October. London: Institute of Personnel Management.

JACKSON, S.E. and SCHULER, R.S. (1995) Understanding human resource management in the context of organizations and their environments. *Annual Review of Psychology.* Vol. 46. 237–264.

JACKSON, T. (2000) *Career development.* London: Institute of Personnel and Development.

JAVAID, M. (2002) Seismic levelling. *People Management.* Vol. 8, No. 2, 24 January. 18.

JOHNSON, R. (2001) Lessons for learndirect. *People Management.* Vol. 27, No. 23, 22 November. 7.

JOHNSON, R. (2003). Coaching and leadership: the inside view. *Training Journal.* October. 12–15.

JOHNSTON R. (1996) Power and influence and the L&D function. In J. STEWART and J. MCGOLDRICK (eds) *Human resource development: perspectives, strategies and practice.* London: Pitman. 180–195.

JONES, R.A. and GOSS, D.M. (1991) The role of training strategy in reducing skills shortages: some evidence from a survey of small firms. *Personnel Review.* Vol. 20, No.2. 24–30.

JUDGE, E. (2004) 'Stealth chancellor' cashes in on new business link status. *The Times.* 25 November. 65.

KANDOLA, R. and FULLERTON, J. (1998) *Diversity in action: managing the mosaic.* 2nd edn. London: Chartered Institute of Personnel and Development.

KAPLAN, R. and NORTON, D. (2001) Marked impact. *People Management.* Vol. 7, No. 21, 25 November. 52–57.

KARTEN, N. (2001) *How to establish service level agreements.* Randolph, MA: Karten Associates.

Order from slaO@nkarten.com, or see excerpts on http://www.ServiceLevel Agreements.com [accessed 19 September 2004].

KAZMIER, L.J. (1964) *Principles of management: a program for self-instruction*. New York: McGraw-Hill.

KEALEY, T. (2004). Only Lenin would rejoice in how we fund our universities. *Daily Telegraph*. 2 December. 26.

KEEP, E. (2002) Joined up thinking. *People Management*. Vol. 8, No.18, 12 September. 53.

KENNY, J. et al (1979) *Manpower training and development*. 2nd edn. London: Institute of Personnel Management.

KERSTEN, A. (2000) Diversity management: dialogue, dialectics and diversion. *Journal of Organisational Change Management*. Vol. 13, No. 3. 235–248.

KESSELS, J.W.M. (1996) Knowledge productivity and the corporate curriculum. In J.F. SCHREINEMAKERS (ed) *Knowledge management, organization, competence and methodology*. Würzburg: Ergon Verlag. 168–174.

KESSELS, J. and HARRISON, R. (1998). External consistency: the key to management development? *Management Learning*. Vol. 29, No.1. 39–68.

KESSLER, I. (2001) Responsibility can work wonders for customer care. *People Management*. Vol. 7, No. 23, 22 November. 56.

KING, D. (1964) *Training within the organization*. London: Tavistock.

KING, Z. (2004) *Career management: A CIPD guide*. London: Chartered Institute of Personnel and Development.

KINGSTON, P. (2004) Crisis, what crisis? *Guardian 'Further'*. 13 April. 15.

KIRJAVAINEN, P. (2001) Strategic learning in a knowledge-intensive organisation. In H.W. VOLBERDA and T. ELFRING (eds) *Rethinking strategy*. London: Sage. 172–190.

KIRKPATRICK, D.L. (1960) Techniques for evaluating training programmes. *Journal of the American Society for Training and Development*. Vol. 14. 13–18, 25–32.

KOENIG, C. and VAN WIJK, G. (2001) Managing beyond boundaries: the dynamics of trust in alliances. In H.W. VOLBERDA and T. ELFRING (eds) *Rethinking strategy*. London: Sage. 116–127.

KOLB, D. A., RUBIN, I. M. and MCINTYRE, J. M. (1974) *Organizational psychology: an experiential approach*. Englewood Cliffs, NJ: Prentice Hall.

KOTTER, J.P. (1996) *Leading change*. Boston, MA: Harvard Business School Press.

LANDALE, A. (2003) Distance mentoring: a must-have alternative to training. *Training Journal*. October. 32–35.

LANK, E. (2002) Head to head. *People Management*. Vol. 8, No. 4, 21 February. 46–49.

LANK, E. and WINDLE, I. (2003) Catch me if you can. *People Management*. Vol. 9, No. 3, 6 February. 40–42.

LARSEN, H.H. (1994) Key issues in training and development. In C. BREWSTER and A. HEGEWISCH (eds) *Policy and practice in European human resource management: the Pricewaterhouse Cranfield survey*. London: Routledge. 107–121.

LAVE, J. and WENGER, E. (1991) *Situated learning – legitimate peripheral participation.* Cambridge: Cambridge University Press.

LEARNING AND SKILLS COUNCIL (2004a) *National employers' skills survey, 2003: key findings.* Coventry: LSC. Online version also available at http://www.lsc.gov.uk [accessed 22 August 2004].

LEARNING AND SKILLS COUNCIL (2004b) *Widening adult participation: policy and strategy.* Coventry: Learning and Skills Council, Skills and Education Network. email: senet@lsc.gov.uk. Online version also available at http://senet.lsc.gov.uk/guide2/wide participationpolicy/index.cfm [accessed 25 August 2004].

LEE, G. and PICK, L. (2004) How to buy coaching. *People Management.* Vol.9, No. 5, 11 March. 50–51.

LEE, R. (1996) The 'pay-forward' view of training. *People Management.* Vol. 2, No. 3. 30–32.

LEGGE, K. (1995) *Human resource management: rhetorics and realities.* London: Macmillan.

LEGGE, K. (1998) The morality of HRM. In C. MABEY, G. SALAMAN and J.STOREY (eds) *Strategic human resource management: a reader.* London: Open University and Sage. 18–29.

LEONARD, T. (2004) BBC's £35m training course is a fiasco, says expert. *Daily Telegraph.* 2 October. 9.

LIDBETTER, K. (2003). For good measure. *People Management.* Vol. 8, No. 1, 9 January. 46.

LIKERT, R. (1961) *New patterns of management.* New York: McGraw-Hill.

LIPPITT, G. (1983) Management development as the key to organisational renewal. *Journal of Management Development.* Vol. 1, No. 2. 36–39.

LITTLE, S. QUINTAS, P. and RAY, T. (eds) *Managing knowledge: an essential reader.* London: Sage.

LLOYD, C. (2003) *High involvement work systems: the only option for high skills sectors.* Oxford and Warwick Universities: SKOPE. Online version also available at: http://www. econ.ox.ac.uk/skope [accessed 25 August 2004].

LOCKETT, J. (1992) *Effective performance management: a strategic guide to getting the best from people.* London: Kogan Page.

LORENZ, C. (1994) Dissent in the measurement ranks. *Financial Times.* 25 March. 16.

LYNCH, S. (2003) Is it safe to hand HR tasks over to non-experts? *People Management.* Vol. 9, No. 18, 11 September. 56.

MABEY, C. and ILES, P. (eds) (1994) *Managing learning.* London: Routledge and Open University.

MABEY, C. and RAMIREZ, M. (2004) *Developing managers: a European perspective: a survey of management training & development in the United Kingdom, France, Germany, Spain, Denmark, Norway & Romania.* London: Chartered Management Institute. Online version also available at: http://www.managers.org.uk/institute/content_toc_description_1.asp? category=3&id=234&id=211&id=44 [accessed 1 October 2004].

MACAULAY, S. and HARDING, N. (1996) Drawing up a new careers contract. *People Management.* Vol. 2, No. 7, 4 April. 34–35.

MACKINNON, I. (2003) Too much of a good thing. *People Management*. Vol. 9, No. 6, 20 March. 50.

MACKINNON, I. (2004) Make the grade. *People Management*. Vol. 10, No. 20, 14 October. 50.

MAGER, R.F. (1984) *Preparing instructional objectives*. California: Fearon.

MAHONEY, C. (2003) On good authority. *People Management*. Vol. 9, No. 5, 6 March. 28–31.

MANOCHA, R. (2002) Partnership on the line. *People Management*. Vol. 8, No. 2, 24 January. 12.

MANOCHA, R. (2003) Catch-22. *People Management*. Vol. 9, No.20, 9 October. 40–43.

MANOCHA, R. (2004) Skill shortages 'are overstated'. *People Management*. Vol. 10, No. 9, 6 May. 12.

MANWARING, T. and WOOD, S. (1985) The ghost in the labour process: job redesign. In D. KNIGHT (ed) *Critical perspectives on the labour process*. Aldershot: Gower.

MARTON, F. and RAMSDEN, P. (1988) What does it take to improve learning? In P. RAMSDEN (ed) *Improving learning: new perspectives*. London: Kogan Page.

MASON, G. (2002) High skills utilisation under mass higher education: graduate employment in service industries in Britain. *Journal of Education and Work*. Vol. 15, No. 4. 427–456.

MASON, R. and MITROFF, I. (1981) *Challenging strategic planning assumptions*. New York: John Wiley & Sons.

MATTHEWS, J.H. and CANDY, P.C. (1999) New dimensions in the dynamics of learning and knowledge. In D. BOUD and J. GARRICK (eds) *Understanding learning at work*. London: Routledge. 47–64.

MAYO, A. (2004) *Creating a learning and development strategy: the HR partner's guide to developing people*. 2nd edn. London: Chartered Institute of Personnel and Development.

MCGREGOR, D. (1960) *The human side of enterprise*. Maidenhead: McGraw-Hill.

MERALI, Y. (1999) Informed decisions. *People Management*. Vol. 5, No. 12, 17 June. 59–62.

MERRICK, N. (2004) Modern romance. *People Management*. Vol. 10, No. 6, 25 March. 16–17.

MERRICK, N. and PICKARD, J. (2002) Whistle and bells. *People Management*. Vol. 8, No. 3, 7 February. 44–45.

MEZIROW, J.A. (1985) A critical theory of self-directed learning. In S. BROOKFIELD (ed) *Self-directed learning: from theory to practice*. San Francisco, CA: Jossey-Bass.

MILES, R. and SNOW, C. (1995) The new network firm: a spherical structure built on a human investment philosophy. *Organizational Dynamics*. Vol. 23, No.4. 5–18.

MILLER, L., RANKIN, N. and NEATHEY, F. (2001) *Competency frameworks in UK organisations: Research report*. London: Chartered Institute of Personnel and Development.

MILLER, R. and STEWART, J. (1999) Opened university. *People Management*. Vol. 5, No. 12, 17 June. 42–45.

MILLER, S., HICKSON, D.J. and WILSON, D.C. (1999) Decision-making in organizations. In S.R. CLEGG, C. HARDY and W.R. NORD (eds) *Managing organizations: current issues*. London: Sage. 43–62.

MINTZBERG, H. (1973) *The nature of managerial work*. New York: Harper and Row.

MINTZBERG, H. (2004) *Managers not MBAs*. FT Prentice Hall.

MOHRMAN, S.A. and LAWLER III, E.E. (1999) The new Human Resources management: creating the strategic business partnership. In R.S. SCHULER and S.E. JACKSON (eds) *Strategic human resource management*. Oxford: Blackwell. 433–447.

MORGAN, G. (1997) *Images of organization*. 2nd edn. London: Sage.

MORTON, B. and WILSON, A. (2003) Double vision. *People Management*. Vol. 9, No. 20, 9 October. 37–38.

MOXON, G.R. (1943) *The functions of a personnel department*. London: Institute of Personnel Management.

MOYNAGH, M and WORSLEY, R. (2001) *Tomorrow's workplace: fulfilment or stress?* The Tomorrow Project, tel. 0115 925 1114. See also http://www.tomorrowproject.net [accessed 21 September 2004].

MUMFORD, A., ROBINSON, G. and STRADLING, D. (1987) *Developing directors: the learning processes*. Sheffield: Manpower Services Commission.

NADLER, L. (1970) *Developing human resources*. Houston: Gulf.

NADLER, L. (1992) HRD – where has it been, where is it going? *Studies in Continuing Education*. Vol. 14, No. 2. 104–114.

NATIONAL COMMITTEE OF INQUIRY INTO HIGHER EDUCATION (1997) *Higher education in the learning society ('The Dearing Report')*. London: HMSO.

NEWTON, T. and FINDLAY, P. (1998) Playing God? The performance of appraisal. In C. MABEY, G. SALAMAN and J. STOREY (eds) *Strategic human resource management: a reader*. London: Open University Business School and Sage. 128–143.

NOE, R.A. (1986) Trainee attributes and attitudes: neglected influences of training effectiveness. *Academy of Management Review*. 11. 736–749.

NONAKA, I. (1991) The knowledge-creating company. *Harvard Business Review*. November–December. 96–104.

NONAKA, I. (1994) A dynamic theory of organizational knowledge creation. *Organization Science*. Vol. 5, No.1. 14–37.

ONIONS, C.T. (ed) (1973) *The shorter Oxford English dictionary*. 3rd edn. Oxford: Oxford University Press.

OPEN UNIVERSITY (2004) *History of the Open University*. Online version also available at: http://www3.open.ac.uk/media/factsheets [accessed 25 August 2004].

ORGANISATION FOR ECONOMIC CO-OPERATION AND DEVELOPMENT (2001) *The well-being of nations: the role of human and social capital*. Paris: OECD.

ORR, J.E. (1990) Sharing knowledge, celebrating identity: community memory in a service culture. In D.S. MIDDLETON and D. EDWARDS (eds) *Collective remembering*. Newbury Park, CA: Sage. 169–198.

PAN, S.L. (1999) Knowledge management at Buckman Laboratories. In H. SCARBROUGH and J. SWAN (eds) *Case studies in knowledge management*. London: Institute of Personnel and Development. 76–84.

PARTRIDGE, B. (1989) The problem of supervision. In K. SISSON (ed) *Personnel management in Britain*. Oxford: Blackwell. 203–221.

PASCALE, R. (1990) *Managing on the edge*. New York: Viking.

PASSMORE, J. (2003) Goal-orientated coaching. *The occupational psychologist: Special Issue Coaching Psychology*. No. 49, August. 30–33.

PATRIOTTA, G. (1999) Multicorp: knowledge management in product development. In H. SCARBROUGH and J. SWAN (eds) *Case studies in knowledge management*. London: Institute of Personnel and Development. 68–75.

PATTERSON, M. G., WEST, M. A., LAWTHOM, R. and NICKEL, L. S. (1997) *Impact of people management practices on business performance*. London: Institute of Personnel and Development.

PEARSALL, J. and TRUMBLE, B. (eds) (1996) *The Oxford English reference dictionary*. 2nd edn. Oxford: Oxford University Press.

PECCEI, R. and ROSENTHAL, P. (2001) Delivering customer-oriented behaviour through empowerment: an empirical test of HRM assumptions. *Journal of Management Studies*. Vol. 38, No. 6.

PEDLER, M., BURGOYNE, J. and BOYDELL, T. (1991) *The learning company: a strategy for sustainable development*. Maidenhead: McGraw-Hill.

PENNINGS, J. M. (2001) Configurations and the firm in current strategic management. In H.W. VOLBERDA and T. ELFRING (eds) *Rethinking strategy*. London: Sage. 240–244.

PEOPLE MANAGEMENT (2002a) World Bank fails to 'set an example on corruption'. *People Management*, letter. Vol. 8, No. 21, 24 October. 26.

PEOPLE MANAGEMENT (2002b) Trainers face race risk. *People Management*, letter. Vol. 8, No. 9, 2 May. 11.

PEOPLE MANAGEMENT (2003) Quality of adult learning has risen. *People Management*. Vol 9, No. 24, 4 December. 10.

PEOPLE MANAGEMENT (2004a) Firms 'must invest' to plug skills gap. *People Management*. Vol. 10, No. 13, 30 June. 10.

PEOPLE MANAGEMENT (2004b) Police diversity drive fails. *People Management*. Vol. 10, No. 13, 30 June. 11.

PEOPLE MANAGEMENT (2004c) Britannia focuses on attitude, not skills. *People Management*. Vol. 10, No.1, 3 June. 12.

PERFORMANCE AND INNOVATION UNIT (2001) *In demand: adult skills for the 21st century Part 1*. Printed copies available from strategy@cabinet-office.x.gsi.gov.uk. Online version also available at http://www.strategy.gov.uk/su/wfd_1/report [accessed 17 July 2004].

PETTIGREW, A.M. (1985) *The awakening giant: continuity and change in ICI*. Oxford: Blackwell.

PETTIGREW, A.M. (1987) Context and action in transformation of the firm. *Journal of Management Studies*. Vol. 24, No 6. 649–670.

PETTIGREW, A.M., ARTHUR, M.B. and HENDRY, C. (1990) Training and human resource management in small to medium sized enterprises: a critical review of the literature and a model for future research. *Research Paper No. 56*. Sheffield: Employment Department.

PETTIGREW, A.M., JONES, G.R. and REASON, P.W. (1982) *Training and development roles in their organisational setting.* Sheffield: Manpower Services Commission.

PETTIGREW, A.M., THOMAS, H. and WHITTINGTON, R. (2002) Strategic management: the strengths and limitations of a field. In A. PETTIGREW, H. THOMAS and R. WHITTINGTON (eds) *Handbook of strategy and management.* London: Sage. 3–30.

PHILLIPS, J. (2001) How to measure returns on HR investment. *People Management.* Vol. 7, No. 23, 22 November. 48–50.

PHILLIPS, P.P. and PHILLIPS, J.J. (2001) *In action: measuring return on investment, volume 3.* VA: American Society of Training and Development.

PHILPOTT, J. (2003a) Hit the right note. *People Management.* Vol. 9, No. 19, 25 September. 22.

PHILPOTT, J. (2003b) The great stakeholder debate. *People Management.* Vol. 9, No. 16, 7 August. 20.

PHILPOTT, J. (2003c) Boxing clever. *People Management.* Vol. 9, No. 25, 18 December. 20.

PHILPOTT, J. (2004a) A product of our imagination. *People Management.* Vol.10, No. 6, 25 March. 24.

PHILPOTT, J. (2004b) Training: the economic context. In CHARTERED INSTITUTE OF PERSONNEL AND DEVELOPMENT. *Reflections: new trends in training and development.* London: CIPD. 5–9.

PICKARD, J. (1995) Food for thought. *People Management.* Vol. 1, No. 20. 30–31.

PICKARD, J. (1999) Sense and sensitivity. *People Management,* Vol. 5, No. 21, 28 October. 48–56.

PICKARD, J. (2001) How Abbey are they? *People Management.* Vol. 7, No. 25, 27 December. 27.

PICKARD, J. (2002) An ideal solution. *People Management.* Vol. 8, No. 6, 21 March. 33–34.

PICKARD, J. (2003a) A clearer provision. *People Management.* Vol. 9, No.12, 12 June. 28–34.

PICKARD, J. (2003b) Traditional jobs 'are here to stay'. *People Management.* Vol. 9, No. 14, 10 July. 11.

PICKARD, J. (2003c) Joint effort. *People Management.* Vol. 9, No.15, 24 July. 33–35.

PICKARD, J. (2004) One step beyond. *People Management.* Vol. 10, No. 13, 30 June. 27–31.

POLANYI, M. (1966) *The tacit dimension.* New York: Anchor Day Books.

POTTINGER, J. (1989) Engineering change through pay. *Personnel Management.* Vol. 21, No. 10, 10 October. 73–74.

PRAHALAD, C.K. and RAMASWAMY, V. (2002) The co-creation connection. *Strategy and Business.* Issue 27, 2nd quarter. 50–61.

PRATT, M.G. and FOREMAN, P.O. (2000) Classifying managerial responses to multiple organisational identities. *Academy of Management Review.* Vol. 23, No.1. 18–42.

PURCELL, J., KINNIE, N., HUTCHINSON, S., RAYTON, B. and SWART, J. (2003) *Understanding the people and performance link: unlocking the black box.* London: Chartered Institute of Personnel and Development.

PUTNAM, R. (2000) *Bowling alone: the collapse and revival of American community.* New York: Simon & Schuster.

RAINBIRD, H. (2003) A further education. *Personnel Management*. Vol. 9, No. 18, 11 September. 48.

RAINBIRD, H., MUNRO, A. and HOLLY, L. (2004). Exploring the concept of employer demand for skills and qualifications: case studies from the public sector. In C. WARHURST, I. GRUGULIS and E. KEEP (eds) *The skills that matter*. Houndmills, Basingstoke: Palgrave Macmillan.

RAINBIRD, H., MUNRO, A. and SENKER, P. (2003). Running fast to stay in the same place: the intended and unintended consequences of government policy for workplace learning. *Paper presented to the Network/SKOPE meeting, University of Warwick*. 14 March. Helen.Rainbird@northampton.ac.uk.

RANA, E. (2002) A class above the rest. *People Management*. Vol. 8, No.9, 2 May. 15.

RANA, E. (2003) Council appraisals discriminate. *People Management*. Vol. 9, No. 2. 11.

RANKINE, K. (2004) Putting customers first helped store come from behind in High St stakes. *Daily Telegraph*, 21 April. 6.

RAPER, P., ASHTON, D., FELSTEAD, A and STOREY, K. (1997) Toward the learning organisation? Explaining current trends in training practice in the UK. *International Journal of Training and Development*. Vol. 1, No. 1. 9–21.

RAY, T. (2002) Managing Japanese organizational knowledge creation: the difference. In S. LITTLE, P. QUINTAS and T. RAY (eds) *Managing knowledge: an essential reader*. London: Sage. pp102–138.

REFAUSSE, J. (1996) Self-knowledge to lift career spirits. *People Management*. Vol. 2, No.10, 16 May. 34–35.

REID, M.A., BARRINGTON, H. and BROWN, M. (2004) *Human resource development*. 7th edn. London: Chartered Institute of Personnel and Development.

REYNOLDS, J. (2002) Method and madness. *People Management*. Vol. 8, No.7, 4 April. 42–43.

REYNOLDS, J., CALEY, L. and MASON, R. (2002) *How do people learn?* London: CIPD. For an online module see: http://www.cipd.co.uk/subjects/misc/_ppllrnidx.htm?IsSrchRes=1 [accessed 25 August 2004].

REYNOLDS, J. and SLOMAN, M. (2004) In the driving seat. *People Management*. Vol. 10, No. 3, 12 February. 40–42.

RICE, R., MAJCHRAZAK, A., KING, N., BA, S. and MALHOTRA, A. (2000) Computer mediated interorganizational knowledge sharing: insights from a virtual team innovating using a collaborative tool. In Y. MALHOTRA (ed) *Knowledge management and virtual organizations*. Hershey: Idea Group Publishing. 84–100.

RILEY, K. and SLOMAN, M. (1991) Milestones for the personnel department. *Personnel Management*. Vol. 23, No. 8. 34–37.

ROBERTS, Z. (2003) Fast-track learning. *People Management*. Vol. 9, No. 14, 10 July. 14–15.

RODGER, D. and MABEY, C. (1987) BT's leap forward from assessment centres. *Personnel Management*. Vol. 19, No.7. 32–35.

ROGERS, M.S. (2004) Power to the people managers. *People Management*. Vol. 10, No. 18, 16 September. 25.

ROONEY, B. (2003) Embracing the office revolution. *Daily Telegraph*. 5 June. 12–16.

ROSSET, A. (2002) Marquee competencies. *People Management*. Vol. 8, No. 23, 21 November. 38–41.

RUBERY, J., EARNSHAW, J., MARCHINGTON, M., COOKE, F. and VINCENT, S. (2002) Changing organisational forms and the employment relationship. *Journal of Management Studies*. Vol. 39, No. 5. 645–672.

RYAN, C. (2004) Opinion. *Guardian, Further*. 13 April. 15.

RYLATT, A. (2004) Metrics reloaded. *People Management*. Vol. 10, No. 2, 29 January. 50.

SAMPSON, H. (1992) Vorsprung durch training: how the Germans do it. *Human Resources*. Spring 1992, Issue 5. 41–43.

SANCHEZ, R. (1995) Strategic flexibility in product competition. *Strategic Management Journal*. Vol. 16. 135–159.

SCARBROUGH, H. (2003) Food for thought. *People Management*. Vol. 9, No. 2, 23 January. 32–35.

SCARBROUGH, H. and SWAN, J. (eds) (1999) *Case studies in knowledge management*. London: Institute of Personnel and Development.

SCARBROUGH, H., SWAN, J. and PRESTON, J. (1999) *Knowledge management: a literature review*. London: Institute of Personnel and Development.

SCHEIN, E. H. (1978) *Career dynamics: matching individual and organizational needs*. Reading, MA: Addison Wesley.

SCHENDEL, D. and HOFER, C. (1979) *Strategic management: a new view of business policy and planning*. Boston, MA: Little, Brown.

SCHUCK, G. (1996) Intelligent technology, intelligent workers: a new pedagogy for the high-tech workplace. In K. STARKEY (ed) *How organizations learn*. London: International Thomson Business Press. 199–213.

SCHULTZ, T.W. (1961) Investment in human capital. *American Economic Review*. Vol. 51, No. 1. 1–17.

SENGE, P. M. (1990) *The fifth discipline: the art and practice of the learning organization*. New York: Doubleday.

SENGE, P.M. (1996) The leader's new work: building learning organizations. In K. STARKEY (ed) *How organizations learn*. London: International Thomson Business Press. 288–315.

SEYMOUR, W.D. (1959) *Operator training in industry*. London: Institute of Personnel Management.

SIMMONDS, D. (2004) *Designing and delivering training*. London: Chartered Institute of Personnel and Development.

SIMMONS, C. and VALENTINE, E. (2000) Good mixers. *People Management*. Vol. 6, No. 7, 30 March. 48–50.

SIMMS, J. (2004) Home or away? *People Management*. Vol. 10, No. 11, 3 June. 35–36.

SIMON, H.A. (1945) *Administrative behaviour*. New York: Free Press.

SIMON, H.A. (1955) A behavioural model of rational choice. *Quarterly Journal of Economics*. Vol. 69. 99–118.

SKAPINKER, M. (2002) *Knowledge management: the change agenda*. London: Chartered Institute of Personnel Management.

SLOMAN, M. (2001) *The e-learning revolution*. London: Chartered Institute of Personnel and Development.

SLOMAN, M. (2002a) *Focus on the learner: a change agenda*. London: CIPD. Online version also available at: http://www.cipd.co.uk/changeagendas [accessed 25 August 2004].

SLOMAN, M. (2002b) Outlook expressed. *People Management*. Vol. 8, No. 23, 21 November. 41–42.

SLOMAN, M. (2003) *Training in the age of the learner*. London: Chartered Institute of Personnel and Development.

SLOMAN, M. (2004) Learner drivers. *People Management*. Vol. 10, No. 17, 2 September. 37–38.

SMEWING, C. (2004) Feeling the way. *People Management*. Vol. 10, No. 21, 28 October. 66.

SOLOMON, N. (1999) Culture and difference in workplace learning. In D. BOUD and J. GARRICK (eds) *Understanding learning at work*. London: Routledge. 119–131.

SPARROW, P.R. (1999) Is human resource management in crisis? In R.S. SCHULER and S.E. JACKSON (eds) *Strategic human resource management*. Oxford: Blackwell. 416–432.

SPARROW, P and COOPER, C. (2003) *The employment relationship: key challenges for HR*. Oxford: Butterworth-Heinemann.

SPARROW, P. and HILTROP, J-M. (1994) *European human resource management in transition*. Hemel Hempstead: Prentice Hall.

SPENCER, S. (2004) Size matters. *People Management*. Vol. 10, No. 11, 3 June. 19.

STARKEY, K. (1996) Executive tourism: the dynamics of strategic leadership in the MNC. In K. STARKEY (ed) *How organizations learn*. London: International Thomson Business Press. 368–380.

STERN, E. and SOMMERLAD, E. (1999) *Workplace learning, culture and performance*. London: Institute of Personnel and Development.

STERN, S. (2004) HR: Heading the Revival. *Daily Telegraph Business 2+Jobs*. 26 February. A3.

STEVENS, C. (1985) Assessment centres: the British experience. *Personnel Management*. Vol. 17, No. 7. 28–31.

STEVENS, J. (2000) *High performance working is for everyone*. London: Institute of Personnel and Development/International Labour Organisation.

STEVENS, J. (2001) Summary report of seminar proceedings. In CHARTERED INSTITUTE OF PERSONNEL AND DEVELOPMENT. *Workplace learning in Europe* [summary of the European Workplace Learning Seminar, London, 2 April]. London: CIPD. 7–12.

STEVENS, J. (2003) Employers should lead in developing staff skills. *People Management*. Vol. 9, No. 8, 17 April. 29.

STEVENS, J. and ASHTON, D. (1999) Underperformance appraisal. *People Management*. Vol. 5, No. 14, 15 July. 31–32.

STEWART, J. and HARRIS, L. (2003) HRD and HRM: an uneasy relationship. *People Management.* Vol. 9, No. 19, 25 September. 58.

STEWART, J. and TANSLEY, C. (2002) *Training in the knowledge economy.* London: Chartered Institute of Personnel and Development.

STOREY, J. (1992) *Developments in the management of human resources.* Oxford: Blackwell.

STRATEGY UNIT (2002) *In demand: adult skills for the 21st century Part 2.* Available from strategy@cabinet-office.x.gsi.gov.uk (020 7276 1881). Online version also available at: http:// www.strategy.gov.uk/su/wfd_2/report [accessed 17 July 2004].

STURGES, J., GUEST, D., CONWAY, N. and MACKENZIE DAVEY, K. (2002) A longitudinal study of the relationship between career management and organisational commitment among graduates in the first ten years at work. *Journal of Organisational Behaviour.* Vol. 23. 731–748.

SUNDAY TIMES (2004) Stand up and fight. *Sunday Times* (leader). 17 October. 1.18.

SUTCLIFFE, G. (2004) A problem shared. *People Management.* Vol. 10, No. 21, 28 October. 29.

SWAILES, S. (2002) Organisational commitment: a critique of the construct and measures. *International Journal of Management Reviews.* Vol. 4, No. 2. 155–178.

SWART, J., KINNIE, N. and PURCELL, J. (2003) *People and performance in knowledge-intensive firms: a comparison of six research and technology organisations.* London: Chartered Institute of Personnel and Development.

SWIDLER, A. (1986) Culture in action: symbols and strategies. *American Sociological Review.* Vol 5. 273–286.

TAYLOR, C. (2002) Gold standards. *People Management.* Vol. 8, No. 5, 7 March. 14–15.

TAYLOR, F.W. (1947) *Scientific management.* New York: Harper and Row.

TAYLOR, H. (1991) The systematic training model: corn circles in search of a spaceship? *Management Education and Development.* Vol. 22, part 4. 258–78.

TAYLOR, J. (2001) Growth treatment. *People Management.* Vol. 7, No. 20. 11 October. 48–51.

TEMPLE, M. (2002) Lessons from the real world. *People Management.* Vol. 8, No. 12, 13 June. 25.

TENNANT, M. (1999) Is learning transferable? In D. BOUD and J. GARRICK (eds) *Understanding learning at work.* London: Routledge. 165–179.

TERRY, M. and PURCELL, J. (1997) Return to slender. *People Management.* Vol.3, No. 21, 23 October. 46–47.

THACKER, K. (2002). How to take advantage of diversity. *People Management.* Vol. 8, No. 5, 7 March. 52–53.

THOMSON, I. (2004) The power and the impact. *People Management.* Vol. 10, No.8, 22 April. 15.

TJEPKEMA, S. (2002) Conclusions from case studies and survey. In S. TJEPKEMA, J. STEWART, S. SAMBROOK, M. MULDER, H. TER HORST and J. SCHEERENS (eds) *HRD and learning organisations in Europe.* London: Routledge. 156–177.

TJEPKEMA, S., TER HORST, H. and MULDER, M. (2002a) Learning organisations and HRD. In S. TJEPKEMA, J. STEWART, S. SAMBROOK, M. MULDER, H. TER HORST and J. SCHEERENS (eds) *HRD and learning organisations in Europe*. London: Routledge. 6–19.

TJEPKEMA S., STEWART, J., SAMBROOK, S., MULDER, M., TER HORST, H. and SCHEERENS, J. (eds) (2002b) *HRD and learning organisations in Europe*. London: Routledge.

TORRINGTON, D. and WEIGHTMAN, J. (1985) *The business of management*. London: Prentice Hall.

TRAPP, R. (2004) Measured response. *People Management*. Vol. 10, No. 23, 25 November. 44–45.

TRIST, E. and BAMFORTH, K. (1951) Some social and psychological consequences of the long-wall method of coal-getting. *Human Relations*. Vol. 4. 3–38.

TRUSS, C. and GRATTON, L. (1994) Strategic human resource management: a conceptual approach. *International Journal of Human Resource Management*. Vol. 5, No. 3. 663–686.

TULIP, S. (2003) Added value. *People Management*. Vol. 9, No. 2, 23 January. 50–54.

TYLER, R. (2004a) Basic skills 'should be taught by schools, not by business'. *Daily Telegraph, Business 2+Jobs*. 2 December. A1.

TYLER, R. (2004b) Skills Council in dark over where the apprentices are. *Daily Telegraph Business 2 + Jobs*. 22 July. 1.

ULRICH, D. (1987) Organizational capability as a competitive advantage: human resource professionals as strategic partners. *Human Resource Planning Part 4*. 169–184.

ULRICH, D. and SMALLWOOD, R. (2002) *Why the bottom line ISN'T!: how to build value through people and organization*. New Jersey and Canada: Wiley.

VAILL, P.B. (1996) Purposing of high-performing systems. In K. STARKEY (ed) *How organizations learn*. London: International Thomson Business Press. 60–81.

VENKATRAMAN, N. and SUBRAMANIAM, M. (2002) Theorizing the future of strategy: questions for shaping strategy research in the knowledge economy. In A. PETTIGREW, H. THOMAS and R. WHITTINGTON (eds) *Handbook of strategy and management*. London: Sage. 461–474.

VON KROGH, G., ROOS, J. and SLOCUM, K. (1994) An essay on corporate epistemology. *Strategic Management Journal, Summer Special Issue*. Vol. 15. 53–71.

VROOM, V.H. and DECI, E.L. (eds) (1970) *Management and motivation: selected readings*. Harmondsworth: Penguin.

VYGOTSKY, L.S. (1978) *Mind in society: the development of higher psychological processes*. Cambridge, MA: Harvard University Press.

WALKER, B. A. (1994) Valuing differences: the concept and a model. In C. MABEY and P. ILES (eds) *Managing learning*. London: Open University and Routledge. 211–223.

WARD, L. (2004a) Drive to tackle failures focuses on key skills. *Guardian*. 18 February. 4.

WARD, L. (2004b) Diploma plan to reward lower and higher abilities. *Guardian*. 18 February. 4.

WARR, P. B. and BIRD, M. W. (1968) Identifying supervisory training needs. *Training Information Paper No. 2*. London: HMSO.

WARR, P., BIRD, M. W. and RACKHAM, N. (1970) *Evaluation of management training*. Aldershot: Gower.

WATSON, I. (2004) A hidden agenda? *People Management, Letters*. Vol. 10, No. 12, 17 June. 21.

WEST, M. and JOHNSON, R. (2002) A matter of life and death. *People Management*. Vol. 8, No. 4, 21 February. 30–36.

WESTWOOD, A. (2001) Drawing a line – who is going to train our workforce? In D.WILSON, E. LANK, A. WESTWOOD, E.KEEP, C. LEADBEATER and M.SLOMAN. *The future of learning for work: executive briefing*. London: Chartered Institute of Personnel and Development. 17–22.

WHITE, D. (2004) How to keep a spanner out of the works. *Daily Telegraph, Business2+Jobs*. 15 April. A4.

WHITE, M. (1996) Flexible response. *People Management*. Vol. 2, No. 6, 21 March. 33.

WHITE, M., HILL, S., MILLS, C. and SMEATON, D. (eds) (2004) *Managing to change? British workplaces and the future of work*. Basingstoke: Palgrave Macmillan.

WHITTAKER, J. and JOHNS, T. (2004) Standards deliver. *People Management*. Vol. 10, No. 13, 30 June. 32–34.

WHITTAKER, M. (2003) Cinderella treatment. *People Management*. Vol. 8, No.1, 9 January. 27–30.

WHITTINGTON, R. (2002) Corporate structure: from policy to practice. In A. PETTIGREW, H. THOMAS and R. WHITTINGTON (eds) *Handbook of strategy and management*. London: Sage. 113–138.

WHITTINGTON, R. and MAYER, M. (2002) *Organising for success in the twenty-first century*. London: Chartered Institute of Personnel and Development.

WHITTINGTON, R., PETTIGREW, A. and THOMAS, H. (2002) Conclusion: doing more in strategy research. In A. PETTIGREW, H. THOMAS and R. WHITTINGTON (eds) *Handbook of strategy and management*. London: Sage. 475–488.

WOLF, A. (2004) *The impact of government skills initiatives on employers. Reflections: new trends in training and development: Experts' views on the 2004 training and development survey findings*. London: Chartered Institute of Personnel and Development. 22–25.

WOODRUFFE, C. (1991) Competent by any other name. *Personnel Management*. Vol. 23, No. 9. 30–33.

WOODRUFFE, C. (2001) Promotional intelligence. *People Management*. Vol. 7, No.1, 11 January. 26–29.

WOOD, S and DE MENEZES, L. (1998) High Commitment Management in the UK: Evidence from the Workplace Industrial Relations Survey, and Employers' Manpower and Skills Practices Survey. *Human Relations*. Vol 51, No 4. 485–515.

WOODS, R. (2003) High cost of the glittering prizes. *Sunday Times*. 26 January. 1.16–17.

WORK FOUNDATION *The missing link: from productivity to performance*. London: Work Foundation.

WORKING GROUP ON 14–19 REFORM (2004) *The final report of the working group on 14–19 reform, February 2004*. Nottingham: DfES Publications. Online version also available at http://www.14-19reform.gov.uk [accessed 19 January 2005].

ZACHARIAS, L. (2003) Small change. *People Management*. Vol. 9, No. 9, 1 May. 24–27.

ZOHAR, D. and DRAKE, J. (2000) On the whole. *People Management*. Vol. 6, No. 8. 55.

ZUBOFF, S. (1988) *In the age of the smart machine*. New York: Basic Books.

Subject Index

Author Index

STUDENTS

Save 20% when buying direct from the CIPD using the Student Discount Scheme

Order online at www.cipd.co.uk/bookstore or call 0870 800 3366

The Chartered Institute of Personnel and Development (CIPD) is the leading publisher of books and reports for personnel and training professionals, students, and for all those concerned with the effective management and development of people at work.

The CIPD offers ALL students a 20% discount on textbooks and selected practitioner titles.

To claim your discount, and to see a full list of titles available, call 0870 800 3366 quoting '*Student Discount Scheme*', alternatively visit us online at **www.cipd.co.uk/bookstore.**

N.B. This offer is exclusive of any other offers from the CIPD and applies to CIPD Publishing textbooks and Revision Guides only.

2005

Learning and
Development

Rosemary Harrison

Need help studying for your exams?

The 2005 Revision Guides are here to help you!

Based on the experience and skills of the CIPD Chief and Associate Examiners, the 2005 CIPD Revision Guides provide comprehensive and relevant information and are an invaluable resource for students in the lead-up to their examinations.

The Revision Guides available include: *Employee Relations, Employee Reward, Employment Law, Learning and Development, Managing Activities, Managing Information, Managing in a Business Context, Managing People, People Management and Development, and People Resourcing.*

Students SAVE 20% when buying direct from the CIPD

To order, visit us online at www.cipd.co.uk/bookstore or call us on 0870 800 3366

The Guides include:

- advice on how to prepare for the exams;
- pointers on how to avoid common mistakes and how to maximise students' potential;
- advice on how to approach exam questions;
- examples of past exam questions with suggestions on how to answer (including examples from the May 2004 exam paper); and
- examples of responses students have given and explanations of why these were good, poor or average.

The Chartered Institute of Personnel and Development is the leading publisher of books and reports for personnel and training professionals, students, and for all those concerned with the effective management and development of people at work.

Also from CIPD Publishing . . .

Developing and Applying Study Skills:

Writing assignments, dissertations and management reports

Donald Currie

Having trouble writing your assignment?

Do you want to improve your study skills and write successful reports?

Help is at hand with this latest title from CIPD Publishing. A practical guide to help you prepare, write and complete assignments, dissertations and management reports. This text looks at the skills required to produce successful documents, how to gain these skills and how and when to use them.

Taking a straight forward, hands-on approach, you can use this book as an ongoing tool to aid you in your studies. It offers guidance on getting the best from lectures, tutorials, seminars, structured learning sessions and group work.

Included throughout the book are exercises, case studies and self-test questions that can help you increase your experience of tackling organisation-based problems, addressing issues, increasing your academic understanding and monitoring your progress.

Order your copy now online at www.cipd.co.uk/bookstore or call us on 0870 800 3366

Donald Currie worked as a personnel officer for more than 15 years before joining the Southampton Institute as a Lecturer in personnel management. In 1990 he was appointed Fellow In Human Resource Management and for more than 10 years led the CIPD Professional Education Scheme. Donald continues to work as a consulatnt to the Southampton Business School, and has been running the CIPD CPP course since 1995.

Published 2005   1 84398 064 9   Paperback   240 pages

The Chartered Institute of Personnel and Development is the leading publisher of books and reports for personnel and training professionals, students, and for all those concerned with the effective management and development of people at work.

Membership has its rewards

Join us online today as an Affiliate member and get immediate access to our member services. As a member you'll also be entitled to special discounts on our range of courses, conferences, books and training resources.

To find out more, visit www.cipd.co.uk/affiliate or call us on 020 8612 6208.